Postmodern Marketing Two

Postmodern Marketing Two

Telling Tales

Stephen Brown
University of Ulster

INTERNATIONAL THOMSON BUSINESS PRESS
I(T)P An International Thomson Publishing Company

London • Bonn • Boston • Johannesburg • Madrid • Melbourne • Mexico City • New York • Paris
Singapore • Tokyo • Toronto • Albany, NY • Belmont, CA • Cincinnati, OH • Detroit, MI

British Library Cataloguing-in-Publication Data
A catalogue record for this book is available from the British Library

First edition published by Routledge 1995
This edition published by International Thomson Business Press 1998

Typeset by J&L Composition Ltd, Filey, North Yorkshire
Printed in the UK by The Alden Press, Oxford

ISBN 1–86152–018–2

International Thomson Business Press
Berkshire House
168–173 High Holborn
London WC1V 7AA
UK

International Thomson Business Press
20 Park Plaza
13th Floor
Boston MA 02116
USA

http://www.itbp.com

Amor fati

Do you wanna get rocked?

It's been a long time since I rock 'n' rolled

Well, I got this guitar and I learned how to make it talk

Hello, hello, it's good to be back

'No.'

'Yes.'

'No!'

'But why not?'

'Stephen, how many times do I have to tell you? The answer is no.'

'Come on, Francesca, it's a great idea for a book and you know it.'

'It may well be, Stephen, but Routledge doesn't do that sort of thing. I'm sorry.'

'Well, I'll just take my idea to another publisher, then.'

'From what I hear, you've already done the publishing rounds without success and now seem to think you can come crawling back to me. Read my lips, Stephen, the answer is no, N-O spells no!'

'But think of my public.'

'Your public?'

'Yes, my public. Just think how disappointed they'll be.'

'Your disappointed public?'

'Yeah, what's wrong with that?'

'So, you really think that the marketing world is waiting agog for the next bulletin from Stephen Brown, do you?'

'Well, agog's a bit strong. But I think there's some enthusiasm out there, Francesca. In all modesty of course.'

'Call me a cynic, in all modesty of course. But what makes you think there's some enthusiasm out there?'

'The sales of Postmodern Marketing, for one.'

'The sales of Postmodern Marketing?'

'Francesca, why do you keep repeating everything I say in such a sarcastic voice? Do you deny that Postmodern Marketing sold well?'

'It certainly exceeded our expectations . . . '

'Right, there you go. Now . . . '

'. . . *but our expectations were pretty low to start off with.*'

'*Come on, Francesca, the bloody book sold well and don't pretend otherwise.*'

'*Yes, fair enough, it sold, though I'm not so sure about the "well".*'

'*Very funny. It sold. It sold more than you expected. So, let's stop the nonsense and get down to business.*'

'*Hold on a minute, Stephen. Let's get one thing perfectly clear, I don't care about the sales. It's who* bought Postmodern Marketing *that bothers me.*'

'*What on earth are you talking about? A customer's a customer. End of story. The marketing concept states that . . .* '

'*Spare me the marketing concept. You didn't have a kind word to say about the marketing concept in your book. Don't start spouting it to me when it suits you.*'

'*So, your customers don't matter, is that what you're telling me Francesca? I've heard the book business is production oriented, but this is beyond belief.*'

'*No, Stephen,* our *customers do matter. Its* your *customers I'm worried about.*'

'*My customers?* My *customers? What do you mean, my customers? Okay, so they're a sad bunch of inadequates, losers, malcontents and, let's face it, sado-masochistic dullards, but there's no need to insult them.*'

'*Do you really think we don't know what's been going on?*'

'*Just what do you mean by that, Francesca?*'

'*We know what you've been up to.*'

'*Sorry? I'm not with you. I may be Irish, but I've no idea at all . . .* '

'*At all, at all . . .*'

'*Yeah right, very good. Now, what exactly are you insinuating?*'

'*Stephen, with our software, we can track the sale of every single copy of your book.*'

'*So?*'

'*Well, let's have a look, shall we? Heavy concentration of sales in Northern Ireland, as you can see.*'

'*Yes, but it's recommended reading on some of my own courses. What's wrong with that?*'

'*Recommended reading? Required reading, according to some of the letters we've received.* Demanded *reading, from what we hear. If-you-don't-buy-this-book-you'll-never-get-through-the-course-there's-a-compulsory-question-on-your-examination-paper-oh-and-by-the-way-the-library-copies-are-still-being-catalogued sort of reading so we're reliably informed.*'

'*Who's been telling tales?*'

'*We have our methods, Stephen.*'

'*Fair enough, Francesca, I have pushed it a little bit at home, but your own figures show a reasonable spread of sales around the country.*'

'*Indeed. Pity about the reports from the bookshops.*'

'Reports, what sort of reports?'

'Reports about a little old woman, a little old grey-haired woman who's been buying lots of copies of Postmodern Marketing.*'*

'Perhaps you haven't noticed, Francesca, but there are quite a few little old grey-haired women in the country. Perhaps they're buying it for their sons and daughters . . . as a present . . . I don't know.'

'Or perhaps it's just the one little old grey-haired woman who's buying up copies to boost the sales of her son, the author. I do know.'

'How dare you. How dare you suggest such a thing.'

'Stephen, she was found pressing copies of your book on innocent shoppers in Foyles. She was singing its praises to all and sundry in the Business section of Waterstones in Edinburgh. She was forceably ejected from Blackwell's in Oxford for complaining long and loud about it being out of stock and taking a swing at a sales assistant when he made disparaging noises about your, er, oeuvre. *You sent your own mother on a book-buying tour of the country. You should be ashamed of yourself.'*

'She needs the exercise. She likes to get out and about. She enjoys meeting people. Okay, so she bought a few extra copies for the extended family. You know how it is, Francesca, mother's pride and all that.'

'How many copies, exactly?'

'Three or four.'

'Three or four hundred, you mean.'

'Well, we have a big family. I'm Irish, remember.'

'Trying to pin the blame on your race now? You really are the lowest of the low, Stephen Brown.'

'Look, Francesca, let's cut the crap. The book has sold. It doesn't matter who bought it or what it was bought for . . . .'

'No. I'm sorry, you're wrong. You see, it's not just a matter of sales or your pathetic attempts to rig the figures. It's a question of standards.'

'Standards? Come again?'

'For your information, we've had a number of very serious complaints about Postmodern Marketing.*'*

'Oh, you mean the reviews? Bunch of know-nothing, back-stabbing score-settlers. Don't pay any attention to reviewers. You should know better than to listen to that lot.'

'They're hard to ignore, Stephen. When someone describes your book as "completely incomprehensible" and another calls it "unspeakably vile", questions have to be asked.'

'Let me ask you a question, Francesca. Since when have the words "completely incomprehensible" ever dented anyone's academic reputation? Academics love *obscurantism, haven't you realized that by now? If they can't understand something it must be*

profound and then they blame themselves for not being able to understand it. I mean, come on!'

'I'm not so sure marketing *academics feel that way.'*

'You're not suggesting that my esteemed colleagues are incapable of appreciating works of scholarship, that they can't comprehend words of more than one syllable, that they trace each sentence with a finger whilst silently mouthing the cadence as they read. Are you?'

'Don't exaggerate, Stephen. Incomprehensible I can live with, it's the "unspeakably vile" that worries me.'

'Wake up, Francesca! Unspeakably vile is perfect. You couldn't ask for more. Put it on the back cover, I say. You know, you should be selling my new book on a shock-horror ticket. The book everyone loves to hate, sort of thing. Get some of those "this book could seriously damage your intellectual health" stickers for the front cover. Sales would go through the roof.'

'Is that with or without your parental payola? Look, Stephen, we don't go in for unprofessional behaviour like that. We don't put stickers on front covers. We're serious academic publishers. And as I've already told you, there's not going to be a new book.'

'So, you're not going ahead on account of a few bad reviews and the fact that my aged mother, in her misplaced enthusiasm, bought a couple of spare copies. Get real.'

'No, it's not just that. We've had other complaints.'

'What sort of other *complaints?'*

'Well, there's the companies for a start.'

'The companies?'

'Yes, Stephen, the companies. It seems that you mentioned several companies by name in Postmodern Marketing *and they all went belly up.'*

'Such as?'

'Oakdale Batteries . . . The Modern Review *. . . do you really want me to go on?' The Body Shop was on its knees for a while, Laura Ashley almost went to the wall . . . '*

'No, no, I see what you mean, but they can hardly blame me for their difficulties.'

'It may be irrational, Stephen. It may be, indeed it is, *pure superstition. But it seems that many marketing-oriented organizations consider you the kiss of death and they don't want you mentioning their names, or their products, in anything you write. We have the solicitors' letters to prove it. If you so much as allude to any of these companies, you'll be in the High Court before you can say Beanz Meanz Heinz.'*

'Goodness, that's some list. You mean to tell me I can't even say Heinz?'

'Especially not Heinz.'

'But it's going to be a book about marketing theory, Francesca. I'll just do it without brand names.'

'Just do it?'

'Yeah.'

'Sorry, Stephen, advertising slogans are out too.'

'Jeez, that's bad.'

'It gets worse.'

'What do you mean it gets worse, Francesca?'

'Why do you keep repeating everything I say, Stephen? It gets worse because we've had several, well, how can I put this, strange *letters about* Postmodern Marketing.*'*

'What is it this time?'

'Well, there's a slight, er, "local difficulty" with the footnotes.'

'Oh yes, of course, the footnotes. I could've kicked myself about the footnotes. I blew it completely, you know. I should've put a footnote in my first footnote and a footnote in my first footnote's footnote. It could have gone on for ever and a day, though I'm a bit surprised that someone complained. I didn't think anyone actually read *the footnotes. Bloody lawyers, I should have guessed.'*

'No, no, you don't understand, Stephen. This has nothing to do with companies or their lawyers. We've had an official complaint from the British Footnote Protection Society.'

'The what*? You're taking the Mickey, aren't you?'*

'Afraid not. I wish I were. Believe me, BFPS is an old-established association devoted to the preservation of the footnote and policing its use and abuse.'

'A sort of literary PLO?'

'Something like that. Anyway, it appears you breeched their code of conduct in Postmodern Marketing.*'*

'You cannot be serious. Are you telling me that there's a fatwa *on my footnotes?'*

'We have the injunction to prove it. You are prohibited from using footnotes in any future works of literature.'

'But the footnotes were the best bit.'

'Your words not mine.'

'Okay, Francesca. I'll do it without footnotes. I'll do it without brand names. I'll do it without companies.'

'No you won't.'

'What next? A writ from Mixed Metaphors R Us? Similes U Like? The Tropes Out Movement?'

'Oh God, no. If they'd read Postmodern Marketing *you'd have been incarcerated by now. Bread and water. Slopping out. Bullwhip. The lot!'*

'Francesca, you're forgetting something. I was at the MEG conference in Cardiff. I survived the MEG conference in Cardiff. Bread and water I can live on. Slopping out I*

can handle. Bullwhip, I'm quite looking forward to. No problem, believe me. You'll have to do a lot better than that.'

'I can, Stephen. Have you ever heard of the X-Philes?'

'The X-Files? Yes, of course. Television series about the paranormal, UFOs, the unexplained and what have you.'

'No, the X-Philes, the fan club of the TV series.'

'It's a good show, Francesca, but I'm not the fan club type.'

'Maybe not, but you used the words "the truth is out there" in Postmodern Marketing. *Page 94 to be precise.'*

'OK, so I accidently employed the show's tagline. Big deal.'

'You wrote the book before *the television series was broadcast. You also mentioned "the usual suspects" before the release of the film. Spooky, or what? Some would call it uncanny. A bit too much of a coincidence for certain people's liking. We've had letters. Strange letters. Green ink. You name it.'*

'Sorry, Francesca, I forgot to tell you I was abducted by aliens as a child. Keyser Soze is a friend of the family. I keep an effigy of Shelby Hunt in the drawer of my desk and stick pins in it to pass the time. You're not going to pay any attention to train-spotting, bird-watching, list-writing, anorak-wearing, acne-ridden, hairy-palmed knuckle-draggers, are you?'

'No – and that's why we're going to pass on your new book.'

'I may not be the most handsome marketing academic in the world and my shell-suit may have seen better days, but there's no need to make gratuitously offensive remarks about my personal appearance.'

'You're right, Stephen. I'm sorry. Your eczma has cleared up so well that we could almost put a photo of you on a back cover, providing we airbrushed the tattoo on your forehead, of course.'

'Great, that's settled. Now, let's talk turkey. As I see it, the book will . . . '

'Woah. Hold your horses. You just don't seem to understand. There isn't going to be a back-cover photo. There isn't going to be a book to put it on. The answer is still *no.'*

'Jesus Christ Almighty! If it's not extraterrestials, or my subhuman physiognomy, what on earth is it? Don't tell me I'm the wrong bloody star sign.'

'Inspection copy review forms.'

'Inspection copy review forms?'

'Correct.'

'You mean the comments people made about their inspection copies of Postmodern Marketing*?'*

'Yes, we pay more attention to them than anything else. In our experience, inspection copy comments are a very reliable source of information.'

'But I saw the comments on the book. They were all right. Everyone seemed to think it was "quirky".'

'Exactly!'

'What's wrong with quirky? Idiosyncratic. Mannered. Offbeat. I can live with that.'

'No, Stephen, you don't quite get it. We find that inspection copy comments are written in a sort of secret code. People use certain words when they actually mean something else.'

'What, like estate agents' brochures where "interesting" means grotesque, "compact" means miniscule and "period features" an outside toilet?'

'Precisely, except in the academic publishing game "interesting" means unpublishable, "debatable" means drivel, "contentious" means complete drivel and "controversial" translates as "lock them up and throw away the key".'

'And where exactly does "quirky" fit into the pantheon?'

'Hmmm, how can I put this? It means, er, two papers short of a conference proceedings, total headbanger, Care in the Community school of marketing scholarship. That sort of thing.'

'You're joking, Francesca.'

'I'm trying to put it to you gently, Stephen. It's actually a lot worse than that.'

'So they think I'm mad?'

'Barking.'

'How barking?'

'Hound of the Baskervilles.'

'That's barking, Francesca.'

'That's barking, Stephen.'

'Why do you keep repeating everything I say, Francesca?'

'Running postmodern joke, Stephen?'

'Nah, they'll never fall for it.'

'Yeah, you're right there.'

'You're not going to budge on this book idea, are you?'

'Look, Stephen, I want to help you. I do. To be perfectly honest with you, however, your proposal just isn't good enough. In my experience, reviewers are either sycophants or score-settlers, so we ignore them most of the time. All publishers get their fair share of writs and cranky letters. We can live with that. Most authors try their damnedest to rig the charts in their favour, so to speak. It's all part of publishing's rich pageant. But we can do absolutely nothing when the basic idea doesn't work. Your book proposal doesn't work Stephen. I'm very sorry.'

'What don't you like about it?'

'Well, the title for starters.'

'The title? For goodness sake Francesca, the title is one of the book's strong points. I reckon it will sell by the truckload on the strength of its title alone!'

'I can't deny that Kotler is Dead! *has a certain robustness, a definite ring to it even. But academics are a funny lot, as you well know. A title like that is bound to upset people, many of whom may well write for us already and probably sell a lot more copies than you. We're a very big publishing house . . . '*

Oh, I see. Yes. I'm beginning to catch your drift.'

'Glad you understand how things really are.'

'I could call it something else if you prefer, a whole new title. What about Who Killed Kotler?'

'I don't think so, Stephen. You see, it's not just the title. Phil Kotler is still very much alive and well, thank goodness, but you know what American lawyers are like.'

'But it's not about the *Phil Kotler. It's about a marketing professor called Phillipa Kotler who's appointed in the belief that she is* the *Phil Kotler.'*

'A pretty feeble premise for a novel, if you don't mind me saying so, even a campus novel.'

'Yes, but it's not really a novel. It's a textbook written in a novel form . . . in the form of a novel. You know what I'm trying to say. It's a murder mystery set in the marketing department of a university.'

'Stephen, we doesn't publish novels. We don't publish campus novels. We don't publish murder mysteries. We don't publish novel novels, you know what I'm trying to say? End of story.'

'I appreciate that. I understand what you're telling me, Francesca. The whole point, however, is that it's not a novel. It's a book about marketing theory.'

'If it's a book about marketing theory, why don't you just write a book called Marketing Theory?'

'Because I teach a course on marketing theory and it's very tedious, very dry. The students get bored. Writing it in the form of a novel is a good way of keeping them interested in the content, that's all.'

'I don't quite know how to put this to you, Stephen, but have you ever considered the possibility that the tedium of your course may have nothing to do with what's taught and everything to do with the teacher?'

'Yeah, well, um. I may not be the most charismatic marketing academic in the world . . . '

'Really.'

'. . . but . . . ah . . . but . . . you've confused me now . . . made me lose my train of . . . my train of . . . .'

'This is a book on marketing thought, *isn't it? Marketing theory, you tell me? You'll be*

wrestling with profound philosophical problems, will you? Are you really sure you're up to this, Stephen? Does your brain hurt, at all?'

'At all, at all.'

'Quite.'

'I can see I'm wasting my time, Francesca. I can see I'm wasting your time, Francesca. I take it Kotler is Dead! *is dead.'*

'Yes, Stephen, I killed Kotler.'

'And don't think you'll get away with it . . . '

'Very funny, very good.'

'It's no joke!'

'Look, I'd love to spend more time chatting with you, Stephen, but I have another meeting. Sorry I couldn't do anything for you. If you come up with any other interesting ideas, please get in touch . . .'

'I won't stand for this!'

'Sorry?'

'I'M AS MAD AS HELL AND I WON'T TAKE IT ANY MORE.'

'Ever the movie buff, Stephen. Network, *right? Stephen? Stephen! Stephen!! Stephen, come off that window ledge.'*

'I'm going to jump!'

'Now, just calm down, Stephen. Calm down. Don't do anything silly.'

'Sorry, Francesca, but it's either Kotler is Dead! *or Stephen is dead! Make up your mind.'*

'That's a tough one. Come on, Stephen. Be sensible. Act your age. Come back inside and we'll talk about it.'

'We've already talked about it. I've had enough, Francesca. Don't try to stop me.'

'OK, then, I won't try to stop you.'

'You won't?'

'No. And, don't forget to say "farewell cruel world" before you take the plunge.'

'God, you're a cynical bitch. Farewell cruel world it is then.'

'Just get on with it, will you.'

'I said, farewell cruel world.'

'I'm waiting.'

'My heart aches and a drowsy numbness pains my sense . . . '

'What's this? Keatsaoke night?'

'It's a far, far better thing I do than I have ever done . . .'

'Yes, I know. If you see Sidney Carton, tell him. Hurry up, Stephen, I've got a meeting in a couple of minutes.'

'Riverrun, past Eve's and Adam's, from swerve of shore to bend of bay, brings us by a commodius vicus of recirculation . . . '

'Jesus, James Joyce. We could be here all day. Stephen, I hate to spoil your fun, but just look down for a second.'

'I don't want to look. It's a long way. I'll be down there soon enough.'

'If you look down you'll see a big net, a very big net that stretches all the way across the courtyard. I've got news for you Quasimodo, we have disgruntled authors on the window ledges all the time. You've heard of the Internet? Well, we call ours the author-net.'

'This sort of thing has happened before, then?'

'You're not even the first marketing academic on that ledge. We've had more authors on that ledge than you've had sales of Postmodern Marketing, *take it from me. But, we got fed up with giving in to academic blackmail and publishing no-hope books as a consequence. So, we decided to take some precautions.'*

'Who . . . who else has been out here . . . up here . . . Francesca?'

'I've lost count of how many times Malcolm McDonald's been on that very spot. Every spring, regular as clockwork. Like a homing pigeon. Christ, we thought he was going to build a nest at one stage.'

'I always wondered how he managed to get so many books published.'

'Not any more. Those days are gone, Stephen. If you want to surf the author-net, feel free. Jump. Go ahead. Suit yourself. Just keep it quiet on the way down. People are trying to work.'

'I can't see any net.'

'Oh, shit. What day is it?'

'Tuesday.'

'Shit, shit, shit! We always take down the net on Tuesdays. That's the day the literary agents come around and, well, hope springs eternal.'

'Farewell cruel world.'

'Look, Stephen, I tell you what. If you come back in, we'll do something for you. It won't be Kotler is Dead!, *but we'll sort something out. I swear it.'*

'You swear it?'

'Why do you keep repeating everything I say, Stephen?'

'Running jump, Francesca?'

'Running joke. It was running joke! Give me your hand. Steady now. Steady! Atta boy. Atta boy. Take a seat. Just relax. Take it easy. Everything's going to be fine.'

'I'm OK now.'

'Of course you are.'

'Everything's under control.'

'You weren't really going to go through with it, were you, Stephen?'

'My negotiating skills are legendary.'

'Ledgendary, certainly.'

'So, Francesca, if it's not going to be Kotler is Dead!, what do you suggest?

'Let me see, have you ever considered a follow-up to Postmodern Marketing?'

'I'm not with you.'

'A sequel. Like the movies. You could call it Postmodern Marketing Two.'

'But I thought you weren't happy with the original. Why on earth would you want a follow-up?'

'Well it works in the film indusrty. It might be worth trying in academic publishing. Who knows. As I recall, you mentioned the possibility of a sequel in the last paragraph of Postmodern Marketing.'

'That was just a joke.'

'So was the one about Alan Smithee, Stephen, and nobody got it. So was your use of modernist four-cell matrices to illustrate your postmodernist arguments. And no one got those either. Academics don't like to have tricks played on them. They believe everything they read is true.'

'Francesca, are you seriously telling me that there are people who thought in all seriousness, that I was being serious?'

'The truth is out there, Stephen.'

'Strange. There are some strange people in academic life.'

'You should see some of the people we get in here, Stephen. Only the other day, we had a guy who wanted to start and end his book with an imaginary conversation between himself and a commissioning editor. Would you believe it?'

'Now, that's what I call barking, Francesca.'

'American Werewolf in London.'

'American Werewolf in London's big brother!'

'Anyway, strange as it may seem, Stephen, your public is expecting a second volume, believe me.'

'My public, Francesca?'

'Your public, Stephen.'

'I'm not sure my mother can afford another . . . '

'Hmmm. How's your father?'

'Well, that's a very interesting offer, Francesca. I never knew you cared.'

'No, you misunderstand, big boy. Cool it. What I meant was, how's your father's health, these days?'

'He's very well.'

'Very well, then.'

'I'm not sure I can lean on my students to buy it like before. There were official complaints, you know.'

'Those students will be long gone by the time it's published. And, anyway, I've always believed that Business Studies students should be exposed to the sorts of unethical acts of extortion that they'll eventually face in the real world. Don't you agree?'

'But what about the crazies, the companies, the writs, the X-Philes?'

'Don't you worry your pretty little head about all that, Stephen. Just do it.'

'Footnotes?'

'Hmmm. better not risk it.'

'Mixed metaphors? I can't manage without mixed metaphors.'

'Can you write about *mixed metaphors rather than wrestling with them?'*

'Do bears shit on Catholics?'

'Does the pope live in the woods?'

'There's just one problem, Francesca.'

'What's that, Stephen.'

'I don't know what to write about.'

'Of course you do.'

'I do?'

'Yes, of course you do. It's real simple. You rewrite Postmodern Marketing. *Make a couple of changes. Move things around a bit. Easy-peasy. Sure you've been doing it for years with your academic papers.'*

'That's true. But what sort of changes have you got in mind?'

'Well you could change the overarching metaphor.'

'No movies. No movies? You talkin' to me? Are you talkin' to me? I just have one word to say to you, Francesca . . . '

'Frankly, my dear, I don't give a damn about the movies. Stephen, you must have some other interests besides going to the cinema.'

'Not really.'

'You must have. Poetry? Art? Wine? Food? Television? Literature? Music?'

'I quite like music, I suppose.'

'Right, that's it. An orchestral metaphor. Opera possibly. I can just see it now.'

'Well, I'm more the heavy metal type, Francesca.'

'Heavy metal?'

'Yeah. Metal. Rock. Punk. You know, rock 'n' rooollllll.'

'I know.'

'I have a CD in my car. The volume control goes up to eleven. By the time I get to the university in the morning, I'm bleeding from every orifice.'

'You're an aesthete, Stephen, no doubt about it.'

'Yeah. Now that you mention it, I am. Never quite thought of it like that before. But you're right. Have you ever heard Ballbreaker *by AC/DC? What an album . . . '*

'Another time, Stephen. Let's save it until you've finished the book.'

'So, we're agreed then. If I rewrite Postmodern Marketing *using a musical metaphor, you'll definitely publish it?'*

'Well, yes, though you understand I can't guarantee *publication. Refereeing process and all that. However, I can assure you that we are likely to be very favourably disposed towards such a book. Very favourably disposed.'*

'Right, I'll do it.'

'Great stuff, Stephen.'

'Just one question, Francesca. What about the quotations from Alan Coren? Do I keep them?'

'Yes, absolutely. They were the only decent bit of writing in Postmodern Marketing.'

'The only decent bit?'

'Sorry, the best bit. I meant the best bit. It was all wonderful, Stephen, believe me. It's just that Alan Coren is a little bit better than you. A tiny bit. He's so much older than you. He writes for a living. You'll be as good as him one day.'

'I will, won't I?'

'No question.'

'Just need a bit more practice. A bit more practice, that's all.'

'Well, that and a touch of scholarship.'

'Scholarship? What's scholarship got to do with it, Francesca? This is show business.'

'Break a leg, Stephen.'

'What, from this height?'

'Stephen, can I ask you something?'

'Sure.'

'Have you ever seen 101 Dalmatians?'

'Seen it? Seen it? I can sing it. Cruella, Cruella de Vil . . .'

'Quite. What about Lassie Come Home?'

'No, but Lassie Goes Rabid *is one of my favourites.'*

'Thought it might be.'

'Way to go, Francesca.'

'Long way to go, Stephen.'

Chapter 1

We're on the road to nowhere, come on inside

Come with me to the margin. That is where real life happens. It always does. [Consider] . . . newspapers. Page after page of notional pith and moment from every fraught cranny of the globe, yet so little of it touching our core, until, suddenly, there is a single paragraph . . . on, let us say, page nine of The Times *yesterday:*

> Twenty-nine people wanted for failing to attend court, or who had been sentenced in their absence, were arrested after police lured them to a hotel in Liverpool by offering free camcorders. They had all received letters asking for volunteers in a market survey.

Real life or what? Apart, of course, from the sheer relish of the scenario: . . . a dozen CID officers in shiny suits and cheesy smiles welcoming the slavering audience of 29 camcorder-ravenous wallies to the marketing opportunity of a lifetime, the joyous denouement as, on a synchronised nod, the doors are locked, the badges flashed, the rights read out . . .

But it is much more than this. It is more even than a wondrous shaft of clear cold light into the murky corners of our huckstering, double-dealing, free-offering, card-scratching, prize-grubbing, something-for-nothing world. . . . What makes the fell swoop of the Mersey Bill even more than this is the strong possibility that their action may well kill all the geese that lay tin eggs. For how many of us can be certain ever again that the appealing con we have just been junk-mailed does not conceal a greater con calculated to get us where we have hitherto managed not to be got? Is any of us so confident of spotlessness as to take that risk?

A cold call, say, informs me that my house has been selected from thousands for the trial of an astonishing new Tonkinese fitted kitchen worth twenty grand, which will be installed for nothing in return for my allowing it to be used in future publicity, and their team will be in my area tomorrow. Shall I invite them in, only to have them whip off their dungarees and begin asking me about apparent discrepancies in my Schedule D tax return? A letter arrives, fifth of a sequence, pleading that if I do not turn up tomorrow at the spot arrowed on the enclosed map, then my absolutely free Ford Granada/diamond Rolex/fortnight with Sharon Stone will be forfeit: if I rush round, will I discover not only that I cannot get any of these unless I agree to buy Benidorm, but also that two large men from the Serious Stationery Squad are waiting to arrest me for the theft of corporate ball-points, typing paper, rubber bands and deluxe box files, going back to 1965?

Never mind the normal errors that too often accompany the kind of constabulary enthusiasm shown in Liverpool: it is not impossible that, should I accept the offer of a buckshee personal organiser for joining The Cricklewood Book Club, I might open the door to take delivery only to find my collar being felt by a man in a flak jacket informing me that they have got me bang to rights for the Abbey National ram-raid, do not argue, sunshine, it is all on the computer, prints, DNA, everything.

Real life has just changed. From today, there is no such thing as a free carriage clock.

(Coren 1996a: 18)

Teenage kicks

Twenty years ago, just as punk rock was exploding on to the British music scene, I moved into a house with three acquaintances I'd met at university. As it was my first experience of living away from home, I confidently anticipated the life of dissolution, dissipation and depravity that I'd always aspired to and fantasized about as an adolescent. Needless to say, my dreams of late nights, wild parties and, let's be honest, compliant women never quite materialized. Or, to put it another way, they materialized all right, but they materialized for everyone else in the house except me. I slept through the late nights, was not invited to the wild parties and, understandably enough I suppose, all the compliant women in the vicinity gravitated towards my three more glamorous companions. I did, admittedly, strike up a pretty close relationship with the next-door neighbours, but this was predicated on the premise that if I didn't turn down that bloody music they'd call the police. Naturally, I refused to accede to these totally unreasonable demands, though in the interest of good neighbourliness I offered to play them a couple of requests.

Now one of the guys in the house had a particular facility with the opposite sex. I don't know what it was about him – well, I do, albeit in these politically correct times I'm not prepared to divulge it – but hardly a week went by without a new and unfailingly alluring addition to his entourage. Charlie's success, unfortunately, went to his head and, in a moment of rampant egomania-cum-sartorial eccentricity, he took to wearing dark glasses and black leather gloves on a semi-permanent basis. Come winter, come spring; come rain, come shine; come day, come night, Charlie was poised to pose in his Ray Bans, kid gloves and ubiquitous untipped cigarette (his eyes, you understand, were very sensitive and the gloves prevented nicotine stains).

Pride, needless to say, comes before a fall and it wasn't too long before nemesis came knocking on the cool dude's door. One scorchingly hot summer's evening, when almost everyone in the street was sitting on their doorstep enjoying the unseasonable weather, my car refused to start. After several unsuccessful attempts to get it going, we were about to give up and go for a drink, when Charlie chose to come to our assistance. Sensing, I suspect, an opportunity to parade his freshly tanned physique in front of every hitherto unvanquished female in the terrace, the Lothario of Elaine Street descended to join us. Fresh from the shower and wearing only a minuscule midriff-hugging towel, his shades and – I swear – the ever-present black leather gloves, Charlie instructed us to raise the bonnet so that he could 'listen to the tappets', even though he knew absolutely nothing about motor car mechanics.

However, as he was peering into the bowels of the machine, pretending to be preoccupied with its timing, whilst clenching his buttocks for the benefit of any admiring onlookers, I whipped away his bath towel. It almost goes without saying that Charlie's initial howl of rage turned every head in the street, but, in an uncharacteristically modest attempt to shield his nakedness, he instinctively pressed himself against the burning metal of my clapped-out Escort. I would have thought Charlie was well used to blisters and friction burns on that particular part of his anatomy, yet the screams suggested otherwise. We let him wrestle with this 'frying pan or fire' decision for a few more minutes and then decided *not* to return his towel. Charlie was forced to slope back into the house covering his embarrassment with the black leather gloves, though I maintain to this day that if he had any genuine panache he would have pressed his sunglasses into potentially trend-setting service.

The above incident can readily be dismissed as youthful high spirits, as androcentric behaviour of the most recondite and reprehensible kind, or indeed as some sort of Freudo-Lacanian, deep-fried phallusy. But, to my mind at least, Charlie's impossible position, his mission impossible, his missionary position, is strongly reminiscent of the state of contemporary marketing scholarship. Like Charlie, marketing is endowed with considerable personal charm and has enjoyed more than its fair share of conquests. Like Charlie, marketing is a bit brash, a bit macho, a bit of a lovable rogue that likes to think of itself as a cool academic dude (marketing is the Sam Malone, the Jack Nicholson, the Dave Lee Roth of scholarship). And, like Charlie on that hot and sticky summer's evening, marketing has to decide whether to expose its intellectual nakedness for all to see or press itself against the searing heat of postmodernism, with all the likely long-term consequences. Forced to choose, I much prefer the latter option – albeit my predilection for placing private parts and scalding metal in close proximity is none of your goddamn business – though, as this book will endeavour to demonstrate, another alternative is available, an academic equivalent, if you will, to Charlie's black leather gloves and Ray Bans.

This time it's for real

At this early stage in the proceedings, I suppose some readers, especially those fortunate enough to have avoided *Postmodern Marketing* (S. Brown 1995a), are wondering what on earth I'm talking about (better get used to it, there are 300 odd pages still to go). Academic marketing, after all, may have manifold shortcomings, but it is by no means intellectually naked. If the burgeoning numbers of under-graduate and postgraduate students, degree programs, endowed chairs, university departments, professional associations, international conferences, books published and appropriately learned scholarly journals are any indication, then marketing is not only fully clothed, it is wearing formal attire, sporting a natty top hat and carrying an overcoat, umbrella and galoshes for good measure. Indeed, the increas-ing academic attention that is being devoted to marketing and consumption-related phenomena by non-business disciplines such as sociology, anthropology and history, (e.g. Miller 1995) suggests that far from being the second-hand rose of scholarship, marketing is now something of a fashion leader. Granted, it may not yet have attained the dizzy heights of high-brow haute couture, but surely it is no longer reliant on the conceptual equivalent of musty thrift shops, sterile factory outlets or dubious car boot sales for its cerebral ensemble and accessories.

Yet despite its developing intellectual chic, the Georgio Armani of the academy has not been striking poses, preening itself or generally admiring its sylph-like reflection in the full-length mirror of pedagogic approbation. Quite the reverse. As a glance at our discipline's glossy magazines and not quite so glossy periodicals amply demonstrates, marketing's leading scholarly costumiers are uniformly pessi-mistic about the theoretical collections that are currently on show.

- Peter Doyle, one of the UK's foremost marketing thinkers and one of the very few that enjoys international celebrity status, has recently reflected on the state of contemporary marketing. He concludes that it has fallen from its hitherto unassailable position as 'the all-conquering discipline' (1995: 23). Not only is it in decline; not only is it failing; not only is it anachronistic; not only is it being abandoned by its erstwhile advocates; it is simply no longer appropriate to the changed socio-economic circumstances of the late twentieth century.

- Michael Thomas (1995), a distinguished past president of the Chartered Institute of Marketing (the UK's leading professional body), commences his latest book, not with a ringing declaration of marketing's continuing rude health, but an announcement that it is in an unprecedented state of crisis. Although such contentions are two-a-penny these days, the context in which it was made – a 650-page compendium showcasing the very best of marketing theory and practice – speaks volumes about the discipline's current lack of self-confidence.

- Robin Wensley (1995), another internationally renowned member of the marketing intelligentsia, has also delivered a decidedly downbeat state-of-the-nation address. Concentrating on three key areas of academic research – market segmentation, marketing orientation, and networks and relationships – he posits that, despite an enormous amount of scholarly endeavour, very little progress and almost nothing of lasting value has been achieved in the post-war period.

- Michael Baker, the major-domo of British marketing and an academic ambassador *par excellence*, notes a 'decline in the incremental value added by current research/publication' (1995: 1003) combined with a grotesque over-extension of marketing's domain into areas that rightly belong to other disciplines. The upshot of these developments is that marketing's own intellectual heritage is being ignored in favour of fashionable but ephemeral panaceas or imported nostrums which are often no better and frequently worse than the indigenous concepts they supersede.

- Francis Buttle, one of the most prominent new-wave marketing theorists, describes 'a crisis of confidence in the dominant paradigm' (1994: 8–9) and, in a devastating assessment of what is currently on offer, concludes that 'New paradigm researchers have found mainstream marketing theory wanting. Consumer behaviour is a theoretical black hole. We do not understand how advertising works. . . . The only thing we know with certainty is that we do not know very much at all. Not much of an outcome for 50 years' scientific endeavour' (1994: 8–9).

- Douglas Brownlie, yet another unreconstructed, out-and-out, bona fide, if-he-didn't-exist-we'd-have-to-invent-him marketing iconoclast, is equally scathing about the present state of academic play. After traversing the boondocks of published research, he maintains that 'marketing as a domain of knowledge and practice is itself becoming as myopic, complacent and inward looking as all the once great but now defunct myopic companies. Is the end of marketing as we once knew it in sight?' (Brownlie *et al.* 1994: 8).

- Even Malcolm McDonald, doyen of detailed marketing planning, Director of the demurely named Institute for Advanced Research in Marketing,[1] proselytiser nonpareil, and possibly the most published marketing intellectual this side of Phil Kotler, is now willing to concede that, 'Perhaps classical 4Ps marketing, with changes in emphasis to its constituent parts, is not as relevant a framework outside the FMCG domain as we have become prepared to accept' (Denison and McDonald 1995: 55).

Some, of course, may say that these concerns, cavils and complaints are a manifestation of that peculiarly British plegmaticism – many call it masochism – whereby the worse things get the more there is to grumble about and the more perversely enjoyable the whole experience becomes. Convenient though such appeals to the public-school, stiff-upper-lip and blitz-spirit stereotypes undoubtedly are – not that I would ever resort to such a cheap, nasty and utterly fallacious line of argument – they cannot account for the almost identical set of anxieties currently being expressed by leading European and American marketing authorities. Amongst the Europeans, for example, Giles Marion (1993) avers that, conceptually speaking, there has been 'nothing new' in marketing since the 1960s; Christian Grönroos (1989, 1990, 1991, 1994, 1995) submits that it is time to bid a fond farewell – or, rather, good riddance – to traditional marketing frameworks of the 4Ps variety; and Evert Gummesson (1987, 1993, 1996a, 1996b, 1996c) has roundly, repeatedly, well-nigh recklessly ridiculed the all-conquering Kotlerite model of modern marketing scholarship.

While the savagery of this European academic assault is doubtless partly

---

1 Is there, I sometimes wonder, an inverse correlation between the grandeur of the title and a research centre's academic achievements? I certainly hope so, because the institute I once directed was called the Centre for Research and Analogous Publications Pertaining to Education in Retailing, albeit within Ireland it was known as the Centre for Retail Education and Training in the North. (Hope you like the 'real' footnote, by the way. None of your back-of-the-book-lump-them-all-together-because-nobody-reads-them-anyhow rubbish this time around. How did I get away with it? You'll just have to wait and see.)

attributable to an Oedipal desire to break away from American disciplinary strictures, recent evidence suggests that US marketing scholars are no less contrite
about their sins of omission, commission and general theoretical misdemeanours.
None other than Shelby Hunt, Fred Webster, Jagdish Sheth and, believe it or not,
slick Philly Kotler himself have latterly high-tailed it from the essentially transac-
tion-based 'marketing as exchange' nexus, thrown their not inconsiderable intellectual weight behind the burgeoning relationship marketing paradigm (Figure
1.1), and, in so doing, they merely serve to undermine further the very premises
of marketing understanding that *they* have been enthusiastically promulgating for
more than twenty years (F. E. Webster 1992; Kotler 1994; Sheth and Parvatiyar
1995; Hunt and Morgan 1995). When asked, moreover, to comment on the current
state of marketing thought and practice, a distinguished panel of American academic thinkers noted how 'AMA journals are not at the cutting edge of research
. . . one rarely sees marketers interviewed on television or quoted in major news

Figure 1.1 The Blois are back in town

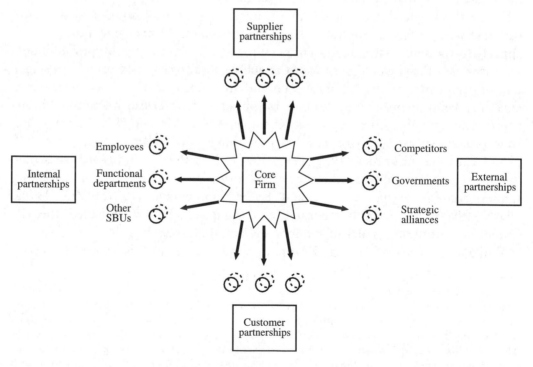

Source: adapted from Doyle 1995.

publications. Marketers have had little or no impact on major national issues, from health care to social security to welfare . . . one can conclude that all is not well with our field' (reported in Mowen and Leigh 1996: 1).

Similarly, albeit on a slightly less elevated plane, Pradeep Rau attributes the 'declines in journal subscriptions and the generally low importance attached to academic marketing research' to the fact that 'we are only recycling old knowledge for the benefit of a narrow audience' (1996: 2). As a result, 'our batting average has actually been declining from the early decades, and truly meaningful research efforts are getting fewer and farther between' (1996: 2). Indeed, in what must be the ultimate embodiment of the utter bankruptcy of contemporary US marketing scholarship, a well-meaning if impolitic contributor to the latest *Academy of Marketing Science Newsletter* explains his reluctance to switch allegiance to the relationship marketing paradigm, not on the basis of its shortcomings, its inappropriateness, or its intellectual and empirical poverty, but because – wait for it – 'I still need to attain tenure' (Stafford 1996: 4).

This manifest lack of faith in dat ole time marketing religion is not confined to the scholarly patriarchs, pontiffs, priests and parishioners, however. Practitioners are purported to be equally apostate, albeit in light of the manifold opportunities for managerial/academic interaction (short courses, training programmes, consultancy exercises, etc.), this perfidy is likely to be inflamed by – and reinforces in turn – the faithlessness of the intellectuals (Kell *et al.* 1996). Be that as it may, the past few years have been characterized by what, to put it at its most charitable, can best be described as a marked loss of confidence in marketing. For example, a much-publicized report by McKinsey has concluded that the marketing function is facing a mid-life crisis (Brady and Davis 1993); Coopers and Lybrand (1994) suggest that marketing departments are critically ill; *The Economist* (1994) has composed an obituary for the brand manager; Unilever, Procter and Gamble and BT, to name but three blue-chip companies, have abolished the position of Marketing Director (Doyle 1995). 'Many public policy and opinion leaders', as Sheth and Parvatiyar coyly note, 'think that marketing practices are designed to manipulate the consumers and, therefore, that consumer protection and vigilance are critical to balance the abusive powers of the marketers' (1995: 264). And, for Weir at least, 'the depressing reality of many marketing campaigns [is], that after comprehensive market research, panel testing, test marketing and carefully orchestrated launch, the customer simply decides to do something else that day. The secret history of marketing, like that of most management, is one of crisis, failure, confusion, misunderstanding, and occasional joyous, inexplicable, successful hitting of the jackpot' (1996: 28).

Perhaps the most poignant example of this self-abnegating turn occurred a couple of years ago, when the good ship *Oriana*, packed with the cream of British and European marketing managers, plus the illuminati of the Marketing Forum, set sail for a three-day voyage of discovery, during which the sole topic of discussion was the chronic condition of contemporary marketing. Now, I have absolutely no idea what was said on board, and I know I am only 22 pages into a book where I resolved to avoid plumbing the depths of metaphor, steer clear of the reefs of allusion, skirt the shallows of conceit, evade the sirens of synecdoche and generally refuse to set sail on the metonymyical briny. But this *Titanic*, this *Marie Celeste*, this *Exxon Valdez* of marketing is such a sitting duck that it is all I can do to refrain from referring to running aground, nautical gaits, walking planks, manning life-boats, Captain Ahabs, Davy Joneses, deserting rats, men overboard, full fathom fives, ships of fools, great white whales, muster stations, hunt the bismarketing, rimes of the marketing mariners and many more seafaring allusions besides.

Arc of a diver

In light of the foregoing comments on the marketing condition, it would be easy to conclude that our discipline is sliding below the intellectual waves to the affecting strains of 'Abide With Me' or, depending on your personal preferences, a rousing medley of 'I Am The Walrus' and 'Yellow Submarine'. Before abandoning ship, however, it may be prudent to pause for a moment and reflect on the causes of marketing's ostensible foundering. Perhaps, as some of the cynical old seadogs (or should that be P-dogs?) among you may have surmised, marketing hasn't foundered at all. Perhaps marketing is more buoyant now than it has ever been. Perhaps, certain unscrupulous, self-aggrandizing individuals are concocting an 'iceberg, what iceberg?'-style crisis as part of their nefarious desire to promote the post-modern marketing paradigm. Perhaps they are massaging, maltreating, misreporting and generally manipulating the evidence to suit their mendacious purposes. Perhaps the real problem is not marketing *in* crisis but the marketing *of* crisis. Marketing is not so much facing a crisis of representation as representations of crisis.

As you can no doubt imagine, I'm completely lost for words when confronted with such scurrilous insinuations. What's more, I'm shocked, not to say deeply disappointed, that you think so little of me. I am, after all, merely the messenger, an interpreter, a neutral channel – who said empty vessel? – for the freely expressed opinions of marketing's great and good. While I recognize that crisis-mongering per se can be construed as a studied act of post-teenage rebellion, a crude attempt to capture the cockpit of disciplinary power, which is in the process of being vacated by the current crop of scholarly plenipotentiaries. Yet, it is the *older* generation of marketing academics – the Kotlers, the Bakers, the Druckers, the Thomases of this world – who are proving most vocal about the present parlous state of the subject area. Granted, their prominence means that they have easy access to communication channels and, hence, their voices are more likely to be heard, and indeed attended to, by practitioners in particular (some of whom recycle, reinforce or act upon the words of the gurus, and so the whole process is perpetuated). But it cannot be contended that the present crisis of marketing confidence has been engineered by a few fascistic, megalomaniacal marketing academics and their misguided followers (if you so much as mention Brownshirts, my lawyers will be in touch). Nor, for that matter, is it solely attributable to the dyspeptic cavils of older 'things were better in my day' intellectuals, since they were largely responsible for articulating and codifying the position that is currently being called into question.

If, after dismissing the possibility that marketing's 'mid-life crisis' is an instantiation of an internecine intergenerational power struggle or, conversely, a romantically thanatic desire on the part of the captains of marketing consciousness to go down with their unseaworthy ship, the only meaningful alternative is that our discipline is facing some sort of 'genuine' crisis of representation. In these circumstances, it seems reasonable to ask the questions: why?, and why now? The first and most obvious answer is that the current loss of conceptual self-esteem is a direct reflection of unprecedented upheaval and turmoil in the marketplace itself – that is, the real, everyday, earn-an-honest-crust-is-that-your-best-price-where's-the-delivery-you-promised-me-you-bastard world of the marketing manager. While it is easy to slip into chrono-solipsism, the assumption that today's business conditions are somehow tougher, more competitive, faster moving, less ethical or whatever than at any time in the past (when, in all probability, they are neither more nor less turbulent, tougher, unethical or what have you – just different), many prominent commentators contend that the contemporary socio-economic environment is undergoing a period of profound, prolonged and possibly unprecedented change (e.g. Dicken 1992; Naisbitt 1994; Handy 1994, 1995). Certainly, in today's paradoxical marketing milieu where organizations are exhorted to be both global and local, centralized and decentralized, large and small, and planned yet flexible, and are expected to serve mass and niche markets, with standardized and customized products, at premium and penetration prices, through restricted and extensive distribution networks and supported by national yet targeted promotional campaigns, it is perhaps not surprising that the traditional, linear, step-by-step marketing model of analysis, planning, implementation and control no longer seems applicable, appropriate or even pertinent to what is actually happening on the ground (S. Brown 1995b).

With this is mind, it is arguable that the real problem is not so much the chaotic business environment – difficult though it undoubtedly is – as our extant marketing conceptualizations; the metaphors, models and theoretical frameworks through which we view, interpret and act upon the marketplace. The traditional constructs no longer apply. They are not up to the challenge. Just as Peter Drucker, the founding father of the modern marketing concept, blames the malaise of many hitherto large and successful organizations on the fact that 'their theory of the business no longer works' (1994: 96), so too marketing, as a theory of business, no longer works. Marketing's hegemonic claims to universal applicability have been found wanting, exposed for the hubristic bombast that they are and always have been. And exposed, ironically, at the very time when marketing is being enthusiastically embraced in fields as diverse as health care, public administration and not-for-profit, not to mention the erstwhile command economies of eastern Europe (S. Brown 1995a).

Paradoxical though this simultaneous success and failure seem to be, it is very much in keeping with the spirit of our postmodern times. As McGinn (1995) observes, it is invariably at the very moment of a concept or culture's greatest triumph that doubts start to accumulate, that premonitions of decline transpire, that terminal visions materialize. Or, in the arresting words of the high priest of postmodernism, Jean Baudrillard, 'Ideas proliferate like polyps or seaweed and perish by suffocating in their own luxuriant vegetation. . . . Every idea and culture becomes universalised before it disappears. As with stars, their maximum expansion comes at the point of death, their transformation into red giants and then black dwarfs. . . . The elevation of a value to universality is a prelude to its becoming transparent, which itself is a prelude to its disappearance' (1994: 103–5).

Another closely related consideration, and one that is likely to appeal to my small but vocal 'green-ink' constituency, is the fact that we are not alone. The merest glance across the current intellectual landscape reveals that marketing's aura of unease, its sense of crisis and impending collapse, is very widely shared. It is shared, moreover, by all manner of academic specialisms – economics (Ormerod 1994), anthropology (van Maanen 1995), history (Jenkins 1995), sociology (Lemert 1995), cultural studies (R. J. C. Young 1996), theology (Grenz 1995), architecture (Jencks 1995) and physics (Lindley 1994), to name but a few (take it from me, when economists succumb to self-doubt you can be pretty sure that something serious is amiss). Indeed, certain wild and woolly individuals contend that this penumbra of perplexity is an instantiation of PMT (pre-millennial tension), the almost palpable ethos of despondency, lassitude, stasis, melancholia and diffidence that is symptomatic of the present *fin de siècle*. Now, *fins de siècle*, as Kermode (1967, 1995), Kumar (1993, 1995a), Showalter (1991) and Meštrović (1991), among others, have shown, are entirely arbitrary calendrical artifacts – Judeo-Christian calendrical artifacts – and there is no 'rational' reason why they should be tainted by an air of decadence and despair, infused with a feeling of doom, gloom and foreboding. Yet they are, they long have been and, as evinced by the plethora of books, films and television series premised on the imminence of the purportedly apocalyptic year 2000, *they continue so to be* (Grosso 1995; Dellamora 1995; Thompson 1996; Briggs and Snowman 1996).

For literary critic Frank Kermode, in fact, this *fin de psychosis* (which is not confined to the ends of centuries, but tends to be accentuated at such temporal turning points) is nothing less than a fundamental correlate of the human condition, a means of making transcendental sense of the flux, chaos and fragmentation of the quotidian round. The idea that we live within and experience a sequence of events between which there is no relation, pattern or progression is simply unthinkable. Hence, he argues, humankind is inclined to foist a beginning, middle and end upon time, whether it be the changing of the seasons, the ticking of a clock (tick-tock being a complete narrative, as opposed to the unending succession that is tick-tick-tick) or periodic predictions of the end of the world (Bull 1995), the end of nature (McKibben 1990), the end of history (Fukuyama 1992), the end of philosophy (Cahoone 1995), the end of science (Horgan 1996), the end of work (Rifkin 1995) or, for that matter, the end of marketing (S. Brown, Bell and Carson 1996).

It cannot be denied that such X-Filesque arguments are tempting, not to say seductive. They help us comprehend the trajectory of twentieth-century marketing scholarship, the entire history of which has been littered with intermittent announcements of crisis, calamity and catastrophe (G. Fisk 1971; Austen 1983; Lynch 1995). However, it seems to me that there is yet another important issue which impinges upon the present uncertain state of the marketing discipline, and that is the radical implications of postmodernism for the so-called 'Art or Science?' debate. Few people, after all, would deny that the utopian pursuit of scientific status, and the intellectual legitimacy it confers, has been the leitmotif of post-war marketing endeavour (Bass 1993; Bass and Wind 1995; S. Brown 1996a; Kerin 1996). It goes to the very heart of modern marketing understanding, our sense of ourselves. It represents the axiology, the purpose, the ultimate destination of the discipline's academic odyssey and it follows that any alteration in the balance between Art and

Science (or swing of the art/science pendulum, if you prefer) has significant implications for the underpinning premises of marketing theory and practice.

Clearly, it is impossible to do justice to such a complex topic in an essay such as this and, let's be frank, I have no particular desire to alienate my admittedly small (but beautifully formed) readership in the very first chapter. That comes later. However, since this issue is so central to marketing's self-image, comprises an essential element of the emerging postmodern critique of modernity and, most importantly of all, gives me an opportunity to demonstrate my familiarity with, if not understanding of, all manner of pretentious phraseologies, terminologies and expressions, a lightning sketch of the 'art or science?' controversy may prove illuminating. It also gives me a chance to rewrite history, revel in invective and generally display my pseudo-intellectual credentials, such as they are, but that is by the by. (Look, I'm really sorry about the next section, but if I don't resort to academese at an early stage in the proceedings – and thereby establish my right to speak, so to speak – I'll get into all sorts of trouble. Just hang in there. We'll rip it up later, I promise you. Please excuse me while I clear my throat and adopt a 'scholarly' tone of voice.)

Once upon a time

Although some distinguished authorities demur (Kerin 1996), it is widely accepted that the great 'marketing: art or science?' debate began approximately fifty years ago, when Paul D. Converse alluded to the 'classified body of knowledge which we call the science of marketing' (1945: 14). While these were little more than throw-away remarks in a paper primarily devoted to the results of a questionnaire survey of sixty-four marketing researchers, it wasn't long before marketing's scientific aspirations and credentials were called seriously into question. Vaile (1949), for example, asserted that marketing was an art where innovation, creativity and extravaganza prevailed, and where the sheer complexity of marketplace behaviours rendered impossible the development of a general theory or theories. In a similar vein, Bartels (1951) emphasized that marketing was not and could not be considered a science, since work that warranted the appellation 'science' was simply not being conducted by marketing researchers and, while it may be possible to study marketing phenomena scientifically, the very idea of establishing a science called marketing was questionable. That said, Bartels found *some* evidence of the use of the scientific method in marketing research and concluded that, with further theoretical speculation and systematic scholarship, marketing may well become a science in the fullness of time.

Bartels' suggestion, coupled with the growing preparedness to speak openly of 'marketing science' (e.g. L. O. Brown 1948; Alderson and Cox 1948; Cox and Alderson 1950), prompted Hutchinson (1952) to pen a tart rejoinder. 'In appraising the progress which has been made in developing a science of marketing,' he contended,

> one is tempted to make allowances for the relatively short period of time in which the issues have been under discussion. But whatever allowances are called for, one is likely to be somewhat disappointed over the lack of progress to date. . . . There seems to be little evidence to support the claim that all is needed is time and patience until there will emerge the new and shining science of marketing. . . . There is a real reason, however, why the field of marketing has been slow to develop a unique body of theory. It is a simple one: marketing is not a science. It is rather an art or a practice, and as such more closely resembles engineering, medicine and architecture than it does physics, chemistry or biology. It is the drollest travesty to relate the scientist's search for knowledge to the market research man's seeking after customers. In actual practice . . . many and probably most of the decisions in the field resemble the scientific method hardly any more closely than what is involved in reading a road map or a time table.
>
> (Hutchinson 1952: 287–91)

Notwithstanding Hutchinson's heroic attempt to emasculate marketing's insatiable 'physics envy', it is fair to say that by the early 1960s the battle had been decisively won by the scientific emulators (S. Brown 1996a). In an era informed by the Ford and Carnegie Reports and the celebrated Two Cultures controversy, the establishment of the Marketing Science Institute, combined with the AMA's stated aim of advancing the science of marketing and the publication of Buzzell's (1963) famous paean to the scientific worldview, ensured that no one seriously questioned the appropriateness of marketing's aspiration to scientific status. Granted, there was a great deal of discussion about whether the discipline had or had not attained its ultimate objective. For some commentators, marketing was already a science or proto-science (M. D. Mills 1961; Lee 1965; Robin 1970; Kotler 1972; Ramond 1974). For others, it had either a considerable way to go or was pursuing a pleasant if somewhat idealistic daydream (Borden 1965; Halbert 1965; Kernan 1973; Levy 1976). Nonetheless, as G. Schwartz stressed at the time, 'the various expressions of opinion have not revealed anyone who is opposed to the development of a science of marketing' (1965: 1). Indeed, the culmination of the 'debate' occurred in 1976, when Shelby Hunt, in a much-cited, award-winning article, evaluated the state of marketing scholarship against the three characteristic features of science (distinct subject matter, underlying uniformities and intersubjectively certifiable research procedures) and found that it passed, or certain aspects of it passed, on all counts. 'The study of the positive dimensions of marketing', he triumphantly concluded, 'can be appropriately referred to as marketing science' (Hunt 1976: 28).

Hunt's exultations, however, were comparatively short-lived thanks to the intervention of Paul Anderson (1983, 1986, 1989), who challenged the fundamental philosophical premises of marketing science. The received view, variously described as 'positivist', 'positivistic' or 'logical empiricist' rested on the assumption that a single external world existed, that this social reality could be empirically measured by independent observers using objective methods, and that it could be explained and predicted through the identification of universal laws or law-like generalizations. Aided and abetted by like-minded revolutionaries (Peter and Olson 1983; Despande 1983; Hirschman 1986), Anderson contended that marketing was ill served by the traditional positivistic perspective – what he termed *science*[1] – and argued that a relativist approach – dubbed *science*[2] – had much more to offer. This maintained that, although an external world may well exist 'out there', it was impossible to access this world independently of human sensations, perceptions and interpretations. Hence, reality was not objective and external to the observer but socially constructed and given meaning by human actors. What counted as knowledge about this world was *relative* to different times, contexts and research communities. Relativism held that there were no universal standards for judging knowledge claims, that different research communities constructed different world-views and that science was a social process where consensus prevailed about the status of knowledge claims, scientific standards and the like, though these were not immutable. Science was *so* social, in fact, that Peter and Olson (1983), in their ringing endorsement of the relativist position, concluded that science was actually a special case of marketing, that successful scientific theories were those which performed well in the marketplace of ideas thanks to the marketing skills of their proponents.

It almost goes without saying that this eschewal of the orthodox idea of marketing science – as objectively proven knowledge – and its attempted replacement with the notion of science as societal consensus provoked a ferocious reaction. The foremost defender of the faith, Shelby D. Hunt (1984, 1990a, 1992) was particularly scathing about relativism, arguing that not only would its pursuit lead inexorably to nihilism, irrationalism, incoherence and irrelevance, but it also threatened to subvert the past 400 years of scientific and technological progress (Western Civilization in Peril – Shock!). Battle was thus joined, and over the subsequent decade or thereabouts the heavyweights of marketing scholarship slugged it out . . .

('Hold on a minute, Stephen.'
'Francesca, what on earth are you doing in here? You're part of the framing device, not the body of the text. How do you expect the readers to suspend their disbelief if you're going to start blundering into the narrative?'
'Butt out, Brown. I'm the commissioning editor of this book and I'll butt in if I want to.'
'Oh, so it's like that, is it? Well, make it quick, what do you want?'
'It's about the passage you've just written.'
'Yeah, pretty good, isn't it? Cynical yet scholarly, just the sort of postmodern mood I'm trying to convey.'
'That's one way of describing it.'
'Sorry, Francesca, is this a stylistic thing?'
'No, though you do seem to have a somewhat liberal view of what constitutes literary style.'
'What exactly is your problem?'
'It's just that I've read that passage before. In Postmodern Marketing One. *Page 143 to be precise, Stephen.'*
'Correct me if I'm wrong, but you were the very person that told me to rewrite the first book.'
'Not word for word!'
'It's postmodern Francesca. We don't subscribe to old-fashioned notions of plagiarism and authorial authority. Barthes' "always already written", don't you know.'
'Bullshit. No more recycling, Stephen, you hear? No more fun and games. Got it?'
'What, you mean no more frame-breaking textual intrusions by a fictional editorial figure?'
'Just get on with it, Bozo!')

Anyway, to cut a long story short, the Hunt–Anderson contretemps opened the door for apocalyptic postmodern critiques of the western scientific worldview. Now, 'postmodern' is one of those slippery words that, if you are so inclined, enables you to write several hundred pages of text and still fail to come up with a satisfactory definition. For some commentators, it is a distinctive, late-twentieth-century artistic and cultural movement. For others, the term pertains to latter-day developments in social, economic and political life. For yet others, it is essentially a periodizing concept or, indeed, a fashionably chic – some would say passé – post-ure espoused by the fashion victims of thought (Hollinger 1994; Dickens and Fontana 1994a; Seidman 1994; Adam and Allan 1995; Cahoone 1996; Appleby *et al.* 1996). For the purposes of the present chapter, however, it can be contended that the postmodern consciousness is premised upon the repudiation of the western scientific paradigm. Or, to be more precise, it is exemplified by its renunciation of 'scientism', the long-standing assumption that science is capable of solving all our problems (provided enough resources are made available), that science is a force for the good, that science is unproblematic (Sorrell 1991). While postmodernists recognize the enormous material benefits that western science has provided, they draw attention to the dark side of science, to the fact that it brings costs as well as benefits, that it is not the be-all and end-all, that the achievements of western science have been accomplished at a very heavy social, environmental and political price (S. Brown 1995a).

For postmodernists, then, the appellation 'science' is no longer considered honorific. On the contrary, it is an epithet of opprobrium. Science, to put it crudely, is seen as cold, calculating, austere, authoritarian, sterile, inhuman, uncontrollable, Frankensteinian, deceptive, self-serving, patriarchal, rapacious, destructive and downright dangerous. It is a force for human immiseration rather than liberation. It is morally bankrupt, spiritually bereft and intellectually barren. It has given us a very great deal – where, after all, would we be without the Pot Noodle? – but it has not made us any happier or succeeded in explaining the meaning(s) of life (Appleyard 1992; Midgley 1992; Haynes 1994).

Although such antinomian sentiments are not shared by everyone (Wolpert 1992; Jacques 1993; Carey 1995; Dawkins 1996; Durant 1996), this latter-day denial of scientific authority cannot fail to strike a chord with observers of the contemporary marketing scene. In a recent devastating assessment of the discipline's post-war academic achievements, for example, L. McTeir Anderson maintains that 'the dogged pursuit of the mantle of sciencehood has severely damaged marketing's credibility at a time when international competitiveness demands acumen and leadership – not the continued railings of pseudo-scientists' (1994: 14). Kavanagh (1994), likewise, has excoriated marketing science for its utter lack of moral, spiritual and ethical fibre, as have many academic advocates of an ecologically informed marketing worldview (McDonagh 1995; G. Fisk 1995). In fact, even prominent proponents of marketing science have attempted to step back from their earlier extravagant expectations (Buzzell 1984; Hunt 1994; Kotler 1994) and, irony of ironies, none other than Shelby D. Hunt has recently acknowledged that scientists are marketers, the very position he condemned out of hand when it was articulated a decade or so ago by Peter and Olson (Hunt and Edison 1995).

Countdown to ecstasy

In light of these developments, it may be worth attempting to draw some tentative lessons from the great 'art or science' debate and thereby set the scene for the remainder of this book. The first, and arguably most self-evident, point is that despite half a century of academic endeavour, the holy grail of marketing science has not been achieved (see Willmott 1993; Desmond 1993; L. McT. Anderson 1994). In 1963, during the salad days of pro-science enthusiasm, Buzzell maintained that by the turn of the millennium marketing would become 'a full-fledged science'. Well, the millennium is now upon us and the anticipated model of science – rigorous, objective, predictive, theory-building, law-giving, etc. – has simply not transpired, nor is it ever likely to transpire. Notwithstanding Hunt's specious claims to the contrary and macho-modellers' much-repeated contention that this land of marketing milk and honey is just around the corner, provided we all pull together and refuse to be distracted by the siren voices of postmodern promiscuity, importuned by the sodomites of post-structuralism or seduced by any analogous whores of intellectual Babylon, this academic Arcadia has not been attained by any other social sciences, most of which are longer established and more intellectually cultivated than ourselves. These days, only the most arrogant, recidivist or – dare one say it? – myopic marketing academic continues to assume that we can succeed where our elders and betters have demonstrably failed (Bass 1993; Little *et al.* 1994; Bass and Wind 1995).

A second and closely related point is that even if scientific status *were* attainable, or could be achieved with one last superhuman effort, the question has to be asked: is it something that we really want any more? When we look back at the great debate, the early days in particular, we cannot help but be struck by the sheer naïveté of the assumption that, regardless of its realizability, western science was an unproblematic role model for marketing. In truth, and not to put too fine a point on it, we are appalled by early commentators' preparedness to hold up the atom bomb as an exemplar of scientific achievement (L. O. Brown 1948; H. D. Mills 1961); now find the very idea of a single, all-embracing General Theory of Marketing laughably absurd (Figure 1.2); consider the advocates of 'broadening' somewhat overambitious at best or suffering from delusions of grandeur at worst; and, to be frank, increasingly regard our discipline's pseudo-scientific aspirations, its underpinning progressivist, gung-ho, we-have-the-technology metanarrative more a manifestation of 1960s-style American intellectual imperialism than a meaningful aspiration for late-twentieth-century marketing research (Brownlie and Saren 1992; S. Brown 1995a). Continuing to aspire to 'scientific' status

Figure 1.2 Levitt be, Levitt be, Levitt be, Levitt be

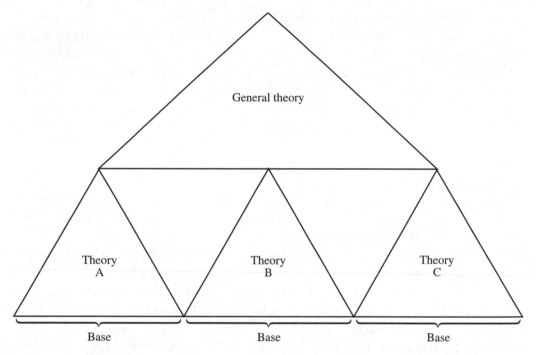

General theory

Theory
A

Theory
B

Theory
C

Base   Base   Base

Source: adapted from Bartels 1968

when all our sister disciplines have renounced it merely serves to reinforce marketing's reputed lack of intellectual sophistication. We are the academic equivalent of stack heels, flared trousers, gold medallions and open-to-the-navel wing-collared shirts – the Englebert Humperdinck of higher education, the oldest swingers in town. (Yes, I know these things are back in fashion; I have the sideboards and chest wig to prove it.)

The third distinguishing feature of the great confrontation is what can be described – pretentiously described, I grant you – as its *Zeitgeistian* qualities. When we reflect on fiftysomething years of disputation, it is clear that the exponents of the most cogent and carefully argued positions often failed to carry the day. The undoubted highlight of the earliest exchanges, for example, was Hutchinson's (1952) excoriation of marketing's scientific pretensions, a stance subsequently dismissed as a serious error of judgement. Similarly, Shelby Hunt's (1984, 1989, 1991) undeniably scholarly and philosophically sophisticated critique of relativism is now widely regarded as an irrational rant, a neo–Luddite attempt to prevent, or at least delay, the introduction of interpretivist perspectives. It is thus arguable that the finer points of any stated position are less important to its acceptability or otherwise than the nature of the prevailing intellectual climate. In other words, what the community of marketing scholars *wants* to believe at that particular time (M. J. Arnold and J. E. Fisher 1996). Converse, for example, was not the first marketer to wrap himself in the flag of 'science', yet his utilization of the terminology, at a time when science was in the ascendant, ensured that his name will forever be associated with it. Similarly, Anderson's concern with the type of science considered appropriate for marketing, was expressed by several of his predecessors (e.g. W. J. Taylor 1965; Robin 1970; Dawson 1971; O'Shaughnessy and Ryan 1979). But, it was Anderson's critique, coming at a time of widespread disillusion with the dominant hypothetico-deductive perspective and when the children of the 1960s counterculture were rising to positions of prominence within the marketing academy, that captured the moment, that shaped the contours of the ensuing debate and that is now cited as a milestone in post-war marketing scholarship.

If this *Zeitgeistian* interpretation holds water, then it follows that the key to the future may well be inscribed in the final and, it has to be said, somewhat postmodern aspect of the whole controversy – the appropriately hyperreal fact that the great art/science 'debate' *never actually took place*! Incredible though it seems, not a single person in the entire history of the contretemps attempted to make a case for marketing as an 'art'. True, many people (most notably Hutchinson) maintained that marketing was an art and destined to remain an art, but they did not suggest that marketing should *aspire* to artistic status. In fact, most discussions of the art of marketing focused on art as in artisan (i.e. the craft or technology of marketing), rather than art as in aesthetics, art as the very acme of human achievement, art as a quasi-spiritual endeavour. Interestingly, however, growing numbers of prominent marketing academics are now advocating the study of artistic artifacts, such as books, films, plays and poetry, arguing that they can provide meaningful insights into the marketing condition, or stressing the benefits to be obtained from drawing upon the liberal arts (humanities) end of the academic spectrum rather than the traditional orientation toward the hard sciences (Belk 1986a; Holbrook and Grayson 1986; Holbrook *et al.* 1989; Vargish 1991; Holbrook 1996a). Other prescient thinkers are espousing an increasingly aesthetic-cum-spiritual orientation (Reason 1993; Kavanagh 1994; Chia 1996) and, indeed, certain creative individuals have contended that marketing scholarship can be an artistic achievement *in itself* (Holbrook 1995a; Sherry 1995; McDonagh 1995a; Smithee 1997). Yet despite academic marketers' burgeoning enthusiasm for all things aesthetic, it would appear that its adepts are unwilling to argue for the *superiority* of the artistic 'paradigm' or advocate the abandonment of the discredited scientific model, with its outmoded methods, mechanistic worldview and unattainable axiology. At most, the artistic apologists attempt to make a case for the acceptance of such non-scientific insights, or postulate aesthetics as a useful complement to established approaches.

Until now.

Music for all occasions

The overall aim of this book, then, is to suggest that marketing has much to learn from aesthetics in general and the world of literature and literary criticism in particular. After attempting to show that this storytelling ethos is compatible with the emerging postmodern moment (Chapter 2), the text goes on to examine 'marketing in literature', that is, marketing and consumption phenomena as portrayed in works of fiction (Chapter 3). It continues with an analysis of 'literature in marketing', the use of literary theory to investigate marketing artifacts (Chapter 4), makes a case for 'marketing as literature', the adoption of a more self-consciously literary mode of marketing discourse (Chapter 5), and concludes (Chapter 6) with a few random thoughts, scabrous asides and cheap intellectual shots that you have come to associate with postmodern marketing scholarship (though my harshest comments are reserved for the sorts of readers – cheap thrill seekers, one and all – who flick over to the final chapter in search of gratuitously offensive remarks).

This book, it must be emphasized, does not claim to be the last word on marketing aesthetics – nor the first word, come to think of it. There are several other texts, most notably *The Semiotics of Consumption* (Holbrook and Hirschman 1993), *Consumer Research* (Holbrook 1995a), *Collecting in a Consumer Society* (Belk 1995) and *Artists, Advertising and the Borders of Art* (Bogart 1995), which are much more learned, much better written and, in terms of insights per page, much more of a bargain than *Postmodern Marketing Two*. You know, for the life of me, I can't understand why you've wasted your money on this volume. It contains nothing new; it isn't in the least bit interesting; and the only reason I wrote it was to soften up the publishers for *Kotler is Dead!* So, why don't you just go away and do something useful with your time instead of sitting there reading trash like this. Get a life . . .

Chapter 2
Wild thing, I think I love you

The department store is making a comeback, because customers are coming back to the department store. After a decade of retail flightiness during which they have been seduced into countless brief encounters by each flashy new high street gigolo that cared to wink its neon at them, British shoppers have at last come to their senses. They are returning to the sort of shops that Celia Johnson knew were the best, really. They are flocking back to Selfridges and Harrods and Debenhams and D. H. Evans and John Lewis and all the rest, enabling them, at the eleventh hour, to cheat the bourne from which no Hollingsworth returns.

Nothing, in these harrowing days, could make me happier. For not only have I remained faithful to the department store through thick and thin, I have subjected that loyalty to fine-toothed scrutiny, and am, I submit, in a better position to account for this revival than all the business analysts presently truffling for arcane explanations.

My earliest view of a department store was diamond-shaped. The year was 1944, the store was Selfridges, and I was looking at it through one of those rhomboid peep-holes Mr Churchill had thoughtfully cut into the green mesh designed to stop the Luftwaffe blowing bus-windows all over us. After we got off the bus, my mother, as was her attentive wont, spat on her hankie in order to remove from my face any detritus likely to upset floor-walkers, but for once I did not shrink as my cheeks were shoved this way and that. I stood stock still. Not just still, rapt. Selfridges was the biggest thing I had ever seen. . . . Hitherto, a shop had been a small dark place with a cat snoozing on the bacon-slicer, or a woman saying they only had grey wool due to U-boats everywhere; but here was a shop from one end of which you couldn't see the other . . .

And then we went inside. The inside was bigger than the outside. That is what happens with magic. It had to be big because there were a trillion things for sale; but most astonishing of all, they were different sorts of thing. I had been only in serial shops before: you bought a cabbage in one, then you crossed the road to another one to buy a scarf, and if you wanted a kettle, you had to go into a third one. But Selfridges sold everything there was in the world to sell, and you got to it by going up on electric stairs and coming down in electric rooms. More amazing yet: after my mother had duly bought this and that, we went to another part of Selfridges and had beans on toast. I was eating in a shop!

Dear God, so much plenitude in a time of austerity, so much possibility at a time of circumscription, so much fun in a time of dejection – is it any wonder that that lentitive glow in the infant psyche should have retained a glimmer to be fanned, in an emergency, by adult need?

(Coren 1995a: 113–15)

So far so good

Now, I know what you're thinking. You're thinking, what on earth is going on?; you're thinking, is this book some kind of joke?; you're thinking, is that it?; you're thinking, does he seriously think that starting a chapter with 'now, I know what you're thinking' will make us stop and think (especially when he tried the same thinking thing in his last book). But most of all you're thinking, how can I go about getting my money back? Even those of you who are chary about complaining about authors who reuse old jokes about chary complainers must be reflecting on the fact that you bought this book to be flung into the abyss of postmodern incomprehensibility, to be comprehensively bamboozled by the latest pseudo-intellectual railings from France, to be hit over the head by the hammer of neo-Nietzschean philosophizing. Yet here we are, a mere 36 pages into the text, and Brown – the devious bastard – has not only proffered a comparatively cogent definition of postmodernism but he has told us what this book is going to be about. What is the marketing world coming to, I ask you? Does the author really think he can get away with such pernicious lucidity? It's a sad, sad day for postmodern scholarship when someone who once devoted an entire volume to avoiding easy definitions and explaining his purpose, succumbs to such populism, proceeds to sell out and effectively abandons his academic birthright. How are the flighty fallen.

Setting aside, for a moment, your understandable desire to be up the you-know-what creek of postmodernism without a definitional paddle – hey, we're all *fin-de-siècle* surfers, these days – I fully appreciate that my endeavour to strain the stools of postmodernity through the infiltration plant of aesthetics may strike some readers as deeply disappointing, as a disingenuous cop-out, as merely going through the postmodern motions, so to speak. After all, for many people the 'art or science' debate lost its spark a long time ago and raking over old coals does little to enhance our understanding of marketing in today's paradoxical postmodern world. Others, of course, will appreciate that there is more to postmodernism than the epochal interpretation and recognize that a retro-root through antiquated anthracite is very much is keeping with the postmodern sensibility. At the same time, however, they may well be dismayed by my continuing reliance on conceptual explication rather than empirical demonstration. Surely, the objective of this volume should be to 'cash out' postmodernism, as Rorty (1980, 1989) terms it, to reveal its practical worth, to show what we can 'do' with postmodern marketing, how we can 'use' it most effectively and meaningfully in our day-to-day activities. A third constituency, by contrast, is almost certainly bound to be astonished by the author's brass neck and draw attention to the fact that I have previously lambasted the leading exponents of marketing aesthetics for their misappropriation of the term 'postmodern' (S. Brown 1995a). In other words, the very stance I am seeking to articulate – the position I have previously ruled out of postmodern court – turns out to be nothing less than the centrepiece of *Postmodern Marketing Two*! How, in the words of that intellectual nonpareil, Shelby Hunt (1994), can we possibly *trust* someone who shows us an empty scholarly hat only to extract an aestheticized white rabbit, who unashamedly indulges in such disreputable postmodern prestidigitation, who is seeking to exploit our academic credulity with his three-card trick of 'marketing in literature', 'literature in marketing' and 'marketing as literature'?

If you are prepared to take my position on trust – and, personally, I'm much more inclined to trust someone who says they can't be trusted than people, like Shelby Hunt, who keep banging on about the need for trust (methinks he doth pro*trust* too much) – then feel free to skip the remainder of this chapter. For those of you that remain – oh ye of little faith – I shall examine and attempt to side-step, not very elegantly I grant you, each of the above objections by arguing: (1) that not only is the 'art or science' debate far from settled, its deconstruction helps us comprehend the debilitated state of 'modern' marketing; (2) that postmodernism is not meant to be 'cashed out' empirically, although it can be and continues to be employed in this manner by a number of postmodern marketing exegetes; and (3) that while the emerging postmodern moment is not just about aesthetics, the latter-day textual turn in many social, human and indeed physical sciences is an important aspect of the process.

Beat the retreat

When I was in the throes of writing *Postmodern Marketing One*, I had this horrible recurring nightmare that the reviewers would criticize the book for not being postmodern enough. 'Incomprehensible', I could understand; 'indifferent', I couldn't care less about; 'schizophrenic', I was in two minds over; and 'scandalous',

I was secretly hoping for. But, 'insufficiently postmodern' would have pierced my heart like a silver bullet (sorry, folks, you missed your chance). Indeed, had I been reviewing the book myself, and I was seriously tempted to do so under a pseudonym, that is precisely the line of attack I would have taken. The problem, of course, is that nowadays everyone is up to speed on postmodernism. It is no longer off-limits, 'way out there' or, although it pains me to say so, the preserve of the lunatic fringe. Far from being beyond the pale, the pale is far beyond postmodernism. So much so that a recent commentary by Alex Callinicos, one of the leading critics of the postmodern condition, concluded that it now represented 'normal science', in the Kuhnian sense. In short:

> Postmodernism no longer offers the thrill of scandal and transgression it once had. In some parts of the academy at least, it is now assuming the solemn countenance of orthodoxy. Numerous undergraduate courses introduce students to the ruminations of Lyotard and Baudrillard. Postgraduate theses are written and academic careers launched on the basis of an unquestioning acceptance of the truth of their principal claims. . . . The excitement and controversy generated by the first appearance of the philosophical ideas now marketed under the postmodernist label . . . are long gone.
>
> (Callinicos 1995a: 134)

Since everyone is always already familiar with the salient features of postmodern topography and unlikely to follow the rhetorical false trails that have tempted innocent intellectual itinerants in the past, I realize I can't resort to my favourite and hitherto successful declamatory standby: 'postmodernism is whatever you want it to be and if I say it has something to do with "art or science", it has something to do with art or science – got it mate?!' Obviously, there is no possible way I could persuade a group of sophisticated postmodern marketers like yourselves to entertain such a transparent tissue of lies, though I'll be trying my best later in this chapter. After all, *you know* that 'art or science' is an old-fashioned binary opposition of the pre-post-structuralist variety; *I know you know* that that sort of dichotomy is so far behind the times it's wearing a doublet, codpiece and hose; and *you know I know you know* that it's antiquated enough to make Peter Drucker look like an angry young man, Ted Levitt a dangerous radical and Wroe Alderson the cutting edge of marketing creativity. But, rather than 'knowingly' descend into the abyss of infinite regress, a sub-Derridean deconstruction of this long-standing marketing duality may prove diverting, or, at the very least, provide some textual breathing space to allow the intellectual laggards to catch up with us. (What do you mean you don't know who Derrida is? Look, if you need a primer on postmodernism, you shouldn't be here. Either get with the beat, buddy, or go crawling back to Kotler, where you belong!)

For those of you who are unfamiliar with DerriDada, or Diarrhoeda, as a cynic once described it (S. Brown 1997a: 39), deconstruction is a technique of literary criticism predicated on the inherent instability of language. At the risk of oversimplifying a sophisticated and complex practice, a method that eschews its methodological status, deconstruction is primarily a procedure for interrogating texts which, by means of a careful and detailed reading, seeks to expose their inconsistencies, contradictions, unrecognised assumptions and implicit conceptual hierarchies; to show, as Norris cogently puts it, that a text 'cannot mean what it says . . . or say what it means' (1991: 35). In theory, deconstruction involves the identification of binary oppositions, or polar antitheses, within the text (as per the structuralist orthodoxy), transposing the dominant and subordinate poles, demonstrating that each is inherent in and dependent upon the other, and ultimately that neither pole is privileged or preferable. In practice, however, deconstructive readings of the Derridean kind invariably seize upon a small, seemingly inconsequential aspect of the narrative in question and show how it reflects, infects and unlocks the entire textual edifice (Norris 1992).

With regard to the *soi-disant* 'art or science' debate, the deconstructive key to the text – and, for our present purposes, the entire controversy can be treated as a 'text' – is found in the work of our old friend Shelby D. Hunt. In a landmark contribution, published twenty-odd years ago, he makes an ostensibly innocuous remark, which, on closer examination, tells us virtually everything we need to know about the complexion of modern marketing scholarship and helps contextualize its current malaise. The opening sentences of his classic, award-winning *JM* paper 'The Nature and Scope of Marketing' read as follows: 'During the past three decades, two controversies have overshadowed all others in the marketing literature. The first is the "Is marketing a science?" controversy' (Hunt 1976: 17). Thus, in a single egregious act of omission, the debate formerly known as 'art or science' was consigned to the dustbin of history. By means of the simplest rhetorical manoeuvre, the undefended yet eminently defensible position called Art was completely overrun and the captured territory razed, rotivated and sown with scholarly salt. So successful, indeed, has this scorched-earth (or highly seasoned earth, come to think of it) policy proved that the battle was thereafter fought entirely on the 'nature of science' flank and, as a recent lead article in the diamond jubilee issue of the *Journal of Marketing* clearly indicates, *it still is*.

According to former editor Roger A. Kerin's (1996) 'literary history' of *JM*, the field's premier academic forum and archive of cutting-edge marketing thought, the past four decades of marketing scholarship – that is, from the so-called marketing revolution of the mid-1950s to the present – can be labelled as the eras of 'quantitative science', 'behavioural science', 'decision science' and 'integrative science', respectively. What is more, on at least a dozen occasions during the paper, including the abstract, he vouchsafes that the vital spark of our discipline has been, continues to be and for the foreseeable future will remain 'the advancement of the science and practice of marketing'. Practice, admittedly, hardly warrants a mention, since it was only, apparently, in the ascendant between 1955 and 1964. As for art, it is conspicuous by its absence, even though Kerin's overview adopts an explicitly literary mode of explication, complete with close reading, dominant metaphors and, God preserve us, an underpinning metanarrative.

Yet despite Hunt and Kerin's manifest scientism, it can legitimately be argued that there is an aesthetic – a very important aesthetic – side to marketing endeavour. As the growing preparedness of museums to add marketing ephemera to their collections clearly indicates, marketing artifacts have already had artistic status conferred upon them, whether it be displays of carrier bags in the Design Museum, the celebrated 'High and Low' exhibition in the Museum of Modern Art, the so-called Nike 'museums' in Chicago and Portland, or indeed the latter-day litany of cult-cum-designer products – Apple computers, Mont Blanc pens, Neff cookers, Swatch watches, Starck lemon-squeezers, etc. (Sudjic 1987; Bogart 1995; York and Jennings 1995). Like the works of art that they unquestionably are, truly great marketing achievements are capable of inducing an ineffable sense of awe-struck wonder among observers (merchandise displays in Japanese department stores, British Airways' television advertising, the 'feel' of a Braun electric razor, customer service in Nordstrom, the sheer scale of the West Edmonton Mall, the magic of Selfridges for a youthful Alan Coren). Like the postmodern de-differentiators they undoubtedly are, numerous commercial organizations support, sponsor and indeed appropriate the work of contemporary artists, many of whom find inspiration in the marketized milieu of late-twentieth-century consumer society. Apart from innumerable intertextual allusions to film, television and fine art in advertising campaigns, recent examples of this aesthetic inclination include Habitat's quarterly art broadsheet and exhibition programme (Landesman 1996); Sainsbury's staff drama workshops led by Théâtre de Complicité (Hague 1996); and the limited edition bottle labels for Beck's Bier designed by leading artists like Damien Hirst, Gilbert & George and Rachel Whiteread (Hewison 1995).

These examples, of course, should not be taken to mean that marketing practitioners are endowed with an innate creative genius or artistic flair that has gone unrecognised, unacknowledged and unappreciated by the academic marketing community hitherto. Tempting though it is to apply the 'undiscovered artist in a garret' archetype to the study of marketing aesthetics itself, such myth-making misappropriation does not withstand detailed critical scrutiny. Nor am I suggesting that the distinctions between art and science are somehow cut and dried. On the contrary, numerous physical scientists have attested to the essentially aesthetic qualities of scientific discovery and research – Bohr's injunction that we must try to think like poets being just one among many (Tolstoy 1990; Gillott and Kumar 1995) – and a copious academic literature now exists on the art of science (Gross 1990; Locke 1992; Selzer 1993; Halliday and Martin 1993). The arts, likewise, have not been unaffected by scientific/technological considerations, ranging from Le Corbusier's 'machines for living in', Schoenberg's dodecaphonic or twelve-tone technique of musical composition and the much-vaunted 'factory' of Andy Warhol, to the post-war scientific 'turn' in many of the humanities (cliometrics in history, new criticism in literary theory, spatial science in human geography and the hypothesis-testing endeavours of archaeology, social anthropology and more besides).

By the same token, however, it would be foolish to pretend that academic marketing has aspired to anything other than 'scientific' status in the modern era. There is no question that our attention has been exclusively devoted to a single pole of the science/art binary opposition, that art has been and continues to be the disregarded 'other' of marketing discourse, that the bulk of post-Hunt scholarship can legitimately be described as not so much myopic as cyclopic. With this in mind, it is instructive to alight on Hunt's recent *cri de coeur*, written some twenty years after his earlier airbrush with history. In a characteristically reticent attempt completely to 'rethink' the discipline, practice and methods of marketing, Hunt (1994) maintains that, as a result of its predominantly applied or practitioner orientation and, hence, its excessive reliance on the perceived intellectual authority of other more basic academic disciplines, marketers are all but debarred from making original contributions to knowledge and those who try 'do so at their peril'. Marketing, he goes on, has been open, too open, indiscriminately open to exogenous methods, theories and concepts, a view that is also espoused by George S. Day (1996). Reflecting on the latter-day intellectual retreat, not to say capitulation, of marketing, Day despairs of the discipline's ever-increasing dependence upon the theoretical largesse of adjacent subject areas, notes that its admittedly tiny treasure trove of indigenous concepts is being systematically plundered and successfully repackaged by propinquitous fields of inquiry, and paints a dispiriting picture of the future 'in which marketing as a functional area and academic discipline will have diminished influence' (G. S. Day 1996: 15).

Many of you, I know, may be surprised by Shelby Hunt's ostentatious eschewal of outside sources of scholarly authority, especially since he has always been quite prepared to dragoon passing philosophers of science into the ranks of his Republican Guards of Realism. Many more may be amused by the fact that Day's proposed means of preventing his discouraging prognosis draws inspiration from – get this – the remedial activities of distal academic disciplines! However, if we are prepared to take Hunt and Day's comments on trust – we do, of course, trust them, don't we? – and assume for a moment that marketers have indeed been prevented from making an original contribution to knowledge, it could be counter-argued, with some justification, that the primary cause of this situation is neither our overzealous pursuit of all things applied, nor our fatal weakness for exogenous concepts. After all, one suspects that some, if not most, practising managers might be pleasantly surprised to hear that improving their everyday lot has been uppermost in the minds of marketing academics for the past half-century or so. Many, indeed, may be wondering when the fruits of all this cerebral labour will finally ripen and the bounteous harvest successfully gathered in. When it comes to extra-disciplinary concepts, what is more, marketing's antagonistic response to the advent of – for instance – interpretive research perspectives in the mid- to late-1980s, suggests that the extent of our openness to outside ideas is moot, to put it mildly. If anything, we have not been open enough and if we resort to intellectual in-breeding rather than cross-fertilization, as Sheth *et al.* (1988) recommend, then our conceptual stock will continue to degenerate, our scholarly gene pool will remain stagnant and future generations of mutant marketers will forever be condemned to crawl across the disciplinary desert – to scuttle across the silent seas – on all fours, fives or possibly threes.

In this disconcerting situation, it does not seem unreasonable to suggest that one of the principal reasons why marketers cannot make an original contribution to knowledge is because they are mesmerized by a mirage called Science. It is marketing's short-sighted scientism that lies at the heart of the problem, not our overly applied bent or belief that the intellectual grass is always greener on the other side of the disciplinary fence. If truth be told (and, as you know, you can rely on me to tell the unvarnished truth), the bulk of modern marketing scholarship has proved to be a complete waste of time and effort, an heroic but utterly wrongheaded attempt to acquire the trappings of 'science', a self-abusive orgy of mathematical masturbation that has rendered us philosophically blind, conceptually deaf and spiritually debilitated. Clearly, this contention is unlikely to endear me to the hairy-handed tons of soil who, though few in number, continue to scatter their seed upon the stony ground of marketing science. Yet however much they protest or purport to be on the point of intellectual germination, the simple fact of the matter is that the hayseeds of marketing science have cultivated little or nothing of note in the half-century they have lorded it over our allotment. Don't misunderstand me, there is no shortage of vegetation in Marcadia – this promised land of marketing milk and honey, with its scented bowers of overarching theory, bottomless aquifers of objective knowledge and uxorious water meadows of unified method – but the efflorescence, the abundance, the bough-breaking botanical bounty of science is an illusion. Despite appearances to the contrary and the bland assurances of marketing phytologists, the ground cover is impenetrable, indigestible and poisonous – a thicket in every sense of the word. It is time we faced up to the fact that we will be forever condemned to disciplinary destitution if we continue to try to scratch a living from the ostensibly fertile but ultimately unyielding soil called Science. Slash and burn, I say (S. Brown 1996a).

Modern life is rubbish

As postmodern cowpokes one and all, I'm sure you find the undying faith of the homesteaders of marketing science almost as amusing as I do (many of them have been cleared off the land, I grant you, but the ones that remain are obdurate and seem determined to stay put). It occurs to me, however, that the postmodern cattle barons among you may be having a jolly good laugh – no, splitting your sides – at my expense. Slow-witted wrangler that he is, I hear you say, Brown has committed the cardinal postmodern sin of privileging a particular mode of discourse. Although, in appropriately postmodernist fashion, he has highlighted the hegemony of the scientific pole of the art/science dichotomy and indicated, after a fashion, how each inheres in the other, his stated preference for the former at the expense of the latter is unacceptable from someone who espouses the archetypal postmodern position of 'anything goes'. If anything does indeed go, if heteroglossia obtains, if pluralism prevails and if, as the proponents of postmodernism posit, a thousand discursive flowers are currently in bloom, or budding at least, how can he possibly justify elevating Marketing Aesthetics over Marketing Science? Despite his protestations to the contrary, and that florid, narcissistic, unspeakably preten-tious, pass-the-sick-bag mode of marketing exposition, the author is nothing other than a postmodern poseur, a modernist manqué, a positive positivist!

Laugh if you like. Deconstruct my amateurish attempts at deconstruction if it makes you happy. Cast aspersions on the extent of my engagement with postmodern disengagement if you are sufficiently without sin to launch the first projectile. Break out the postmodern cattle prod, branding irons and gelding shears if that's what you think it takes. I cannot pretend that postmodernism's denial of privilege whilst privileging the non-privileged is inconsistent at best and incoherent at worst, albeit card-carrying postmodernists not only are comfortable with inconsistency and incoherence, but go out of their way to, well, privilege them. What's more, there are so many versions of postmodernism it is quite easy to find one or more that privilege the denial of privilege whilst denying the privilege of those who privilege the denial of privilege, if you see what I mean. Michel Foucault (1977, 1980a), for instance, foregrounds the need to resist the proliferation of normalizing discourses, institutions and decentred apparatus of domination by highlighting the hitherto occluded voices of marginalized, forgotten, deviant and excluded groups within society (McNay 1994). Lyotard (1984, 1993a, 1993b), likewise, stresses that our postmodern incredulity towards metanarratives, or *grand récits*, should be counter-pointed by an emphasis on *petit récits*, local forms of knowledge, the incompatibility of language games and the diverse, often contradictory, perspectives of those who dissent from or seek to destabilize the positions of those in authority (Sim 1996). Roland Barthes (1977a, 1990a), as you know, is renowned for elevating the plur-ivalent interpretations of the reader over those of the author of literary works (Calvet 1994; Rylance 1994) and, indeed, Deleuze and Guattari (1984, 1988) are enthusiastic proponents of the 'micro-politics of desire', a process of overcoming modern, repressive forms of self-hood through the liberation of libido combined with the creation of new types of decentred subjects freed from the restrictions of fixed and unified identities. Like the great pre-postmodernist Friedrich Nietzsche, D&G (the P&G of postmodernity) deem it their duty to undermine the precepts of western philosophy, to reject the idea of a stable and coherent self, to affirm the importance of difference, chance, chaos, becoming and the primordial, and, not least, to seek to create alternative possibilities in both art and life (Best and Kellner 1991).

I could, of course, go on and continue to privilege the positions of prominent theorists of postmodernity. Such an expositional stratagem, however, would merely pander to your insatiable postmodern desire for enigmatic expressions, counterintuitive concepts, obfuscatory circumlocutions and all-round pseudo-intellectualisms. And we simply can't have that, now, can we? Instead, let me just emphasize that, if it is characterized by anything at all, postmodernism is char-acterized by difference, by heterogeneity, by a plurality of perspectives, by the admittedly neo-Orwellian notion that all positions are privileged but some are more privileged than others. Indeed, since every commentator and critic 'constructs' the postmodern in his or her own way, there are almost as many postmodernisms as there are postmodernists (McHale 1987; Hutcheon 1989; Rosenau 1992). Thus, we can identify Lyotard's (1984) postmodern, the condition of knowledge in the late twentieth century; Barth's (1980) postmodern, the literature of replenishment; Jameson's (1985, 1991) postmodern, the cultural logic of late capitalism; Harvey's (1989) postmodern, a new round of time–space compression; McHale's (1987) postmodern, where an ontological 'dominant' supersedes the epistemological 'dominant' of modernity; Bauman's (1987) postmodern, whereby intellectuals are treated as interpreters rather than legislators; Baudrillard's (1983, 1994b) postmodern, in which the signifier breaks free of its restraining referent; Kroker and Cook's (1986) postmodern of excremental culture and hyper-aesthetics; Hassan's (1985) postmodern, as a staging post on the road to spiritual enlightenment; Hutcheon's (1988, 1989) postmodern of self-conscious, self-contradictory, self-undermining statements; Pearman's (1996) postmodern, in which styles are endlessly recycled in a knowing way; and, not least, the apocalyptic postmodern of Baker (1996: 39) – no not that one! – which he aptly describes as the 'Eve of Deconstruction'.

The multi-faceted and discordant character of postmodern discourse – in so far as there is no right or wrong, as such, and several inconsistent positions or interpretations can be held simultaneously (Hoy 1985) – is already apparent within academic marketing, where all manner of divergent approaches are being advanced under the banner of postmodernism. Although it can hardly be described as a new arrival on the marketing scene, postmodernism is still regarded as something of an up-market intellectual emporium which purveys everything from the pin of phenomenology to the elephant of critical theory and trades, suffice it to say, under the time-worn slogan of 'never knowingly understood'. This process of conceptual scrambled merchandising, it must be emphasized, is not a cause for undue concern, unless of course you are one of the few remaining modernist floorwalkers-cum-jobsworths-cum-killjoys who insist on a clear-cut definition before condescending to investigate what all the fuss is about. On the contrary, the kaleidoscopic qualities of the postmodern are very much in keeping with the constituent multiplicities of marketing. Marketing, as Figure 2.1 illustrates, has long considered itself the site, a meeting place, the focal point of the various functional areas within successful organizations and the melting pot of the processed Ps of the McCarthyite marketing mix[1]. These representations, admittedly, have traditionally emphasized

---

1 For the life of me, I can't understand why the 4Ps paradigm has never been described as McCarthyism. I mean, it's perfect: 'are you now or have you ever been a postmodernist?' What do you think of the bigger format of this volume, by the way? Pretty cool, huh? Deep thinkers like myself need a bit of room to express our thoughts; know what I'm saying? If this one sells, we're talking coffee-table format for *Postmodern Marketing Three*. If not . . .

Figure 2.1 Borden the USA

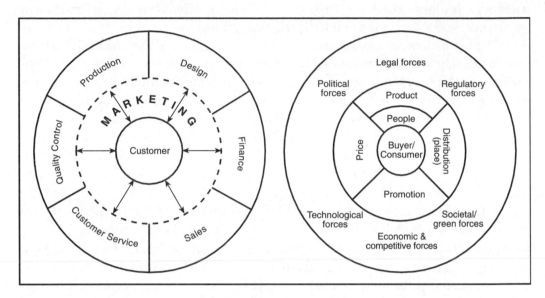

Source: adapted from R. Brown 1987; Dibb *et al.* 1994

harmony, commingling and coherence rather than contrast, variety and divergence, but the former, let's be frank, are manifest more in the breech than the observance. Marketing, for Firat and Venkatesh (1993) at least, has always been postmodern. For Eagleton, furthermore, 'many a business executive is . . . a spontaneous postmodernist' (1996a: 133).

Where angels fear to tread

Just as postmodernism per se has been construed in a host of different ways, so too postmodern marketing comes in many shapes and forms. At the last count, there were no less than twenty-one schools of postmodern marketing thought – approved schools, I grant you – which are outlined in Table 2.1. Ranging from Peripatetic Postmodernists to Promiscuous Postmodernists, these putative 'schools' are not clear-cut entities, established intellectual positions or, indeed, tangible loci of postmodern marketing discourse (so much so, that only the most clod-hopping, unsophisticated philistine would attempt to impose a reductionist classificatory framework upon their essentially ethereal, evanescent ephemerality). For the purposes of recapitulation, however, they can be divided into three main categories:

pragmatic postmodernists; paraclete postmodernists (look it up, you ignoramus!); and *political postmodernists.*

Table 2.1 Honey I want the heart, I want the soul, I want control, right now

Type	Position	Example
Practising postmodernists	desire to 'cash out' postmodernism; practical implications for marketing managers	M. J. Thomas (1996b)
Philosophical postmodernists	accept importance of postmodern position; weakness is its strength	S. Brown (1995a)
Phallopian postmodernists	fusion of postmodernism and feminism	Stern (1993)
Pagan postmodernists	subversion of marketing's established belief system	Brownlie (1997)
Poetic postmodernists	vehicle for introducing humanities into marketing and consumer research	Belk (1991)
Peripheral postmodernists	careerists; no real commitment to postmodern 'cause'	Smithee (1997)
Promiscuous postmodernists	foreground erotic aesthetic of postmodernism	Elliott (1996b)
Prophetic postmodernists	apocalyptics, 'end of marketing' thesis	Brown, Bell and Carson (1996)
Peripatetic postmodernists	constantly shifting position on nature and implications of postmodernism	Firat (1995)
Parodic postmodernists	refuse to take seriously postmodern refusal to take things seriously	McDonagh (1995a)
Phenomenological postmodernists	melding of phenomenology and postmodernism	C. J. Thompson (1996)

Table 2.1 Contd.

Type	Position	Example
Perverse postmodernists	undermine postmodern attempts to undermine marketing scholarship	Grafton Small (1995)
Post-Marxian postmodernists	vehicle for introducing critical theory into marketing and consumer research	Desmond (1995)
Philological postmodernists	application of textual metaphor to marketing scholarship	Hirschman and Holbrook (1992)
Popularizing postmodernists	the postmodern explained to marketing managers	Cova (1996)
Pedantic postmodernists	dogmatic, hair-splitting, 'I'm-right-you're-wrong' postmodernists	S. Brown (1995d)
Periodizing postmodernists	living in postmodern era and must adapt	Denison and McDonald (1995)
Pick 'n' mix postmodernists	postmodernism as bricolage; anything goes	Sherry (1991)
Patrician postmodernists	postmodernism as inverted intellectual snobbery	Holbrook (1995b)
Pretend postmodernists	shameless; recycle anything for a publication	S. Brown (1997c)
Post-partum postmodernists	examine PoMo in specific marketing situations and contexts (advertising, pricing, segmentation, etc.)	Scott (1992)

Pragmatic postmodern marketing is premised, essentially, on the assumption that we are living in, or in the process of entering, a postmodern epoch. This era is qualitatively different from that which has gone before, and hence marketing practice and theory are correspondingly different. The old rules, concepts and approaches no longer necessarily apply, or, rather, only serve to distort and limit the nature and scope of our marketing understanding. In these changed and changeable circumstances, the pragmatics have attempted to identify the characteristics of postmodernism, to explore its implications for marketing, as it is conventionally comprehended and, most importantly of all, to put the postmodern to work, as it were, to cash it out empirically. A broad postmodern slant, for example, has been taken on marketing intelligence (Soderlund 1990; Rothman 1992), marketing strategy (Denison and McDonald 1995; Starkey 1995), segmentation (Firat and Schultz 1997), advertising and promotion (Stern 1994a; O'Donohoe 1997; Elliott 1997), retailing (Hetzel 1996; Jones 1996), pricing (S. Brown and Quinn 1993), products and product design (Cova and Svanfeldt 1993; Meamber 1995), services marketing (T. Wright 1989; Belk 1996a), international marketing (Firat *et al.* 1995a), macro-marketing (Walle 1996) and, especially, consumer behaviour (van Raaij 1993; C. J. Thompson *et al.* 1997; M. J. Thomas 1996a). Likewise, long-established conceptual constructs as diverse as the wheel of retailing theory (S. Brown 1995c), STP (Tornroos and Ranta 1993), the three eras schema (S. Brown 1996b), consumer information processing (Heilbrunn 1996a), marketing as exchange (Belk and Coon 1993), values and lifestyle analysis (Holt 1997), the stages theory of internationalization (J. Bell and Young 1995), general theory of marketing (Firat *et al.* 1995b) and, indeed, the marketing concept itself (S. Brown 1994) have all been interrogated from a postmodern marketing perspective. The postmodern credentials of the new wave of marketing 'paradigms' – maxi-marketing, neo-marketing, after marketing, one-on-one marketing, database marketing, relationship marketing and so on – have also been comprehensively debated (Cova and Badot 1995; Cova 1996, 1997), as have analogous issues like postmodern culture, language, ethics, society and identity, subjectivity, ethnicity and the self (Bouchet 1994, 1995, 1996; Suerdem 1994, 1996; Venkatesh 1994; Bolz and Bosshart 1995; Firat 1995; Holt 1995a; C. J. Thompson and Hirschman 1995; C. J. Thompson 1996).

Perhaps the best-known exponents of pragmatic postmodern marketing are Firat and Venkatesh (1993, 1995, 1996), who have argued, in a series of closely interlinked papers, that the nature of marketing in postmodernity can be described in terms of five key features: fragmentation, hyperreality, reversed consumption and production, decentred subjects and the paradoxical juxtaposition of opposites. (Truth to tell, I have read their comments on the Grand Canyon IMAX centre so many times that Firat and Venkatesh's evocation of this hyperreal marketing environment is doubtless even better than the real unreal thing.) It is arguable, however, that the most cogent explications of the nature and practical implications of postmodernism have been made by marketing practitioners. In a resonant reminder of the premodern marketing era, when practitioners regularly contributed cutting-edge papers to prominent academic journals, Ogilvy (1990) has contended that whereas modernity was characterized by the march of western-style progress, the rise of science, mass-production technologies, bureaucratic hierarchies and the emergence of the nation-state, proponents of postmodernity ostentatiously eschew the idea of a one-path trajectory of development, maintain that there is no such thing as value-free scientific enquiry, have moved beyond mass to flexible forms of production, seek to subvert established hierarchies, be they organizational, social, cultural, political or psychological, and anticipate the withering away of the nation-state and its associated institutional apparatus.

According to C. Petersen and Toop (1994), moreover, these postmodern metamorphoses have major implications for the practice of marketing, which remains – *contra* Firat and Venkatesh – resolutely modernist in orientation. In a world where mass markets have fragmented, advertising costs more and reaches smaller audiences, retail organizations dominate channels of distribution, the range of socially and legally acceptable marketing activities is more circumscribed than ever before (regulations, codes of conduct, green issues, etc.), and consumers are better informed, more sceptical, less predictable, increasingly heterogeneous and, not least, fully *au fait* with the strategies, techniques and lexicon of marketing, postmodern marketers need to cater for diversity and difference whilst avoiding diseconomies and, most importantly of all, endeavouring to establish a dialogue with their customers, whose continuing loyalty is thereby ensured.

Broadly similar sentiments concerning the need to appeal to existing rather than new customers – and the challenge that this presents since the target market is already 'in the know' – have recently been articulated by Forth (1995), who also notes the postmodern propensity among creatives in his own advertising agency, BMP DDB Needham. Whenever a new team starts work on the PG Tips account, which, with its variations on tea-drinking chimpanzees, is one of the longest-running and most consistent advertising campaigns on British television, the scripts invariably comprise a deconstruction of the campaign itself or its intertextual and ontological context.

> Sometimes there is a real-life family drinking tea and our point of view swings round to reveal that the chimps have become cameramen on the shoot. Sometimes a human mask is removed to reveal a chimp (or vice versa). Again, we might find the Tipps family 'coming down the street' in the manner of the original Monkees in the '60s TV series. 'Hey, hey we're the monkeys', they sing, wilfully destroying the suspension of disbelief.
>
> (Forth 1995: 1)

While purists might be critical of practitioners' failure to comply with the niceties of academic argumentation, citation, verification and the like, the fact remains that their insights into marketing in a postmodern era are exceptionally acute. Although the postmodern is often dismissed by its critics as incomprehensible intellectualizing, and therefore very difficult for academics to understand – let alone practitioners! – in my experience, practising marketers are quick to grasp the essence of postmodernism and feel that it provides a meaningful perspective on 'the way things are, at present'. Marketing practitioners may not be familiar with the terminology – though there is mounting evidence to suggest that this is changing – but like the hippopotamus of legend that is impossible to describe yet remains instantly recognizable, they invariably respond positively to the eccentric, reflexive, tangential, idiosyncratic, paradoxical postmodern way of looking sidelong at the world. The Oakies of modern marketing scholarship may be reluctant to abandon their sterile intellectual allotment for academic pastures new, but postmodern practitioners have long since departed our disciplinary dustbowl. Indeed, and at the risk of further mixing my agricultural metaphors, it appears that the fellaheens of marketing science are left to shut the stable door after the, er, cliché has bolted and, if the 'mid-life crisis' literature is any indication, appear to be running around like the proverbial chickens whose decapitation has not yet registered.

Chicken skin music

Few would deny that the contributions of pragmatic postmodern marketers have been manifold and bounteous. They have successfully explicated the nature of the postmodern condition – which is no easy task given the complexity, diversity and inconsistency of the source material – and successfully demonstrated how its premises parallel contemporary marketing practices, subvert traditional conceptual frameworks and undermine established ways of looking at the world. What is more, these contributions have drawn marketers' attention to an extensive body of marketing-related literature in physically propinquitous yet psychically distant fields of academic endeavour, such as cultural studies, media studies and 'new times' sociology (e.g. Storey 1996; Morley and Chen 1996; Marris and Thornham 1996; Turner 1996). Granted, there is considerable dissensus about postmodernism's distinguishing features – any number of inconsistent inventories and itemizations have been posited – and more than a little concern about attempts to pigeonhole the unpigeonholeable in the first place. Nevertheless, it is undeniable that the pragmatics have done much to make the postmodern accessible to the marketing academy at large and in so doing have ensured the triumphant success of our postmodern marketing revolution.

Timely and thought-provoking though it has proved, the principal problem with the pragmatic perspective is, as you might expect, its very pragmatism, its desire to press-gang postmodernism into empirical service, to render the technology useable, to make it earn its intellectual keep, so to speak. Many postmodernists would argue that the postmodern is not designed to be 'cashed out' empirically (Morris 1994; Suerdem 1996; Bonnycastle 1996). It does not claim to provide an alternative approach or menu of methodological procedures (in theory at least). Postmodernism, in short, is a commentary rather than a conceptualization; it provides questions rather than answers; it offers rhetoric rather than reason, illumination rather than generalization, opinion rather than objectivity, edification rather than systematicity, meaning rather than method, enlightenment rather than empiricism, form rather than function, style rather than substance (style, remember, is the substance of the postmodern) and, above all, long lists of contrived antonyms which seek to impress the reader and create an utterly unwarranted impression of effortless scholarship.

This characteristically postmodern propensity for critique rather than conformity, for instability over the immutable, for, as Elias and Scotson (1994) put it, the outsiders instead of the established, is exemplified by the actions of *paraclete* postmodernists, individuals who go out of their way to enunciate, advocate and propagate the postmodern marketing message. Obviously, this group is not readily distinguished from the pragmatics, since the very act of explaining postmodernism comprises a form of proselytization. There is, however, a world of difference between, say, Denison and McDonald's (1995) dispassionate discussion of marketing strategy in postmodern times, Rothman's (1992) systematic assessment of postmodern marketing research techniques or van Raaij's (1993) even-handed adumbration of consumer behaviour in postmodernity, and (say) the rabble-rousing polemic of postmodern standard-bearers like Venkatesh *et al.* who offer the following quasi-Lyotardian call to arms:

> Researchers should not be restricted by frameworks but liberated by frames of mind. We should not be merely writing research proposals, reports and findings. We should embody our varied understandings of marketplace phenomena in as plastic an array of media as our talents permit. We must learn to hallow alterity, not merely manage diversity. Let us explode the modernist myth and celebrate what we find meaningful in postmodernism.
>
> (Venkatesh *et al.* 1993: 219)

Elliott (1993, 1997), likewise, has launched an equally militant attack on the modern marketing mainstream, contending that the advent of postmodernity requires a complete rethink of traditional assumptions concerning consumers, consumption and marketing research methodology. Desmond (1993), moreover, maintains that marketing's basic worldview is a fundamental misrecognition – in a Lacanian sense – as is marketing's image of itself. It sees itself as an integrated whole, a unified discipline, a force for the good, when it is in fact disjointed, fragmented and an unwitting alibi for the machinations of multinational capital.

Indeed, in a particularly high-handed, some would say offensive, passage, Cova and Badot imperiously announce that:

> The anti-universalism and anti-foundationalism of postmodernism have very serious implications for marketing theory, the bulk of whose principles are predicated on the archetypal modernist assumptions of analysis, planning and control. Whether it be marketing planning procedures, the product life cycle, SWOT analyses, Maslow's hierarchy of needs, the Howard–Sheth model of consumer behaviour, the trickle-down principle of fashion diffusion, the strategic matrices of Ansoff, Porter and the Boston Consulting Group, Copeland's classification of goods, the typologies of retailing institutions, hierarchies of advertising effects, the wheel of retailing or, needless to say, the four Ps, the majority of marketing and marketing related conceptualisations are basically modernist in orientation. They represent attempts – admittedly imperfect attempts – to make general statements about marketing phenomena and are thus deemed unacceptable by many postmodernists.
>
> (Cova and Badot 1995: 421–2)

Alongside such intemperate, not to mention irresponsible, outpourings of postmodern marketing vitriol, another group of paracletes . . .

('Not so fast, Stephen.
'Oh God, not you again. What is it this time, Francesca?'
'Well, that's a nice way to make your commissioning editor feel welcome, I must say.'
'Sorry, but I'm right in the middle of something just now. So, what can I do for you?'
'That passage you've just quoted. I'm not very happy with it.'
'Yeah, I see what you mean. The grammar is a bit iffy – that 'whose principles' is wrong for a start – and I know the overall tone is arrogant and offensive, but that's the sort of people we're dealing with here. The paracletes have no time for the subtleties of academic

argument, you know. They just put the boot in. It's a sad reflection of the state of scholarly society, but what else can you expect from . . .'

'That's not what I mean, Stephen.'

'Oh really?'

'I'm not referring to the paracletes, as such, nor the prose.'

'Well, if it's not the tenor or the grammar of the passage, Francesca, what's your problem?'

'You attribute the quote to Cova and Badot.'

'Yeah, that's right. I took it from their chapter in Michael Baker's Marketing Theory and Practice. *Do you have a problem with that?'*

'But you wrote it, Stephen.'

'Pardon?'

'You wrote the passage you've just quoted. I'd recognize that pseudo-style anywhere. You are quoting Cova and Badot quoting yourself and then you try to blame them for the sickening sentiments it contains. That's not the done thing, Stephen, as you well know. You should be ashamed of yourself.'

'Hold on a minute, Francesca. Cova and Badot don't quote me. There are no quotation marks round that passage, thank you very much.'

'So, they've plagiarized your work, then, is that what you're saying?'

'No, no, not at all. How many times do I have to tell you?; postmodernists don't believe in plagiarism; there is no such thing as authenticity; the always already written, don't you know.'

'If postmodernists don't believe in plagiarism and originality, Stephen, why are you drawing attention to the fact that Cova and Badot have quoted you without proper acknowledgement?'

'I'm not drawing attention to it, Francesca, you are!'

'You don't really think the readers will be fooled by that one, do you?'

'Look, just sod off. Any more of these interruptions and I'll jack the whole thing in. I mean it.'

'Is that a promise?'

'I'm not talking to you any more, Francesca. Go away. Just go away and don't come back.'

'Before I go, let me remind you of something, something you should always bear in mind, Stephen.'

'What now?'

'There are only two letters between titan and Titanic.'

'I see.'

'You do, good.'

'No, I C. The letters I C. That's the difference between . . .

'You don't quite get it, Stephen. ICs . . .'
'High seas? I thought it was an iceberg.')

Alongside such intemperate, not to mention irresponsible – yet somehow enga-ging and indubitably scholarly – outpourings of postmodern marketing vitriol, another group of paracletes prefer to make their case in a much less ostentatious but no less effective manner. Employing the characteristically postmodern conceit of *parody* – which, as Hutcheon (1989) points out, simultaneously connives with and conspires against convention – they draw attention to the absurdities of modern marketing, thereby ensuring that it, in effect, both condemns itself and promotes the postmodern *in absentia*. Perhaps the most celebrated instance of this parodic propensity is Russell Belk's (1987a) semi-Swiftian demolition of the infor-mation-processing paradigm of consumer behaviour. Arguing that if real-world consumers are too stupid to behave as the information-processing model envisages, then the only alternative is to make use of latter-day developments in artificial intelligence and modify these recalcitrant, sub-optimal individuals accordingly. Since the conceptualizations are sacrosanct, it follows that the consumer has to be changed, or, rather, disassembled, reconfigured and booted up to perform its task in a suitably efficient, logical and computer-like fashion. Another classic example of postmodern marketing parody is Morris Holbrook's principal compo-nents analysis of a short story, *Close Encounters*, which demonstrates – to a com-mendably high degree of statistical significance – that hypotheses derived from an interpretive research project can be falsified (Holbrook *et al.* 1989). The fact that such crude statistical procedures completely obliterate the subtleties of the market-ing-related narrative is, of course, much less important than the fact that scientific standards have been upheld, scientific rigour exercised and scientific respectability maintained. More recently, McDonagh and Prothero (1996) have written a three-act play set in a dance hall, where, as a result of an outdated musical policy (disco a go-go) and restrictive entry requirements (jacket and tie), things are going from bad to worse, the fashion-conscious in-crowd have fled and it takes a disastrous fire, complete reconstruction and a dramatic change in musical tack to restore the venue's fortunes. Naturally, any similarity between this discourse inferno and the calamitous state of the modern marketing academy is purely coincidental.

Monster

Although it can be a devastating weapon when used effectively, parody is a double-edged sword. In the wrong hands, it comprises little more than crude name-calling and constitutes a singularly unedifying spectacle. (Table 2.2, which purportedly consists of book reviews in the style of famous marketing academics, is a perfect case in point.) More importantly perhaps, the critiques of would-be parodists – and postmodern paracletes generally – are destined forever to fail and fail ignominiously. They are predicated on the outdated assumption that postmodernism comprises the lunatic fringe, the radical cutting edge of marketing scholarship. No-one seems to have told them that postmodern marketing is now the mainstream; that the lunatics have taken over the asylum; that postmodern polemic is par for the course, not a scandalous breech of academic etiquette; and, above all, that the entire contents of every issue of *JMR* and *Marketing Science* are written in parodic mode. There are, admittedly, a few die-hards who continue to believe that the authors of papers like 'Empirical Generalisations and Marketing Science' (Bass 1995), 'Empirical Generalisations: Theory and Method' (Ehrenberg 1995) or 'Good Empirical Generalisations' (Barwise 1995) are perfectly serious when they state that marketing has moved beyond the study of mere regularities to the development of higher-level theory, though I can only say that I found their poker-faced parodies hilariously funny. In these circumstances, it would appear that, far from confronting the mainstream with uncomfortable facts, the postmodern paracletes are pushing at an open door. What is more, if they have nothing to offer other than irony and invective, albeit accompanied by the standard escape clause that their self-appointed task is to criticize the status quo not to provide an alternative modus operandi, then many marketers may conclude that the joke is on the postmodernists, since they are seeking to ironize the ironic, criticize the critics and avoid offering an alternative to the always already avoided.

There are, however, several other groupings of postmodernists who are so dissatisfied with the staple diet of polemic and parody that they have sought to go beyond mere admonition in an attempt to combine censure with substitution. Perhaps the most important of these *political postmodernists* are the critical theorists, the feminists and the post-colonialists. Critical theory, as formulated by Horkheimer, Marcuse, Adorno and their fellow travellers in the Frankfurt School, and latterly revitalized by Jürgen Habermas, rejects both positivistic and interpretivist approaches to knowledge accumulation, since they simply serve to reinforce existing institutions, societal arrangements and conditions of understanding (Bottomore 1984; Bronner 1994; Hoy and McCarthy 1994). Committed, like Marxism, to an emancipatory ideal, albeit by means of critique rather than a specific agency (such as the proletariat), critical theory is dedicated to 'unmasking' the iniquities of capitalism, drawing attention to any discrepancies between the stated goals of contemporary institutions and their actual practices, and subverting self-serving

Table 2.2 I feel so good I'm gonna break somebody's heart tonight

1. Morris Holbrook
I wandered lonely as a consumer researcher
That floats on high o'er a free-form jazz solo
When all at once I saw a crowd,
A host of marketing management textbooks.

I picked one up and read it through
But is showed no sign of an aesthetic plan
I set it down, put on a tape,
And wrote a paper on the ascent of man.

But, oft' times when I lie in bed at night
Wondering just why on earth I bother
I wish I'd written a banausic text,
And sold my soul to the Almighty Dollar.

2. Shelby D. Hunt
In this book review I shall
demonstrate: (1) that the authors are
completely mistaken (2) that they
misunderstand the very nature of marketing
philosophy (3) that they have quoted me
out of context (4) that if I twist their
arguments sufficiently it will look as though
they are contradicting themselves (5) that
I'm right, they're wrong (6) that, contrary
to widespread belief, the 'D.' does not
stand for 'Dogmatic', and (7) that I'm
really a nice guy, so why can't we all
be friends?

3. Elizabeth Hirschman
Help, I'm running out of ideas. I have
written introspective accounts of my
upbringing, education, ethnicity, femininity,
religious beliefs, parental responsibilities,
drug addiction, hospitalization and
shopping behaviour. I can't think of
anything else. How's about the things I
did on my holidays? My pets? My top ten
kosher recipes? Or, my favourite movies,
books and television programmes? Drat,
I've done all of that already. I know what
I'll do, I'll write a phenomenological
account of the book-reviewing process:
'After selecting the book from the
bookshelf and settling into a
comfortable chair, our subject (white,
female, ageing hippy) sharpened her
pencil, stared briefly into space and
read the book from cover to cover,
making notes in her personal log as she
went along.' Yes, that's it. Just perfect
for *JCR*.

4. Jagdish Sheth
These days, it seems that everyone is
talking about 'relationships', 'networks'
and 'de-layering'. They are the latest in a
long line of fashionable marketing
concepts. But, let's get one thing
absolutely straight. I thought of them
first. I first used the term 'relationship'
in a paper that appeared in 1962. True,
it was a love letter to my teenage
girlfriend, but the fact remains that I
thought of it first. Likewise, I was using
the word 'network' as long ago as 1965.
Fair enough, it was in a complaint to the
president of CBS, about a television
programme I'd been watching, but I
thought of it first. Indeed, in 1965 I was
also using the word de-layering, though
it was actually a spelling mistake in a
note I left for the milkman. But that's
quite beside the point, because I
thought of it first.

Table 2.2 Contd.

5. Michael Baker

As Jagdish Sheth has recently pointed out, 'These days it seems that everyone is talking about relationships, networks and de-layering'. But, Elizabeth Hirschman insists that she's 'running out of ideas.' Shelby D. Hunt, moreover, maintains most marketers 'misunderstand the very nature of marketing philosophy'. However, Michael J. Baker emphasizes that 'As Jagdish Sheth has recently pointed out, ''These days it seems that everyone is talking about relationships'''.

rhetorical questions? Do you believe, as I do, that a sentence is not a sentence unless it terminates with a question mark? Do you think, having examined the evidence, that a utopian fusion of marketing, entrepreneurship and strategy is possible? IN OUR LIFETIME? But hold, is that a continuum I see before me? What on earth is happening to marketing textbooks? Why do publishers churn out this rubbish? Stephen, you don't really expect me to say something nasty – in print – about this book, do you? Why can't I just give it a neutral review and let the readers decide? OK then, do you want to see a two-word review, David Carson-style? Buy? Buy!

6. Malcolm McDonald

		Amount of money the book is likely to make me		
		Little	Lots	Loads
Amount of rewriting required from my previous edition	Little			X
	Lots			
	Loads			

7. David Carson

Do you have a weakness for

8. Douglas Brownlie (sung)

Some people call me the space cowboy,
Some call me the gangster of love,
Some people call me barking mad Brownlie,
Cos' I speak of things you can't understand.

. . . Awopbopalubopawopbamboom . . .
Tutti frutti
I'm loopy
Tutti frutti
I'm loopy
Tutti frutti
I'm loopy
I write this way to make you think I'm the man.

Source: S. Brown 1995i: 158–9

ideologies by bringing unsettling or occluded truths to the attention of interested parties.

In light of the manifest disparity between marketing's ostensible intentions (customer care/satisfaction) and practical outcomes (customer exploitation/manipulation), critical theory provides an appealing, intellectually sophisticated, praxis-oriented platform for oppositionally inclined marketing academics, and it has been embraced with some enthusiasm (e.g. J. B. Murray and Ozanne 1991; Alvesson and Willmott 1992; Hetrick and Lozada 1993, 1994; Alvesson 1994; Brownlie and Saren 1995; McDonagh 1995b). Morgan, for example, maintains that:

> the discourses and practices of marketing are productive of, as well as constituted by, a particular society. Marketing is not a neutral way of looking at the world; it has distinctive power effects for organisations, managers, consumers and society as a whole. A critical approach to marketing will seek to uncover those effects that exist beneath the level of everyday consciousness.
>
> (Morgan 1992: 136)

In this respect, Ozanne and Murray (1996) have applied Habermas's theory of communicative competence to consumerism, contending that the development of informed consumer choice (by means of *Consumer Reports* etc.) merely perpetuates the existing system in so far as it entrenches people in their established role as consumers. What is needed, they argue, is a reflexively defiant consumer who refuses to reproduce this form of social domination, who rebels against the system and who chooses to defy traditional conceptions of consumption – though given capital's unerring ability to commodify symbols of resistance, reflexively defiant consumption requires constant vigilance. For Desmond (1995), indeed, commodification represents the appropriation of life force, the replacement of the human by the non-human, the veiling of origins and, in terms of marketing, transforms a potentially emancipatory academic discipline into the 'political wing' of neo-classical economics, a fifth-columnist for the invasion of domains hitherto uncommodified, a means of marketizing the parts that other ideologies cannot reach. Following Habermas, he urges marketers to move away from narrow forms of pragmatic empiricism, to engage with critical theory in a process of systematic self-reflection and, not least, to seek to adopt a tolerant attitude towards the dissenting, the dissident, the different.

Critical theory may well be a 'crouched tiger' (J. B. Murray *et al.* 1994), coiled to pounce, presumably, on the unsuspecting quarry that is marketing, but it remains something of a pussy cat compared to the sheer feral ferocity of feminism. Few would deny that of all the critiques of 'modern' marketing understanding, the most radical by far have been mounted by the women's movement. So much so that if ever the seemingly immovable object of marketing ideology is to be swept aside by an irresistible force, then feminism is perhaps best placed to do the impossible. While many academics have been content to ignore this challenge thus far, a series of dedicated conferences, edited books and special issues of prominent journals suggests that gender is indisputably high on the contemporary marketing agenda (Costa 1993, 1994a, 1996). Published studies range from theoretically informed analyses of androcentrism in the academy (Hirschman 1993a), the phallocentric premises of qualitative research procedures (Catterall *et al.* 1996), the historical foundations of the relationship between consumption and gender (Firat 1994) and the overall implications of feminist thought for consumer research (Bristor and Fischer 1993), to empirically oriented investigations of patriarchal influences on Christmas gift-giving (Fischer and Arnold 1990), representations of womankind in works of popular culture (Hirschman 1993b), the misogynistic milieux endured by female marketing managers (Catterall *et al.* 1997), the deconstruction of gender stereotypes in diverse advertising campaigns (B. B. Stern 1991a, 1993) and the regressive social consequences that such impossibly perfect portrayals of the female body tend to engender (Richins 1991, 1996; M. C. Martin and Kennedy 1994).

Given the multiplicity of perspectives that shelter under the umbrella term 'feminism' (Tong 1989; Nicholson 1990; Watkins *et al.* 1992; Ebert 1996; S. Mills and Pearce 1996), almost all of which have been applied to various aspects of the marketing condition – e.g. woman's voice feminism (Holbrook 1995a), eco-feminism (Lozada and Mintu-Wimsatt 1995), Marxist feminism (Hirschman 1993a), new French Feminism (Catterall *et al.* 1996), etc. – it is impossible to do justice to the recent, rapid and indeed welcome growth of feminist thought within the academy. Nevertheless, by briefly examining a single paper dealing with issues that go to the heart of 'modern' marketing it is possible to provide a indication of the feminist position (under normal circumstances, as I'm sure you appreciate, I'd be indulging in all sorts of flights of literary fancy concerning the 'taste of testosterone', 'whiff of oestrogen' and so on, but discretion, as they say, is the better part of valour). In their post-structuralist feminist deconstruction of the exchange paradigm, Fischer and Bristor (1994) offer a radical reinterpretation of modern marketing discourse. Arguing that consumption has long been regarded as a 'feminine' sphere of activity and marketing essentially 'masculine', they expose the patriarchal premises that inhere in the marketing concept and its principal variants (production concept, sales concept, and so on) as portrayed in the introductory chapters of most traditional marketing management textbooks. Thus, the production concept is predicated on the notion of a passive yet coquettish consumer whom suitably masculine marketers are enjoined to overcome and satisfy; the sales concept rests on an aggressive, hard-sell, rape and pillage model of the female consumer; and the marketing concept on sexual conquest through the 'penetration' of chosen target markets. Even the much-vaunted relationship marketing concept, with its explicit 'marriage' metaphor and associated emphasis on trust, equality and mutual respect, merely reproduces the existing balance of social, economic and political power, which inevitably involves the continuing subordination of women.

While the details of their deconstructive exercise are debatable – as it is primarily a business-to-business construct, relationship marketing might be more fruitfully portrayed as essentially homosexual, hence excluding women completely – Fischer and Bristor have succeeded in highlighting the asymmetrical power relationships and implicit phallocentrism that underpin 'unproblematic', taken-for-granted marketing concepts. This process of unmasking the 'doxa', the what-goes-without-saying (Barthes 1973), also permeates the *post-colonial* critique of modern marketing understanding. Post-colonialism involves questioning the universalist claims made on behalf of the western intellectual tradition – arguing, in effect, that western standards are not timeless or absolute or incontrovertible but an instantiation of imperialism – whilst celebrating the indigenous approaches, perspectives and traditions suppressed or marginalized by the colonial power (Ashcroft *et al.* 1989; Bhabha 1990; Adam and Tiffin 1991; Boehmer 1995). Exemplified by the literary and critical endeavours of Salman Rushdie and Edward Said, respectively, post-colonialism is as much a reaction to as a rejection of the colonial inheritance. On the one hand, it involves the reclamation of local, regional and national forms of expression, combined with a critique of canonical caricatures of the 'native', the 'oriental', the 'exotic'. On the other hand, post-colonial discourse does not involve an irrevocable break, since it invariably employs the 'mother' tongue, comprises a conversation with the 'centre' and, by its very existence, forces the oppressors to reflect on their own racism, to challenge their own sense of superiority, to question their own universalizing predilections.

Unlike feminist approaches to marketing scholarship, post-colonial perspectives are comparatively few in number, though there is a growing literature on the gross ethnocentrism that underpins (mis)representations of the 'strange people with their amusing marketing practices' in the developing world (Table 2.3 epitomizes this pernicious propensity in so far as it 'reveals' the appallingly unsophisticated standards of customer service in China by means of an inventory of the purported patter of sales clerks). Venkatesh (1995), for instance, condemns indiscriminate attempts to apply American conceptual frameworks, or suitably adapted conceptual

Table 2.3 Well, here, we are, here we are and here we go

Concerned about the appalling standards of customer service that continue to prevail in many shops, airports and hotels, the Chinese government recently introduced a 'nationwide politeness campaign'. The following fifty phrases, widely used by sales assistants, have been officially banned:

---

1 Hey!
2 Old man.
3 Hey, soldier!
4 Country bumpkin.
5 Darkie (refers to dark-skinned Chinese).
6 What does it have to do with you?
7 Who told you not to look where you're going?
8 If you don't like it, go somewhere else.
9 Ask someone else.
10 Didn't you hear me? What do you have ears for?
11 Take a taxi if you don't like the bus.
12 Get out of the way, or you'll get killed.
13 That's just the way things are!
14 I don't care whom you complain to.
15 Are you finished talking?
16 If you're not buying, what are you looking at?
17 Buy it if you can afford it, otherwise get out of here.
18 Are you buying or not? Have you made up your mind?
19 What are you yelling about? Wait a while.
20 Don't you see I'm busy? What's the hurry?
21 Hurry up and pay.
22 I can't solve this. Go complain to whomever you want.
23 I don't know.
24 I just told you. Why are you asking again?
25 Don't stand in the way.
26 I have no change. Wait here.
27 Why didn't you choose well when you bought it?
28 Go ask the person who sold it to you.
29 If you don't like it, talk to the manager.
30 Time is up, be quick.
31 The price is posted. Can't you see it yourself?
32 No exchanges, that's the rule.
33 If you're not buying, don't ask.
34 You're asking me. Whom should I ask?
35 Stop shouting. Can't you see I'm eating?
36 It's not my fault.
37 We haven't opened yet. Wait a while.
38 What are you doing? Be quick.
39 I'm not in charge. Don't ask me so many questions.
40 Didn't I tell you? How come you don't get it?
41 I have no change. Go get some yourself.
42 Don't push me.
43 If you want it, speak up; if you don't, get out of the way. Next!
44 Don't talk so much. Say it quickly.

Table 2.3 Contd.

45	Now you tell me. What have you been doing all this time?	48	What can I do? I didn't break it.
46	The busier I am, the more you bother me. How annoying!	49	Don't play the fool with me.
47	Why don't you have the money ready?	50	Get at the end of the line.

frameworks, to non-western cultural contexts, arguing that US-style marketing concepts are both completely inappropriate and utterly irrelevant to the situation in India. Joy and Wallendorf (1996) are equally critical of one-path models of modernization and the analogous assumption that proto-western consumer society is an inevitable consequence of the first world–third world culture clash. As Mead (1994) cogently demonstrates in his case study of contemporary Thailand, a postmodern melange of east and west, old and new, give and take, and adoption and adaptation is a much more likely outcome.

Important, welcome and necessary though such exposés are, it is arguable that the full force of the post-colonial critique will only become manifest in marketing if its basic message is modified. After all, the most pernicious and pervasive form of colonialism in marketing does not involve the relationship between developed and developing worlds, iniquitous though this is. It inheres, rather, in the whole Coca-Kotlerization process, the absolute and seemingly unbreakable dominance of American marketing scholarship in general and the Kotlerite model of analysis, planning, implementation and control in particular. In fairness, many North American marketing academics are cognizant and rightly critical of the narrow-minded parochialism – the 'if it isn't published in *JM*, *JMR* or *JCR* it doesn't count' mentality – that is all too apparent among their countrymen. The colonized, moreover, are often their own worst, we-are-not-worthy enemies when they spontaneously abase themselves before American marketing superiority or, in a classic 'turkeys voting for Christmas' scenario, uncritically reproduce Europeanized editions of best-selling US textbooks, thereby perpetuating the intellectual hegemony of their oppressors (Dibb *et al.* 1994; Kotler *et al.* 1995). There are, of course, a number of forthright, some would say suicidal, individuals who are prepared to break the marketing *omerta* and speak out against the Kotler Nostra (Table 2.4). Nevertheless, it is fair to say that the post-colonialist challenge has yet to make a meaningful impact on the US marketing mainstream. When someone as broad-minded as Elizabeth Hirschman (1993a) can write a paper that condemns gender bias in *JCR*, whilst ignoring the even more blatant bias against non–American academics (not to mention 'doubly silenced' non–American *female* academics), the sheer pervasiveness of this problem is only too apparent.

Table 2.4 What's the frequency, Philip?

Like many marketing academics of my generation, I was brought up on a diet of Kotler. Weaned on *Principles of Marketing*, I progressed to the solids of *Marketing Management* and, in due course, acquired a taste for the exotica of *High Visibility, The New Competition, Marketing for Nonprofit Organisations* and most of the other items on Kotler's impressive marketing menu. I have never met the great man, nor seen Phil perform. However, a colleague of mine once collared him at a conference and it was long my proudest academic boast that I shook the hand that shook the hand of Kotler. As I recall, I refused to wash my hands for a fortnight thereafter, though this is less impressive than it sounds since I usually operate on a monthly ablutionary cycle. (I know that's a lot for an Irishman, but I'm pretty fastidious about personal hygiene.)

In light of my long-felt Kotlerite leanings, my fondness for Phil's pearls of marketing wisdom, and my admittedly impressive party piece – a little recitation entitled 'the generic concept of marketing' – I'm sure you'll appreciate that it gives me no pleasure whatsoever to announce that King Kong Kotler has finally fallen from the Empire State Building of marketing scholarship. I don't know when the colossus began to lose his grip, but the scales started to fall from my eyes on reading his chapter in *Historical Perspectives in Marketing*. Kotler's (1988) essay on the history of the convenience store was so superficial, so uninsightful, so inappropriate to the occasion (a tribute to a genuine marketing intellectual, Stanley C. Hollander) that I came to the deeply depressing – but undoubtedly accurate – conclusion that the chapter was included on account of its contributor rather than its contribution. Why, I wondered, is it that whenever academics make a name for themselves they are allowed to get away with publishing any old nonsense? Do they lose their innate sense of quality control? Are editors unwilling to tell them the uncomfortable truth? Or is it an artifact of our excessively raised expectations, which the authors, no matter how brilliant, are simply unable to satisfy?

At the time, I admit, I dismissed Phil's historical farrago as an unfortunate one-off occurrence, a minor slip, a slight deviation from his otherwise exemplary standards of marketing excellence. I now know better, though I'm not sure if it's me that has changed, having outgrown the infatuations of my intellectual adolescence, or if Kotler has finally given up the fight and is now content to rest on his richly deserved laurels. To be honest, I suspect that it is the former, because I recently reread (as opposed to regurgitated) 'the generic concept of marketing' and found its farcical combination of can-do, counterculture and

Table 2.4 Contd.

conspiracy theory – such as the references to brainwashing, levels of consciousness and the like – as much a manifestation of the late 1960s American *Zeitgeist* as a meaningful guide for today's marketing practitioners. In fact, perhaps the paper's only saving grace is that it is not as bad as 'marketing myopia'. (Let's be honest, most of the confident predictions in Levitt's seminal contribution – rocket-powered cars, ultrasonics, fuel cells, the end of the oil industry by 1985, etc. – turned out to be *completely erroneous*. They represent a hubristic testimony to Levitt's lack of foresight, to his own marketing myopia!)

Kotler and a couple of sidekicks have just brought out a new book called *Marketing Places* and in any other circumstances this occasion would have been the fulfilment of all my academic fantasies. Seven years ago (the same year as our hero's convenience store calamity), I wrote a paper which concluded that 'the marketing of geographical locations . . . may emerge as a major focus of marketing activity in the next few years'. To have this prediction brought to fruition by Philly the Kid, marketing's capo-di-capo, the main man from the windy city, ought to have been my finest hour, my intellectual apotheosis, my moment of vicarious vainglory, my one and only opportunity to boast how 'great minds think alike'.

Regrettably, I find myself unable to bask in Kotler's reflected glow, because *Marketing Places* is utterly devoid of intellectual merit. It is half-baked hack-work of the lowest order. It exhibits not a shred, not a smidgen, not a scintilla of scholarship or academic rigour. It is a gruesome melange of tired and testing truisms, reheated anecdotes, bogus recommendations, pseudo-insights, specious checklists and the sort of simplistic sloganizing that even Tom Peters would be disinclined to disburse. In my more amenable moments, admittedly, I toy with the notion that this catalogue of clichés, this pantheon of platitudes, this inventory of inanities is some kind of a joke – Wild Phil Kotler, the Andy Warhol of marketing scholarship, having a laugh at his credulous disciples' expense. I'm sorry to say that this book *is* a joke . . . but nobody's laughing.

Marketing Places purports to be about 'attracting investment, industry and tourism to cities, states and nations'. According to the back-board blurb, it is required reading for every forward-looking mayor, governor and public official. Well, I'm no local dignitary, and not exactly what you would call a model citizen, but even I can recognize scholarly snake-oil when I see it. The book opens, you'll never guess, with an apocalyptic chapter entitled 'places in trouble'. This is swiftly followed – surprise, surprise – by a ready-made, trip-off-the-tongue, one-size-fits-all, just-add-water solution to a locality's ills, 'strategic marketing planning'. However, just in case the authors might be held responsible for the veracity of their subsequent suggestions, the chapter concludes with that familiar marketing standby, the get-out clause: 'places have to acknowledge that there are

Table 2.4 Contd.

---

no simple panaceas, doctrinaire prescriptions or magical elixirs' (p. 20). Keep taking the tablets, Philip.

The second chapter, on how places market themselves, is a triumph of the trite, with insights of the following well-I-never, you-don't-say, step-back-in-amazement calibre: 'when businesses sell more products to more distant markets, they produce more income and jobs within the local economy' (p. 28); and 'the longer visitors stay, the more they spend. Places would, therefore, prefer to target those visitors who spend the most per day and stay the longest' (p. 24). Sadly, these gems of cutting-edge marketing thinking are as flowers in the desert compared to Chapter 3, which informs us (p. 46) that 'the choice of a two-week vacation destination involves different factors than the choice of a city to move to, or a business firm's choice of a new factory site' (surely not!). Consider, moreover, Chapter 4, which incisively analyses an entire continent's place-marketing problems thus: 'In the short run, India can only tout its strengths. In the long run, it must try to correct its weaknesses' (p. 84). Or what about this from Chapter 5: 'Venice itself is one giant walking area' (p. 125)? Well, Kotler might be able to walk on water, but the rest of us should remember to pack our inflatables. Even Kotler, however, cannot be absolved from the ultimate musical sacrilege perpetrated on p. 217, when he asserts that the Beatles came from Manchester (watch yourself Phil, the lynch mobs are out in Liverpool).

Aside from this litany of banalities, non-advice and occasional old-fashioned factual errors, which continues in an unremitting fashion throughout the text's twelve noisome chapters, there are five things that particularly bother me about *Marketing Places*. First, it is cookie-cutter marketing of the worst kind. As with the vast majority of Kotler's prior publications, it simply applies the tools and techniques of marketing 'technology' to another domain, regardless of its appropriateness or goodness-of-fit. Now, the question isn't whether the marketing concept etc. *can* be applied to these divergent domains – it can, the marketing metaphor is sufficiently vague and all-encompassing to be attached to almost anything – the real question is whether it *should* be applied. This conundrum, admittedly, is ultimately unanswerable, but something is seriously amiss when the application of the marketing concept produces the sort of twaddle we find on p. 12; namely that businesses are more footloose than places. (Let me get this clear, are they really suggesting that places are also footloose to some degree? That if we are displeased with the place of our place, we can re-place our place someplace else? In cyberspace perhaps, on the Internet quite possibly, in the pages of science fiction unquestionably. But somehow I don't think Kotler and his collaborators had these ontological issues in mind when they penned their inexcusably sloppy sentence.)

Second, even if we accept the uncertain premise that sausage-machine

Table 2.4 Contd.

marketing technology is applicable to places, with their infinite variety of social, economic, historical, demographic, environmental, historical, climatic and legislative circumstances, it seems reasonable to expect that the marketing machine on offer will be the very latest model, fully maintained and in perfect working order. Unfortunately, Philip and his pals prefer to peddle a first-generation, steam-driven variant which appears to have been assembled from the spare parts of Kotler's unsuccessful earlier experiments. The model of consumer behaviour in Chapter 3, for example, has not been displayed in the showroom of marketing scholarship for nigh on twenty years; the procedure for image measurement in Chapter 6 is the intellectual equivalent of Caxton's moveable type in an era of desk-top publishing; and the disparaging treatment of homelessness, drug addiction and criminality on p. 127 seems blissfully ignorant of recent academic research into the 'dark side' of consumer behaviour. *Marketing Places*, moreover, abounds with vague generalizations and unattributed assertions (of the 'many marketers say' variety), contemporary academic citations are conspicuous by their absence (though newspaper stories and magazine articles are copiously drawn upon), and the whole book is suffused with the sort of marketing megalomania, gung-ho disciplinary imperialism, we-have-the-technology intellectual arrogance that characterized marketing in the first flush of its youth, some forty years ago. Don't you know, it's time to grow up boys!

This book, to employ an appropriately geographical analogy, is the academic equivalent of the western world's tendency to dump antiquated technology on developing countries (and for which they should be goddamn grateful!). Of course, the problem with such Coca-Kotlerization is that the third world disciplines at the receiving end of marketing's technological cast-offs – geography, regional science, environmental studies, urban planning and the like – are as much if not more sophisticated than the giver (read their journals if you don't believe me). Indeed, on the disappointingly few occasions when the authors actually draw upon the *vast* body of extant research in these particular fields of study, the outcome is excruciatingly inept. On p. 100, we are offered a description of urban development which would not be out of place in a fifth-form geography schoolbook. The authors' declaration on p. 326 that 'clustering has become a key concept of the 1990s' might come as a surprise to spatial scientists, who have been studying the phenomenon for more than sixty years. Latter-day advances in Geographical Information Systems are almost entirely overlooked – there is one brief reference in an exhibit (p. 50) – and, not surprisingly, several erroneous statements flow from Kotler *et al.*'s all-too evident ignorance (e.g. top p. 108). Likewise, Lynch's (1960) celebrated technique of cognitive mapping is alluded to

Table 2.4 Contd.

---

on p. 148 (without due acknowledgement), yet the hundreds of often critical publications on his procedure are apparently unworthy of mention. There is simply no excuse for this. It is downright sloppy scholarship. Philip Kotler should be ashamed of himself.

A third, and almost inconceivable, shortcoming of this book, which purports to deal with spatial issues, is that it is not only academically ethnocentric but geographically ethnocentric! *Marketing Places* is overwhelmingly American in orientation, though in an attempt to save the authors' blushes (a book about places that only deals with one place?) a light sprinkling of other locales is incorporated. Yet a glance through the contents, and a moment's reflection, reveal that this geographical garnish is purely for cosmetic purposes, for *domestic* consumption. It is a cynical attempt to dupe the American readership (hey, who else matters?) into thinking that they are dealing with a cosmopolitan volume. This cosmopolitanism, however, comprises little more than the periodic recycling of gross national stereotypes – lazy Italians, polite Englishmen, untrustworthy Greeks (hell, they'll probably put this review down to the fighting Irish!) – and pseudo 'guidance' of the most vapid and platitudinous kind. According to these self-styled geographical gurus, 'Northern Ireland is urban, brutal and dangerous . . . [and] . . . needs a more believable visual image strategy than pastoral greenery' (p. 154). Holy moly. Hot diggedy daawg. Well blow me down. Now, why didn't we think of that? This nugget alone must be worth $35 of anyone's money. Not!

Fourth, *Marketing Places* is abysmally written and put together. Heaven only knows, we don't expect much of marketing scholars; John Updike, Gore Vidal and Martin Amis are never likely to be casting worried looks in our discipline's direction; and, in fairness, the book never sinks to the fetid depths plumbed by Samli's *Retail Marketing Strategy* or the heights of cliché-mongering attained in McDonald's *Marketing by Matrix*. But, it is still a hackneyed collation of dead metaphors, non-sequiturs, slovenly syntax and substandard journalese (such as bottom p. 283), and exhibits a grasp of grammar which is as tenuous as the rest of its tendentious content. Thus, we are less than one sentence into the text when our old friend anthropomorphism rears its ugly head. Yes folks, the undead of academic discourse, the metaphor you thought was safely buried with a stake through its heart, has risen from the grave! You guessed it – places as patients, on the sick list, road to recovery, clinically depressed, drastic surgery required in some locales, mild sedatives necessary in others. Anyone for Prozac? An enema? Electro-convulsive Therapy? What's the frequency, Philip?

Elsewhere, we are treated to descriptions of cities that are 'investible' (p. 2), 'devolving' into ghost towns (p. 3) or suffering – and I must confess that my imagination imploded at this point – from 'brownouts' (p. 39). Sports arenas are

Table 2.4 Contd.

---

referred to as a 'species' of investment (p. 128); we are advised to 'essentialise' huge amounts of data (p. 141); recommended to 'effectuate' the urban development process (p. 318); and told (p. 197) of the distressing events in Jamaica when, 'its major export, bauxite, collapsed' (some sort of bizarre chemical reaction, or what?). *Marketing Places*, moreover, suffers from repetition (cf. the start of Chapters 1 and 4), mis-sequencing (if the list of points on p. 231 is correct, then Chapters 8 and 9 have been mistakenly transposed), inconsistency (Boston's high-tech Route 128 is paraded as an example of both ineptitude and good practice), incongruity (such as the shift in focus, from place to firm, in Chapter 9), self-contradiction (places are advised to specialize on p. 78 and warned off such a strategy on p. 258) and downright incoherence (e.g. the case study of Detroit which transmogrifies into an analysis of Houston, Alabama and Cleveland). Likewise, the list of ten ways 'to measure your place's export climate' (p. 256), at least two of which are indistinguishable, is the product not so much of authorial inspiration, or perspiration, as of *desperation* (help Phil, we've only got eight, can you think up a couple more?); the 'zero-sum' analogy is employed so often that it has a negative-sum effect upon the reader; and, horror of horrors, the terms 'marketing' and 'selling' are used synonymously throughout! Indeed, the metaphysicians among you might wish to reflect on the sheer profundity of the following sentence: 'The truth is that most troubled places are both victim and cause' (p. 70). Conspiracy theorists, by contrast, might consider certain comments on p. 106 suspiciously prescient: 'what value would Los Angeles's mountainside homes have without flood control works?' (please direct all correspondence, especially items in green ink, to Kotler and his compadres, c/o Northwestern University).

The fifth, final and by far the most fundamental problem I have with *Marketing Places* is the simple fact that it signally fails to adopt the very orientation it endeavours to propagate. The book treats its audience – its market – with total disdain. It appears to subscribe to the view that all place-marketing managers are simpletons, that they are incapable of dealing with complex ideas, or sentences with subclauses, that they require a cavalcade of bullet points, facile exercises and asinine 'exhibits' (which appear to have been faxed into the text from a parallel marketing universe) in order to maintain their interest. This is lowest common denominator scholarship. It demonstrates not an iota of self-consciousness or reflexivity ('smoke-stack chasing' is condemned on pp. 242–6, yet for most non-specialists this approach *is* marketing – marketing is to blame!). *Marketing Places* is flaccid, flawed, fatuous, formulaic and, frankly, an affront to its readership. In fact, if I didn't know better I'd be forced to conclude that this book is written by dullards for dullards. The authors, believe it or not, actually have the audacity to quote Gertrude Stein's celebrated statement on Oakland,

Table 2.4 Contd.

'there's no there there'. Well, I have to tell you Philip, there's no there here either! Now, these remarks may be dismissed as intemperate invective, ivory-tower daydreaming or delusions of scholarship. The harsh reality is that practising managers will not accept anything other than bite-sized, readily digestible, semi-literate, simple-minded bromides, such as those contained herein (hey, you gotta give the customers what they want). I simply don't believe this. On the contrary, I would contend that King Philly's decision to write in this execrable manner merely serves to perpetuate it. For publishers, Kotler represents the gold standard against which all marketing texts are measured; his works comprise the formula that all marketing textbooks are required to employ; and *his* is the approach that readers have become conditioned to expect. Baron Kotlerstein has created a monster which he is incapable of controlling and which cannot be destroyed. Like it or not, Kotler is the personification of marketing for most non-marketers and his endeavours are regarded as representative of the entire field. In my view, the publication of *Marketing Places*, the appearance of this embarrassing mess, has done serious damage to the marketing discipline. We often ask ourselves why marketing continues to be held in such low academic esteem despite its undeniable achievements. Part of the answer lies in books like this. *Marketing Places* is overrated, overwrought and, regrettably, over here.

Source: S. Brown 1995j: 134–8

Sign o' the times

A spectre may be stalking Europe, the spectre of Kotlerism, and the political postmodernists may well wish to change the marketing world, not simply describe it, but their cause has not been helped by the cacophony of competing voices and accompanying internecine conflict. The critical theorists appear to be at each others' throats in a Tarantinoesque 'I'm more radical than you' Mexican stand-off (Larsen and Wright 1993; Murray *et al.* 1994; Hetrick and Lozada 1994); the feminists seem somewhat lacking in brotherly love, so to speak (Costa 1994b; Hetrick and Lozada 1995); and it is ironic that the post–colonialist case is only attended to when it is being made by academics trained or based in the United States (Venkatesh 1995). There is, moreover, considerable debate over the 'post-modern' credentials of critical theory, feminism and post–colonialism in the first place (Nicholson 1990; Adam and Tiffin 1991; Ray 1993; Farganis 1994; Hoy and McCartney 1994). For some commentators of a catholic disposition they are all part and parcel of a grand oppositional alliance, a sort of rainbow coalition of critique (Holbrook 1995a). For the pedantically inclined, however, the exact nature of the relationship between the various positions and postmodernism, both separately and in combination, is highly problematic (S. Brown 1995a). Certain feminists, for example, are very reluctant to associate themselves with the perceived political impotence of the postmodern, as are many critical theorists and post-colonialists. By the same token, most paraclete postmodernists are prone to object, in their characteristic 'anything goes but not that' fashion, to the politicos' promulgation of alternative positions per se. They have, moreover, plenty of vitriol to spare for the pragmatics, those who seek to emasculate postmodernism's subversiveness by portraying it as yet another perspective, a new weapon to stockpile in marketing's extensive intellectual arsenal, a fashionable *pied à terre* to add to our discipline's bulging property portfolio, its many methodological mansions (S. Brown 1995d). The pragmatics, in turn, are less than impressed by the paracletes' anti-alternative alternative and the political postmodernists' manifest enthusiasm for positions, such as the neo-Marxism of critical theory, which are wholeheartedly opposed to the capitalist system that spawned, and to a very large extent sustains, marketing scholarship. Why, after all, bite the ideology that feeds you?

In a situation where some marketers appear determined to recuperate the postmodern and put it to work (Firat and Venkatesh 1995), others are using it to advance the causes of the hitherto excluded or marginalized (Hill 1993, 1995), and yet others seem content to play with the inverted commas of 'postmodern' 'parody', 'by' 'pouring' 'scorn' 'on' 'friend' 'and' 'foe' 'alike' (C. J. Thompson 1997), it is perfectly reasonable to respond to this lack of consensus with 'a plague on all your houses' and to seek succour in the capacious bosom of the 'modern' marketing paradigm. However, in an era when Derrida is *de rigueur*, Barthes is the degree zero of marketing discourse and Lacan's maternal phallus is on almost everyone's lips, sucking on the teats of analysis, planning, implementation and control is no longer a meaningful option. The various schools of postmodern marketing scholarship may disagree on many things but they concur that modern marketing has had its chips, bitten the dust, passed its sell-by date, given up the ghost, shuffled off its mortal coil, and if not exactly on board the Stygian ferry, certainly in the queue at the ticket booth. As we have seen, even the most enthusiastic exponents of the marketing message now acknowledge that the old ways of doing things are hopelessly inadequate, that the traditional models, frameworks and theories no longer work, that the fault lies not in managers' unwillingness or inability to adopt the marketing philosophy but in the utter pointlessness of the principles themselves.

Casual readers – not that you're one of *those*, of course – may conclude that the solution to marketing's current crisis of representation lies in coining new concepts, forging innovative frameworks and promulgating novel perspectives that are more in tune with our perturbed postmodern times. To some extent this is already happening, with the recent rapid emergence of the relationship marketing paradigm, and its epistemological epigones, being perhaps the most obvious case in point (McKenna 1992; Buttle 1996a; Gummesson 1996c). However, the substitution of one representation for another is not necessarily a solution to the problem since postmodernism calls into question the very idea of representation (Marcus and Fischer 1986; Dickens and Fontana 1994b; Eldridge 1996; Gephart *et al.* 1996; G. Rose 1996). The notion that we can somehow capture or portray 'external reality' in an accurate, mimetic, unambiguous, unequivocal, unmediated, essentially truthful fashion, or for that matter discuss it from an Archimedean, objective, omniscient, trans-historical, trans-cultural, value-free, value-neutral, extra-linguistic standpoint, has foundered on the post-structuralists' revelations concerning the inconsistency, instability and ultimate undecidability of language. By undermining the commonsensical or realist view of representation, which presupposes that the sign–referent relationship is transparent, they have succeeded in drawing attention to and challenging the ostensibly direct or natural link between word and world.

In fact, for Baudrillard and like-minded authorities on the apocalyptic wing of the postmodern movement, the always slippery relationship between signifier and signified has been sundered completely, as a result of media metastasis, and all forms of representation now float free, detached from their referents, and merely allude to each other in a complex self-referential arabesque. According to the so-called 'pimp of postmodernism' (Horrocks and Jevtic 1996), there have been four successive stages in the nature of the relationship between representations and reality (Figure 2.2). First, they are a reflection of basic reality; second, they mask and pervert basic reality; third, they mask the absence of a basic reality; and, fourth, they bear no relation to any reality whatsoever. The upshot of this 'precession of simulacra' is a postmodern hall of mirrors where signs, images and representations are reflected, refracted and re-presented in perpetuity. In these disorienting circumstances, where the rug of representation has been figuratively pulled from under our feet, the very idea of developing meaningful marketing frameworks or undertaking associated empirical research has been rendered problematical, possibly impossible (Baudrillard 1983, 1994b).

As you might expect, Baudrillard's position is fairly extreme and for some

Figure 2.2 Wells, it's a one for the money

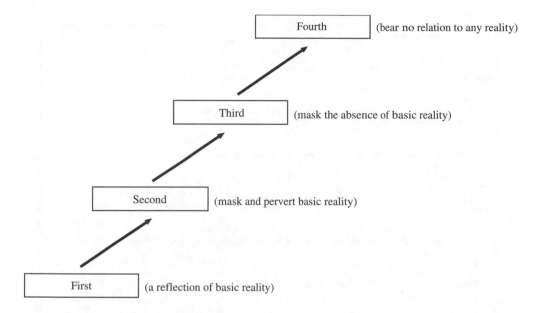

academic authorities it has more holes in it than undergarments washed in Persil Power, the postmodern washing powder that literally eats your shorts (E. Bell 1996). Hutcheon (1989), to cite but a single example, has accused him of metaphysical idealism and unwarranted nostalgia for a non-existent era of pre-mass-mediated authenticity (since we only ever have access to the real through representations, the notion of a pre-lapsidarian linguistic paradise is simply untenable). Yet even if we concede that the relationship between representation and reality is in crisis or under erasure, as opposed to completely eviscerated, then the implications for marketing scholarship are still extremely serious, *because marketing research is inherently representational* (S. Brown 1995d). Whether it be representative samples, the representation of respondents' actions, attitudes and intentions in survey research exercises – which themselves represent researchers' representations of the issues in question – or indeed our very attempts to develop theoretical/ statistical/diagrammatic/interpretive representations of marketing phenomena, representation represents the *raison d'être* of marketing research (Figure 2.3). After all, the output of most marketing research exercises still comprises a representation (verbal delivery) of a representation (academic paper), of a representation (data analysis), of a representation (survey instrument), of a representation (sample), of a representation (respondents' response), of a representation (respondents' mental

Figure 2.3 Drove my Chevy to the Levy but the Levy was dry

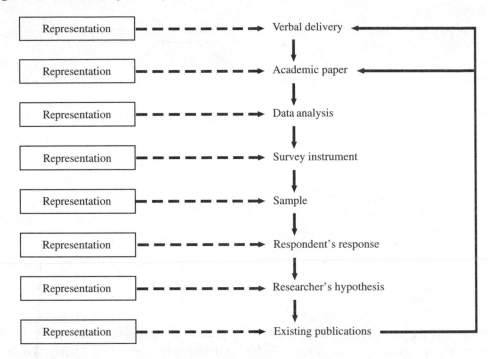

schemata) of a representation (the researcher's assumption that the topic is worth researching), of a representation (the context – published papers, established theoretical frameworks, etc. – from whence this assumption derives). Even discussions of the postmodern crisis of representation represent anti-representative representations of this representational impasse.

If representation *is* in crisis, both in its positivistic and interpretive variants, then the question has to be asked: how can we possibly represent marketing phenomena without resorting to representation? The answer, as Hutcheon (1988, 1989) makes perfectly clear, is that we can't. We can merely acknowledge, in an ironic, suitably self-conscious fashion, our continuing reliance on representation, the fact that we are implicated in the very thing we are seeking to contest. Alternatively, we can confine ourselves to repudiating extant modes of representation by means of Derridean deconstruction, Jameson's cognitive mapping and analogous postmodern procedures (though deconstruction and cognitive mapping also ultimately rely on representation), or choose to remain silent, albeit silence itself can be construed as a form of non-representational representation. Another possibility is to turn to 'unorthodox' forms of representation in the belief that, while they may not provide access to the unvarnished truth or unmediated reality, they may well offer a means of escaping the representational penitentiary or, at the very least, allow us out on postmodern *parole* (as opposed, naturally, to *langue*).

For many commentators, the most promising solution to our 'dead ideology walking' situation lies in the realm of aesthetics in general and literature and literary theory in particular. This latter-day assumption, that the 'artworld' (see Danto 1987) can somehow provide a means of avoiding the intellectual electric chair that is 'sceptical' postmodernism, is predicated on a number of important, mutually reinforcing developments. The first of these is the long-standing, if grandiloquent, belief that works of art can somehow express the inexpressible, describe the indescribable, touch the untouchable, present the unpresentable and, by transporting us beyond the banalities, disappointments and absurdities of everyday existence, enable us to commune momentarily with something eternal, something majestic, something ineffable, something over and above ourselves. Certainly, variants of this viewpoint have been espoused by many prominent thinkers and, as you might expect, by copious creative artists and critics themselves (Said 1984; Kundera 1988, 1995; Steiner 1989; Ozick 1996; Winterson 1996). Friedrich Nietzsche (1974, 1993), for example, avers that great art, music especially, comprises the only meaningful countermovement to the decadence of contemporary religion, morality and philosophy, and a vehicle for overcoming the dangerous illusion that science is capable of knowing, manipulating or 'correcting' our human – all too human – propensities (Nehamas 1985; J. Young 1993). Martin Heidegger (1975, 1993) maintains that art not only preserves us from the depredations of our 'destitute age' but that great art, poetry in particular, also announces, unveils and enshrines the essential 'truths' of an epoch by, in effect, calling them into being, bringing them forth into consciousness, by founding, opening up and *realizing* a world, a people, a way of life (Steiner 1992; Cooper 1996). Similarly, Roger Scruton (1990), like Schiller, Kant, Carlyle, Coleridge, Arnold, Ruskin and Leavis before him, argues that aesthetics provides us with a transcendent sense of the purpose, intelligibility and ultimate meaning of the world, as revealed in and through the life-processes by which we are attached to it (Husserl's *Lebenswelt*), and from which scientific inquiry has progressively, inexorably, inevitably, hopelessly estranged us.

Ars longa vita brevis

While such quasi-spiritual claims about the transcendent power of great art can be, and are, routinely dismissed as metaphysical mysticism or, more often than not, find themselves reduced to aphorisms of the 'life imitates art' persuasion ('art is life, life is art', 'art anticipates life', 'it is the spectator, and not life, that art really mirrors', 'art doesn't imitate life, it imitates bad television', etc., etc.), there is none the less a critical consensus that artistic endeavour, at its best, is somehow capable of articulating the inarticulate, speaking the unspoken, instantiating the incipient, enunciating the embryonic, of rendering the inchoate coherent, of bringing order out of chaos, unity out of diversity, form out of formlessness and, in so doing, offering evanescent intimations of immortality, a momentary yet ineffable sense of rightness, harmony, wholeness, euphony, timelessness. As A. S. Byatt puts it in a sublime passage from her Booker Prize-winning novel *Possession*:

> Now and then there are readings that make the hairs on the neck, the non-existent pelt, stand on end and tremble, when every word burns and shines hard and clear and infinite and exact, like stones of fire, like points of stars in the dark – readings when the knowledge that we *shall know* the writing differently or better or satisfactorily, runs ahead of any capacity to say what we know, or how. In these readings, a sense that the text is wholly new, never before seen, is followed, almost immediately, by the sense that it was *always there*, that we the readers, knew it was always there, and have *always known* it was as it was, though we have now for the first time recognised, become fully cognisant of, our knowledge.
>
> (Byatt 1990: 471–2)

Even the most depraved and cynical vulgarian (yes, friends, I am that soldier) cannot fail to be moved by the sheer power of Byatt's purple prose about the sheer power of purple prose and, thereafter, inclined seriously to entertain the aesthetic sentiments expressed and indeed incomparably exemplified by the passage.

A second key aspect of the recent aesthetic 'turn' is the fact that it is very much in keeping with postmodern sentiment. Regardless of whether you subscribe to the view that postmodernism began in St Louis, Missouri, at 3.32 p.m. on 15 July 1972, when an award-winning landmark of modern architecture, the Pruitt–Igoe housing project, was unceremoniously dynamited (Jencks 1989; Harvey 1989), or consider Frederico de Onis to be its founding father, thanks to his celebrated *postmodern-isimo* typification of early-twentieth-century Latin-American verse (Hassan 1985; Featherstone 1991), or, for that matter, regard postmodernism as merely the most recent manifestation of a tradition that stretches back to Schiller and the Romantic movement of the early seventeenth century, if not earlier (Readings and Schaber 1993; Bertens 1995), the fact remains that the first stirrings of (contemporary) postmodernism occurred in the aesthetic sphere and its initial intellectual impetus derived entirely from the art world (Connor 1989; Waugh 1992a, 1992b, Wheale 1995). Thereafter, the momentum of this intellectual pinball progressively increased, as it ricocheted between the discursive flippers of European post-structuralism and the anti-establishment bumpers of late 1960s American counterculture, until it attained its present (terminal?) velocity. In short, we have reached a situation where postmodernism is widely regarded, especially in light of the implosion of the former Soviet empire, as an historical rupture of epochal proportions, as the apocalyptic end of the progressivist Enlightenment project, as the tumultuous beginnings of a new world (dis)order (McRobbie 1994; Appignanesi and Garratt 1995; Grenz 1995).

Notwithstanding its rapid permeation of social, political, economic, psychological, scientific, ethical and spiritual domains, postmodernism retains its cultural caste, its artistic ethos, its aesthetic aesthetic, as it were. True, the innumerable versions of postmodernism foreground the aesthetic in many different ways, whether it be Lyotard's (1994) slant on the Kantian sublime, Foucault's (1990) technologies of the self, Barthes' (1990a) pleasure of the text, Jameson's (1991) postmodern videodrome, Baudrillard's (1983) televisual black hole, Kristeva's (1982) semiotic disposition or Deleuze and Guattari's (1984) aestheticized liberation of desire and the body. Nevertheless, it is fair to say that, if it is characterized by anything at all, postmodernism is characterized by the salience of art, by the assumption that art plays a central role in the organization of human experience, by 'a sense of the inadequacy of Enlightenment theories of knowledge and traditional rationalist or empiricist methodologies, and a shift towards the *aesthetic* as a means of discovering an alternative to Cartesianism and Kantian Reason' (Waugh 1992a: 4). Even Jürgen Habermas (1985), who can hardly be described as an aficionado of the postmodern, concedes that the increasingly redundant project of modernity can only be rescued by a renewed emphasis on the aesthetic, albeit not at the expense of the cognitive and the practical.

For many authorities, then, the most distinctive feature of our degraded postmodern world is the 'aestheticization of everyday life'. That is, the emergence of a milieu where culture is everywhere and everything is cultural (Featherstone 1991), where people adopt an expressly aesthetic mode of existence (Featherstone 1995), where hitherto sacrosanct boundaries between fact and fiction, image and reality, consumption and production, and, above all, art and life have been eroded, effaced, erased (Maffesoli 1991, 1996). This configuration, of course, is not new. In many respects, it represents a recapitulation of the dandyism of the 'decadents' of the previous *fin de siècle*, yet another attempted valorization of the avant-garde, bohemian lifestyle that has long flourished on the fringes of modern society and periodically moves centre stage (Tester 1994; Frisby 1994). However, this propensity is not only more pervasive than ever before – Waugh (1992b) terms it 'universal aestheticization' – but also involves a comprehensive renegotiation of the relationship between high and low culture. Whereas modernism was characterized by the excavation of a seemingly unbridgeable gulf between élite and popular cultural forms, postmodernism's elevation of the Beatles over Beethoven, Mickey Mouse over Michelangelo, Arnold Schwarzenegger over Matthew Arnold, Levi Strauss over Lévi-Strauss, and Tom Peters over Thomas Paine, Marcel Proust, Ezra Pound and Jackson Pollock *combined* has not so much bridged the chasm between high and low culture as filled it up with hard-core and laid down a twelve-lane motorway complete with flyovers, sliproads, service stations and ever-present triffids of traffic cones.

All this useless beauty

Although there is a widespread consensus that postmodern culture is 'essentially novelistic' (Hutcheon 1989: 54), that 'it carries with it wherever it goes the idea of "telling stories"' (Waugh 1992: 1), that, in many respects, it comprises a rerun of Oscar Wilde's celebrated maxim 'one should either be a work of art or wear a work of art' (1995: 852; see Shusterman 1988), it is important to appreciate that not everyone subscribes to the idea that aesthetics are the essence of postmodernism. For example, its distinguishing features are often conveyed in a scientific-stroke-technological idiom – chaos, complexity, black holes, Gaia, cyberspace and so on. (Haraway 1991; Featherstone and Burrows 1995; Balsamo 1996) – or, alternatively, portrayed as a post-industrial, post-Fordist, post-Marxist, late-capitalist twist on the familiar base–superstructure analogy (Jameson 1991; Harvey 1989; Amin 1994; Kumar 1995b). Even here, however, aesthetics are not entirely absent in that the cybertropers are heavily indebted to latter-day developments in science fiction, most notably the work of William Gibson, while the suspended animation of Marxian cryogenics remains deep frozen in the liquid nitrogen of the grandest – some would say granddaddy – of the grand narratives (and narratives, remember, are about as literary as you can get).

Indeed, in his cogent excursus on the academic postmodern, Simpson (1995) suggests that postmodernism is not so much a new configuration of knowledge in this the twilight of the twentieth century, as the wholesale importation of literary and lit-crit modalities by disciplines that, in their protectionist desire to attain the self-sustaining growth of scientific respectability, have traditionally erected all but impenetrable barriers to academic entry. Set against this, the archetypal postmodern penchant for anecdote, aphorism, autobiography, conversation, confessional, vignette and local narratives – what Simpson describes as an 'epidemic of story-telling' (1995: 25) – represents nothing less than the creation of a free-trade zone, an entrepôt, in literary criticism. It seems that today's itinerant intellectual traders, regardless of their disciplinary domicile, are refusing to continue to pay the exorbitant scientific tariff imposed by the customs and excise officers of the academy. Granted, the happy-go-lucky days of academic bootlegging, speakeasies and shoot-outs at the hyperreal fantasy factory are long gone, thanks to the repeal of prohibition on the highly intoxicating liquor, the firewater, the devil's buttermilk that is literature and literary theory. Nevertheless, as Simpson makes clear:

> it is the reinvention of literature within the contemporary academy as an omnivalent method for the humanities and social sciences that has gone into the creation of an academic postmodern. We seek our inspiration in literature and turn to it for solutions.
>
> (Simpson 1995: 159)

Indeed, in our disconcerting *fin de siècle* world of paradox, contradiction and uncertainty, where it is increasingly impossible to distinguish between knowledge and habit, truth and ideology, and fact and fiction, we appear to be witnessing the re-emergence of the storyteller, a gradual turning away from the impersonality, the objectivity, the inhumanity of western science and ever more insistent attempts to replace the ascetic aesthetic of modernism with the erotic aesthetic of postmodern-ism (Simon 1996; Springer 1996; B. McNair 1996).

Accordingly, our third key reason for applying a literary compress to the con-ceptual bruising caused by the marketing's current crisis of representation is that many other hitherto hard science-oriented academic disciplines have taken the aesthetic treatment with some success. True, we're not talking here about the intellectual equivalent of a life support machine, or even the scholarly surrogate of penicillin, insulin, aspirin or, let's not beat about the bush, Preparation H. For the unconvinced, I grant you, literary criticism comprises a transplant operation at best, cosmetic surgery at worst and, in all likelihood, a worthless paradigmatic placebo of stuff and nonsense. For the cynical, furthermore, postmodernism per se represents nothing less than the CJD, the HIV, the Alzheimer's, the Parkinson's, the lobotomization of contemporary culture. Be that as it may, the aesthetico-literary remedy has been, and is being, tried by a steady stream of academic invalids – economics (McCloskey 1994), sociology (Chaplin 1994), anthropology (Benson 1993), politics (Horton and Baumeister 1996), geography (Brosseau 1994), psy-chology (K. D. Murray 1995), psychiatry (Phillips 1993, 1994), philosophy (Krell

1996), history (Callinicos 1995b), legal studies (Posner 1995), media studies (M. C. Taylor and Saarinen 1994), education (Coles 1989) and, thanks to the astonishing story-telling skills of Stephen Jay Gould (1991, 1996), amongst others, the physical sciences. As Clifford Geertz, arguably the anthropological alchemist of this latter-day literary embrocation, makes clear:

> many social scientists have turned away from a laws and instances ideal of explanation toward a cases and interpretations one, looking less for the sort of thing that connects planets and pendulums and more for the sort of thing that connects chrysanthemums and swords . . . analogies drawn from the humanities are coming to play the kind of role in sociological under-standing that analogies drawn from the crafts and technology have long played in physical understanding. . . . So far as the social sciences are concerned, all this means that . . . it is even more difficult than it has always been to regard them as underdeveloped natural sciences, awaiting only time and aid from more advanced quarters to harden them.
>
> (Geertz 1983: 19–21)

In these circumstances, it is tempting to continue to massage, to manipulate, to resuscitate, to defibrillate, to tracheotomize our medical metaphor, even though it arrested somewhere in the middle of the last paragraph, and conclude this coronary-inducing chapter with the suggestion that marketing has somehow reached the top of the waiting list, that a bed has at last become available, that, in its capacity as the J. Alfred Prufrock of the academy, marketing is lying like a patient etherized upon a table. As Table 2.4 demonstrates, however, such a rheto-rical stratagem is all too readily ridiculed. More to the point perhaps, and in keeping with our characteristically postmodern sense of belatedness (Said 1995; Bloom 1996), it has to be acknowledged that many distinguished marketing medics have already attempted to fit our disciplinary amputees with the aesthetic prosthe-tic. And it is to their radical, remedial, kill-or-cure treatments that we now turn.

(Look, before we plunge into the abyss of sex, drugs and rock 'n' roll that is yawning before us – don't turn over just yet; control yourselves! – I have to digress very briefly. No, this is not the digression on digressions that I promised you in *Postmodern Marketing One* but failed to deliver because I, er, digressed. My point, rather, is that over the next couple of chapters I'll be putting forward some ideas which are pretty old hat (so, what's new?, I hear you say). However, I'll be presenting them *as if* they are the cutting edge of postmodern marketing scholar-ship. Although this expositional stratagem may seem a mite bizarre, there's a perfectly good reason behind it. As you may be aware, there is a very small number of unrepentant, washed-in-the-blood, pre-postmodern marketing zealots hiding out in the scientistic hills. Many people regard them – not unreasonably – as a revolting band of renegades, brigands, cut-throats and guerrillas, but I prefer to think of them as merely misguided, misinformed, mistaken. In the interests of disciplinary unity it behoves us to forgive, to forget, to reach out, to try to attract such sinners back into the postmodern marketing fold. And that is best achieved, I feel, by tempting them with some of our more palatable postmodern conceits. Once they have taken the bait and are safely gathered in, we can of course bring them round to our way of thinking, though we must not be seen to exploit our privileged position by lording it over them. The greater good of the glorious marketing discipline is our primary, our sole concern. What? You don't believe me? Do you really think that I am the sort of person who would take pleasure from downloading World-Wide Webster?; telling Paul Green his number's up?; or issuing commands like 'Peel me a grape, Philip'? You do? You're a sick and sorry bunch.)

Chapter 3
Are you ready for this thing called love?

Say what you like, nothing can kick a hole in the day like a pushy margarine. Hang on, better make that a pushy, extra-light, low-fat sunflower spread high in essential poly-unsaturates: for however much the marketing department of Flora may care about me, and we shall soon see it cares very much indeed, I have little doubt that it's legal department has a flintier heart. And you know lawyers; terminological inexactitude is meat and drink to them: there may be no warning on the Flora carton to the effect that anyone describing the contents as margarine should be advised that a major lawsuit might well result in his barefoot children standing on a street-corner with a tin cup, but don't let that fool you.

The marketing department, however, really does fret about the risk of such comprehensive domestic tragedy. I did not know until I opened a fresh tub of the stuff this morning to spread on my breakfast toast, and saw that the foil protective beneath the lid bore the message, in ostensible handscript: 'If I love you then I need you, if I need you then I want you around.' Even then, mind, I did not know it immediately: my first thought was that some susceptible Waitrose assistant had grown so besotted with me as to have laid her career on the line; but once a moist finger had disappointingly confirmed that the apparent ink was in fact print, I was forced to think again.

This second thought was that the message was promotional. Recalling that the line came from a catchy Eartha Kitt number, I assumed that Flora must be offering a free CD of the singer's greatest hits – send in four lids, complete the following sentence, all that – but further examination of the packaging had nothing to say on the matter. All it said was: 'For more information, call the Flora Care Line on 0800 446464.'

The toast grew cold; the hole in the day widened. 'Flora is rich in Vitamin E' murmured the dulcet Careliner, 'an anti-oxydant which helps to prevent cholesterol from damaging your arterial walls.' What about the loving and needing and wanting, I pressed? Was this the management expressing its desperation for me to stay around longer so that I could buy more Flora? Not at all, she reproved (but charmingly), it was to remind me that I had a responsibility to my loved ones.

I rang off, and sat down at the kitchen table to wonder whether this mightn't be going a bit far. While I was touched that Flora wanted to stop my arteries snapping like pipestems, I should have preferred this to have remained a private arrangement between them and me: a spread warbling ventriloquially on behalf of my wife and children was unacceptably intrusive. It suggested I didn't give a damn. It recalled Victorian temperance posters in which a hapless soak is impeded from finishing his twelfth gin by sobbing waifs attempting to drag him home by his turn-ups . . .

Flora should not get me wrong. I cherish the new caring world in which man and sunflower will always be there for one another. I do not object to being loved, needed and wanted. Just to being nagged . . .

(Coren 1994: 14)

Bring the family

In an essay entitled 'Postmodernism', the novelist and critic Max Apple reflects on the characteristically postmodern worldview or attitude. He describes it as 'a mixture of worldweariness and cleverness, an attempt to make you think that I'm half-kidding, though you're not quite sure about what' (Apple 1984: 39). As you know only too well, there are many better-known portrayals of the postmodern moment; there are many more succinct; there are many more, full stop. But, what makes Apple's especially intriguing, for me at least, is that his account of the postmodern condition was prompted, in a manner of speaking, by an encounter with the marketing condition. Just prior to pronouncing on the postmodern, the protagonist of the essay – an author, naturally, trying to decide what to write about – opens the morning paper in search of inspiration and finds that:

> One column quotes Colonel Muammar Qaddaffi of Libya stating that his nation is ready to go to war against the United States. Directly across the page an ad for Target Stores pictures a Texas Instruments pocket calculator, regularly $9.97: 'today only' $6.97, battery *included*.
>
> The writer is stunned. He has followed this particular calculator since its days as a $49.95 luxury. He has seen it bandied about by Woolco and K-Mart and, under various aliases, by Sears, Penney's and Ward's. Never has it been offered with the battery included. This is something altogether new. He remembers Ezra Pound's dictum, 'Make it new.' Still there is the possibility of an error, a misprint, a lazy proof-reader, a goof by the advertising agency – plenty of room for paranoia and ambiguity, always among the top ten in literary circles. And the sad thing is, this particular ad

will never appear again. Qaddaffi will be quoted endlessly, but the sale was 'today only.' This is one of those ambiguities the writer has to live with.

Of course our writer doesn't equate Target and the battery to war and peace, not even to the United States and Libya. He hardly considers the nuance of the language that uses the same terms for commerce and war: 'Target,' 'battery,' 'calculate,' – he can't help it if the language is a kind of garbage collector of meanings. All he wants to know for sure is if that nine-volt battery is really included. He can, if he has to, imagine a host of happy Libyans clutching their $6.97 calculators and engaged in a gigantic calculating bee against the U.S., a contest that we might consider the moral equivalent of war and save everyone a lot of trouble.

His imagination roams the Mediterranean, but the writer will suppress all his political and moral feelings. He will focus absolutely on that calculator and its quizzical battery. He will scarcely notice the webbed beach chair peeking out of the next box or the sheer panty hose or any of the other targeted bargains.

(Apple 1984: 39)

It is, of course, entirely appropriate that Apple should tell us a story that exemplifies postmodernism rather than seeking to articulate a theory of it ('having no theory to tell, I will show you a little postmodernism'). He is, after all, a story-teller and, as we have seen, the tapestry of the postmodern is woven from the ubiquitous yarn of narration. As Lyotard reminds us in his manifesto for post-modern paganism, 'the intelligentsia's function should not be to tell the truth and save the world, but to will the power to play out, listen to and tell stories' (1989: 153). For Jameson, in fact, 'the all-informing process of *narrative* is the central function or *instance* of the human mind' (1981: 13). According to McHale, more-over, 'story in one form or another, whether as object of theory or as the alternative to theory, seems to be everywhere' (1992: 4). And, as if to demonstrate the point, Barthes announces:

the narratives of the world are numberless . . . narrative is present in myth, legend, fable, tale, novella, epic, history, tragedy, drama, comedy, mime, painting (think of Carpaccio's *Saint Ursula*), stained glass windows, cinema, comics, news item, conversation . . . narrative is present in every age, in every place, in every society; it begins with the very history of mankind and there nowhere is nor has been a people without narrative. All classes, all human groups, have their narratives, enjoyment of which is very often shared by men with different, even opposing, cultural backgrounds. Caring nothing for the division between good and bad literature, narrative is international, transhistorical, transcultural: it is simply there, like life itself.

(Barthes 1977b: 78)

Yet when we, as marketers, read Apple's postmodern ruminations on postmodernism we cannot help but reflect on his thought processes concerning the brand of calculator in question. Indeed, we cannot help but reflect on his compellingly cogent précis of the marketing management paradigm. In the space of a few perspicacious paragraphs, he covers the four Ps of product ('battery included', 'make it new'), promotion ('today only', 'ad will never appear again'), price ('since its days as a $49.95 luxury') and place ('Target Stores', 'Sears, Penney's and Ward's'). He illuminates, furthermore, the information-processing process ('an error, a misprint, a lazy proof-reader, a goof by the advertising agency'), the intra- and inter-market competitive context ('bandied about by Woolco and K–Mart', 'any of the other targeted bargains') and throws in an exegesis on marketing warfare for good measure (bear in mind that this essay was written before marketing's mid- to late-1980s infatuation with the military metaphor). Even the name of the author cannot fail to strike an associative chord with brand-fixated academics (Max Apple? Apple Mac, Pepsi Max, Big Mac – a marketing pseudonym, surely!).

Apple, of course, is not the only postmodern author to offer arresting insights into marketing-related phenomena. For example, in his wonderful and minutely observed novella *The Mezzanine*, which describes a (legendary) lunchtime in the life of an office worker, Nicholson Baker (1989) cogitates briefly on the development of the shampoo market (Table 3.1). In so doing, he not only provides as good an overview of the operation of the product lifecycle as is found in most marketing management textbooks, but, by means of his beautiful allusion to 'the emulsion of our esteem', Baker also offers us a whole new way of thinking about the trajectory of the innovation diffusion process. Equally impressive, in my opinion, is Will Self's (1995) staggering excursus on the service encounter, or, strictly speaking, the service he imagined he encountered whilst on a Virgin Atlantic flight to New York (Table 3.2). Invaluable though the SERQVAL scale undoubtedly is, happy though we are with the dramaturgical metaphor, and critical though the critical incident technique has proved for our peregrinations through the servicescape, only the most positive and least logical of logical positivists would deny that Self's startled realization, 'I spark up. I'm at 22,000 feet, and I'm smoking and drinking *in bed*', says as much, *if not more*, about the nirvana of 'total customer delight' than any number of routine marketing research exercises.

Table 3.1 Shine on, you crazy diamond

[E]motional analogies were not hard to find between the history of civilization on the one hand and the history within the CVS pharmacy on the other, when you caught sight of a once great shampoo like Alberto VO5 or Prell now in sorry vassalage on the bottom shelf of aisle 1B, overrun by later waves of Mongols, Muslims, and Chalukyas – Suave; Clairol Herbal Essence; Gee, Your Hair Smells Terrific; Silkience; Finesse; and bottle after bottle of the Akbaresque Flex. Prell's green is too simple a green for us now; the false French of its name seems kitschy, not chic, and where once it was enveloped in my TV-soaked mind by the immediacy and throatiness of womanly voice-overs, it is now late in its decline, lightly advertised, having descended year by year through the thick but hygroscopic emulsions of our esteem, like the large descending pearl that was used in one of its greatest early ads to prove how lusciously rich it was. (I think that ad was from Prell – or was it Breck, or Alberto VO5?) . . .

I think of the old product managers staring out the window like Proust, reminiscing about the great days when they had huge TV budgets and everything was hopping, now reduced to leafing through trade magazines to keep up with late-breaking news in hair care like outsiders. *Soon, nobody would know that they had introduced a better kind of plastic for their shampoo bottle, a kind with a slight matte gunmetal dullness to it instead of the unpleasant patent-leathery reflectivity of then existing efforts at transparency; that with it they had taken their product straight to the top!* In time, once everyone had died who had used a certain discontinued brand of shampoo, so that it passed from living memory, it no longer would be understood properly, correctly situated in the felt periphery of life; instead it would be one of many quaint vials of plastic in country antique stores – understood no better than a ninth-century trinket unearthed on the Coromandel coast.

Source: N. Baker 1989: 114–15

Table 3.2 I am an Anti-Christ, I am an anarchist

Make no mistake about it, first-class flying is the heroin of travel. A few flights might not give you a bad yen, but push it too far and you'll never, ever escape the consequences: your metabolism will alter at a cellular level; you'll have to become rich – or a whore. Fuck it, I've only had one hit of this shit and I'm still swaddled in its velvet paw ten days later.

But – ah, how did you start? I mean, did someone give it to you, or what . . . ?

Table 3.2 Contd.

It's like this: I've been up all night at the fag end of a rolled-up 72 hours of missed obligations, street corner burns and tiffs with desk clerks. My face is a kind of *impasto* of willed disintegration, and I'm checking in for the Saturday p.m. Virgin flight to New York . . . . It's taking several millennia, Ancient Sumer has risen once more, Gilgamesh appears on the cover of *Radio Times*. Inside my trousers a rain forest is being established, an entire ecosystem. Miniature Colobus monkeys swing from the hairs on my testicles . . . . I approach the white-clad senior angel and cough up some sort of gurgle of discontent. She beckons me round to the Upper Class check in. And then it starts, the plunger is pressed home: the slippery descent into bliss.

The desk clerk slaps and tickles the keyboard, his lovely brow furrows, he can't hack it. He looks up and says: 'I'm sorry, Mr Self, we have no mid-class seats left, we'll have to bump you up to Upper Class . . . ' He's sorry! I do nothing but splutter, and stand there while he goes on slapping and caressing the moulded plastic for about twenty seconds real time (the Queen Mother goes on mega-H.R.T. and is artificially inseminated, the donor is Phil Collins, the intention: to beget a master race . . .). It's too much for me to bear; deranged at the prospect I attempt to run off in the direction of the aircraft, until called back to get a boarding card.

He's thanking me. I'm thanking him. This is a little darling slice of luck. I don't know what's in store yet, but even now I'd give the most fulsome encomiums to V.A. Best Airline 1995? Fuck it: Best Airline of the Whole Fucking Decade. And if I knew then what I know now? No encomium would suffice. If necessary I'd go round to Richard Branson's house, or barge, or whatever it is, and rim him to get another seat in Upper Class.

Then I'm clunking through something called 'fast track.' Not, as I had hoped, a kind of super-rail, running incandescently ahead of my stooped membranes, but really a taped-off extra lane along which the rich limp, burdened by their responsibilities. It has its own metal detectors and security staff, and apparently its own immigration officials. Truly, wealth is another country. . . .

My gate is so far away that I may have to take on bearers. I'm flagging, when another Virgin seraphim appears driving one of those little rubber-wheeled trolleys. 'Virgin Atlantic, sir?' I assent. 'Hop on.' And we're off. I've prematurely aged to this extent: being carted around Heathrow like some thyroid case on a fork-lift. The faces of the healthy, as we pass them, register amusement and contempt. But I don't care. I've lanced into an Arcadia of the idle. We approach the gate, the seraphim says, 'Have your boarding card ready, please,' and then we almost drive *on to* the plane. I totter off the trolley, the cherubim at the door examines my boarding card and directs me all of eight feet to my seat.

Table 3.2 Contd.

I say seat, but really this is a terrible misnomer. It isn't a seat – it's a *bed*. Another heavenly chore-whore appears and sort of tucks me into this thing. 'Champagne, orange-juice or buck's fizz?' she asks. I opt – unsurprisingly – for champagne, and she brings me an *entire bottle* of Tattinger brut. This I cradle protectively, a child safe with its teddy bear in its cot, as we lumber along the runway and take off. . . .

Then we're airborne. We level off (I say that advisedly – I've been levelled off for some years), and the 'no smoking' sign winks out. I spark up. I'm at 22,000 feet, and I'm smoking and drinking *in bed*. A senior sort of *putti* appears. In a New York accent, she asks me if I would like a cocktail. Asks me by name. Asks me as if my welfare really concerns her.

And not just my current welfare, I feel she knows my whole poignant history intimately, just from the tone of her voice. I feel she was with me in the playground when that 13-year-old thug took the piss out of my zip-up, suede ankleboots; and then when I called him out on it, beat me to a reasonable pulp. I whimper, choking back the appellation 'Mummy', that I would like a Bloody Mary. 'Is that with Tabasco and celery salt, Mr Self, or would you prefer a more Worcester sauce-oriented version?' I like it here.

I'm going to crash soon. I can do that here. I've got my window 'seat', but there's enough space between my bed and the aisle bed that I can walk around the end of it without even getting near to the feet of its occupant. Damn it, the guy in the next-door bed is so far away that I could have one of my full-scale *Jacob's Ladder*-type nightmares, complete with arm-thrashing and convulsions, without him even noticing.

There's that, and there's the blissful absence of the video screens as well. They've been stowed somewhere in the interstices of the beds for take-off, and need never be pulled out again. That's fine by me. I've never been able to cope with those miniature LCD video screens since the time I got on a Virgin flight to New York – admittedly well over the herbaceous border – and became convinced that they were accurately portraying the thoughts of the person sitting in the seat in front of me.

Needless to say, it didn't surprise me in the least to learn that at the core of the very being of the women sitting in front of me, Mick Jagger pranced, wearing a leather jacket that had last seen service in an episode of *BMX Bandits*.

Table 3.2 Contd.

When I awake, we're beginning our descent. Mummy appears next to my bed and says: 'Diddums haveums a nice sleepums?' Touchdown is as slight as a repressed homosexual vice cop putting the cuffs on a rent boy. I swing my feet out of bed and stroll off the aircraft, waving goodbye to my close, close Virgin friends. I'm through immigration and customs with indecent haste. Why? Because I'm the first fucker off the entire plane.

Source: From '8 Miles High' from *Junk Mail* by Will Self, published by Bloomsbury in 1995, £9.99

Riding with the king

Sadly, we live in degenerate times and the misanthropic among you doubtless believe I had to 'scour the shelves' in order to unearth the above examples of marketing in literature. This is simply not the case (though if it were, do you really think I would tell *you*?). As a visit to the local library or bookshop quickly demonstrates, the world of literature is literally replete with descriptions of marketing-related phenomena. Not every evocation, admittedly, is in the same league as Apple's cogent summary of the marketing concept, Baker's inspired introspections on hair care, Self's illuminating hallucinations concerning the first-class cabin or, for that matter, Coren's fabulous flight of Floran fancy. Nevertheless, the fact remains that the literary canon is loaded with marketing munitions of the highest calibre. These range, to name but a few of my personal favourites, from Nick Hornby's (1995) acute character sketch of the sad and lonely obsessives who frequent record shops on Saturday mornings, through Martin Amis's (1984) depraved morality tale about the money-grubbing antics of an advertising executive, to Armistead Maupin's (1978) masterful encapsulation of the supermarket singles circuit-stroke-dating game in San Francisco. And how, for that matter, can we forget Bret Easton Ellis's (1991) brand-bespattered depiction of serial killing, cannibalism and dry-cleaning services in New York city?

In light of the manifest richness of this literary seam, it is not surprising that a number of marketing 49–ers have staked a claim and are actively mining this high-grade intellectual ore. It is ten years now since Russell Belk started the gold rush, when he stated that 'art can be a useful way of generating knowledge . . . art has much to contribute to consumer behaviour . . . art may be seen to provide an attractive alternative to more traditional "scientific" means of consumer research' (Belk 1986a: 27), and in that time numerous bookish marketing prospectors (who said panhandlers?) have sought to strike it rich. Ignoring the all too prevalent assumption that lit-crit is the domain of dissolutes, disreputables and suspiciously effeminate daydreamers, they have initiated numerous detailed investigations of marketing and consumption phenomena as portrayed in works of literature. Examples include Friedman's (1985, 1987, 1991) content analysis of brand names in post-war popular fiction; Spiggle's (1986) studies of social values in manifold comic books; Goodwin (1992) and Fullerton's (1994) examinations of consumption behaviour and marketing consciousness in detective stories and nineteenth-century pulp fiction, respectively; Hirschman's (1990) use of Wolfe's *The Bonfire of the Vanities* to illustrate her hypothesis on secular immortality; Belk's (1996a) discourse on diverse novelistic treatments of the magical aura that the marketing system imparts to mundane goods and commodities; McCreery's (1995) explication of early advertising treatments courtesy of a Dorothy Sayers whodunnit; and, not least, Sheth and Parvatiyar's (1993) fanciful contention that, on account of *The Merchant of Venice*, Shakespeare was the one of the first champions of the relationship marketing paradigm! As the man himself might respond to this suggestion: 'The devil can cite Scripture for his purpose' (*The Merchant of Venice*, Act 1, Scene 3).

Perhaps the foremost exponent, and certainly the most articulate champion, of the marketing-in-literature perspective is Morris B. Holbrook (or MoHo, as Elliott (1996a) aptly describes him). As part of his pronunciamento to 'ask not what semiotics can do for marketing but what marketing can do for semiotics' – a pronunciamento, incidentally, that spans the entire cultural spectrum from film, television and photography to music, theatre and fine art (e.g. Holbrook 1985a, 1988, 1993; Holbrook and Grayson 1986; Holbrook and Day 1994) – MoHo has conducted several important studies of prominent literary works. These range from meditations on the 'joys and sorrows' of consumption behaviour found in Homer's *Odyssey*, Virgil's *Aeneid*, Goethe's *Faust* and Joyce's *Ulysses*, amongst others, to attempts to defend his preferred 'subjective personal introspection' research procedure based on readings of the works of Michel de Montaigne and Walter Pater (Holbrook 1991, 1996b). Holbrook, in addition, has been ready, willing and able to persuade poetic masterpieces, such as Wordsworth's *The Recluse*, Milton's *Lycidas*, Shelley's *To a Skylark* and Keats' *On Melancholy*, to speak on behalf of his stated desire for a more aesthetic, increasingly euphoric, well-nigh corybatic approach to consumer research (Holbrook 1990). A desire, as the author himself so eloquently expresses it, to 'recapture, however evanescently, that brief but boundless moment of ecstatic insight in which fleeting truth crashes in around us, arrested in mid-flight by the urgent grasp of our wildest lunging embrace' (Holbrook 1995a: 368).

Although MoHo's learned cogitations on the western canon are brilliantly written, unfailingly incisive and, indeed, comprise a single-handed confutation of the sadly all too common belief that marketing is the Cinderella of the social sciences (no, make that the ugly sister), it is arguable that they have estranged rather than entranced the academic marketing majority and, in so doing, have merely served to frustrate rather than facilitate, hamper rather than hasten, arrest rather than accelerate the intellectual transformation he so ardently advocates. By confining his cerebrations to the high-brow side of the cultural divide, as well as with his outspoken, many would say misplaced, determination to sever the umbilical cord that unites academics and practitioners, Holbrook has succeeded in alienating a constituency who might otherwise be sympathetic to the aesthetic cause (and we can't go round alienating people, now can we?). This rupture is aggravated by MoHo's patent disdain for low-brow cultural forms like game shows and (*gasp*) rock music, and his recent robust defence of élitism in its myriad manifestations (Holbrook 1986a, 1993, 1995b).

Clearly, it is unkind to take the pioneer of 'marketing in literature' to task for his aristocratic aesthetics. After all, books such as this would not have been possible without Holbrook's willingness to suffer the slings and arrows of outrageous reviewers in pursuit of his purist vision (don't even think of saying it!), and he can hardly be held responsible for the foaming-at-the-mouth fulminators who have followed in his wake. In fact, if you are seeking to convince people of the scholarly benefits that are likely to flow from the espousal of an overtly aesthetic ethos, then it seems entirely sensible to start with incontestably exemplary examples from the great tradition rather than somewhat less canonical, if currently fashionable, cultural accomplishments. Be that as it may, Holbrook's laudable aspiration to aestheticize marketing and consumer research is in danger of foundering on his reputation as a New York intellectual far removed from the quotidian concerns of the hoi polloi, the mass, the mob, the herd of plebeian marketing managers and academics. As O'Guinn pointedly, if somewhat churlishly, observes, 'it often appears that Morris is suggesting that he is somehow smarter, better and (whether we like it or not) going to share his personal and epicurean experiences with us' (1996: 86).

Despite his frequently stated fondness for postmodern populism (Holbrook 1994, 1995b), it is evident that Morris represents the 'modernist' wing of the marketing in literature tradition (élitist, autonomous, stream of consciousness, etc.). It is equally clear that his patrician agenda is not only antithetical to the postmodern ethos of inversion, transgression and good old-fashioned vulgarity, but it tends to treat marketing and consumption phenomena with wholly unwarranted reverence (for goodness sake, we're talking about shopping and selling here, not the old masters, not neurosurgery, not rocket science – let's not get carried away!).

While it can doubtless be contended that conferring high regard on low culture is an example of the postmodern propensity, there is a very real possibility that, if the Holbrookian agenda is pursued, the marketing-in-literature paradigm will simply spin off into transcendent otherworldliness. Hence, it has become necessary to demonstrate the utility of rather less exalted literary genres. To some extent, admittedly, this is already happening, what with Belk, Spiggle and Kassarjian's studies of comic books and Goodwin and Fullerton's investigations of crime fiction. It is important to appreciate, however, that detective stories and comic books are generally regarded as élite forms of popular culture. They comprise the highest of the low, so to speak (Moore 1991).

In an attempt, then, to show that meaningful marketing insights can be extracted from what is generally, if unfairly, regarded as the lowest of the literary low, the remainder of this chapter will examine consumer behaviour as portrayed in two best-selling sex 'n' shopping novels, *Scruples* and *Scruples Two*, by Judith Krantz (1978, 1992), the doyenne of raunchy romantic fiction. (No, I'm not joking this time. Look, you have no idea what I have gone through on behalf of marketing scholarship – eyesight ruined, deaf as a post, double pneumonia from the sixteen cold showers per day. And, believe me, you haven't lived until you've ordered *Playboy* through inter-library loans. . . .) If you have any inhibitions about postmodern marketing, prepare to shed them now. If not, then you might as well face it, you're addicted to love . . .

All of a sudden

The protagonist of *Scruples* is Wilhelmina Hunnenwell Winthrop Ikehorn Orsini, or Billy for short. Scion of a rich and old-established New England family, albeit on the impoverished wing, Billy is orphaned at an early age and lives with her father, an underpaid, work-obsessed biomedical researcher. Overlooked at home and ostracized by her socially inferior school friends, she grows up as a morose, grotesquely overweight teenager who is mercilessly teased by acquaintances and extended family alike. Billy fails to get into college, but thanks to the intervention-cum-subvention of her kindly Aunt Cornelia she is sent to Paris for a year, where she resides with Comptesse de Vertdulac and her two daughters, an aristocratic family that has fallen on hard times. Treated with initial disdain and denied access to fattening foods, Billy loses weight, becomes fluent in the French language, develops an exceptionally acute fashion sense and has a doomed love affair with a well-connected if impecunious nobleman, who considers marriage but spurns her on discovering that she lacks the financial resources that the Winthrop name had led him to expect.

Suitably chastened by her first romantic encounter, the former ugly duckling returns to the United States as a beautiful and sophisticated swan. She enrols in secretarial college in New York, where she shares an apartment with Jessica Thorpe, a *summa cum laude* Vassar graduate, part-time magazine editor and full-time man-eater, who introduces Billy to the secrets of successful seduction and sexual conquest. On graduation, Billy joins the firm of Ikehorn Enterprises as assistant personal assistant to Ellis Ikehorn, the conglomerate's fabulously wealthy septuagenarian founder. Due to her superior's indisposition, Billy accompanies Ellis Ikehorn to a business meeting in Barbados which is interrupted by inclement weather. They have a passionate affair, marry on impulse and spend several happy years enjoying the fabulous, jet-setting, high-profile lifestyle of the impossibly rich and famous. Ellis, however, is struck down by a debilitating and ultimately terminal medical condition; they relocate to the more congenial climate available in California; and, from being a permanent fixture on the élite social circuit and Best Dressed list, Billy becomes a virtual recluse, a housebound nursemaid whose physical urges are assuaged by a succession of pro tem medical attendants. After Ikehorn's death, Billy inherits his entire fortune and, as an extremely affluent young widow, she indulges in an orgy of compulsive consumption – a shopping frenzy – which the emporia of Rodeo Drive are incapable of satisfying. So much so that Billy decides to establish her own speciality clothing store, the eponymous Scruples.

Although it is the last word in retailing luxury, selling the most exclusive brands of designer clothing, occupying one of the prime locations on prestigious Rodeo Drive and boasting an interior that is an exact replica of Christian Dior's flagship store in Paris, Scruples proves to be spectacularly unsuccessful. Faced with the prospect of an humiliating failure, Billy is duped into appointing Spider Elliott, a glamour photographer and incorrigible womanizer, and Valentine O'Neill, a temperamental Franco-Irish fashion designer, to the posts of store manager and chief buyer, respectively. Despite Billy's serious misgivings, and his total lack of retailing experience, Spider completely reorganizes, re-arranges, restocks, revamps and eventually relaunches the new, improved Scruples to enormous acclaim, instant success and unparalleled profitability. Secure in her position as a fashion retailing superstar and, thanks to Valentine's remarkable bespoke creations, restored to her rightful place on the Best Dressed list, Billy is invited by one of Scruples' regular customers, Susan Avery, to join her and her studio-executive husband at the Cannes film festival. There she meets, is charmed by, falls in love with and subsequently marries a dynamic, wheeler-dealing, somewhat unscrupulous film producer, Vito Orsini. She assists with the making of his next film, *Mirrors*, which, after a carefully orchestrated publicity campaign and notwithstanding the studio's attempts at sabotage, succeeds in winning the Oscar for best picture. The book ends on Oscars night with Billy pregnant, Vito triumphant and Spider and Valentine in *love*.

Scruples Two opens on Oscars night with Billy pregnant, Vito triumphant and Spider and Valentine in love, but the euphoria does not last for long. Billy quickly realizes that she takes second place to Vito's career, which blossoms in the wake of his award, and discovers that he has a 16-year-old daughter from a previous marriage, Gigi Orsini. Outraged at Vito's neglect of his offspring, traumatized by a miscarriage and betrayed by her husband's infidelity with an old flame, television presenter Maggie McGregor, Billy initiates divorce proceedings, takes Gigi under her wing and derives grim satisfaction from the abject failure of Vito's next motion picture, *The WASP*. These personal disasters, however, are offset to some extent by the continuing success of the retail store. A chain of Scruples outlets is established in prime locations throughout the world, but after an accidental fire which kills Valentine O'Neill and completely destroys the original store, Billy closes the shops, sells the sites and winds up the entire retail organization. Scruples, 'the most opulent and successful speciality store that has ever existed' (p. 20), ceases to exist.

Devastated by the death of his wife, Spider Elliott buys a yacht and sets off to sail around the world. Billy returns to Paris, where she throws herself into the élite social round, acquires a dilapidated seventeenth-century mansion in a fashionable location and sets about its painstaking restoration. Encouraged by Cora Middleton, a scheming social climber, Billy develops a passion for antiques, collectibles and *objets d'art*, which she pursues with her customary vigour. Indeed, it is in the course of an antique hunt that she meets Sam Jamison, an impoverished American sculptor with a ramshackle studio in the Latin Quarter. Determined to avoid revealing her true identity, because of the distorting effect that her vast wealth has on personal relationships, Billy poses as a schoolteacher on sabbatical. They have a passionate affair and Billy is precipitated into a hectic double life, which is eventually uncovered when Sam accidentally encounters her – in her full super-rich regalia – at the Paris Opéra.

Profoundly upset by Sam's outraged termination of their relationship, Billy retreats to New York, where she proceeds to catch up on the progress of her step-daughter Gigi Orsini. Having decided to pursue a career in catering, Gigi shares an apartment with Sasha Nevsky, an ebullient lingerie model and self-proclaimed 'Great Slut of Babylon' (p. 245). Despite Sasha's attempts to convert Gigi to her 'men must suffer' philosophy (p. 246), Gigi falls madly in love with Sasha's brother, Zach Nevsky, a talented and dynamic theatrical director. Unfortunately, a skiing holiday goes disastrously wrong when Gigi breaks an ankle and, in her heavily medicated state, discovers Zach being seduced by a female admirer – in his sleep! Misinterpreting the situation, Gigi spurns Zach and turns to the other passion in her life, collecting antique lingerie. Although she considers it simply as a means to her Christmas gift-giving ends, the collection is shown to Sasha's employer, Herman Brothers, and seized upon as a potential gold-mine. A contract to reproduce the antique lingerie collection is negotiated, but on Herman's sudden death Gigi and Sasha are left high and dry.

Never at a loss for ideas, Sasha suggests to Billy that they develop a Scruples mail-order catalogue featuring Gigi's creations. Outraged at the very thought of debasing Scruples' good name, Billy flies in high dudgeon to Los Angeles and calls to see Spider Elliott, recently returned from his travels. Spider recognizes the potential of the catalogue shopping concept and persuades Billy, against her better judgement, that it might just work. After the development of an appropriate format, Sasha and Gigi relocate to Los Angeles, where the former meets and falls in love with Billy's lawyer, Josh Hillman, and the latter renews contact with her father, who is having difficulties securing finance for his next motion picture. Gigi asks Billy to help and she agrees to underwrite the movie provided Zach Nevsky is appointed director. Unsurprisingly, therefore, the book concludes with Gigi and Zach happily reunited, Sasha and Josh duly married, Vito's career resurrected, Billy and Spider in love, the Scruples Two catalogue a triumphant success and sufficient loose ends to eke out another episode of this literary soap opera.

Stolen moments

Now it cannot be denied that works of romantic literature are routinely dismissed as mass-produced fantasies which are atrociously written, mindlessly consumed, concocted according to the same tired and tiresome recipe (Figure 3.1) and, for first-generation feminists at least, sugar-coated instantiations of oppressive patriarchal ideology (Greer 1971; Firestone 1971; Douglas 1980; Lamb 1982). On flicking through the Scruples novels, however, it is impossible to overlook the sheer pervasiveness of marketing phenomena and consumption-related behaviours. The books are absolutely replete with references to national brands, designer labels and famous personalities, from Coca-Cola and Kleenex to Calvin Klein and Clint Eastwood (S. Brown 1995e). They incorporate detailed discussions of speciality retailing operations, the mechanics of the mail-order business, the functioning of the film industry, the world of high fashion and, not least, the nature, characteristics and consequences of shopping activities-cum-pathologies.

Figure 3.1 Sherry, Sherry baby

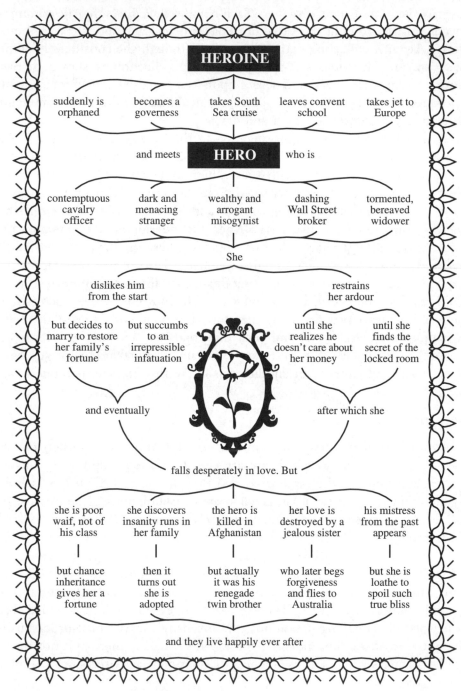

Source: adapted from Berger 1992

They provide, in short, a wealth of insight into marketplace behaviours. They deal with issues that are high on the agenda of contemporary consumer research. They offer representations of marketing phenomema untainted by positivistic research techniques and perspectives.

Naturally, these textual representations can be examined in a variety of ways, ranging from quantitative content analysis of brand-name citation – what Friedman (1987) terms 'word of author' advertising – to essentially qualitative attempts to interpret the meaning or meanings of the books as refracted through the manifold schools of literary criticism – psychoanalytical, reader response, Marxist, feminist, structuralist, post-structuralist, new historicist and so on (see Jefferson and Robey 1986; Lodge 1988; Selden and Widdowson 1993; Eagleton 1996b; R. Webster 1996). For our present purposes, however, discussion will be confined to a straightforward comparative analysis of consumer behaviour and retailing evolution as portrayed in the novels and the relevant academic literature, respectively. Five aspects of consumer behaviour feature prominently in the Scruples (S1, S2) corpus – *hedonic consumption*, *shopping addiction*, *obsessive collecting*, *gift-giving* and *shopper apathy* – as does the seemingly unending process of *retail institutional change*.

A glance at almost any page of either book clearly reveals that they are extended, occasionally ecstatic, encomia to the joys of *hedonic consumption* and the profligate lifestyle of the impossibly rich and famous. Almost without exception, the characters dress in the most elegant outfits, dine in the most exclusive restaurants, disport the most extravagant displays of jewellery, drive, or are chauffeur-driven in, the most expensive automobiles, decamp to the most select suites in the most exorbitant hotels and purchase aeroplanes, vineyards, Parisian mansions or retail stores on the merest whim. *Scruples Two*, admittedly, adopts a pseudo-admonitory stance, in that it attempts to condemn the activities it so lovingly describes, but the overall effect is much the same. The unremitting drip of prominent brand names, designer labels and famous celebrities ensures that the books reek of affluence, excess, immoderation, untrammelled materialism and naked hedonism. As the quotations in Table 3.3 amply testify, the novels are paeans to the thrill of possession, the sybaritic pleasures of unrestrained, irresponsible, irrepressible acquisitiveness, the fantasies, feelings and fun noted by several prominent consumer researchers (Hirschman and Holbrook 1982; Holbrook and Hirschman 1982; Hudson and Murray 1986), and the inevitable behavioural consequences of pampered self-indulgence. If, as Hirschman and Holbrook (1982) suggest, reading a novel is a form of hedonic consumption in itself, the emotional consequences of hedonically consuming a book about hedonic consumption can hardly be imagined.

The Scruples novels, however, do more than explicate and indeed embody the

Table 3.3 All I want is everything

When Billy was twenty-four they bought a villa at Cap-Ferrat with legendary gardens and grassy terraces that descended towards the Mediterranean like a vast Matisse; they maintained a permanent suite of six rooms at Claridge's for their frequent trips to London, where Billy collected Georgian and Queen Anne silver whenever Ellis had to spend part of the day in business meetings. They bought a hide-away house on a hidden cove in Barbados, to which they often flew for a weekend; they travelled widely in the Orient; but of all their homes, they both preferred the Victorian manor house in the Napa Valley, where they could watch the grapes for their Château Silverado wines being tended in a countrywide as pastoral, as comforting to the spirit as that of Provence . . .

(*S1*: 148)

As the years went by she lived entirely within this magic circle, forgetting more and more of even the most minor problems of ordinary life, becoming so accustomed to having her every desire fulfilled that she grew gently yet totally autocratic without either of them realizing it. With a limousine and chauffeur at her disposal twenty-four hours a day, it quickly became unimaginable that she had ever owned an umbrella. Wet feet became as remote a possibility as bed linens that weren't changed every day. A room that wasn't filled with fresh flowers was as foreign to Billy as the idea of running her own tub. . . . She grew spoiled in a way only a few hundred women in the world would begin to understand. This particular kind of spoiling, no matter how graciously accepted, has a subtle way of changing a woman's character, giving her a thirst for control that becomes as natural as a thirst for water . . .

(*S1*: 150)

She had just barely attained the prime of a beauty that would last for many years; she was rich beyond even her ability to comprehend the extent of her wealth – and she was bored. . . . The entire world was available to her, she observed, as she flipped over the pages of *Architectural Digest*. For three hundred thousand dollars she could own an air-conditioned pavilion in Bali, built in a coconut grove next to the ocean, with a swimming pool of course. In Eleuthera there was a house for sale that had twelve hundred feet of pink sand beach and a private overseas telephone system – all for less than three million dollars, furnished. . . . Or, if she preferred something less tropical, she could live in England at Number 7, Royal Crescent, Bath, for no more than seventy-five thousand pounds, owning a house that had been built in 1770 as part of the most splendid example of Georgian architecture in the world, and which now possessed a sauna and a five-car garage. . . . She could have anything in the world she wanted. Just name it. She couldn't – that was the problem. She didn't want another house. She still

Table 3.3 Contd.

---

maintained a plane, a new Learjet now, but only Valentine and the other buyers used it for their trips. The St Helena vineyard made a substantial profit and there was no reason to sell it. Perhaps a horse? Adopt a baby? A pet mouse? Obviously there was something wrong with her.

(*S1*: 369–70)

Source: Krantz 1978

carnality of consumption and the lifestyles of the impossibly rich and famous. They also provide insights into the pleasures of possessions and their ostentatious exhibition. According to a number of analyses of conspicuous consumption, the nouveaux riches take enormous pride in the possessions that their achievements have made possible; find it necessary to demonstrate their elevated status through highly visible displays of appropriate product arrays; and, as a rule, are preoccupied with collecting, philanthropy, home ownership, health, beauty, personal security and, inevitably, entrée into the upper upper class of old money (Hirschman 1990; LaBarbera 1988; Mason 1992). All of these traits are referred to in the Scruples novels, as is another interesting facet of the new rich – status anxiety (Costa and Belk 1990; Solomon 1994). Despite their wealth, the nouveaux riches are unfamiliar with what is expected of them – what is deemed appropriate – in their elevated social circumstances, whether it be in terms of possessions or behaviour. To this end, they require guidance and, on reading the Scruples novels, it is clear that they provide a form of 'socialization' for those with more money than taste (Moschis and Smith 1985; O'Guinn and Faber 1989). The books offer copious detailed, 'how-to' descriptions of complete outfits, interior designs, fashion advice and social etiquette, ranging from party planning to table manners, for the super-rich or, rather, the super-rich aspirants-cum-fantasizers among the novels' mainly lower-middle-class readership (Schiffman and Schnarrs 1981). Thus, on asking Valentine to design some riding apparel, the wife of an ambassador is sharply reminded, 'For that you must go straight to Hermès . . . I can make you anything but that – it simply would not be correct' (*S1*: 19). Billy, likewise, discovers, 'It was perfectly correct to address a duchess simply as "Madame" after you had met her, but you must take care to address the concierge by her full name' (*S1*: 71). And, on the thankless task of buying clothes for truculent teenagers, readers are reminded, 'Just as good shoes and a good bag were essential for a woman, they could be a sign of overcalculation on a teenager. New sneakers could ruin everything' (*S2*: 55).

Indeed, in addition to disbursing do's and don'ts for super-rich wannabees and emulators, it is arguable that the books provide a form of vicarious acculturation into many other walks of life or unfamiliar subcultural milieux – high fashion, glamour photography, glossy magazines, homosexual encounters, movie-making, the mail-order industry and, above all, speciality retailing.

Although they are often – and rightly – considered to be celebrations of the hyper-affluent lifestyle, the Scruples novels offer occasional arresting insights into what academic researchers variously describe as 'consumer misbehaviour' or 'the dark side' (Holbrook 1987; Hirschman 1991). These include overeating, bulimia, child abuse, sexual promiscuity and the obsessive pursuit of physical perfection. More importantly perhaps, both books contain some remarkable portrayals of *shopping addiction*. During the incapacitation and after the death of her first husband, Ellis Ikehorn, Billy indulges in a prolonged spending spree, which the author memorably describes as follows:

> There was something which almost relieved her constant tension in prowling daily through the boutiques and department stores of Beverly Hills, buying, always buying – what did it matter if she needed the clothes or not? She had hundreds of elegant robes to wear at dinner; dozens of pairs of beautifully tailored pants; forty tennis dresses; silk shirts by the hundreds; drawers and drawers full of handmade lingerie from Juel Park, where a pair of panties could cost two hundred dollars; closets full of two-thousand-dollar dresses from Miss Stella's Custom department at I. Magnin to wear to the few dinner parties to which she was invited; three dozen bathing suits, which she kept in the elaborate pool house where she changed for her daily swim. Three empty bedrooms in the mansion had been turned into closets for her new clothes.
>
> Billy knew perfectly well, as she walked into the General Store or Dorso's or Saks, that she was falling into the classic occupation of rich idle women: buying supremely unnecessary clothes to feed, but never fill, the emptiness within. It's that or get fat again, she told herself, as she walked up Rodeo or down Camden, feeling a sexual buzz as she searched the windows for new merchandise. The thrill was in the trying on, in the buying. The moment after she had acquired something new it became meaningless to her; therefore, each time she went out looking for something to purchase it was the same need that drove her.
>
> (Krantz 1978: 205–6)

What is more, after her divorce from Vito Orsini and the pre-emptory eradication of the Scruples retailing empire, Billy:

> was in the mood to buy, and buy instantly, buy big and buy recklessly, a mood she'd believed she'd never feel again, with the listless, empty indifference of someone who has outgrown a vice. But now she felt herself being lured into the thrilling undertow of her old passion to own, to possess, to acquire; she was being filled by the old covetousness, the frenzied impatience to make something hers. Caution and common-sense were equally absurd, for she was feeling desire again, desire, that life-giving force; desire, that need that can't be called up by any force of will, by whose rules she had lived for so long; desire, the pleasure that had given her up after her divorce.
>
> Billy signed the check slowly, forming each letter of her name with mounting pleasure, utterly indifferent to the exorbitant fees of the *notaires*, the twelve different taxes she deliberately hadn't asked about, the commissions on commissions that would curl Josh's hair when he saw the documents. Christ, it was bliss to spend too much money again.
>
> (Krantz 1992: 253–4)

In recent years an extensive academic literature has accumulated on the topic of compulsive or addictive shopping, and articles on 'shopaholics' are a commonplace in newspapers and magazines (e.g. Valence *et al.* 1988; O'Guinn and Faber 1989; d'Astous 1990; Hirschman 1992; Shoaf *et al.* 1995). As Elliott (1994) points out, these papers present a consistent picture of consumers who buy for motives not directly related to the possession of goods, who persistently repeat the behaviour despite its adverse consequences, who may be prone to cross-addiction (eating disorders, for example), and who feel compelled to continue for a combination of reasons including low self-esteem, high levels of personal anxiety and, not least, the emotional succour or 'mood repair' that these shopping bouts engender (notwithstanding post-purchase feelings of remorse). A close reading of the above passages demonstrates that, despite the literary establishment's disdain for her low-brow endeavours, Judith Krantz perfectly captures and synthesizes many key aspects of shopping addiction, as identified by consumer researchers employing 'scientific' research procedures. What is more, in her intimation that addictive shoppers anticipate, yet continue to disregard, their post-purchase feelings of self-abasement, Krantz draws attention to an important yet under-researched aspect of compulsive consumption (Rook 1987; Hoch and Loewenstein 1991). Her representation of the whole experience is not only 'accurate', so to speak, suggestive of future research possibilities and much more succinct than most, but also considerably *predates* the bulk of the published research in this rapidly growing field. Most importantly of all, she gives us a real experiential sense of the emotions involved, a 'sense' that simply cannot be obtained from more traditional research techniques.

Alongside the analyses of shopping compulsion, the topic of *obsessive collecting* figures prominently in the Scruples novels, though it involves several characters in addition to Billy. For Cora Middleton, 'The purchase of things, things of all sorts, so long as they were genuinely fine or, if not fine, highly original, and the arranging of them into collections that complemented each other' (*S2*: 200) was the primary interest of her life. She had 'learned to worship antique furniture and porcelain, old glass, old silver and carved ivory: precious *things* became her religion, her children, her contentment' (*S2*: 200). Indeed, when asked to define what she meant by 'things' and to justify her obsession with collecting, Cora described the former as 'an addiction, a little object you hadn't intended to buy and certainly don't need, but end up paying too much for and take away with you, filled with the thrill of possession' (*S2*: 212). The latter, likewise, was exonerated in the following manner:

> a collector always wakes up excited by the thrill of the chase – it's like having a full-time job, except that you spend money instead of making it. I've always thought that the only way to be rich and stay interested in life was either to collect with passion – collect anything, it doesn't matter what – or be very competitive at something you do well – some sport, for example.
>
> (Krantz 1992: 307).

Just as academic studies of addictive shopping have come to the fore in recent years, so too the topic of collecting behaviour is attracting the attention of social scientists in general and consumer researchers in particular (Dittmar 1992; Muensterberger 1994; Elsner and Cardinal 1994; Belk *et al.* 1988; Belk 1995). Once again, however, it seems that the foregoing quotations capture many of the salient aspects of collecting mania and more besides. In their comprehensive review of the extant literature on collectors, Belk *et al.* (1991) note how this form of behaviour is characterized by a constant quest, the euphoria of the find, the pleasures that inhere in the display and rearrangement of the collection, a willingness to acknowledge the power of the addiction and the overwhelming importance – equivalent to religious devotion or surrogate parenthood – that a collection plays in the lives of its assemblers. In addition, the Scruples novels refer to collectors' well-established tendency to confine themselves to certain specific categories of object; to the unalloyed pride they take in their treasures; to the friendship and rivalries that a passion for collecting engenders; to the close but uneasy relationship between acquisition and disposal; to the voyeuristic, emotionally charged process of contemplation; and, to objects' remarkable ability to evoke past times and places (Table 3.4). Similarly, the influence of family circumstances on collecting behaviour is suggested and the propensity towards cross-addiction is amply illustrated by one collector's defiant determination to 'do some meaningful shopping, antique shopping, for there was a limit to how much serious money you could spend on clothes' (*S2*: 118).

Table 3.4 No, you ain't got me

Categories of object	The Lioncourts bought no painting and sculpture. They settled the question quickly; fine art, by the time it was accepted, was far beyond their means, and when it was experimental and still affordable it was too much of a risk. They crowded their walls with remarkable engravings and mirrors, and so rich with objects was their environment that no one had ever noticed the lack of art. *(S2: 202)*
Sense of pride	Valentine was speechless. This was such a complete work of art that she really felt nothing yet but astonishment. Wilton waited, drinking in with pleasure this reaction on the part of his guest . . . and began to show her around the two floors and the small formal garden with unabashed pride in his treasures. *(S2: 186)*
Friendship and rivalry	Harriett was as totally in thrall to collector's mania as Cora, and equally knowledgeable. They developed a genuine affection and true respect for each other as they lunched together on Saturdays and then went off to the auction at Parke Bernet, or drove out for a day to investigate country dealers; not even a suburban garage sale could fail to inspire the thrill of the hunt for women who knew that you could never guess where a great or merely desirably amusing object might turn up. . . . Harriett Toppingham and Cora [Middleton] collected different kinds of objects and used them in different ways in their complicated, beloved interiors, so the element of competition, which might have been a problem, was absent. *(S2: 218–9)*

Table 3.4 Contd.

Acquisition and disposal	Every good antiques dealer in Europe shuddered when they walked into his shop, for they bought the very pieces the dealer, against his own principles, had been covetously contemplating reserving for himself; antiques that were just on the verge of coming into fashion or objects so curious, so unusual that they had been overlooked until the Lioncourts started poking into the corners of the shop. (*S2*: 210)
Contemplative pleasures	She unwrapped the bottle from its layer of protective newspaper and placed it carefully on the table to give herself something, no matter how small, to gloat over. . . . She'd put each item on once to see how it looked and then tuck it away carefully in a special drawer, protected by tissue paper, for her own future delectation. (*S2*: 261, 297)
Evocative power	Each bit of lingerie that she brought home seemed to her to have a history, each one could tell a wondrous story if she could only be alive to its vibrations. . . . 'To view oneself in such a mirror is to see oneself reincarnated in another era, do you not think so, Madame?' (*S2*: 297, 310)
Family circumstances	She had been one and a half when her mother died, Billy mused. Her father, that overworked doctor whose free time he dedicated entirely to research, had never had more than a few minutes to spend with her, and even then his mind was visibly far away. . . . She *had* been a neglected child, Billy realized. . . . She had not been loved in the only way that would have given her the inner sense of selfhood she was still struggling to find. If you don't grow up with that sense of selfhood, how could you ever get it? Not from all the Burmese rubies in the world. Not from being given your weight in diamonds on your birthday. (*S2*: 368–9)

Source: Krantz 1992

Another, and in some ways the most intriguing, facet of collecting behaviour portrayed in the Scruples novels concerns Gigi Orsini's fondness for antique lingerie. Like many collections, it started almost accidentally ('it was while she was looking for something special' (*S2*: 297); its assembly necessitated a prodigious amount of time and effort ('hundreds of garments in dozens of little stores before she finds one that she buys' (*S2*: 351); and one of its chief attractions was an ability to evoke a gentler, kinder, ineffably romantic era (Table 3.4). More importantly perhaps, the collection eventually formed the basis of Gigi's Christmas *gift-giving* behaviour. Each item of lingerie was lovingly restored, carefully wrapped and, not least, purchased with a particular individual in mind, herself included. Indeed, each gift from Gigi was accompanied by an illustrated, handwritten card which comprised a little retro-romantic fantasy concerning the recipient, or rather a lightly fictionalized 'characterization' of the recipient and their various erotic adventures whilst wearing the garment concerned. Thus, Billy was portrayed as 'Georgie', a blue-blooded, fabulously wealthy Englishwoman who enjoyed a succession of athletic lovers and recuperated by taking afternoon tea in her elegant underwear. Sasha, similarly, was synonymous with 'Nora', an exotic dancer and camiknicker-clad exhibitionist, with three men in tow at any one time.

Although this aspect of the narrative can be dismissed as a mildly diverting interlude, a subversive intertextual skit on the conventions of romantic fiction, a crude plot device to introduce the catalogue shopping concept or the author's attempt to answer the perennial yet impossible question, 'what do you give someone who has everything?', it goes to the very heart of gift-giving behaviour as it has been described by numerous consumer researchers (e.g. Belk 1976, 1979, 1988; Sherry 1983; Mick and DeMoss 1990; Belk and Coon 1993; Otnes *et al.* 1993; Wolfinbarger and Gilly 1996). Not only do Gigi's romantic vignettes encapsulate the fact that gift-giving has been likened to the imposition of an identity on the recipient (B. Schwartz 1967; McCracken 1986), but she also succeeds in elevating what many people might consider to be irredeemably contaminated objects – second-hand underwear (see O'Reilly *et al.* 1984; Belk 1988) – from the arena of the profane to the realms of the sacred (Belk *et al.* 1989). When shown to a group of professional lingerie models, the collection is treated 'reverentially' (*S2*: 345); the romantic fantasies are listened to in 'starry-eyed, all but trance-like enchantment' (*S2*: 346); the garments appear to possess an almost magical ability to transform the wearer; and seem capable of putting people in touch with something profound, something eternal, something beyond time and place (Table 3.5). Furthermore, when the money-spinning possibilities of an antique lingerie 'collection' are explained to her, Gigi is deeply offended by the immorality of the suggestion

Table 3.5 In the name of love, once more in the name of love

Transformation	'My God', she breathed, 'I feel . . . oh, I can't even say how I feel . . . certainly not like mean, horrid old me. Oh, Sasha, do I ever have to take it off?' 'Eventually, I'm afraid'. (*S2*: 346)
Timelessness	Gigi's cards had given them the clues they needed to feel that each garment wasn't merely an example of antique lingerie but a tangible connection to a piquant, attainable dream, sealed with a promise of timelessness, a dream in which they could so easily imagine themselves starring. They felt sensuously alert to another world, in a graceful and right relationship to an erotic sensitivity they hadn't known before. (*S2*: 348)
Immorality	Gigi felt torn between his enthusiasm and her reluctance to broadcast something that had been her private, intimate pleasure, something she shared only with a few close friends in mind. '"Almost-antique" – did you just invent that?' 'I must have', he said proudly. 'Not bad, is it?' 'But, excuse me, Mr Jimmy, is it honest to call something brand-new an almost antique?' (*S2*: 352)
Secularization	'Wait a minute, Mr Jimmy', Gigi protested, 'you keep talking about "reproducing" them. The whole point to my lingerie is that everything's unique, one of a kind, the real thing.' (*S2*: 352)
Quintessence	'Gigi!' Sasha burst into tears. 'Gigi, you can't give that to Billy. You know you meant it for me! Say you did, say you just wanted to see if I liked it!' 'Oh, Sasha, I didn't mean to make you cry! Of course it's for you! It's pure you, not Billy at all.' (*S2*: 341)
Liminality	They walked about, getting the feel of the garments, and soon they pranced, paraded and capered, admiring themselves and each other with delighted, flushed faces. (*S2*: 348)

Table 3.5 Contd.

Kratophany	Unquestionably the nameplate had somehow helped Josh, that much was sure, or he would never have kept it all this time. . . . But if there was any comfort on earth he could bring to Billy, if this fragment of marble had one-hundredth of the power Josh said it had, he had to give it to her.
	(*S2*: 554, 557)

Source: Krantz 1992

and by the secularization, the commodification, the loss of authenticity of her idea through its endless, profane reproduction. The importance of authenticity, of the quintessential, 'just right' aspect of gift-giving is perfectly captured by Sasha's reaction to an item which she erroneously believes is destined for Billy, as is the ecstasy, the liminality, the communitas and, not least, the kratophany (overwhelming power) that sacred objects engender or exude (see Table 3.5). Even hierophany, the act of manifestation of the sacred, is captured by Sasha's employer's comment: 'If I'd seen your old things just sitting on a shelf somewhere, I wouldn't have had this idea, but the way Sasha and the girls reacted to them and the cards you wrote came together in my head the other afternoon' (*S2*: 351). All told, Krantz's evocation of Gigi's collecting-cum-gift-giving behaviours perfectly capture, 'the processes used by consumers to remove an object or experience from a principally economic orbit and insert it into a personal pantheon, so that the object or experience becomes so highly infused with significance . . . that it becomes a transcendental vehicle' (Belk *et al.* 1989: 32).

Despite their emphasis on consumption as an emotionally charged, occasionally ecstatic, spiritually uplifting experience, the Scruples novels also highlight the secular, the utilitarian, the mundane side of consumer behaviour – or *shopper apathy*, as it is sometimes termed. For example, the sheer physical effort that shopping requires is referred to on several occasions ('we wore ourselves out shopping' . . . 'shopping leaves me wilted on the vine' (*S1*: 60, 166)), as is the associated need for rest and recuperation (Table 3.6). The ambivalence, or even outright hostility, that shopping activities induce in certain individuals is much in evidence ('I consider that activity called "going shopping" a kind of terrible torture' . . . 'shopping's a *nightmare* for most women', (*S1*: 212; *S2*: 487)). The complex relationship between consumption and mood repair – that is, shopping's therapeutic rather than hedonic function – is encapsulated in statements like 'she thought she might order one of everything . . . she deserved her little rewards' (*S2*:

Table 3.6 I've been down but not like this before

'Suppose this customer had arrived at Scruples at eleven in the morning and suppose she had spent two hours looking and trying on things and hadn't finished yet?'

'Well?'

'Would she be hungry? Would her feet hurt? Billy, I see you've taken off your shoes.'

'What has that to do with retailing, Spider?' In one minute she'd tell him about her investigation of his non-existent credentials.

'Your shoes? Nothing. Your customer's shoes? Everything. Your customer's empty stomach? Even more. It is the *key*.'

'You'll have to be a little more explicit. We don't sell shoes. We're not running a restaurant – we're running, or trying to run, a store.'

'Not until you start running a restaurant.' Spider smiled at her benevolently.

'What happens when your hungry customer's feet begin to hurt? Her blood sugar goes down. If she continues to try on clothes she gets irritable and difficult, and she decides that nothing she sees suits her. If she stops to get dressed to go somewhere for lunch, the chances are that she'd have to be absolutely desperate to find a particular dress on that particular day in your particular store for her to come back to Scruples after lunch. If you lose her at lunch-time, she'll try another store later. So, first we're going to build a kitchen by shutting off part of the garage, which is much bigger than you need. Then we hire a couple of cooks, maybe only one at first, and some waiters and offer our customers lunch on the house. Nothing too fancy, Billy, just salads or open-faced sandwiches. I noticed that there's a chaise longue in each fitting room. Our customers can sit and eat there while they get a foot massage. A good one can rejuvenate the whole body.' He quirked one eyebrow at Billy. 'You probably know the best masseurs in town? I doubt you'll need more than three of them in the beginning. Then, after lunch, we'll sell those ladies the whole fucking store.'

Source: Krantz 1978: 275–6

117–8), 'could there be a better way to cure [an anxiety attack] than to catalogue shop' (*S2*: 498), or in what can only be described as a quasi–cathartic refusal to buy, 'As she had expected, she saw nothing worth a second of her time, but she wanted to reject and reject, and reject again, with pointed, spiteful, accurately disdainful words, to vent some of the rage Spider Elliott had aroused in her' (*S2*: 216). In a similar vein, the retail store's almost total dependence on 'rich idle women' (*S1*: 205), 'very rich, very bored, very elegant women' (*S1*: 571) suggests a significant association between shopping behaviour and sheer boredom and one well worth investigating. What is more, the uncertainty, the dismay, the guilt and embarrassment that erroneous shopping decisions bring is perfectly evoked in Gigi's 'policy statement' for the mail-order catalogue:

> I know some secrets you hide in your closet that you won't tell your best friend about. . . . For example, there's that beautiful, ruffled, real lace blouse you bought because you were feeling so romantic that you couldn't resist it, and when you got it home and tried it with all your skirts it made you look weirdly like your mother. But it's too good to give away and too small to give her. . . . I know about those elephant-retreating-into-the-jungle pants that you bought without checking in a three way mirror and I know about that practical, sensible coat you wore for two years, hating every minute of it, because you're practical and sensible only to a point – and it went too far!
>
> But enough of these tales of closet woe. Why torture yourself about that bright red, sparkly cocktail dress you bought for Christmas parties and regretted even before you had it shortened – and that was three years ago!
>
> My point is that we all make mistakes. *Everyone*. People who boast that they never make the same mistake twice make new ones all the time. The best-dressed man I know once told me that two out of three things he bought were mistakes and he only wore the one that wasn't. I don't know anyone who can *afford* to make mistakes like that. But you can afford to take all the things in your closet that make you feel a nasty little 'yucch' in your heart and give them away to the Salvation Army, because, face it, you're *never* going to wear them again anyway.
>
> (Krantz 1992: 498–9)

The picture of shopping orientation contained in *Scruples* and *Scruples Two* is thus very much in keeping with that in the academic literature. In the fortysomething years since G. P. Stone's (1954) seminal study, numerous attempts have been made to explore consumer attitudes to shopping and develop meaningful shopper typologies. Understandably, in light of the obvious managerial implications, the bulk of these studies have concentrated on consumption-prone individuals, be they impulse shoppers (Kollat and Willet 1969; Rook and Hoch 1985), bargain hunters (Darden and Reynolds 1971; Blattberg *et al*. 1978), browsers (Bloch and Richins 1983; Bloch *et al*. 1989), recreational shoppers (Bellenger *et al*. 1977; Bellenger and Korgaonkar 1980) or whatever (e.g. Lesser and Hughes 1986; Lunt and Livingstone 1992). Yet these exercises also highlight – almost without exception – the existence

Table 3.7 To win just once, to win just once

No woman left Scruples until Spider had approved of what she had bought. He was always in at the kill. His taste was literally flawless and his speciality was twofold: to convince a wavering woman that she did indeed look beautiful in a particular garment, or to talk her out of something she adored but which didn't suit her. He operated independently of concern about any individual sale. He would far rather see a customer leave without having made a single purchase than have her go home and decide, regretfully, that she'd made a mistake. If Spider detected that slight hanging back that a women feels when she is compromising on something she isn't truly enthusiastic about, he used all his wiles to dissuade her. He was only really happy with a sale in which the customer displayed her conviction by trying to sell *him*. And, with deliberation, he invariably managed to make each customer decide against at least one thing she loved so that when she got home, any pangs of guilt she might feel over having spent so much money would be annulled by her feeling of virtue in not having bought that one thing she had *really* wanted.

(*S1*: 336)

'Reading catalogues, disappointing as they always are, is more like going shopping when I don't have the time to waste in a crowded store, or the money for impulse buying. It's basically a fantasy trip, I guess. A cheap thrill. See, all this stuff in the catalogues *is* actually available – it's not like a fashion magazine, where they show clothes that aren't in the stores yet. With a catalogue, all I have to do is call a toll-free number and it's mine – so even if I don't want it and can't afford it I'm having the fun of being impossibly choosy without a salesgirl glowering at me. I can turn down a diamond necklace and one of those china Boehm birds for almost five hundred dollars, and a Vuitton bag and thirty different velour bathrobes that all look alike . . . Since I'm not going to buy the kneesocks with jingle bells or the whipsnake – whipsnake? – sounds kinky – handbag, I can also not buy the condo. It's more fun to *not* buy the condo. It makes me feel richer . . . and that I'm above temptation. It's probably the nun-like, non-consumer side of my personality trying to grow. Next year I'm going to throw them all out unopened because they'll just be more of the same.'
'I bet you don't', Gigi said morosely.

(*S2*: 418–19)

There was nothing morally wrong with buying things, she told herself as she walked, shopping was rooted in the human psyche, people waited eagerly at every oasis for the sight of camel trains bearing goods; itinerant peddlers had been sure of a welcome wherever they went, cavemen must have held cave swap meets. When in human history had shopping not been a normal human

Table 3.7 Contd.

---

occupation? But not for her, not today. She had to endure the wait until she heard from Sam without recourse to her old ways of keeping from feeling emotion. She didn't know why, only that it was necessary. Not for anyone else, but for her. Perhaps it was superstition? A form of test? If she didn't buy anything, was it a charm to make Sam call the Ritz in the next fifteen minutes?

No, magical thinking of that childish sort didn't work. Did she honestly believe that if she thought about nothing but Sam reading her letter and rushing to a telephone, she'd send a strong enough psychic message to make it happen?

(S2: 366)

Source: Krantz 1978, 1992

of so-called 'apathetic shoppers', people who are not interested in, are frustrated by, or actively dislike shopping and who endure rather than enjoy the whole experience (G. P. Stone 1954; R. H. Williams *et al.* 1978; Westbrook and Black 1985). As the foregoing quotation indicates, the apathetic shopper and the unfulfilling side of the shopping ordeal are very clearly illustrated in the Scruples novels. Indeed, and in line with Babin *et al.*'s (1994) timely study, the books suggest that individuals may be *both* pro- and anti-shopping on occasion, and hence belong to more than one shopper type. Likewise, they raise the intriguing – and hitherto under-researched (Campbell 1987; Hoch and Loewenstein 1991; Brown and Reid 1997) – possibility that enjoyment can be derived from *not* shopping, from the self-satisfaction of self-denial, from the superstitious assumption that personal restraint will be rewarded in some sort of magical or thaumaturgic manner (Table 3.7).

Love gets strange

Scintillating though the Scruples sex 'n' shopping opera undoubtedly is – at least for aesthetically minded high-brows like myself – I fully appreciate that there may be a modicum of disappointment, not to say frustration, out there. For some of you, I have failed to engage with the titillating (sorry, substantive scholarly) issues of, well, sex and shopping. For others, I have been content with a 'parallel reading' of the Krantzian corpus-cum-academic literature when deconstructive, post-structur-alist firecrackers are warranted. For yet others, I have focused on recognizably 'realist' works of literature and thereby squandered an opportunity to interrogate some of the manifold 'postmodern' novels in which consumption-related behaviours figure prominently (*Generation X*, *Bright Lights, Big City*, *American Psycho*, etc). To these charges, I can only assure you that, *contra* the assumptions of the premature ejaculators, sex will raise its ugly head in a shopping context before this chapter is out, believe me. To the post-structuralist fire-crackheads, I would not only reply that when it comes to lighting blue touch paper and retiring Judith Krantz is pretty well placed, but also remind them that there is more to post-modern literary criticism than deconstruction. In fact, the foregoing analysis is very much in keeping with the new historicism paradigm (S. Brown 1997b), which in certain respects comprises the post-post-structuralist perspective within contemporary literary theory (Veeser 1989, 1992; Cunningham 1994; Ryan 1996). To the 'unscrupulous' coterie of lit-crit élitists I can but protest that, in my opinion, the Scruples novels are *more* postmodern than many of the works that are traditionally held up as exemplars of the form. Yes, they are the lowest of the literary low, seemingly suitable only for summertime, semi-somnambulant, pool-side consumption. Yes, they are formulaic, best-selling 'brands' of book that are produced, distributed and sold like any other fast-moving consumer good. Yes, they have no elaborate literary devices, stylistic quirks or artistic pretensions and don't claim to be anything other than 'rattling good reads'. But, and this is a very big but, the same is true of postmodernism! PoMo, as we have seen, is characterized by its celebration of low culture, and in the strata of low culture Judith Krantz is positively subterranean, if not Palaeozoic. The postmodern movement, unlike its modern predecessor, is not opposed to popular acclaim; on the contrary, it flaunts its commodification, its complicity with the capitalist system. Postmodern works of literature, what is more, are *not* identifiable by their use of flamboyant literary devices – unreliable narrator, metafictional confabulation, *mise en abyme* and so on – since such procedures were standard in the classics of high modernism (though I accept that these devices are often used parodically by postmodern authors and that many scholars consider the works of Proust, Joyce, Beckett and so on as post-modern precursors). If literary postmodernism is distinguished by anything at all, it is distinguished by the return of the storyteller. And, despite the opprobrium that is often heaped on her head, the author of the Scruples novels is pre-eminently, undeniably, indubitably, a storyteller of the first magnitude.

Few people, I suspect, have ever considered Judith Krantz to be a postmodern author, albeit the fact that she has occasionally (like Jeffrey Archer and, allegedly, Phil Kotler) been accused of not writing her own books, the sex scenes in particular, give a distinctly hyperreal hue to her corpus and a whole new meaning to the 'death of the author' thesis. By the same token, a careful reading of the Scruples novels reveals that they make frequent use of purportedly post-structuralist procedures such as irony, playfulness and self-referentiality. For example, Krantz makes copious – occasionally anachronistic (cf. an allusion to 'the vision thing' (*S2*: 384) in a novel set in the early 1980s) – intertextual references to the conventions of romantic fiction ('did she have to react as violently as an insulted maiden in a Victorian novel?' (*S2*: 405)) and aspects of popular culture ('Lipsmakin', finger-lickin' good' (*S2*: 332)). What is more, she expounds on the problems of being an author (*S2*: 234), takes a sideswipe at know-nothing critics (*S2*: 131) and, as the flag-bearer of a debased cultural form, is happy to debunk the pretensions of the literary canon's guardians, Norman Mailer in particular (*S2*: 128). Indeed, *Scruples Two* contains one glorious moment of ironic self-referentiality when Billy muses, 'Sex and shopping . . . where had she heard that catchy, promising phrase before? In a song? In a book?' (*S2*: 258).

Above and beyond post-structuralist playfulness, however, *Scruples* and *Scruples Two* deal explicitly with certain characteristically post-structuralist themes, most notably the nature of the relationship between real and fake, past and present, and male and female. As the briefest acquaintance with the works of Jean Baudrillard (1983), Frederic Jameson (1991) and Umberto Eco (1986) amply demonstrates, the propinquity of true and false, fact and fiction, and the fake and the real is one of the prime concerns of prominent postmodern commentators. It is also a constantly recurring motif in the Scruples novels. For example, the inherent pretence of the fashion industry, the film industry and the retailing industry is routinely referred to, as is the unreality of the west-coast setting ('Does anyone ever become a real Californian?' (*S1*: 301)). Most of the principal and many of the minor characters – Billy, Gigi, Vito, Spider, Valentine, Maggie McGregor, Susan Avery among them – have changed their names, pursue a secret life or are not what they seem. And, as Table 3.8 indicates, replicas and imitations abound in the novels, be they houses, gardens, rooms, restaurants, places, people, outfits, advertisements, motion pictures, television programmes or indeed retailing environments. Thus, the studio of fashion designer Prince is a recreation of an English gentleman's club; the interior of the original Scruples is an exact copy of Dior in Paris; Spider's successful reinvention of the retailing concept is modelled on that monument to kitsch and talisman of first-generation postmodernists – Disneyland; and, with all due respect to T. Wright (1989), the superb description of the 94th Aero Squadron Restaurant is as good an evocation of hyperreality as anything that has been published in the academic marketing literature hitherto.

Alongside and interpenetrating the nature of the relationship between truth and falsity – which culminates, incidentally, with Billy's remarkable declaration, 'I've had a real life with real love and real friends and real achievements. Real ups, real

Table 3.8 Why don't you try me tonight, why don't you try me?

Topic	Examples
Houses	The Ikehorn mansion in Los Angeles is a replica of a Spanish-Moorish castle and 'as authentic as many millions could make it' (*S1*: 201). Billy's house in the Hollywood Hills is designed to look distastefully dishevelled, an 'immaculate reflection of studied disorder' (*S2*: 16), in a pseudo-English style ('mellow European splendour', p. 44).
Gardens	The greenhouses in Billy's 'English walled garden' were 'patterned after the glasshouses at Kew' (*S1*: 406). Billy's hideaway is an all-white 'secret garden', designed by Russell Page, akin to that at Sissinghurst Castle, Kent (*S2*: 99)[1]
Rooms	On moving into the splendour of Billy's abode, Gigi finds it difficult to believe that 'everything in this room must be real. She's seen rooms like this in old movies' (*S2*: 40). The main room in Valentine and Spider's apartment was 'a piece of Paris in Los Angeles, a make-believe Paris in which the single most authentic and unmistakably French element was Valentine herself' (*S2*: 104).
Restaurants	'Peppone's was the kind of authentically old-fashioned Italian restaurant that might be expected to exist almost anywhere except California, all well-worn leather and candlelight and dark wood, without a ray of sunshine piercing its intimate dimness' (*S2*: 430). 'The 94th Aero Squadron . . . was an authentic oddity, a restaurant constructed exactly like an old French farmhouse built of weathered bricks and crumbling plaster, which, one was asked to believe, had been commandeered by a British flying unit during World War I. It has hundreds of sandbags piled high around its ground floor, with early sten guns concealed behind them, a farm wagon full of hay by the front door.

Table 3.8 Contd.

	Muzak that played ''It's a Long, Long Way to Tipperary'' and ''Pack up Your Troubles in Your Old Kit-Bag'', signs directing guests to the ''Briefing Room'', and faded photographs of brave, dead pilots on the walls. An old biplane was parked between this apparition from another world and the real end of Van Nuys Airport, where some seventeen hundred private planes landed or took off every day of the year. Josh enjoyed the nostalgia and sweet melancholy of the place, which somehow managed not to feel fake no matter how much it had to be' (*S1*: 298).[2]
Places	*Mirrors* is filmed in the town of Mendochino, described as 'California's true Brigadoon', where any new construction 'must exactly duplicate this Cape Cod-style of architecture' (*S1*: 438).
	Hollywood was 'a city that managed reliably to fool the public', that 'primped itself silly and presented its best face when the world was watching' (*S2*: 20–1).
People	Valentine and Spider, after talking their way into Billy's employ despite their lack of retailing experience, conclude that 'we're a couple of complete fakers . . . we're both illusionists' (*S1*: 285).
	Valentine 'had spent the last few years with men who weren't men, or men who might be men but whose main interest in life was buying and selling women's clothes. Enough! She was ready for a serious man, but not a solemn one, a man of substance, but not a stuffy man – in short, a real man!' (*S1*: 299).
Outfits	When she worked for fashion designer Prince, Valentine's task was to reproduce his look, a job which 'gave her less personal satisfaction than that of a professional art forger, since she couldn't even feel that she was putting something over on a gullible public' (*S1*: 257).
	On being commissioned to design the costumes for a film set in the 1930s, Valentine states 'I would never design strict period clothes, since what women actually wore in that era would be shockingly

Table 3.8 Contd.

	unattractive to us now . . . I will approximate the period, interpret it, design whatever it is that your own look demand, and still give the audience the impression that you are dressed in the height of fashion of those years. What I will avoid . . . is the disillusionment of reproducing reality' (*S2*: 147).
Advertisements	It is suggested to Billy that she should appear in the advertisements for Scruples, to which Spider cautions, 'I don't know that you'd want to be the symbol of the Scruples customer . . . look Billy, I have to deal with them directly and ninety-nine . . . per cent of them can't wear clothes the way you can. They're used to seeing photographs of models looking better than they ever will, but you're a real person and that could be annoying to them, a kind of turn-off' (*S2*: 213).
Film and television	The audience of Maggie McGregor's television show, which purports to offer an 'inside' account of the film industry, 'thought they were getting a peek at something with a grain of reality at its core' (*S1*: 337).
	'Susan was always amazed at the people who thought that one went to the Cannes Film Festival to see movies. If you had a film in competition you had to show up, but otherwise – goodness, what a bizarre idea' (*S1*: 372).
Others	'Gigi was without words. Everything she'd seen and done since she'd arrived at Billy's had been part of a dream that had nothing to do with life as she knew it' (*S2*: 52).
	"O.K., you two, this hasn't happened." "Not a word to anyone," Lester assured her. "I've forgotten already," said Dolly "I always wanted to hear people talk like that in real life," said Maggie' (*S1*: 533).

Notes:
1 This bears a striking resemblance to the package holiday for the *nouveaux riches*, described by LaBarbara (1988: 195).
2 An academic analysis of the 94th Aero Squadron Restaurant has appeared in the marketing literature, though it is arguable that Krantz better captures the essence of his hyperreal consumption site than T. Wright (1989).

downs, like everyone else. *There is a real me*' (*S2*: 560) – the novels are noteworthy for their characteristically postmodern treatment of time, *Scruples Two* in particular (Nowotny 1994). Like the real–fake dichotomy, this retro orientation is made manifest in all manner of ways. Certain characters, most notably Gigi, are described as belonging to another era ('the 1920s Jazz Baby quality . . . a reincarnation of an idealised flapper' (*S2*: 295)) or as having some sort of preoccupation with the past (her love of old films, music, lingerie, etc.). Numerous individuals, including Billy, Cora Middleton and Susan Avery, have a passion for antiques; Lester Weinstock (Dolly Moon's husband) makes his fortune by buying up the rights to old television series; Valentine is working on reproduction costumes for a period film when she meets her untimely end, and, blaming herself for the fire, Billy attempts to breathe life back into a 400-year-old Parisian mansion. The mail-order retailing concept, moreover, consists of clothes aptly described as 'new classics' (*S2*: 465); the catalogue also incorporates Gigi's antique lingerie collection; and the Scruples Two launch party serves as a sad reminder of the 'last great party' which had relaunched the retail store some seven years beforehand (*S2*: 535). Indeed, in one of the most evocative moments of the entire narrative, the marble nameplate of the original Scruples store, which miraculously survived the fire, is taken to Billy as 'a remembrance of what they used to have' (*S2*: 554), in order to alleviate her profound depression and give her the strength to soldier on.

The paradoxical treatment of time in *Scruples* and *Scruples Two* is paralleled by an unconventional approach to the male–female dichotomy. In keeping with the frequently observed fact that sex 'n' shopping novels are distinguished by their eschewal of the traditional Harlequin or Mills & Boon-style heroine – passive, flighty, loving and subordinate to the aggressive, pagan, domineering qualities of the heroic male – the Scruples saga comprises a complete reversal of the archetypal romantic fiction schema, in so far as the female protagonist is endowed with many of the 'standard' (if stereotypical) male characteristics (S. Brown 1996c). She is tall, dark, handsome, temperamental, unpredictable, impetuous, driven and totally indifferent to wedded bliss, parenthood and the pleasures of procreation (see Cawelti 1976; Pearson and Pope 1981; Flynn and Schweikart 1986). Blessed, moreover, with a voracious sexual appetite (cf. the succession of nurses during Ellis's incapacitation), the heroine is more than capable of treating men as sexual playthings and readily disposable commodities (Hirschman and Stern 1994).

If, as her name implies, Billy is a female embodiment of the masculine qualities of the romantic hero, Spider Elliott exemplifies the traditional romantic heroine. He may be a man among men, a rampant heterosexual in the notoriously homosexual milieu of high fashion and glamour photography, but he is endowed with numerous ostensibly 'feminine' characteristics. Not only is he intuitive, creative, sensitive, artistic, trusting, empathetic, caring, desperate for romantic fulfilment and determined to find the one true love of his life, but:

> he ha[s] a passion for everything and anything that was part of the female element in the world . . . [and possesses a] . . . very special knack for moving through a women's mind, trading easily in her idiom, speaking directly to her, cutting across the barriers of masculinity and femininity.
>
> (Krantz 1978: 14, 84)

Although this blurring of gender boundaries is very much in keeping with postmodernity (Peñaloza 1994; Joy and Venkatesh 1994), as indeed is the melding of past and present and fake and real, perhaps the single most remarkable aspect of the Scruples novels is the *direct connection* that is made, again and again, between shopping behaviour and sexual gratification. For example: 'buying clothes should be as satisfactory as a good fuck' (*S1*: 303); 'her sex life existed only in the moment of purchase' (*S1*: 303); 'shopping is a sensuous experience' (*S1*: 314); 'you had to be hot for them [purchases], dizzy with a desire that can't be forced, any more than a faked orgasm can be enjoyed' (*S1*: 336); 'where there is shopping, sex would somehow follow' (*S2*: 259); 'people want to be *loved* when they buy their clothes – especially rich people!' (*S2*: 315); 'feeling a sexual buzz as she searched the windows for new merchandise' (*S2*: 205); and, as cited earlier, the positively orgasmic 'Christ, it was bliss to spend too much money again' (*S2*: 253). This relationship, admittedly, has been discussed by a number of prominent thinkers such as Marx, Freud, Baudrillard and Lyotard (Sherry *et al.* 1993, 1995) addressed in best-selling glossy magazines (e.g. Maxted 1996) and is starting to attract the attention of several leading consumer researchers (e.g. Hirschman and Holbrook 1982; Belk 1988; Belk *et al.* 1991, 1996; Gould 1991; Deighton and Grayson 1995). However, as Joy and Venkatesh have recently and rightly pointed out, 'while the study of consumer behaviour focuses on categories such as human needs, wants and motivations, it seldom concerns itself with the issue of "human desire"' (1994: 336).

Slow turning

Having transported you to the heights of textacy, I am very seriously tempted to withdraw from this chapter (the rhythm method of writing, as it's known in the trade), thereby ensuring that you are sufficiently aroused to want to read on. However, and at the risk of instant intellectual detumescence, I'm afraid I have to introduce an anti-climactic consideration concerning retailing. Look, I'm really sorry about this; I don't mean to upset you; I know I should have told you earlier;

but you must understand that I have other commitments. I'm supposed to be a retailing person, you know, and people are starting to talk about my postmodern inclinations. I've tried telling them that everything is completely innocent and above board, that our relationship is purely platonic, that our assignations are occasional, unremarkable, business-like. But they are a suspicious lot, rumours are circulating and the Dean – my boss – has started calling me 'the professor formerly known as retailing'. So, I'm going to say a few words about the Scruples novels and the wheel of retailing theory. No, don't leave me. Everything will be all right. I'll make it up to you, I swear. I know the wheel was my first love, but that was a long time ago. I've got to do this. I have no choice. The books are directly relevant to the concept. If you really cared for me, you would understand. At least wait until you hear what I have to say before walking out on me. Okay, then, go. See if I care. There's lots more philosophical fish in the sea.

Figure 3.2 Stan by your man

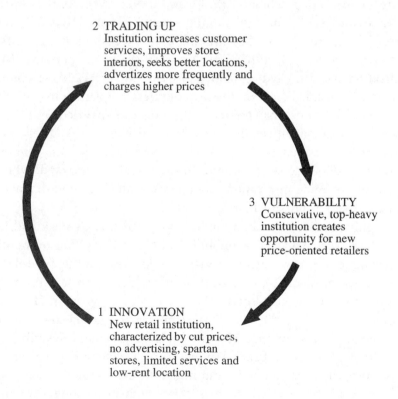

Source: Brown 1988.

It has often been stated that the wheel theory states that new forms of retailing start as cut-price, low-cost, narrow-margin operations which subsequently trade up (cf. department stores, supermarkets, discount houses, etc.). Improvements in display, more prestigious premises, increased advertising and the provision of credit, delivery and many other customer services all serve to drive up expenses, margins and prices (Figure 3.2). Eventually they mature as high-cost, conservative and moribund retail institutions with a sales policy based on quality goods and services rather than price appeal. This, in turn, opens the way for a new low-cost, cut-price retailing format; and so the wheel revolves (M. P. McNair 1958; Hollander 1960; S. Brown 1988, 1991, 1995c).

It has also often been stated that the wheel theory's statements concerning the state of retail institutions have proved highly controversial. At one extreme, the model has been described as 'powerful and fascinating' (Stern and El-Ansary 1977: 243), 'the dominant concept in retailing' (Greyser 1976: iii) and 'a perennial favourite of marketing scholars' (S. Brown 1992: 180). At the other extreme, it has been castigated for having 'limited clarity' (Savitt 1988: 38), being 'vaguely conceived' (Gripsrud 1986: 252) and failing to 'meet the criteria for formal theory' (Hirschman and Stampfl 1980: 72). More to the point perhaps, McNair's conceptualization has attracted an enormous amount of academic commentary (for, against and undecided), given rise to countless 'explanations' of the trading-up process (secular trends, managerial sloth, etc.) and spawned innumerable alternative conceptualizations of retailing change (S. Brown 1988). These range from the 'retail accordion', which posits perpetual alternation between generalist and specialist retail outlets (Hollander 1966), to the so-called 'reversed' wheel of retailing theory, where retailing innovations commence at the high end of the cost spectrum and progressively trade down (Mun 1988).

As a highly successful retailing innovation, which at its peak had outlets in Los Angeles, New York, Chicago, Honolulu and Hong Kong, not to mention the mail-order catalogue, it seems entirely reasonable to examine the Scruples operation in light of the wheel theory. Although it pains me deeply to say so, the concept does not fare well from this encounter. True, Scruples' proprietor, Billy Ikehorn, is an embodiment of the dynamic, charismatic, imperious, go-getting, no-nonsense, risk-taking retailing innovator that McNair eulogizes over and describes so eloquently (he cites John Wanamaker, Frank Woolworth and Eugene Ferkauf, amongst others). What is more, the extent of her commitment to the retailing cause gradually wanes in the course of the novels, which is very much in keeping with the managerial deterioration, 'fat cats' explanation of the trading-up process (though Billy would not be pleased to be so described). It is fair to say, however, that the evolution of the Scruples operation does not accord with the wheel theory.

When the store is first opened, for instance, it sells a narrowly focused range of exclusive fashion merchandise and is positioned at the very top end, the apex, of the market. Incredible though it is, the initial Scruples concept proves unsuccessful, and it is only rescued by Spider Elliott's repositioning exercise. This involves moving the store slightly *down-market* – relatively speaking, of course – that is, from serving the mega-rich to the mere super-rich market segment, dramatically increasing its hedonic-to-utilitarian ratio by implementing his 'shopping is show-business' dictum, and by broadening out the range of goods and services on offer. The new, improved Scruples retailing concept thus comprises high-fashion apparel, a bespoke design department, gifts and accessories, a restaurant, bar-cum-gentleman's club and all manner of personal services including manicure, massage, pedicure, luxurious changing facilities, dancing lessons, party planning and, not least, Spider's personal seal of approval on every item of clothing purchased (Table 3.9). Much the same evolutionary pattern is apparent with the Scruples Two catalogue retailing concept, which comprises yet another move down-market, albeit the position that is eventually occupied, as with the original Scruples store, is considered exclusive and up-market compared to the norms of the mail-order industry. Similarly, the range of goods carried by the Scruples Two catalogue – principally Gigi's antique lingerie and separates, 'the twenty per cent of the stuff she buys that she wears ninety per cent of the time' (*S2*: 468) – is much narrower than that of the extinct retailing organization, though this too is eventually broadened out to include maternity wear, children's wear, designer labels, a collection for the extra large and so on.

Table 3.9 First we sterilize it, then we merchandise it

'Look at the facts. In Beverly Hills you have a shopping area that equals, in sheer luxury and choice, the best of New York. It's not as big, but neither is the population. Now obviously, this area wouldn't be here, and growing every day, if the customers weren't here to support it. But Scruples isn't getting them, Why? Because it *doesn't work*.'

'Doesn't work?' Billy glared. 'It's a more elegant and comfortable store than any store in the world, including Paris! I made sure of that.'

It doesn't work as ENTERTAINMENT!' Both Valentine and Billy just stared at Spider as he went on. 'Shopping has become a form of entertainment, Billy, whether you like it or not. A visit to Scruples *is just not fun* and your potential

Table 3.9 Contd.

customers demand fun from the stores they visit. You can even go all the way and call it the Disneyland concept of retailing.'

'Disneyland!' Billy said it in a low, horrified, repelled voice.

'Yes, Disneyland – shopping as a trip, shopping as a giggle. The same money changes hands, no mistake about that, but if your customer, your local customer or your customer from Santa Barbara or a tourist from another country, has a choice between Scruples and Giorgio's, your neighbour across the street, which will she pick? You walk into Scruples and you see a vast, ornate space decorated in twenty-five shades of supremely subtle grey, with little gilt chairs here and there and a terrifying herd of chic, elderly, haughty sales women who all act as if they would far rather speak French than English – or you go into Giorgio's and you see a crowded, merry mob of people drinking at the bar, playing pool, sales ladies who wear nutty hats and look at you as if they've been hoping you'd come in for a good gossip, and all of them ready to make you feel expansive and cosseted.'

'Giorgio's happens to stand for everything that Scruples is NOT,' Billy said in a glacial voice.

'Giorgio's is the number-one retail specialty store in the country, including New York City.'

'What? I don't believe it!' . . .

'No matter. The point is that I'm convinced that unless you accept the Disneyland concept of making retailing fun, there isn't any point in my staying here. You can have my resignation if you want it.' Billy looked at him testily. He wasn't using that astonishing smile for a change. He was really in dead earnest. She had had enough experience with men to know a ploy when she heard one. This creature meant every word he was saying.

'Christ, I'm beginning to think I should have bought Giorgio's instead of building Scruples!' she said with a bitter laugh and sudden tears in her eyes.

'Wrong! Scruples can be ten times the store Giorgio's is because you have three things they don't have: *space – Valentine – and me.*' Spider had already smelled a change in her.

Billy had abandoned something with her last remark and stepped an inch away from a fiercely defended position.

'And what do you plan – to put in a pool table and ask my sales people to dress funky?'

'Nothing that simple, or that copycat. Complete redecoration, including your immaculate fitting rooms. They have to be made sexy, individual, and amusing. It may mean another seven or eight hundred thousand dollars spent on top of the millions you've sunk in her already – but it will be enough to turn the store around. Example: When you walk in the front door of Scruples *after* we redecorate, you'll find yourself in the most extraordinary, charming country store

Table 3.9 Contd.

in the world: bulging, chockablock full of everything necessary and unnecessary from antique buttons to lilies growing in pots, penny candy in Waterford glass jars, antique toys, the most expensive pruning shears in the world, handmade writing paper, pillows made from grandmothers' quilts, tortoiseshell boxes and bird whistles to – you name it. And the country store is so much fun that it puts you in a good mood, whether you buy or not. The way I've planned it, they'll buy there on the way out, impulsive gifts, but it's planned to be the entrance to the Fun Fair.

'The Fair, Billy – that's the main part of the ground floor. For the men, we'll have a pub. And while they're waiting for the women to shop, and so they don't feel silly, as if they're trapped in some embarrassingly feminine place, we'll give them all kinds of those new pinball machines, the electronic ones, and at least four backgammon tables and, of course, a men's department, accessories only, but the finest in the world. Maybe a couple of Ping-Pong tables – I'm not sure about that yet. Now, the rest of the room, except the back end, is going to be accessory heaven for women – just heaps and heaps of gorgeous goodies, only the best, the most expensive, the latest, the newest, most exclusive beautiful things – you know what I mean – but all done with such a sense of abundance, of accessibility, of touchability that they won't be able to resist. The Arabian Nights. The Sultan's Treasures. That's why they shop, Billy – not because, God knows, they *need* another bag or scarf but because it just feels so damn good. They *want to be tempted* – they can afford it. And in the back, an Edwardian winter garden, cosy, intimate, old-fashioned, just the place to revive yourself with tea and crumpets or a chocolate soda or a glass of champagne. And, of course, all the showcases and display pieces will be easily movable – even the walls in between the country store and the winter garden can be sliding walls – so that when you give the parties there'll be lots of room for the orchestra and dancers— ' He paused for breath.

'Dancers?' said Billy in a strange tone of voice . . .

'Would I be wrong in saying that you want to turn Scruples into a kind of penny arcade with pinball machines and penny candy and free lunch and sexy fitting rooms and a hoard of models prancing around and foot massage and gambling and dancing parties, or am I exaggerating?' She bit off each word as if she were reading from a laundry list.

'Basically, yes.' There was much more, but he'd stand on that, Spider decided. If she couldn't see—

'I LOVE IT!' Billy leaped up from behind her desk as if she'd been detonated and kissed a dazzled Valentine who had yet to open her mouth. 'Valentine! Darling! *I LOVE IT.*'

Source: Krantz 1978: 313–18

The Scruples operation, in sum, completely refutes the celebrated and much-loved wheel of retailing theory, insofar as it involves trading down rather than trading up. If anything, it corroborates the reversed wheel of retailing concept and, to some extent, the retail accordion (i.e. specialist to general to specialist to general). As I'm sure you must appreciate, this conclusion comes as a deep personal and professional blow to me, since my academic career, such as it is, is in ruins. Although I could attempt to bluster my way out of this impasse by reminding you of the fact that Scruples is a fictional retail store – and we shouldn't place too much reliance on what we read in books, now should we? – this would be contrary to the spirit of the present volume, which maintains that marketers have much to learn from works of literature. Indeed, careful examination of the Scruples operation suggests a form of retailing evolution that has never been articulated by retailing theorists hitherto; that is, from an essentially utilitarian to an overwhelmingly hedonic shopping experience and back again (Table 3.10). Hold on a minute, that *is* the wheel of retailing theory, albeit shorn of its cut-price/premium-price, low-margin/high-margin, bare-bones/service-rich dialectic! The essence of the wheel theory, surely, is that the shopping experience *itself* swings from utilitarian, functional, austere and so on to hedonic, fantastic, sybaritic, etc. (regardless of price point or margin). The Scruples novels *do* conform to the wheel of retailing theory. I was right all along. Oh happy day. Oh happy, happy day. Peel me a grape, Philip . . .

Table 3.10 She said the same thing to me

'I think Gigi's right about that, Sasha,' Billy said. 'You need a lot of merchandise and you need a name. Every one of these catalogs you have here is from a famous store; people order from them largely because the gift box has instant name recognition and it comes from a place they consider to have status, like Neiman's or Tiffany. Nobody's ever heard of Gigi Orsini . . . not yet.'

'Wait a minute, Billy, what you just said about recognition, did you hear yourself?' Gigi asked, suddenly excited. 'You're absolutely right, it takes recognition, that's the key – Billy, *what about Scruples*?'

'Scruples?' Billy said blankly. 'What are you talking about?'

'Scruples – *a catalog like Scruples*!'

'Oh please, Gigi!' Billy said, instantly offended. 'Scruples was the most exclusive specialty store in the world. Scruples would never, *never* have had a catalog! I would not have allowed it, not in a million years. And anyway, there are no Scruples anymore. No, absolutely not!'

'But listen, Billy, that's the thing, there are no more stores, but the Scruples name and reputation and mystique and status have never lost their power. It's

Table 3.10 Contd.

---

only been . . . what? . . . not even two years . . . you could bring it back, but in a different form . . . the first really great catalog for fashion!'

'Oh, Gigi, do you have any idea of how expensive we were?' Billy snapped, deeply irritated. 'There were enough women in Beverly Hills and New York and Chicago to support three boutiques, not big department stores, but large boutiques located in the centers of wealthy areas. The other Scruples were all in other countries. Most people never had the kind of money you needed to shop at Scruples, and the ones who did *certainly* don't shop by mail order! Mail order! Even if I liked the idea . . . and I have to say I most definitely don't . . . you could never sell clothes as expensive as Scruples clothes without fitting rooms and perfect alterations and personal attention – no, it couldn't work, it simply *cannot* be done.'

'But what if the clothes weren't so expensive?' Gigi insisted. 'What if they were affordable?'

'Then they wouldn't reflect Scruples. It's out of the question.' Billy spoke angrily. Gigi simply had no idea why the idea of Scruples as a catalog assaulted and damaged her memories of her perfect store, her exquisite, exclusive boutique, the dream she had created to satisfy no one but herself, the dream that was over forever.

'Billy,' Gigi said intently, 'Scruples was a concept before it worked – remember how you told me that you started with one concept – to bring the elegance of Dior to Beverly Hills – and then Spider changed it into a fun Disneyland for grownups? Why couldn't you change it again? Make it a moderate-priced concept, but with just as much taste? Call the catalog Scruples Two, so people wouldn't think it was the same thing . . . it would be about taste and quality and the youth and style that Sasha keeps wanting—'

'And it wouldn't have to arrive only at Christmas, like the others,' Sasha interrupted, galvanised. 'It wouldn't have to contain this gifty-gifty stuff – it could come twice – or maybe even four times – a year, the way the stores change their merchandise by the season. Oh, Billy, it could be done! I'm your customer, Gigi's your customer, even you might find out that you'd be your own customer!'

'Scruples Two,' Gigi said. 'Just the name alone makes it different – the "Two" part shows that it's not trying to be like the store, it's its own self.' She grabbed her crutches and got up to get the photocopies of her cards. 'Look, Billy, it could have a section for my antique lingerie, with these cards as copy – come on, read them, Billy. Hell, I could write the whole catalog if I had to, couldn't I, Sasha? How hard could it be? I couldn't get the merchandise designed or made, but you could, Billy, and Sasha could help, and . . . oh, Billy! You've got to say yes!'

'No.'

'No?' Gigi asked reflexively. She knew that when Billy said no, she meant it . . .

'A catalog called Scruples Two? I do *not* think so, thank you very much,' Billy

Table 3.10 Contd.

---

said disdainfully, shaking her head in vigorous repudiation.

'Say again?'

'Her idea was to start a new, reasonably priced clothing catalog, and call it Scruples Two since that would give it an immediate name to attract people. And Sasha wanted it to come out each season, not just at Christmas the way they do now. Of course I told them it was out of the question.'

'Of course. Just like of course Scruples, the original boutique, was all done up to the teeth in deadly Parisian gray silk and gilt and haughty salesladies so that it intimidated shoppers right out of the door.'

'Spider! You *can't* possibly think it's a good idea!'

'Why not, Billy?'

'But . . . listen, Spider, we were about the very best, we were the most exclusive . . . Valentine's custom designs . . . the elegance . . . Spider, a catalog is so . . . *available*! Anybody, just absolutely anybody could order from it,' Billy spluttered, outraged at his lack of agreement.'

'But Scruples doesn't exist anymore, Billy, Scruples is over. Very much over,' Spider said patiently, with a touch of grimness.

'But, Spider— '

'Hell, Billy, even if all the Scruples were still there, you could put out a catalog without going into competition with yourself. You'd be showing a less expensive version of the Scruples *attitude* towards clothes. Our customers never wore only our stuff, Billy, they wore all sorts of things at just about every price range. You were one of the few people who could afford to dress from head to toe at Scruples, and when you wanted anything in denim or jeans, even you had to go elsewhere. We showed the ultimate designers because we were carving out a position for the Scruples name, making it the top store for special occasions. But that was in real life, with money-making boutiques in the most affluent areas in the country. A catalog would have to be much less expensive and very different in its orientation . . . but since I live in the present tense, I see no reason not to think about it.'

'I still think it's indecent!'

'No way. It's a good idea, there's nothing wrong with it.'

Source: Krantz 1992: 420–2, 436–7

Chapter 4

Bakhtin the US, Bakhtin the US, Bakhtin the USSR

I have a homunculus on my right buttock. When I move one way, he smiles; another, and he grows glum. Grave and gay by turns, as he himself put it when he was a touch more alive than he is now . . .

He arrived yesterday, from Lloyds Bank, wrapped in a letter. We enclose a replacement cheque card for your use, *said the letter*, please sign the card immediately. *It has been the work of a moment to do this, and it would have been the work of another to slip the new card into my wallet had I not, as I did so, noticed a fuzzy little face in the corner of it. Hello, I said, a breakthrough. What a good idea, sticking the cardholder's face on a card, that is one in the eye for mugger and pickpocket. And I put my glasses on to check the likeness.*

It was a bloke with a beard. As I turned the tiny hologram, his expression changed several times, but it never became mine. Here we go, I said – as I have said so often when colliding with a technological glitch – they have sent me someone else's card. Is it not amazing, I said to the manikin, that, in this day and age, we can put a man on the moon, but we cannot guarantee that it will be the right man?

I uncrumpled the binned letter. If the card is lost, *it said*, please inform the Chief Inspector, Lloyd's Bank plc, 071–626–1500.

'You have got the name right,' I informed Cashplod, 'but the picture is not of me.'

'It is not supposed to be of you. It is William Shakespeare.'

I looked again. It was a photograph.

'How did you get a photograph of Shakespeare?' I inquired.

'It is an actor,' said the Chief Inspector, 'dressed up.'

'All right,' I said, because I am a reasonable man. 'I can accept the how. What about the why? Why is there a hologram of William Shakespeare on my cheque guarantee card?'

'Not my department,' said the Chief Inspector. 'I suggest you speak to Jim Parsons. He handles corporate communications . . . '

'Hello, Jim,' I said, after a bit, and popped the question.

'We call it the Bard Card,' said Jim. 'It facilitates recognition.'

'Only of Shakespeare,' I said. 'I can see where if Shakespeare fetched up at the Tesco's till they would be more than happy to accept his cheque. Mind you, that said, it does occur to me that he never signed his name the same way twice. It is quite possible that if he put Shagsper, your Chief Inspector would have his glove on the Bard's collar before he'd got his trolley half way to the Volvo.'

I was losing Jim. You can sense things like that.

'It is not about identifying the cardholder,' said Jim, a mite testily, 'it is about identifying the card. When the retailer sees Shakespeare, it triggers the correct procedures. Remember, retailers may be foreign or illiterate, but they can all be trained to recognise Shakespeare . . . '

'To what base uses we may return, Horatio!' I said. 'I mean, Jim.'

But I rang off cordially. After all, when you get right down to it, if imperious Caesar, dead and turned to clay, might stop a hole to keep the wind away, so what?

Provided it triggers the correct procedures in Tesco's.

(Coren 1991: 32–4)

(What's the story) morning glory?

When the academic roll is called up yonder, I very much doubt if I'll be there. As intellectual chaff rather than wheat, as a pedagogic goat not a sheep, as a scholarly sinner instead of a saint, I'm pretty sure that the lake of cerebral fire awaits me. It is, admittedly, a mite depressing to think that on the day of academic marketing judgement Phil Kotler will be welcomed with open arms and, presumably, a tidy consultancy package (Hereafter Marketing has a ring to it, I'm sure you agree, albeit they're-after-your-money marketing is perhaps more in keeping with the prevailing consultancy ethos). Shelby Hunt, similarly, will doubtless be duly and deservedly cannonized (that's right, two n's – he is a big shot, after all) and David Aaker will not only have the opportunity to count his blessings but can be relied on to conduct multivariate analyses, conjoint contortions and report a four-factor solution. However, when my own academic exploits are eventually weighed in the celestial balance, I'll be very surprised if my achievements on the sex and shopping front are weighty enough to tip the scales in my favour. Patriarchy probably prevails in paradise and reading romantic fiction when more (spiritually) uplifting books are to hand is a one-way ticket – a business-class, full-fare, extra leg-room, fully reclining seat, triple Air Miles, first-name terms with the flight attendant, none of your Standby or Apex rubbish ticket – to hell fire and damnation.

While I cannot deny that my perverse academic inclinations are destined, assuredly, to transport me directly from the nether regions to the nether world, as it were, there are a number of ostensible short-term benefits to be had from by long-term trajectory. Apart from the obvious physical effects – I weighed 240 lb when I started work on the Krantz novels and am now the desiccated husk that you know and, er, love – I have discovered that 'sex' can do wonders for one's scholarly standing (S. Brown 1995e, 1997b). For years and years I trudged around the conference circuit presenting, if I say so myself, erudite and learned papers on the wheel of retailing theory. In fact, they were so erudite and learned that I invariably found myself scheduled for the very last session in the programme (when all the delegates are heading in the general direction of the airport) or, conversely, for the first session in the morning after the conference dinner, when the only person in attendance is a still-stotious, somewhat disoriented reveller from the night before (and that, dear reader, is the chairperson of the session). Since I started talking about sex and shopping, however, I have found – for some strange reason – that my presentations are scheduled for the primest of prime spots on the programme and the room is unfailingly full to overflowing with distinguished academics, all of whom are dedicated to the ceaseless pursuit of disinterested, rigorous and objective marketing knowledge.

As you can imagine, this sudden change in scholarly fortune has come as something of a shock to my somewhat timorous system. After years of talking to a combination of slumbering senior citizens, academic tyros who have misread the conference programme but are much too polite to leave the room, and, as often as not, an ocean of empty seats (some of my best friends are empty seats; hell, I could write a book on empty seats I have known; undertake cross-cultural comparative analyses of empty seating arrangements . . .), it is very unsettling to have to deal with an alert, agog and, worst of all, querulous audience. Not only do these people insist on asking all sorts of (im)pertinent questions about methodology, procedure, findings and other things that are no concern of theirs, but they also occasionally attempt to collar you afterwards in order to continue the inquisition over coffee and biscuits. What on earth is going on? Have these people no shame? Don't they have anything better to do with their time? Have they no Homes to go to, or sheltered accommodation at least?

Anyway, a couple of years ago I was at an academic marketing conference in some godforsaken spot, when something remarkable happened. I had delivered my standard 'sex and shopping' presentation to its standard round of tumultuous apathy (sadly, my performances never quite match up to audience expectations), when I was approached by someone who introduced herself as a marketing practitioner. My heart, needless to say, plummeted Hush-Puppywards, since I was anticipating a tirade about being sick in the head, taxpayers' money being squandered on perverts or, the standard when-oh-when-oh-when will academics produce something of use to practitioners. To my astonishment, and the blessed relief of my blue suede shoes, she informed me that in her long and successful career as marketing manager for a succession of major multinational clothing manufacturers, her decisions often relied more upon books, television programmes and glossy magazines than formal market research exercises. Sure, the companies she worked for had all sorts of sophisticated marketing intelligence systems, commissioned copious quantitative and qualitative research reports, modelled buyer/consumer/competitor behaviour like it was going out of style and bought into all the longitudinal data bases that are known to man – and some that aren't. But, when it came to the crunch, *Dallas*, *Dynasty*, *Cosmopolitan* and bonkbuster novels provided more insight into the workings of the marketplace, as far as she was concerned, than the very best endeavours of the marketing research department.

Although it is easy to make light of this anecdote or attempt to explain her behaviour away as aberrant, unrepresentative, an artifact of the notoriously unpredictable clothing market, a demonstration of intuitive marketing abilities or – why not? – an unfortunate but all too typical example of underperformance (just think how much *more* successful she *could* have been had she only analysed, planned, implemented and controlled her marketing activities). Yet, whether you accept it or not, it seems to me that this episode raises a very simple question. If marketing practitioners can get something meaningful from works of literature, broadly defined – and seem prepared to make multi-million-dollar decisions on the basis of such insights – why are certain marketing scholars still unwilling to do likewise (present company excepted, of course)? It's not as though there are any *real* risks in doing so (financial, house and home, bankruptcy courts, etc.), other than to our old-fashioned, albeit difficult to eradicate, notions of rigorous marketing science. It can hardly denude our standing in the eyes of our principal constituents, marketing managers and prospective managers, since they already consider most academic publications to be next to worthless. Indeed, if the above story is in any way typical, a literary turn may go some way towards repairing the breach that patently exists between academics and practitioners.

As a bare minimum, even the most backward backwoodsman of marketing science – stop laughing there, these people can't help themselves; you shouldn't mock the afflicted – must be prepared to concede that potentially researchable hypotheses are obtainable from works of literature. The Scruples novels, for example, are literally full of throwaway remarks that cannot fail to whet the appetites of or strike a chord with students of marketing and consumer behaviour – 'sales-women . . . had a habit of falling in love with the dress that would have looked well on them rather than on the woman who would wear it' (*S1*: 14), 'the fierce look in her eyes informed him of five of the most welcome words in the jewellery business. Rich. American. Woman. Impulse. Shopper.' (*S2*: 364), and, not least, 'going into research is the only way a doctor can positively insure himself against ever making a decent living' (*S1*: 37)! Such turns of phrase exemplify Norman Mailer's cogent observation that 'fiction can serve as our reconnaissance into all those jungles and up those precipices of human behaviour that psychiatry, history, theology, and sociology are too intellectually encumbered to try' (1991: 159).

The study of 'marketing in literature', however, is not just about hypothesis generation. Works of literature can offer insights into marketing- and consumption-related phenomena that are otherwise unobtainable. Consider the short extract from *The Diary of Virginia Woolf* reproduced in Table 4.1. It describes the author's experience of having her handbag stolen whilst purchasing Christmas presents in Marshall & Snelgrove, a leading London department store. There is no doubt that in its intimation that the victim feels tainted by the guilt of the criminal ('I was admitted to the underworld') the passage provides an interesting proposition suitable

Table 4.1 What's her name? Virginia Plain!

Tuesday 23 December

I will make this hasty note about being robbed. I put my bag under my coat at Marshall & Snelgrove's. I turned; & felt, before I looked 'It was gone'. So it was. Then began questions & futile messages. Then the detectives came. He stopped a respectable elderly woman apparently shopping. They exchanged remarks about 'the usual one – no she's not here today. Its a young woman in brown fur.' Meanwhile I was ravaged, of course, with my own futile wishes – how I had thought, as I put down my bag, this is foolish. I was admitted to the underworld. I imagined the brown young woman peeping, pouncing. And it was gone my 6 pounds – my two brooches – all because of that moment. They throw the bags away, said the detective. These dreadful women come here – but not so much as to some of the Oxford St. shops. Fluster, regret, humiliation, curiosity, something frustrated, foolish, something jarred, by this underworld – a foggy evening – going home, penniless – thinking of my green bag – imagining the woman rifling it – her home – her husband – Now to Rodmell in the fog.

Monks House, [Rodmell, Sussex]

Source: A. O. Bell and McNellie 1980: 339–40

for subsequent empirical testing. But, like Krantz's superb description of compulsive shopping behaviour, Woolf's compelling use of language – *futile* (twice), *foolish* (twice), *ravaged, frustrated, jarred, penniless, fluster, regret, humiliation* – also comprises a very powerful evocation of the distress, dismay, anger, self-loathing and overwhelming feeling of personal violation that the theft of one's possessions is known to induce (Belk 1988). We get a very real sense of what it's like to suffer such indignity. As Belk (1986a) rightly observes in his comparison of artistic and scientific approaches to consumer research, 'only art is able to convey the specific, personal, and experiential knowledge . . . of, say, a day in Victorian England, in a way that approaches the intensity and intimacy of the actual experience' (p. 23), . . . 'One can learn more about the complexity of motives and mutual perception from a reasonably good novel than from a "solid" piece of social-science research' (p. 24, quoting Sennett), . . . 'what good art can do is reveal the essence of that which it concerns' (p. 25).

Rocket to Russia

There is, of course, more to marketing aesthetics than culling the literary canon for references to marketing artifacts, or phenomenological accounts of consumption experiences, important and necessary though such endeavours undoubtedly are. A number of prominent researchers have, in effect, turned the 'marketing-in-litera-ture' perspective on its head by applying the tools and techniques of literary criticism to certain key elements of the marketing mix, most notably advertising and promotion. Before we examine this 'literature-in-marketing' tradition in detail, however, it is necessary to emphasize that, within literary circles, criticism has traditionally enjoyed a somewhat ambivalent relationship with the canon or corpus of great and not so great works (Eagleton 1984, 1996b; Jefferson and Robey 1986; R. Webster 1996). On the one hand, it is often dismissed as secondary, subservient, parasitic or, indeed, a sheet anchor on artistic attainment. As a glance at any anthology of quotations amply testifies, creative writers have coined any number of derogatory comments on the function, discernment and, as often as not, parentage of literary critics (Muir and Brett 1981; Metcalf 1987). According to the celebrated Irish playwright and dipsomaniac, Brendan Behan, 'critics are like eunuchs in a harem; they know how it's done; they've seen it done everyday; but they are unable to do it themselves'. For Archbishop Garbett, 'any fool can criticise and many of them do'. Or, in the oft-cited epithet of John Osborne, 'asking a working writer what he feels about critics is like asking a lamp-post what it feels about dogs'.

On the other hand, there is the no doubt equally stereotyped notion of critic as connoisseur, as the defender of the literary faith, as the disseminator of the great tradition, as the last bastion, in direct line of descent from Matthew 'sweetness and light' Arnold and F. R. 'scrutiny' Leavis, of moral probity and the rule of literature. When viewed from this perspective, indeed, it is clear that far from being subordinate to, or leeches upon, the working author, critics actually *create* and maintain the canon though their commentaries on the merits of individual works, artists, genres, interpretations and schools of thought (Selden and Widdowson 1993; Bennett and Royle 1995; Barry 1995). Literary criticism may be chronologically posterior to the texts which it addresses and assesses, but it also serves to identify, classify and, not least, disqualify the works that are deemed worthy of critical attention in the first place. Adair (1992), in fact, has gone so far as to suggest that criticism constitutes the essence – the driving force – of contemporary cultural discourse. These days, you don't have to attend all the plays, films and operas on offer, or read all the books. You simply have to possess the requisite degree of critic-induced familiarity to participate in the surrounding debates, discussions and controversies. Works of literature and art, in other words, are unimportant in themselves; they are simply canon fodder, so to speak, for the after-dinner conversations of the chattering classes.

Although the author/critic distinction continues to be made, and their respective positions adumbrated, it is important to emphasize that the cleavage is neither clear cut nor immutable. Just as the traditional division between high art and low has gone the way of long-dead brand names like Treets, Marathon and Spangles, so too the long-standing demarcation dispute between artist and critic has been all but abandoned (if it ever really existed). In our present postmodern times, it appears that many, perhaps most, literary luminaries also serve in a critical capacity, as occasional book reviewers, and equally many critics seem keen to try their authorial hand. As the contents pages of the Sunday supplements or literary periodicals amply testify, the Martin Amises, Will Selfs, Gore Vidals and John Updikes of this world are quite prepared to prostitute themselves on the (lucrative) altar of the review pages, while critics ranging from Umberto Eco and Sarah Dunant to David Lodge and Terry Eagleton are more than capable of tilting at the bestsellers list. It cannot be denied, furthermore, that many of the most influential writers of the late twentieth century – Jacques Derrida, Roland Barthes, Michel Foucault, Fredric Jameson, etc. – not only hail from the critical end of the literary spectrum, but also that their work routinely serves as a catalyst for novelists, essayists and the tellers of tall tales and short stories (see, for example, Burnham 1995; Duncker 1996; Litt 1996a).

Be that as it may, the apparatus of literary criticism has recently been applied, with some vigour and not a little success, to the 'text' of marketing artifacts, advertising and promotion in particular. The *primum mobile* of this methodological transfiguration is Barbara B. Stern, a consumer researcher with a doctorate in English Literature. Arguing that 'literary criticism can contribute to marketing theory in several areas, among which are idea generation, development of new theories, enrichment of existing ones and evaluation of the discipline's theoretical underpinnings' (B. B. Stern 1990a: 24), she has undertaken a series of detailed analyses which treat magazine and television advertisements as works of literature. These commenced with a close New Critical explication of the principal concerns of literary theorists – syntax, sense, sound, symbol, structure, style – coupled with a demonstration of their relevance in a commercial context (B. B. Stern 1988a), and continued with a cogent summary of the various schools of literary theory as applied to a single 1929 advertisement for Ivory Soap (B. B. Stern 1989). Stern, in addition, has examined advertisers' use of diverse literary devices such as allegory, symbol, metaphor, irony and humour; explored the conventions of classical drama and vignette in a sample of forty television ads; offered instructive insights into company personae, the author 'function' and *fin-de-siècle* effects; and, in what is arguably her single most important contribution, applied Northrop Frye's celebrated fourfold classification of narrative forms – comedy, romance, tragedy and irony – to the myths and rituals that inhere in the annual Thanksgiving festival (B. B. Stern 1988b, 1990b, 1990c, 1991b, 1992, 1994a, 1994b, 1995, 1996a).

Alongside Stern, a number of other prominent marketing academics have sought to apply the tools and techniques of literary criticism to advertising artifacts. To cite but a few examples: McQuarrie has drawn upon a comprehensive 317-item archive of magazine ads to demonstrate the prevalence and characteristics of what he terms 'resonance' (the use of puns, wordplay and analogous figures of speech) and developed a three-level, hierarchical classification of advertising rhetoric (McQuarrie 1989; McQuarrie and Mick 1992, 1996). Grafton Small and Linstead (1989), furthermore, have uncovered the subtext of seduction–cum–sexual politics in an advert for a chauffeur-driven limousine service and, in another virtuoso display of textual interpretation, articulated the élite culture/popular culture divide that inheres in a big-budget, sub-Christo commercial for Silk Cut cigarettes (Linstead and Grafton Small 1990). Linda Scott (1990, 1994a), likewise, has sought to expose the shortcomings of the information-processing orthodoxy by highlighting the integral parts played by music and visual rhetoric in successful marketing communications. She has also made a convincing case for reader-response theory, a school of literary thought that shifts the focus of critical attention away from its traditional preoccupation with authorial intention, textual content or indeed the socio-economic context of its creation, to the often highly variegated, not to say conflicting, circumstances of its reception. In other words, to the *audience*'s understanding, interpretation and utilization of the work in question and, moreover, to the assumptions, expectations and pre-understandings that they bring to bear upon commercial messages generally – scepticism in particular (Scott 1994b).

Scepticism, of course, is not confined to the watch-out-the-bastards-are-trying-to-sell-me-something defence mechanisms of the audience for advertisements. It is equally apparent in academic reader's response to this literary theory–advertising practice nexus. Some hair-splitting, self-serving cynics, for example, have drawn ostentatious attention to the fact that, despite a certain congruence in overall outlook, literary criticism and postmodern marketing are not one and the same (S. Brown 1995a). On the contrary, it is evident that the principal exponents of a lit-crit approach to marketing phenomena have championed schools of critical thought that are anything but postmodern in spirit. Other narrow-minded dyspeptics have noted the curious fact that in-depth 'readings' of individual ads are almost always predicated upon the interpretations of marketing intellectuals, not those of the actual target market for the advertising campaigns (S. Brown *et al.* 1997). While this propensity is a commonplace of cultural studies (e.g. Williamson 1978, 1986; Wernick 1991; Goldman and Papson 1994a, 1994b; Fowles 1996; Stallabrass 1996), it is unbecoming when it comes from supposedly customer-oriented marketing academics, individuals who repeatedly call for, but never quite get round to delivering, empirical confirmation of their contentions or, incredibly, make a case for reader-response theory without so much as a sniff of reader response.

In fairness to the researchers concerned – and, as you know, I am nothing if not totally fair – Stern has progressively moved away from her initial assertion that literary criticism was 'scientific', in a manner of speaking, and therefore comprised a useful complement to more conventional forms of marketing research. Of late, she has plunged headlong into the depthless depths of Derridean deconstruction, concluding that its greatest contribution 'is as an agent provocateur, a force for making the field revisit itself' (B. B. Stern 1996b: 145). Scott, moreover, has been responsible for perhaps the most lucid explanation of post-structuralism in the marketing literature, as well as a masterful historical overview of the figure–discourse dialectic (Scott 1992, 1993). The meanings and understandings that 'real' readers derive from 'real' advertising campaigns have also been examined at length by researchers espousing what could be described as para-lit-crit positions. These include empirical analyses of the so-called 'hell of connotation' (Mick and Politi 1989); the impact of consumer life histories and themes (Mick and Buhl 1992); the affective effect of figures of speech (McQuarrie and Mick 1992); consumer reactions to treatments of the 'new man', sexuality and personal identity (Elliott *et al.* 1993, 1995; Elliott and Ritson 1995; Ritson *et al.* 1996); and the diverse uses and gratifications, such as entertainment, escapism, aspiration, information, education, ego enhancement, surveillance, reassurance and play, that young people derive from their everyday encounters with the advertising condition (O'Donohoe 1994).

While fairness, to be fair, has its place, it would be grossly unfair of me not to draw your attention to another significant shortcoming of the lit-crit approach to advertising and promotion. Although its adepts have been assiduous in their attempts to press the many and varied schools of literary theory into service – and, indeed, have been at pains to point out that no single school provides a complete reading – they have tended to treat marketing communications in a somewhat monolithic fashion. To be sure, there are any number of detailed content analyses of the history and development of the genre (Belk and Pollay 1985; Pollay 1985, 1986, 1991) and Scott (1992) has pointed out the post-structuralist propensities of contemporary advertisers. Yet marketing researchers of a lit-crit persuasion have not, in the main, foregrounded the stylistic fads, fashions, trends, movements, cults and – yes – schools of thought that characterize the trajectory of twentieth-century *advertising* (Haug 1987; Ewen 1988; Davidson 1992; Bogart 1995). It would appear that marketing's literary theorists, to put it in an irritatingly scientific idiom, have differentiated one side of the 'advertising = art' equation and one side only (interestingly, in cultural studies, where discussions of postmodern advertising campaigns are almost old hat, the opposite propensity is apparent). We are still awaiting the first avowedly postmodern analysis of an avowedly postmodern advertisement.

Naturally, such an ambition is not easily attained since it necessitates definitional criteria for *two* all but indefinables – namely, what exactly is postmodern analysis and what exactly is a postmodern advertisement? – not to mention the underlying difficulty of defining postmodernism itself (if it can be described as an *it*, that is). However, for the purposes of our present discussion, and in an admittedly desperate attempt to perk this chapter up a little, I would like to place before you a brief Bakhtinian interrogation of an advertisement that exhibits many of the allegedly distinguishing features of postmodernism. As postmodernists through and through, you will doubtless be familiar with the work of Mikhail Mikhailovitch Bakhtin (1895–1975), albeit his place in the postmodern pantheon is perhaps less well established than (say) Derrida's, Foucault's, Lacan's, Baudrillard's or Barthes'. Indeed, as subscribers to the 'death of the author' hypothesis you are presumably indifferent to the biographical details of this supremely gifted thinker and simply require a cursory reminder of his key constructs. Still, it would be unforgivably remiss of me if I failed to acknowledge that Bakhtin's *real* claim to fame is the incredible fact that at the height of the Siege of Moscow in 1942–3, when cigarette papers were unobtainable, he famously smoked the *only copy* of his manuscript – his masterwork – on the history of the novel. (I've heard of book-burning but this *Walpurgisnacht* of the soul is just too staggering for words. Did he reread what he'd written before he puffed it away? Did he smoke it in sequence or the worst bits first? Did he try to cut down in order to save at least some of his opus?) Bakhtin, for good measure, miraculously survived the Stalinist purges; lived and worked in poverty-stricken internal exile, whilst denied access to the bare necessities of academic life; had his PhD thesis on Rabelais rejected when it was examined in 1946, some ten *years* after submission; may or may not have been responsible for two seminal books on Marxist literary criticism which were published under the names of his associates P. N. Medvedev and V. Volosinov in the mid-1920s; and, as if he didn't have enough problems to contend with, had one of his legs amputated when he was in his mid-forties (I don't know if this happened before or after the book-smoking incident, but the thought of a half-starved Bakhtin gnawing on his own severed limb, interspersed with hits on his footnotes, is way beyond surreal).

Mikhail Bakhtin is a marvellously fecund, if occasionally inaccessible, literary theorist, and aspects of his corpus have been claimed by commentators hailing from all points of the critical compass – formalists, structuralists, Marxists, feminists, semiologists, discourse theorists and many more besides (Hirschkop 1989; Lodge 1990; Holquist 1990; Morris 1994; Docker 1994; Dentith 1995). Apart from his preoccupation with *parole* (to employ the Saussurean terminology), as opposed to the *langue* leanings of orthodox structuralists, and lifelong concern for the dialogic or polyphonic novel (where the narrator's voice is not privileged but just one among many), Bakhtin is best known for three key concepts: *carnivalesque*, *heteroglossia* and *chronotope*. Most fully articulated in his book on Rabelais, 'carnivalesque' refers to the inversions, transpositions and temporary reversals that typify the medieval marketplace (Bakhtin 1984). These are locations where fools become wise, kings turn into commoners, the sacred is profaned, authority is subverted, rogues run wild and unmentionable bodily functions are frequently and freely mentioned. Carnival, in effect, comprises a physical manifestation of the deeply ironic, inherently irreverent outlook that finds expression in the works of a long line of satiric, parodic and erotic novelists such as Cervantes, Swift, Sterne, de Sade, Dickens, Wilde, Joyce and, of late, the postmodernists. This anti-authoritarianism is equally integral to 'heteroglossia', Bakhtin's idea that language is not an abstract and unified system, as traditional Saussurean linguistics suggests. Language, rather, is always in a state of flux, where meanings are never singular or uncontested but plural, debatable, contradictory, open to multiple interpretations, sites of perpetual struggle and prone to periodic revolts against stultifying orthodoxy, standardization, convention and false unity. It is a place where a multiplicity of voices obtain at any one time (Bakhtin 1981a). However, just as the novel is the locus – the quintessence – of this heteroglossic linguistic inclination, so too, according to Bakhtin, it is distinguished by a clearly discernible 'chronotope'. Predicated, in part, upon Einsteinian astrophysics, chronotopes comprise the distinctive syntheses of time and space contained in works of literature. Novels, in other words, unfold in imagined, phenomenological worlds where the normal laws of time and space may be suspended, transformed, broken or dissolved, and where the characters may experience time and space in an idiosyncratic, fluid, open-ended, relational or, to introduce a timely Nietzschean note, perspectival fashion (Bakhtin 1981b).

Every picture tells a story

I appreciate that the foregoing synopsis is somewhat austere, but before you flounce back to Philip, take a look at Figure 4.1, which is a wonderful example of postmodern marketing. This advert for Moët & Chandon champagne, which ran in a number of British glossy magazines in the mid-1990s, exhibits many of the stylistic hallmarks commonly associated with postmodernism – de-differentiation, intertextuality, chronology, hyperreality and so on (S. Brown 1995a). It melds high art and low, in so far as it is a clear homage to the work of Alphonse Mucha (1860–1939), a celebrated late-nineteenth-century artist renowned for his Art-Nouveau studies of beautiful, bejewelled women with swirling pre-Raphaelite tresses (Ulmer 1994; Duncan 1994). Indeed, as the artist was the de-differentiator of his time – much of Mucha's prodigious and much-imitated output was commissioned by commercial organizations like breweries, cigarette manufacturers and entertainment venues – Moët's allusion to Mucha is not only accurate but singularly apt. This double-coded intertextuality is equally evident in the advertising copy which refers, on the surface at least, to the technical process of producing champagne through carefully controlled pressures exerted by the company's traditional wooden presses. However, the copy is also an allusion to the manifold sex scandals that occurred at around about the time of Moët's advertising campaign. Since these involved members of the British royal family, government ministers and diverse pillars of the Establishment, they prompted numerous outraged calls to control the power of the press, the sorts of unsavoury organs that delighted in prying into and publicizing the untoward activities of the great and good.

As Foucault (1979), Showalter (1991, 1993), Schorske (1980) and Eagleton (1995), amongst others, have demonstrated, sexual impropriety-cum-aestheticism was also a prominent feature of the last *fin de siècle* (Max Nordau, Toulouse

Figure 4.1 Weird scenes inside the Gould mine

Lautrec, Oscar Wilde, Lily Langtree, Gustav Klimt, etc.). Hence, the Moët & Chandon ad is *triply* chronological in so far as it is nostalgic not simply for the decadence, deviance and sexual anarchy of Mucha's *fin de siècle*, nor indeed for the 250-year history of the company and its tried and trusted methods of production, but it is nostalgic for the *fin de siècle*'s nostalgia for the temptresses of pre-classical times – Cleopatra, Helen of Troy, Jezebel, Judith, Nefertiti and, above all, Salome (Dowling 1986; Schweik 1987; Showalter 1991; S. M. Gilbert 1996). We are forced to conclude, then, that this recent advertisement for an historic product, which comprises a painting of a mythical seductress who inspired numerous works of art at the turn of the twentieth century and continues to appear in movies, plays, novels and television programmes, is irredeemably, unalterably and unashamedly hyperreal. So much so, that we are inclined to doubt the 'real' existence of Monsieur Philippe Saunier, his great wooden presses and the venerable production processes lovingly described in the advertising copy.

Before we elevate Moët & Chandon champagne to the quasi-mythical status of its wanton champion, it is worth noting that this advertisement's postmodern oscillation between past and present, real and fake, and myth and reality is very much in keeping with Bakhtin's notion of the 'chronotope'. If we ask ourselves about its position or setting in time and space, the answer is far from clear. It is a contemporary advert that refers us back, stylistically at least, to the dog days of the late nineteenth century, an era that has much in common with our own decadent postmodern times (Meštrović 1991; Ledger and McCracken 1995; Pykett 1996). In terms of content, we are catapulted back some 250 years to the establishment of the company and, more to the point, to the indeterminate, archaic, prehistorical past of the ancient world, or, rather, to the ancient world as we imagine it to be, thanks to centuries of artistic and media representations. Our spatial coordinates are equally imprecise, since this is an advertisement for a manufacturer of French champagne, which appeared in British magazines, employing the techniques of a Czech artist who is regarded as the acme of the Art-Nouveau movement that swept throughout the whole of western society, depicting the (placeless) boudoir of an archetypal *femme fatale* of Middle Eastern extract, and, as Moët's by-line boasts, whose brand name is world renowned.

This time–space uncertainty is reinforced by the (outside) possibility that the advertisement might *not* be contemporary or, alternatively, might be sourced from another locale in the latitudinous brandscape. As the company has been in existence for hundreds of years, it could well be an old *fin-de-siècle* ad updated for the 1990s (cf. M. Saunier's shirt and tie), or one that was first produced sometime between the late nineteenth century and the present (viz. the 1970s-style hair of the workers). Is it actually a redrawing of an original Mucha/school of Mucha poster[1] for another product? The unopened bottle, after all, seems ever so slightly out of place; the half-full glass has that not-quite-right look of being inserted into the drawing (if the bottle is unopened, where did her champagne come from?); and, the figure is leaning forward in an unnatural position (what are her arms resting on? – not the seat, clearly). Is this an old ad, a new ad, a new old ad, an old new ad or something from somewhere else entirely? We could ask, admittedly, but we can't tell. Do we really want to be told? Would the company tell us the truth? Would we believe them if they did?

Just as Bakhtin's chronotope swirls in and around this particular champagne advertisement, so too his idea of the 'carnivalesque' is readily apparent. The most obvious instantiation of this inclination is the product itself, which is and long has been associated with celebration, revelry, special occasions, emotion, euphoria, laughter, tears, transgression, bacchanalian excess and letting our hair down as a prelude to the pleasures of the lower body. This voluptuous air of exotic, champagne-fuelled aphrodisiacal abandon is also embodied in the central figure with her heavy-lidded, half-closed, amatorial eyes, sideways glance, sensual mouth, seductive posture (draped over a chair, leaning toward us) and the less than subtle symbolism of glass, jewellery, crumpled bedclothes, serpent-headed armrest and an unopened, doubtless ready to burst, bottle of champagne. In fact, we are so captivated that we almost fail to notice the complete absence of a cooler, cease to care about the prospect of quaffing warm bubbly, wrapped as it is in the libidinous folds of the material, and only vaguely register the company's puritanical desire to limit the power of the press of our flesh (quick, someone throw a bucket of cold water over me!).

The Bakhtinian carnival may be characterized by eroticism and titillation, by ribaldry and irreverence, by subversion, inversion, diversion and perversion, but the possibility always remains that these reversals, overturnings and profanities are permitted or licensed rather than spontaneous outpourings of emotion. In time-honoured 'bread and circuses' fashion, they represent ordered disorder, regulated deregulation, organized chaos, authorized anti-authoritarianism, controlled decontrol of the emotions, and thereby serve to reinforce rather than subvert the status quo (Stallybrass and White 1986; Brandist 1996). After the temporary transgres-

---

1 A little bit of empirical research – revolting, I know, but someone has to do it – reveals that Mucha actually produced ads for Moët & Chandon. For what it's worth, Salome's dress and jewellery in Figure 4.1 were taken from the *standing* figure in Mucha's original, while the chair came from another work entirely (Mucha's poster for the American actress Leslie Carter).

sion, order will be restored, the rule of law will once again obtain; the doxa will continue as before. A price, in short, will have to be paid for our misdemeanours with Ms Moët & Chandon. Like Herod (metaphorically) and John the Baptist (literally), we may lose our heads and ultimately our souls if we choose to partake of her forbidden fruit. We hover between resistance and temptation, attraction and repulsion, control and abandon, advance and retreat, composure and carnality, aestheticism and asceticism. Mercifully, the company promises to preserve us from this Madonna/Medusa thanks to the protection of its great wooden prophylactics (WorkMates?); no colour from the diseased grape skins will find its way into our juices; M. Saunier, our personal, white-coated physician may look disapprovingly upon our licentious behaviour, but he won't let us down like the manufacturers of rival brands or inform the tabloid press of our human, all too human, frailties. We can confide in him. Our secrets are his. He is there to take care of us, to serve our best interests.

Peel me a grape, Philippe.

Alongside and interpenetrating the orgiastic celebrations of the carnivalesque, Moët's ostensibly monoglossian Muchaesque advertisement is interrupted by heteroglossian murmurings. Seemingly a stylish and subtle serenade from the world's leading champagne producer, a far from harmonious chorus of other voices is audible behind the soloist. We can detect, for example, the voice of the past, of the decadence of *la belle époque*, of the corrupt and dissipated society that was eventually called to account in the trenches of the Western Front. We can hear the voice of the target market, the upper or, as the affected lift of Salome's little finger indicates, the *aspirant* upper classes, those who wish (or wish to wish) to have their peccadillos hidden from the prying eyes of the gutter press. We can discern the voices of the company's competitors, those unscrupulous organizations that adulterate champagne by failing to adhere to the time-honoured methods of wooden presses and carefully controlled pressure. In this respect, can we also pick up a *sotto-voce* descant from viticultural publications or the ubiquitous taste-testers in glossy magazines, who may have been critical of the colour/flavour/bouquet of the Moët product and require vigorous rebuttal (and the power of whose damaging presses should be severely limited)?

If, to switch to a more appropriate metaphor for a moment, it is possible to taste several distinct flavours in our mouthful of Moët & Chandon, perhaps the greatest gustatory impact emanates from vintages cultivated on those heavily tilled, some would say exhausted, slopes of colonialism, capitalism and gender. With its evocation of Salome, Jezebel and similar concupiscent sirens, the advertisement is implicated in the Orientalism that Edward Said (1978) rails against, the illusory world of man-eating maidens, magic carpets and exotic eroticism – in short, the Other – that exercised imperial imaginations at the *fin de siècle* and which is equally evident today. The colonialism of the late twentieth century, however, is a commercial colonialism, a coca-colonization, an empire of the brand. Label epoch, no less. Thus, by dint of a hint of British Airway's by-line, the world's most famous champagne extends its *entente cordiale* – or should that be *cordial entêtant?*, to the United Kingdom and beyond. It does so, what is more, not only by exploiting the faceless, nameless and bowed but not beaten workers who labour on Moët's great wooden presses, but also by valorizing the gender agenda, by expropriating the archetype of wanton womanhood that feminist theorists have traditionally condemned. At the same time, and in keeping with contemporary feminist thought, which foregrounds and refuses to apologize for female sexuality (Estés 1993; Vice 1995; Pearce and Stacey 1995), the ad exploits the exploiters, to some extent, in so far as it employs the archetype of the mesmeric vamp to strip away the latter-day veneer of equal opportunities. Patriarchy's post-Adamite susceptibility to the primal, procreative urge serves to reveal the hypocrisy – the macho-masculinist masquerade – that inheres in stated male support for female emancipation, egalitarianism and sexual equality. Phallocentrism thus exposes itself for all to see.

('Stephen Brown, please.'
'He speaketh.'
'Sorry, can I speak to Stephen Brown, the marketing person?'
'It is I. What, pray, is the purpose of this telephonic communication?'
'Stephen, is everything all right? Are you OK?'
'Perfectly, my dear young lady. And you are?'
'It's Francesca. Who do you think it is? Why are you talking in that strange voice? You sound as though you've been on tour with the Royal Shakespeare Company.'
'Ah, the Bard, the Bard. The Swan of Avon. The . . . '
'Jesus, Stephen, you haven't gone all artsy-fartsy on us, have you? Don't tell me all this aesthetic stuff and nonsense has gone to your head.'
'All art is quite useless, I assure you madam.'
'That's Oscar Wilde, isn't it? Picture of Dorian Grey. *I hope you haven't had an attack of the Oscar Wildes.'*
'Oscar Wilde, Billy Wilder, Stephen Wildest, don't you know.'
'Get a grip on yourself, Stephen. You'll be wearing knee breeches and ruffs next . . . and carrying a lily.'
'Knee breeches, my dear, are very fetching at this time of year, especially when set off by

a well-turned ankle, and the lily, I have always maintained, is a much underrated accessory. The ruffle, I grant you, can prove a sartorial problem . . .'

'Especially when you slobber uncontrollably at meal times.'

'You took the words right out of my mouth, young lady.'

'When are *they going to aestheticize the bib? I suppose you'll be coining aphorisms next.'*

'I have nothing to declare except my Guinness.'

'What did I tell you about brand names, Stephen.'

'Drink is the work of the cursing classes.'

'Don't give up the day job.'

'I can tempt everything except resistance.'

'It gets worse.'

'A little flattery is a dangerous thing, but a great deal of it is sincere.'

'Sorry, Stephen, but your epigrams are not in the Wilde league.'

'May I remind you, your majesty, it was epipounds and ounces in Oscar's time. We've had the metrication of meter since then.'

'You're no Oscar Wilde, Stephen. You're not even Oscar Ever-so-slightly-miffed, or Oscar Wouldn't-say-boo-to-a-goose, come to think of it. You're a marketing man, for God's sake. Don't get carried away on some Wilde goose chase.'

'Marketing men know everything of price and nothing of value.'

'Academics excepted, Stephen; they don't even know everything of price.'

'Academics know everything of nothing and nothing of everything, madam.'

'You're right there.'

'Pray, what is *the purpose of this call? Do you have anything to say, young woman, besides your stream of, if I may be so bold, rather offensive remarks?'*

'Well, I was just ringing up to see how things were going.'

'You will doubtless be delighted to hear that I have completed an entire chapter since our last conversation.'

'Great, what's it about?'

'Sex and shopping, shopping and sex, sexing shops, shopping sexes.'

'Not too much sex I hope. We don't want to lower the tone of the book, now do we, Stephen?'

'I wouldn't dream of such a thing. The manuscript will be as pure as the driven.'

'Glad to hear it.'

'Is there anything else you wish to say, my dear? I'm so terribly, terribly busy at present.'

'Yes, I've just received another review of Postmodern Marketing *and I thought you might be interested.'*

'Somewhat tardy, but encomia to its intellectual rigour and depth of scholarship are always welcome. How did they describe me this time? A titan? A colossus? A mere giant?'
'Well, no. She calls you the Malcolm McDonald of postmodernism.'
'The what?'
'The Malcolm McDonald of postmodern marketing. Aren't you pleased?'
'Infamy! Perfidy! An icy hand has grippèd my heart. A dagger is plungèd into my fluttering breast . . .'
'Steady on, Stephen.'
'Oh tiger's heart wrapp'd in a woman's hide.'
'Quite.'
'I am a man, more sinned against than sinning.'
'Just calm down, will you?'
'Reputation, reputation, reputation! O, I have lost my reputation! I have lost the immortal part of myself, and what remains is bestial.'
'Don't exaggerate.'
'Finish, good lady; the bright day is done, And we are for the dark.'
'Yeah, gotta go, Stephen. Jonson is on the other line and I've got a meeting with Donne and Sidney this afternoon.')

Back in black

As a reflexive, hermeneutics-of-suspicion kind of guy, I know only too well that the sceptics among you are making seditious remarks, fomenting rebellion and muttering dark oaths about yours truly, your humble interlocutor, your postmodern troubadour. It's a bit rich, I hear you say, when someone criticizes the existing academic literature for its excessive reliance on the 'readings' of marketing intellectuals, as opposed to the interpretations of the actual consumers of advertising messages, only to turn around and offer his own reading of a purportedly postmodern ad. A reading, incidentally, that should perhaps be described as idiosyncratic at best and fetishistic at worst. (Who said perverted? How dare you make such unfounded insinuations? Leave this book forthwith.) There is, of course, an infallible, iron-clad defence against such unwarranted, unconscionable and unprovoked attacks, and that is to remind you that I criticized the readings of marketing *intellectuals*. As I manifestly do not fall into this particular category, I am free to say what I like about postmodern advertising. My conscience is clear. If only my thinking could be so described.

Rather than become embroiled in a slanging match with the principal exponents of the literature-in-marketing perspective – abusive comments are so unseemly, don't you agree? – it may be more appropriate to highlight the innumerable opportunities that this particular approach to marketing research affords. When the lit-crit corpus is examined in detail, it is clear that its proponents have been assiduous in their applications of the various schools of critical thought and diligent in their discussions of the deployment of diverse literary devices. However, they have tended to concentrate on a single aspect of marketing; namely, advertising and promotion. As advertising is very amenable to textual analysis – and custom cannot stale its infinite variety – this preoccupation is entirely understandable. There is, nevertheless, no reason why such approaches cannot be meaningfully applied to other marketing institutions or elements of the marketing mix. Not only is this very much in keeping with the postmodern notion that everything can be considered a text – 'be it a haircut, holiday, personal crisis or political upheaval' (S. Brown 1995a: 166) – but it may also help lift the literature-in-marketing tradition out of the ghetto, the *barrio*, the *favela* that is advertising and promotion.

Fortunately, a number of upwardly mobile marketing scholars have sought to gentrify the lit-crit neighbourhood by demonstrating the utility of literary approaches to extra-advertising marketing phenomena. Some fifteen years ago, for example, Levy (1981) contended that marketing researchers could use literary theory to help investigate the stories consumers tell about products (see also Levy 1994a). To this end, he conducted six in-depth interviews, during which the informants were encouraged to recount family anecdotes concerning food preferences, and from which Levy was able to identify the various Lévi-Straussian myths – origin, emergence, migration, etc. – that inhered in these marketing-inflected narratives. In a similar vein, Durgee (1988) has argued that the interview transcripts from the celebrated Consumer Odyssey can be examined from a literary theory perspective. Working on the definitional premises that 'stories' have a beginning middle and end, one or more protagonists, obstacles to be surmounted, improbable occurrences, a degree of suspense over the outcome, and contain some sort of underlying moral, message or homily, he identified over 300 such narratives in the Odyssey field notes and classified them according to clearly identifiable stages of the consumption process. In the event, it seems that there were comparatively few stories pertaining to the actual manufacture or purchase of products, whereas many anecdotes were recorded about consumer perceptions of product quality and the ways in which the wares were sold. Seven of these stories were examined in greater detail, leading Durgee to conclude that their ultimate message concerned consumption's tendency to beget consumption – ownership of a '57 Chevy influenced 'consumption' of a marriage partner; over-consumption of food affected 'consumption' of romantic encounters; and food consumption patterns in the Great Depression determined lifelong perceptions of what could and could not be eaten.

Unsurprisingly perhaps, Barbara B. Stern is yet another leading advocate of literary methods in non-advertising contexts. Her above-mentioned application of Northrop Frye's typology of narrative types to the traditional Thanksgiving festival involved a detailed myth-crit interrogation of interview protocols derived from a separate, interpretive study of consumption behaviours associated with the occasion (Wallendorf and Arnould 1991). Arguing that 'extending mythic analysis to the way . . . consumers shape stories enriches the understanding of consumer behaviour by shedding light on the consumer's perception of the experience' (B. B. Stern 1995: 183), she demonstrated that the events in each reported story could be analysed in terms of Frye's four mythoi of comedy (joyful or happy occurrences), tragedy (sadness or wisdom related), romance (nostalgic, the way things were) and irony (tales with a twist in the tail). When these findings were combined with the associated evidence from Thanksgiving advertising treatments, it was abundantly clear that 'even though consumer respondents do not set out to create works of literature, their stories do contain plots that are traceable to mythoi found in the oldest works of western culture' (B. B. Stern 1995: 184).

The rise and demise of motivation research, which flourished in the 1950s and was all but abandoned during the subsequent decade, has also been examined by Stern (1990d) in terms of three 'authorial' schools of literary criticism: *psychobiographical*, *editorial* and *structural*. The psychobiographical interpretation intimates that Ernest Dichter's dramatic fall from grace was attributable to his status as a maverick and outsider (born, educated and trained in Europe, with no ties to American research universities). The editorial school explains his precipitous plunge in terms of his preference for unorthodox, non-academic channels of communication (trade press, semi-autobiographical, tub-thumping textbooks). Structural analysis, by contrast, suggests that his stylistic idiosyncrasies were the root cause of his Icarusian descent. Dichter, apparently, refused to report his findings in standard, impersonal, 'scientific' forms of expression and, for that heinous crime alone, he was lucky to escape with ostracism, if you ask me. Frankly, he should have been thrashed – no, make that buggy-whipped – to within an inch of his life.

Significant though Levy's, Durgee's and Stern's contributions undoubtedly are, by far the most impressive applications of critical methods to extra-advertising marketing artifacts emanate from continental Europe. In a *tour de force* of semio-narrative literary explication, Floch (1988) has interrogated the interview protocols of 400 French hypermarket shoppers and used them to help develop a new store layout, one which is radically different from the traditional arrangement of right angles, grid lines and serried ranks of monotonous display racks. Heilbrunn (1996a, 1996b), likewise, has recently employed the principles of narratology to examine the nature of the relationship between consumer and brand. Drawing upon the Russian folklorist Vladimir Propp's (1958) celebrated contention that fairy tales have an invariant plot structure comprising thirty-one separate functions or elements, Heilbrunn highlights how the four basic stages of this narrative chain – acquisition of competency, contract, performance and sanction – can be applied to ongoing contacts between the buyer and his or her preferred brand. In line with Propp, he argues that the various narrative functions need not occur in each and every purchasing occasion (straight re-buy situations, presumably, obviate the necessity for competency acquisition), although he also maintains – *contra* Propp – that the functions may fail to unfold in the same preordained sequence. Heilbrunn, what is more, wraps up his remarkable narratological excursus with the suggestion that Propp's seven spheres of action or *dramatis personae*, which may or may not coincide on a one-to-one basis with specific characters in each individual story, are implicitly employed by brand managers as positioning strategies (Table 4.2).

While few would deny that the above publications comprise the cutting edge of literary approaches to non-promotional marketing milieux, it is fair to say that many other studies of a broadly bookish bent have been reported. To be sure, the literary character of these exercises is rarely, if ever, emphasized or proclaimed, but it is no less apparent for all that. Consider, for instance, the increasingly widespread use of projective techniques – such as the TAT – which specifically require respondents to 'tell a story' about the behaviours under investigation (E. Day 1989; Aaker and Stayman 1992; Sherry *et al.* 1993, 1995; Hassay and Smith 1996). The critical incident technique, beloved by academics from the services marketing end of the research spectrum, is highly literary in ethos, as is the analogous dramaturgical metaphor (Bitner *et al.* 1990; Bitner *et al.* 1994; Czepiel 1990; Deighton 1992; R. P. Fisk and Grove 1996). Semiotics, hermeneutics and discourse analysis, which have become something of a cult – many would say convention – in contemporary consumer research, are so closely intertwined with literary criticism that it is almost impossible to separate them (e.g. Mick 1987; Sherry and Camargo 1987; C. J. Thompson *et al.* 1994; S. J. Arnold and Fisher 1994; Pennell 1994). The textual metaphor, moreover, suffuses the study of scripts, schemata and frames in memory (Baddeley 1990; Alba *et al.* 1991; Mick 1992); creative writing is the kernel of the controversial 'subjective personal introspection' procedure espoused by several prominent consumer researchers (S. J. Gould 1991, 1993; Holbrook 1995a; Hirschman 1996); the relationship

Table 4.2 Just give me one good reason

Contact occasions with the brand	Related behaviours	Corresponding stage in the narrative chain
Information contact	Read newspapers or billboards Listen to radio commercials Listen to sales persons	Acquisition of competency
Brand contact	Locate product in store Obtain product	Acquisition of competency
Transaction	Exchange funds for product Take product to use location	Contract
Consumption	Consume/use brand Dispose of packaging/used product	Performance
Subsequent contacts	Repurchase Brand switching	Sanction
Communication	Tell others of product experience Fill out warranty cards	Sanction

Source: Heilbrunn 1996b.

marketing literature is replete with organizational parables of the 'I was lost but now I'm found' variety (McKenna 1992; Kanter 1994; Heskett *et al.* 1994); and it is hard to conceive of more overtly fabulous artifacts than the countless case studies that punctuate each and every chapter of each and every marketing textbook. Not only are the writers of case studies advised to adopt an explicitly storytelling posture, but the whole genre is nothing less than a latter-day revival of the *Bildungsroman* and its copious eighteenth-century variants (*Erziehungsroman*, *Kunstlerroman*, etc.). Indeed, it is profoundly ironic that Harvard Business School, having stuck with their renowned case study approach throughout the whole of the 'modern' marketing era, should be debating its abandonment – at the very time when storytelling is back in postmodern vogue (Lataif 1992; Linder and Smith 1992; Mintzberg 1992; Mitroff and Churchman 1992).

Without doubt, this chronicle-cum-narrative mode of marketing exposition is most fully developed in the sub-field of consumer research (e.g. Mick 1987; Rook 1985, 1987; Fournier and Guiry 1993; B. B. Stern 1994a, 1996c; L. A. Williams and

Burns 1994; Dodson and Belk 1996). The semi-detached status of CR, coupled with its critical mass of charismatic figureheads – Mahatma Belk, Beth de Beauvoir, Bronislaw the-natives-are-revolting Sherry, Wacko-Jacko Jacoby, Tom O'Gump *et al.* – and what appears to be a general counterculture orientation, has been sufficient to ensure a somewhat warmer welcome for the literary than for the literally minded (well, some of them at least). However, as the extensive literature on managerial storytelling indicates, there is considerable scope for intra-organizational analyses, for telling tales, so to speak, of the marketing department (Boje 1991, 1994, 1995). In this respect, the recent work of Brownlie and Desmond (1996) is highly instructive. According to their ethnographic account, which is reproduced in Table 4.3, one of the authors interviewed a senior marketing manager and he recounted an arresting story of the relationship between marketing and his rise to power within the organization. So spellbinding, indeed, was this raconteur's tale that the researcher reflected on his experience as follows:

> After the interview, when I was transcribing it, I wondered about the story he told me. During the interview I felt I had to believe him, or at least to feign it, just to keep engaged in the discussion. But now as I sit here trying to make sense of it all, I wonder was he having me on? After all, if he had been able to outflank some senior people in the company, could he not easily outflank me? He seemed to speak a language I could understand. In retrospect, he often spoke to me just as another academic would do. I felt he was organising me, just as he probably would do his colleagues. My ethnography was his impression management test. The idea that he might have been spinning me a clever yarn never entered my head until I sat down to analyse the transcript. And you know, I have conducted many research interviews. But, I've always ended up taking what was said at face value.
>
> (Brownlie and Desmond 1996: 73–4)

Brownlie and Desmond's post-partum ruminations on that particular interviewing experience could quite easily be dismissed as a postmodern shaggy-dog story – as a story about a story about a story (can we believe what they tell us?; can you believe what I tell you about what they tell us?) – but it highlights the principal shortcoming of literary approaches, broadly defined, to extra-advertising marketing phenomena. With the noteworthy exception of the theoretically informed, lit-crit-oriented analyses of Levy, Durgee, Stern and so on, the majority of contributions to the storytelling school of marketing scholarship have tended to take the content of the tales at face value. True, Holbrook (1988) seems to have treated his personal introspections to a three-sessions-a-week-money-no-object-just-lie-down-on-this-couch-and-tell-me-about-first-time-you-wet-the-bed course of Freudian psycho-analysis (and we all feel much better because of it, thank you for asking). What's more, the semioticians and hermeneuticists routinely search for subtextual meta-phors, as do some users of projective research techniques (Mick *et al.* 1992; C. J. Thompson *et al.* 1994; Babbes 1996; C. J. Thompson 1996). Nevertheless, it is no exaggeration to state that a largely uncritical – essentially realist – assumption of unproblematic linguistic transparency is all too prevalent. In classic, New Criticism fashion, the marketing literati seem to believe that texts mean what they say and say what they mean.

Table 4.3 That's the glory, yeah

I was interviewing the marketing director of a large engineering company the other day and we wandered on to the topic of his involvement in company marketing strategy activities. He'd told me that he'd done an MBA in 1988 and was familiar with marketing strategy theory. He could even cite a few authors and wondered whether he might get a job as a visiting lecturer sometime. I wanted to know what use he made of the typical marketing techniques in his strategy and planning work, you know, the SWOT, BCG, Marketing Audit, Environmental Scanning, etc. Anyway, he knew my agenda. I didn't know his – at least at the outset. He said that he'd found the ideas useful. He'd used them and told me this interesting story as a way of relating the hows and whos. After his MBA he'd been promoted out of sales and into his current job – the first board member with direct marketing responsibilities. He saw this as his finest moment. He'd been disagreeing with the sales director for some time over the direction of their European sales effort, which was costing the company serious money. The sales director had spearheaded their efforts with, initially, the support of the MD and the finance director, who ruled supreme. Their disagreements were kept internal to sales, and were never really aired at company level, at least while my informant was studying his MBA. The problem seemed to be that the company was happy to push for sales development overseas – whilst its product technology and quality seemed to suffer. He saw it as too much hassle to get involved in the wider discussions and felt that events would eventually take their toll anyway. He was, however, a bit concerned that he might become the scapegoat if events arrived more quickly than he expected. So he said he really never took his eyes off the ball.

Anyway, after his MBA, the sales director suggested to him that he'd better begin to look elsewhere for promotion, as it wasn't going to come to him just because he'd gone back to university for three years – and anyway a shake-up was coming in the company and his position would be under review. According to my informant, he seemed to be taking an active interest in making things difficult for

Table 4.3 Contd.

him, by cutting him out of discussions. In the meantime his sales work and his attitude seemed to have suffered – at least that was my informant's representation of the sales director's view at the time. My informant said that he foresaw that some sort of realignment was in the offing and that the sales director must have been threatened by something to be so public in his defence, by dint of attack.

The story went that the bleeding sore of European sales had reached a crisis and the company had to decide to stay in Europe, or retrench and rationalise. But, meanwhile, events had rather overtaken them. The company finances were in poor shape. Advances had been made by a predator company and were being actively pursued. European customers were getting upset at the company's problems and were raising some serious concerns about future relationships. The company was involved in some long-term supply deals with those customers which the sales director had taken them into. It was having to fight the predators off and raise some serious money to do so, as well as to fund the retrenchment. And at this time the finance director left, and there was a rumour that he had taken up with the predator. A team of consultants were brought in by the MD as a condition of going to the City for more capital. The informant saw his opportunity and managed to get involved in their work through some careful politicking with the MD, who was really isolated since losing the finance guy and he didn't really trust the sales director. The informant said he could speak the consultants' language. He had learnt it through his MBA. Anyway, the MD could see the sense of having someone from the company involved with the consultants. And this he did. The consultants were critical of the European strategy. They quickly detected the lack of direction. Their incisive cost/contribution analysis showed the problem with margins, product quality and delivery performance. They drew attention to the threats. And fingers were pointed.

During his MBA studies, the informant had made contact with an engineer in the same line of business, as a supplier of small high-machined parts that went into their down-hole pumps. He had mentioned that some Japanese company had developed a new alloy that vastly improved bearing life in the highly corrosive conditions of down-hole operation. Post-MBA he looked into the Japanese company. So when it came to the internal battling over European strategy, he built on what the consultants had done, speaking their language and using their concepts. In addition he put forward the idea of seeking a licence from a Japanese company to use its alloy and some of its designs in their pumps. This would update their product line as well as their management practices, particularly on quality. He had also received, off the record, some positive signals from one of their major European customers.

So, after the bloody coup, he was promoted to marketing director on the back

Table 4.3 Contd.

of his contribution. He more or less designed his own job. The sales director left, as did two of his appointees, and the sales team was totally restructured. After some pretty tough negotiations a licensing deal was set up with the Japanese company. He said that all that would never have happened if he had not been able to link up with the consultants and subtly shift the agenda from defence to attack. The language of the BCG and marketing strategy analysis had been a major resource for him. It allowed him to appropriate the discussions of marketing options and to cleverly de-personalise the issues.

I took what he said seriously. He was really convincing and seemed glad to be able to tell someone else about his success, as if he was getting some sort of kick out of it. At times I felt like a voyeur. Not in a predatory way, almost as if I was being manipulated by my intended victim. Do you think I should believe him though? Was he telling me the truth? I mean, I couldn't really go and publish this stuff if he wasn't telling the truth, could I? It seems to open up too many cracks that have been plastered over. No one has really considered the conceptual colonisation. During the interview, I was trying to be the objective outsider. But, I was a conspirator, a participant in the discussion we had. I provided cues which he responded to. He also provided me with cues which I responded to. And so he was interviewing me as much as I was interviewing him.

Source: Brownlie and Desmond 1996: 71–3

Before we leap to the blindingly obvious solution that subjective introspectionists, critical incident technologists, case study perpetrators and their ilk require a good, old-fashioned dose of literary theory to protect them from the intellectual ebola virus that is realism, it must be stressed that the key word here is *old-fashioned*. Priceless though Stern's application of Frye's taxonomy, Levy's Lévi-Straussian insights and Floch and Heilbrunn's narratological investigations have proved to be, almost all of the lit-crit readings of extra-communications marketing artifacts are premised on structuralist or para-structuralist schools of critical thought. They seek to identify the deep, inviolate, universal structures or functions (or archetypes in Frye's case) that underpin the marketing 'texts' in question. Make no mistake, this aspiration is entirely laudable. Structuralist perspectives have contributed much and have much to contribute to academic marketing discourse. The very fact, for example, that major Hollywood studios are prepared to produce multi-million-dollar movies on the basis of sub-structuralist analyses of film plots (Figure 4.2) is proof positive that there is merit in the method, if not method in their meretriciousness. Be that as it may, in our present, postmodern, post-structuralist times, the 'modernist' idea of deep universal structures of meaning has been abandoned by literary theorists as an impossible dream, an unrealizable aspiration (Cunningham 1994; Veeser 1996; Bonnycastle 1996). The once-accepted assumption that is possible to analyse all myths according to the famous Lévi-Straussian (1968: 228) 'formula', F_x (a): F_y (b) $\simeq$ F_x (b): F_{a-1} (y), is now widely regarded as a myth in itself. Propp's narratology and Frye's archetypal techniques have been roundly condemned by latter-day literary critics and, as you know only too well, none other than Roland steak-and-chips Barthes ostentatiously abandoned his quest for the 'the structural analysis of narratives' and thereafter took a sensual polysemous turn on the pleasure of the text.

Passé though they are, it cannot be denied that structuralist or para-structuralist approaches to literary criticism are inherently appealing to marketing researchers. Let's be honest, at the end of the day, when push comes to shove, the chips are down, the fat lady is about to sing and *soi-disant* marketing literati are reduced to cobbling together a clatter of clichés, the bottom, bottom line is that marketing is a structuralist academic discipline, or semi-structuralist at least. It attempts to identify and encapsulate the configurations – the processes, patterns and propensities – that underpin exchange-related activities. The vast majority of modern marketing concepts, from the seven Ss, through the five forces and the four Ps, to the one and only general theory of marketing (still waiting!), may not be structuralist in the sub-Saussurean, binary oppositions, without-positive-terms, 8.45 p.m. train to Geneva sense of the word, but they do endeavour to capture deep, underlying structures of a sort.

As prime movers of the post-Philip, post-everything, post-early-for-Christmas school of marketing thought, you don't need me to tell you that the rationale for our postmodern marketing revolution – if it can be described as having a rationale – is very severely compromised by the application of 'modernist' schools of literary theory to marketing phenomena, especially when so many of today's marketing practices and institutions are manifestly postmodern in spirit. Granted, making use of essentially modernist lit-crit methods under the guise of 'postmodern marketing' is, well, almost postmodern in its breathtaking audacity. But contending, in effect, that it is their very inappropriateness that makes them appropriate for our postmodern marketing agenda is little short of disingenuous (and that would never do). In these circumstances, one of our principal research priorities must be to interrogate a postmodern, non-advertising marketing artifact using techniques of literary criticism that can reasonably be described as postmodern. To this end, a succinct Bakhtinian interpretation of the bewitching *Riverdance* experience is about to appear

Figure 4.2 Swallow it down (what a Jagged little pill)

The 12 Steps of the Hero's Journey	Four Weddings and a Funeral	The Wizard Of Oz	Star Wars	Romancing the Stone
1 ORDINARY WORLD	Charles is a serial monogamist who goes to other people's weddings but can't imagine getting hitched himself. His heroic lack is the ability to say, or know, what he feels.	In the black and white world of Kansas, Dorothy gets into trouble when Toto digs up a flowerbed, and gets no sympathy from her uncle and aunt. Her parents dead, she does not feel at home.	Restless teenager Luke Skywalker is bored with life on the remote farm where he lives with his uncle and aunt. Like Dorothy's, his parents are presumed dead and he feels incomplete.	Romantic novelist Joan Wilder lives in a cluttered New York apartment and there is no partner in her life. She dreams of finding true love and adventure.
2 CALL TO ADVENTURE	At the first wedding he is strongly attracted to Carrie, a mysterious woman from outside the circle of his friends.	Dorothy's unease crystallizes when Miss Gulch takes Toto away. Toto escapes and she follows, running away from home.	Luke accidently finds the beautiful Princess Leia's desperate plea for help, addressed to Obi-Wan Kenobi and stored in the droid R2D2.	Joan receives a phone call from her sister, who has been kidnapped by thugs in Colombia.
3 REFUSAL OF THE CALL	Charles refuses the call of his heart several times, starting with the first wedding, when he does not have the courage to speak to Carrie.	Dorothy gets as far as the carnival wagon of Professor Marvel, who convinces her to return home.	Luke seeks out Obi-Wan but doesn't dare take up the challenge, saying that his uncle and aunt need him.	Joan is a willing hero, but the refusal is acknowledged in a scene with her tough, cynical agent who tells her: 'You're not cut out for this.'
4 MEETING THE MENTOR	Charles has several mentors: Carrie, who warns of missed opportunities; Gareth, who says how wonderful Carrie is; his deaf-mute brother, who forces him to speak the truth.	Dorothy has many mentors, including Professor Marvel, who sends her on a quest for Home; Glinda, the Good Witch, who helps her out in the Special World, and the Wizard himself.	Luke finally puts himself in the hands of Obi-Wan and begins to learn about the Force.	Joan's agent is a negative influence and attempts to prevent her from answering the call.
5 CROSSING THE FIRST THRESHOLD	Charles crosses, or half-crosses, many thresholds, most notably when he makes an attempt to tell Carrie how he feels after helping her with her wedding dress.	Dorothy is trying to get home when a storm flings her into the Technicolor, special world of Oz.	Luke takes up the challenge when Imperial troops barbecue his uncle and aunt.	Joan arrives in Colombia and is immediately misdirected on to a bus that is going nowhere.
6 TESTS, ALLIES, ENEMIES	As he enters the special world of love, Charles is hounded by ex-girlfriends, shadowed by a friend who would like to be his lover, and finds he has a rival for Carrie's love.	Dorothy starts down the Yellow Brick Road, earns the loyality of the Scarecrow, learns the Wicked Witch is out to get her, befriends the Tin Woodman and then sees through the bluster of the Cowardly Lion.	Luke and Obi-Wan head for a spaceport bar, meet up with Han Solo and the Wookie and make a bitter enemy of Jabba the Hut.	Joan is followed by a sinister man, the bus crashes, she is 'rescued' by the archetypal Shapeshifter, Jack, more a mercenary than an ally.
7 APPROACH TO THE INMOST CAVE	The series of weddings becomes trying for Charles as the object of his love seems to grow more desirable and remote, and finally marries Hamish.	Dorothy and friends quickly come within sight of the Emerald City, but they are repeatedly attacked by the Wicked Witch and blocked by various Threshold Guardians.	Luke and company have a series of adventures that culminate in an attempt to break Princess Leia out of the Deathstar.	On the run from the baddies, Joan and Jack seek out the hiding-place of El Corazon, a giant emerald, using the map the kidnappers are after.
8 SUPREME ORDEAL	At the third wedding, Charles loses hope of ever winning Carrie as she speaks of her love for Hamish; when Gareth collapses of a heart attack he has lost a dear friend.	Dorothy and friends are captured by the Wicked Witch and face death. The Witch sets the Scarecrow on fire, but Dorothy douses him with water, accidently splashing the Witch and causing her a slow, melting death.	The ordeal is made up of a series of adventures in the Deathstar, including a near-death experience in a garbage compactor.	Joan and Jack quickly locate the emerald in a real inmost cave, but that is too easy and their car plunges over a waterfall. Joan disappears for several seconds, finally struggling to a rock on the opposite side from Jack.
9 REWARD (SEIZING THE SWORD)	The reward, if any, is self-knowledge, but for Charles it is not simple. He learns from Gareth's death that love does not have to mean marriage. He has also learned to lower his expectations.	Dorothy gets the broomstick that the Wizard demands as payment for getting her home, but he balks at paying up. Toto discovers, behind the curtain, the meek little man controlling the illusion, who is powerless to help them – a typical, post-ordeal insight.	Luke and company escape with the Princess and the information needed to destroy the Deathstar, but not without the sacrifice of Obi-Wan.	The obvious reward is possession of the gem, but Joan has also found romance and new self-knowledge.
10 ROAD BACK	A sadder, but not much wiser man, he gets over Carrie and (somehow) rebounds into the arms of 'Duck Face'.	The Wizard has prepared a hot-air balloon to take Dorothy back to Kansas, but Toto runs after a cat and Dorothy after him. The balloon leaves without them.	The worst is not yet over; the Deathstar, moving within range of the rebel base, still has to be destroyed.	The river separates them and the two have to make their own way out of the jungle. Joan has to trust that Jack, who has the gem, will keep his promise.
11 RESURRECTION	Charles's real ordeal comes on his own wedding day, when he finds out that he could have had Carrie and recognizes his own feelings. His heroic flaw almost brings him to ruin, but his brother forces him to speak the truth.	Dorothy survives the death of her hopes of getting home, but the Good Witch reappears to tell her that she had the power all along. She had to learn it for herself.	Luke trusts the Force and destroys the Deathstar by sacrificing an old part of his personality, his dependence on machines.	Joan and Jack unite to rescue her sister, but Jack immediately pursues his own interest, the money. She has to give up her hopes of love, but is changed by her adventures.
12 RETURN WITH ELIXIR	In a touching, rainy reconciliation scene, Charles demonstrates that he has learned his lesson, speaking honestly about his feelings for Carrie and of his now severe allergy to weddings.	Dorothy says farewell to her allies, who have also learned that they already had what they sought, and taps the red shoes together, saying; 'There's no place like home.' Back in Kansas, she feels complete, possessing the elixir of self-knowledge.	Luke and friends are decorated as heroes, in front of a large crowd. Luke's internal elixir is his new self-knowledge and control of the Force.	A changed Joan, more 'together' and a better writer, has surrendered her old fantasies about men, when Jack appears with the sailing-boat he has always dreamed of, to whisk her away.

Source: adapted from Widdicombe 1994.

before your very eyes. (Provided you go immediately to the checkout counter of your nearest bookshop and say the magic words: 'A copy of *Postmodern Marketing*, my good man.' If that doesn't work, and you may have to try it in several shops to be sure, use the following infallible incantation: 'A copy of *Postmodern Marketing* by Stephen Brown and throw in a couple of copies of *Postmodern Marketing Two* while you're at it.')

Feats don't fail me now

By any reckoning, *Riverdance* must rank as one of the most remarkable achievements in the annals of services marketing (Ó'Cinnéide 1995, 1996). It began as a seven-minute interlude in the 1994 Eurovision Song Contest – a contemporary celebration of traditional Irish music and dance relayed to an estimated television audience of 300 million – and blossomed into a 98-minute stage show that has played and is playing to packed houses around the world (450 plus performances and counting); shattered box-office records in every venue bar none; earned approximately £40 million in ticket sales alone; and transformed its principals, Jean Butler and Michael Flatley, from overnight sensations into international celebrities. The *Riverdance* single spent eighteen weeks at No. 1 in the Irish charts (top ten in the UK), the album went double platinum (double gold in Britain), merchandising sales at Radio City Music Hall (NY) comfortably exceeded the previous record set by *Teenage Mutant Ninja Turtles* and, incredibly, the video not only outsold Disney's *The Lion King*, but, at 2 million copies purchased to date, it is the best-selling music video of all time (Donnelly 1996; Pielou 1996; Quantick 1996).

Riverdance, however, is more than a mere example, admittedly a dazzling example, of our postmodern 'society of the spectacle', Debord's (1990, 1994) contention that we live in a world increasingly characterized by a ceaseless parade of incredibly vivid, if fleeting, images, events and occurrences (Venkatesh 1992). It is also a well-nigh perfect example of a postmodern marketing 'product'. Like all services, of course, *Riverdance* only really exists, as it were, in the moment of its production and consumption, and hence the show can legitimately be described as an example of hyperreality. Similarly, the receipts from tie-in merchandise and associated activities (CDs, videos, books, etc.) are much greater – in 'classic' postmodern marketing fashion – than those derived from ticket sales. And, in equally timeless postmodern marketing fashion, the show has stimulated any number of intertextual allusions and advertising parodies (the most bizarre of which comprised step-dancing teabags). Furthermore, the single biggest setback of the show's otherwise triumphant progress, which involved the forced departure of one of its stars, revolved around the thorny but typically postmodern

Figure 4.3 Lutz dance

issue of *authenticity* (Belk 1990; B. B. Stern 1994a; Grayson and Shulman 1996): in other words, the originality and/or ownership of the always already written ideas that form the core of the show (i.e. who actually 'owns' the dance steps?, or the Celtic heritage of the story line?, or the airs, reels and jigs that inform the musical accompaniment?).

More meaningfully perhaps than the attendant postmodern apparatus, it is the nature and content of the stage show itself that gives *Riverdance* its overwhelmingly postmodern aspect (Figure 4.3). According to Banes (1987), there are many forms of 'postmodern' dance – breakaway, analytic, metaphor and metaphysical, etc. – but they are as one in their abandonment of the reductionism, minimalization and denial of meaning that typified 'modern' dance. Postmodern dance, rather, is marked by the reintroduction of meaning (in the form of narrative, character and extravagant expression) and characterized by pastiche, playfulness, vernacular and ethnic quotation, theatricality, musicality and, above all, *radical juxtaposition* (see Levin 1990; Brinson 1991; Mackrell 1991; Copeland 1993). All of these distinguishing features are readily discernible in *Riverdance*. The show not only quotes but completely reinterprets the Irish step-dance tradition by introducing flowing movement, choreographed ensemble work, principal dancers and even shafts of amusement into this somewhat rigid, highly formalized, largely anonymous and deadly serious mode of Terpsichorean expression. With regard to radical juxtapositions, moreover, *Riverdance* draws freely upon and intermingles a multiplicity of ethnic traditions, such as Russian, Scottish, Spanish and American tap, square dance, break-dance and Hollywood musical. The music is equally eclectic, with its mélange of medieval chant, flamenco, Ole Man River-style basso profundo and Irish traditional music played in a heavily amplified rock 'n' roll manner (complete with solos, call and response, extravagant gestures, flamboyant stagecraft *et al.*). As Table 4.4 reveals, moreover, the fractured narrative of the show is premised on a highly allusive, dreamlike melding of Irish myth, legend and historical events (prehistoric settlement, Chú Chúlainn, Shivna, famine, emigration), set within an overarching framework of the primordial Great Year (the unending cycle of the heavens and seasons), and, not least, the River of Life as it flows on its journey from source to sea (Campion 1994; Eliade 1996). *Riverdance* thus comprises an evocative postmodern fusion of old and new, past and present, myth and history, east and west, north and south, here and there, us and them, rural and urban, birth and death, war and peace, feast and famine, earth and water, sea and sky, home and away. It has often been described, in that most postmodern of oxymorons, as a 'modern classic'. It is narrowly ethnic yet has managed to transcend national, linguistic, cultural and socio-economic barriers. It is, so the producers maintain, about the roots of all nations finding themselves in dance. It is 'nothing less than the story of humankind' (Brophy 1996: 7).

Table 4.4 Oh, the horizontal mambo

Act One

INTRODUCTION

At the root of all native cultures is the primal quest to come to terms with spiritual and elemental forces.

Just as they harnessed fire, water, wood and stone, our ancestors also learned to harness their creativity. They quickly learned also how to express and celebrate their own lives and spirits, their own human relationships and their bond with the place they called home. The first half of this performance deals with the native imagination as it embraces the great forces and challenges of life.

REEL AROUND the SUN

This opening dance sequence starts with a slow air, then develops into a full-blown, energetic reel by the Irish Dance Troupe in praise of the sun's great power. It comprises three dances: *Corona* (slow air), *The Chronos Reel* and *Reel Around the Sun*.

THE HEART'S CRY

A haunting song reminds us that from earliest times we have known that the key to everything is love.

WOMEN OF IRELAND

Here we see two images of woman in Celtic tradition. *The Countess Cathleen*, a slip jig, reflects Yeats' metaphor of nurturing Irish womanhood, while in the second dance, *Women of the Sidhe* (*The Fairy Women*), their sexuality is portrayed as they challenge the men.

CAOINEADH CHÚ CHÚLAINN

A lament for Chú Chúlainn, probably the greatest figure in all of Celtic mythology, hero of many an epic battle, who fought even the sea itself before he died.

THUNDERSTORM

The energy and potency of one of nature's most dramatic forces is echoed in a hard-shoe unaccompanied dance by the male troupe.

SHIVNA

Each culture has its tales and legends, and Ireland is particularly rich in them. Shivna was a 7th century chieftain who ran foul of a saint and was cursed to spend his remaining years in the branches of oak and yew forests which then covered Ireland. Bill Whelan's music is set to a 12th century verse.

FIREDANCE

Fire was one of humankind's greatest benefactors, but also one of its biggest dangers. In this dance, the woman appears as its embodiment, conveying its allure in her graceful hand movements and its power and danger in her dance.

Table 4.4 Contd.

SLIP INTO SPRING – THE HARVEST

The circle of the seasons is evoked in a virtuoso violin and orchestral piece. Beginning gently with the first shoots of Spring, it swells in energy and passion to celebrate Summer's ripening and the gathering of Autumn's bounty.

RIVERDANCE

Now comes the seminal set piece from which everything else has flowed: In *Cloudsong*, the spirit of the Riverwoman is summoned up by song and ushered onto the land. The *Dance of the Riverwoman* is as soft and fluid as the river's movement over the land. She wakes the earth from its barren sleep and it responds with energy and vital movement, symbolised in the dramatic hard-shoe tap dancing of *Earthrise*. Finally, in *Riverdance* itself, the two great forces of earth and water come together, tentatively at first, but with the return of the drums it becomes a rousing jig and, with massed dancers and orchestra in full flight, it builds and builds to spectacular climax.

Act Two

INTRODUCTION

To leave the homeplace because of war, famine or slavery has been the fate of many native peoples. Such a dislocation is the central theme of Act Two.

AMERICAN WAKE

From the mid-19th century, poverty and famine drove the Irish to emigrate in their millions, many to America. Families and communities were sundered, never to meet again; so grew the American Wake, an extraordinary communal leavetaking that combines the desolation of parting with a defiant note of festivity in the *Nova Scotia Set*. *Lift the Wings* is a song of parting as the lovers face out into the New World.

HARBOUR OF THE NEW WORLD

The music and dance that forged a sense of identity are now exposed to new and unfamiliar cultures. Ultimately, in the blending and fusion that follows, the emigrants find that the totality of human experience and expression is greater even than the sum of its many diverse parts.

I) HEAL THEIR HEARTS – FREEDOM

From the darkness a lone voice sings and is then joined by other immigrants, reflecting the universal yearning of the dispossessed wherever they make their home.

II) TRADING TAPS

On the sidewalks of New York, our travellers meet new cultures and new challenges. Immigrants from other places display their native styles and steps and the newly-arrived respond with their own display of skill. The contest

Table 4.4 Contd.

---

develops into a celebration of shared dexterity and pride in their distant heritage.

III) Morning in Macedonia

A plaintive air reminds us of the loneliness of other travellers for their homeland in the heart of Europe. But sadness gives way to celebration as they dance *The Russian Dervish*, a dynamic acrobatic routine, drawing inspiration from folk traditions that range from Siberia to Eastern Europe.

IV) Oscail an Doras (Open the Door)

In the flight from famine and poverty, musical instruments were an unknown luxury. 'Mouth music' often used by the Celtic nations in the past was now revived as a substitute dance accompaniment and also as relief from the tedium of manual labour.

V) Heartbeat Of The World – Andalucia

In the cauldron of the big city, the pulsing energy of the streets is reflected in the fiery Latin rhythms of percussive Spanish dance.

Home and the Heartland

Going home – as our immigrants prosper and flourish in the New World, the call to return home is finally answered in a joyous celebration of music, song and dance.

Riverdance International

Journey's end, history's resolution. The circle of river and ocean returns us to the source. In this climactic piece, the hope and energy of the New World is borne back to the island home of the children to the diaspora. Their inherited cultural expressions remain vital and strong, but now they are coloured and energised by the influence of world music, world dance. As the island finds its place in the world, the entire company celebrates, uniting the many strands of the performance in a rousing reprise that echoes what has gone before.

Source: Abhann Productions 1996: 30–1. (*Riverdance the Show*: producer Moya Doherty; composer, Bill Whelan; director, John McColgan)

Just as *Riverdance* is a supreme example of postmodern marketing practice, so too its text can be treated to a postmodern marketing interrogation. As with Moët's mucho–macho Mucha mimicry (yes, it's horrible, I'm sorry, but I simply can't resist an alliterative opportunity like that), the Bakhtinian concepts of carnivalesque, chronotope and heteroglossia are readily discernible. By its very nature, of course, dance is inherently carnivalesque. Not only is it a form of social and self–expression that has been around since the very dawn of civilization, but it has always been very closely associated with fertility rites, orgiastic behaviour, liminality, licentiousness, abandonment, ecstasy and frenzied outpourings of emotion (Sporre 1989; H. Thomas 1995). True, the pagan, profane, Dionysian side of dance is periodically subject to sacralization, sanctification and Apollonian-style censure – the strictures of St Augustine, for instance – yet the history of Terpsichorean accomplishment reveals that these spells of formalization, standardization and stasis are eventually destroyed by the sudden, explosive irruption of dance's basic instincts (the Ballets Russes controversy at the turn of the twentieth century being just one occasion among many). Thus, it comes as no surprise to discover that *Riverdance* is routinely described in this liberatory, transformational fashion, as a joyful release from stultifying orthodoxy, as a sensuous, sinuous, serpentine antithesis to the sterile rigidity, formality and angularity of the step-dance tradition, as a return to the 'uninhibited earthiness that must once have been there' (Brophy 1996: 7).

Indeed, in a remarkably revealing interview with Michael Flatley, a less than enamoured (female) reporter states:

> First he wants to talk about sex or dance, how they are the same thing. He wants to know, do I understand masculine and feminine energy? 'A man should dance like a man. The energy he creates is a sexual energy: that's what dance is all about. I've discussed this with different people and I don't know why, but sometimes they just don't get it. But the audience understand. That's why they are there.' So the Irish dancing phenomenon started by *Riverdance* wasn't about tapping into the *Zeitgeist*, about Flatley's charisma, the whimsically dramatic musical score, the heavenly choir, the roots of all nations finding themselves, or some such rubbish that its producer, Moya Doherty, talked. It wasn't about a dance format available in all body formats. It was about sex.
>
> (Iley 1996: 32)

At one level, then, *Riverdance* can be regarded as a much-needed carnivalesque cure for Ireland's step-dance sclerosis. The show, after all, contains many elements of the carnivalesque, ranging from the covert sexual symbolism that inheres in its celebration of the lunar and the land (Jung 1964; Becker 1994), to scenes which overtly address the voluptuary-cum-bacchanalian-cum-procreative sides of life ('The Heart's Cry', 'Women of Ireland'). In truth, this Rabelaisian spirit is nowhere better illustrated than in the professional spat that led to Michael Flatley's abrupt departure and ensuing oedipal ambition to oust *Riverdance* with his competing, belligerently entitled production, *Lord of the Dance* (Dougill 1996; Harlow 1996; Tedre 1996). Nevertheless, the possibility must also be entertained that *Riverdance* represents a form of controlled madness, of permitted promiscuity, of Apollonian

Dionysianism, in so far as it ultimately serves to underpin rather than undermine the powers that be. It is generally acknowledged, for example, that by turning the Irish step-dance tradition on its head, the show has succeeded in stimulating prodigious interest in, and attracting a host of new recruits to, this venerable if hitherto moribund mode of cultural expression (Pielou 1996; Smyth 1996). But, the question has to be asked: will these new recruits be inducted into anything other than the traditional, formal, orthodox style? The answer is probably not and, hence, the aesthetic status quo is not merely reinforced or revitalized – it is redoubled. Likewise, it is noteworthy that audiences invariably remain seated throughout performances of *Riverdance*. Unlike the rock concert format from which the show derives so many of its stylistic motifs, there is no evidence of step-dancing, break-dancing, idiot dancing or any other type of dancing in the aisles. There is no audience participation. Everything is strictly under control. Subversive? Certainly not!

The controlled decontrol that permeates *Riverdance* is perfectly captured in Iley's (1996: 32) aside in her above-mentioned interview with Flatley. She responds to his suggestion that the show represents carnality unleashed with the rider that its sexuality is covert, sanitized, unthreatening, acceptable: 'A multi-class version of the Chippendales, suitable for family viewing.' Similarly, the very fact that the President of the Irish Republic – *the* voice of the Establishment – can unreservedly recommend *Riverdance* as a 'fresh impetus to the consciousness of our Irish culture . . . [that] . . . has brought an uplifting pride to ourselves and friends of Ireland at home and abroad' (Robinson 1996: 5) confirms that the show represents not so much an anti-authoritarian release of primal, orgiastic forces, as a mechanism for keeping them under lock and key. Terpsichore in chains.

At the same time, however, the comments of Iley and President Robinson are indicative of, and highly relevant to, the chronotope of *Riverdance*. Despite the fact that the show is patently an act of patriotic boosterism, narcissistic nationalism and ethnic self-glorification, it has proved to be an unalloyed international triumph. It has transcended cultural differences and demonstrably succeeded in countries without obvious Irish connections or substantial communities of expatriates and descendants. With two separate touring companies (and plans for a third), *Riverdance* is rapidly developing into a global brand. It is the Disney, the Diners Club, the Dunkin-Donuts, the Dyno-Rod, the McDonalds of dance. Indeed, by telling us, in effect, to 'think local, act global', *Riverdance* offers an adroit postmodern alternative to the global→local orthodoxy of international marketing (Levitt 1983; Dunning 1993; Ohmae 1990, 1995; Clegg and Gray 1996; Hirst and Thompson 1996).

Although it exemplifies Lyotard's description of the postmodern condition – a world where 'one listens to reggae, watches a western, eats McDonalds food for lunch and local cuisine for dinner, wears Paris perfume in Tokyo and retro clothes in Hong Kong' (1984: 76) – the chronotope of the *Riverdance* phenomenon is not limited to its *siècle*-surfing mélange of local and global. Nor, for that matter, is it confined to its pre-millennial torsion of mythical Irish past (of heroes and warriors) and equally mythical present (of cultural leviathan). The stage show itself has a very distinctive chronotope, albeit a chronotope that is distinctly indistinct. If we ask when and where the action occurs, no clear-cut answer is forthcoming. *Riverdance* is set in another time and another place that is recognizably Ireland at various points in its history and in various spaces of its geography. But, these settings are filtered through a sort of spatio-temporal haze, a mist of myths, a shimmer of symbols, a cloud of archetype, that gives the show its striking atmosphere of archaic contemporaneousness and transnational parochialism. This sense of distant familiarity is reinforced by the choreography, which is innovative yet orthodox and flowing yet formal, while the music is an extraordinary combination of conventions that can perhaps best be described as ole time rock 'n' reel, rock 'n' canticle, rock 'n' oratorio.

Thus, by drawing upon the primeval concepts of cyclical time, of eternal recurrence, of the Great Year, coupled with the seemingly ubiquitous spatial cycle of nationhood, diaspora and homecoming, *Riverdance* manages to capture the universal in the particular, the past in the present, the future as past, the world in a grain of sand. It provides nothing less than an ephemeral postmodern illumination of Heidegger's *being-in-the-world*, a fleeting glimpse of the fact that we, in our innate *thrown-ness* and state of *inauthenticity*, are as much a part of the world as it is of us. The *Dasein* of dance affords a momentary means of surmounting *Gestell*, our technocratic worldview, grants us unmediated, if passing, access to *The One* and thereby enables us to commune temporarily with the transcendental truth of *Being* (and if you believe all that Heideggerian guff, you're even more gullible than I thought).

Martin Heidegger may have been something of a brown-shirted tree-hugger, the eco-friendly wing of the Nazi party, a pre-postmodern cross between Greenpeace and the Gestapo, yet his metaphysical ruminations accord, after a fashion, with the truly astonishing outpouring of emotion that greeted the first performance of *Riverdance* during Eurovision. For those in the auditorium, and many more at home, it provided a genuine, tingle-in-the-spine, tears-in-the-eyes, once-in-a-life-time aesthetic epiphany. At the time, it seemed to be drawing directly from the bottomless artesian well, the irrepressible geyser of Irish cultural accomplishment and, having done so, not only quenched the unquenchable thirst of the intoxicated audience but soaked it to the seventh skin of the seventh skin and swept the entire Song Contest away in a swirling current of ethnic euphoria. Terpsichore *in excelsis*. Terpsichore *in celtus*.

Drenched by the rapturous *Riverdance* downpour, it is all too easy to get caught up in an ersatz hibernian whirlpool; to shoot the white-water rapids of sham Irish heritage, to lose oneself in the bogus bayoux of the Celtic delta, or, worse still, to attempt to identify the spurious source somewhere in the watersheds of cultural prehistory. A cursory examination of the *Riverdance* phenomenon, however, indicates that there is much more to the show than its ostensibly monoglossian glorification of counterfeit Irish ethnicity (or, indeed, the limitless opportunities it provides for mixing aquatic and acoustic metaphors). On the contrary, a cacophony of competing heteroglossian voices is very clearly audible. There are, for instance, polysemous voices from within the production itself – the demands of the market, the interjections of promoters, the soliloquy of ticket sales, the asides of tie-in merchandise, the rhyming couplets of the press release. It is impossible, moreover, to turn a deaf ear to the unmentionable but none the less detectable professional aspirations of the principals, the producers, the musicians, the chorus and the troupe. The stage show, furthermore, endeavours to translate several musical and Terpsichorean tongues – Russian, Spanish, American, etc. – into pidgin Irish.

Eavesdropping and back-stage gossip aside, it is clear that two of the voices within *Riverdance* are particularly insistent and difficult to ignore. The first of these is the voice of dance itself. Long the thin and intermittent rivulet of Irish culture, seemingly overpowered by a cascade of achievements in the adjacent streams of literature (Joyce, O'Brien, Doyle), drama (Shaw, Beckett, O'Casey), poetry (Yeats, Heaney, Muldoon), music (U2, Morrison, The cranberries) and film (Jordan, Neeson, Brosnan), dance has leaped, in a single fluvial bound – a spring, no less – to the forefront of national aesthetic consciousness. Thanks to *Riverdance*, Irish step-dancing is no longer a babbling brook but a raging torrent. It is a raging torrent that has burst its parochial banks and, in a Terpsichorean inundation the like of which has not been felt since the (equally ethnic) Ballets Russes of the last *fin de siècle*, the unashamed genre-bending populism of *Riverdance* has succeeded in irrigating the parched floodplains of postmodern dance per se (cf. Joaquín Cortés' subsequent (Wood 1996) Armani-clad, rock 'n' roll-based reinvention of flamenco).

A second and even more emphatic utterance that expresses itself through *Riverdance* is the voice of Ireland, or, rather, the voices of Ireland. Euphonious though the *Riverdance* experience undoubtedly is, the Ireland it articulates is the Ireland of myth, of legend, of half-remembered historical facts. It is the Ireland of the heritage trail, of the tourist trap, of Bloomsday, of Paddy's Day parades, of the *craic*, of a land before time – O'Topia – that never existed and doesn't exist, except in our dreams, travel brochures and, naturally, advertisements for Ballygowan water, Irish Mist soap, Caffrey's Ale and Lucky Charm breakfast cereal. The Ireland of crime, drugs, delinquency, prostitution, terrorism, urban blight, traffic jams, air pollution, unemployment, homelessness, teenage abortions, child abuse, patriarchy and religious discrimination (and that's just a typical Monday morning) has been silenced, swallowed and scrubbed clean by the melodious, mellifluous, magical waters of *Riverdance*. Granted, the show never quite descends to the priest-ridden, pig-in-the-parlour, shillelagh-wielding, leprechaun-baiting stereotype – though *Lord of the Dance* comes within spitting distance – but it is undoubtedly closer to the Ireland of *The Quiet Man* than the Ireland of *The Commitments*. It is nothing short of astonishing that a society which has latterly gone out of its way to emphasize its progressive, egalitarian, business-like, ultra-modern, cutting-edge cosmopolitan credentials, should completely capitulate and willingly participate in this communal, pseudo-Celtic regression therapy at the first sound of the uilleann pipes and the clicking-clacking of the high-heeled shoe. *Riverdance*, in sum, is a potent, if ultimately parochial, irredeemably philistine and utterly phoney celebration of cod-Irish culture. It is hiberno-hokum writ large.

Postmodernists, of course, are perfectly at home with the philistine, the fake, the phoney, the pseudo, the kitsch, the ersatz, and if it comes in retro or tribal packaging, so much the better. False consciousness may be alive, well and step-dancing at twenty-eight beats to the bar, but does anyone really care any more, so long as it's a good night out? If *Riverdance* uses the Irish Muse as a shamrock-bedecked ventriloquist's dummy, is it reasonable to expect a Habermasian ideal speech situation, especially when we can't see its lips move? In this respect, it is surely no accident that the original principals of *Riverdance*, Michael Flatley and Jean Butler, are not native-born Irish. They are American-Irish and it is their (mis)perception of Ireland that permeates the show (this is particularly true of Flatley's rival production, *Lord of the Dance*). But what is wrong with that? Irish culture has never been pure; it was largely an invention of the last *fin de siècle*, thanks to Yeats and the nationalist revival (Hobsbawm 1983; Regan 1995; Kiberd 1995; Boyce and O'Day 1996; Foster 1996). In our postmodern world, Irish culture does not and, as a consequence of the imperialistic artistic ambitions that *River-dance* exemplifies, simply *cannot* belong to Ireland – nor should it. If someone wants to exploit a 'degraded' version of Irish culture for their commercial purposes, why make a song and dance about it?

While *Riverdance* in many ways exemplifies late-twentieth-century, neo-Celtic culture – the new baseline against which 'Irishness' is measured and which will doubtless be 'debased' in the fullness of time – it seems to me that the real problem with this *Riverdance*-inspired cultural catholicism, this Ireland-lite, this Celtic simulacrum, is that its prevailing ethos of 'I'm Irish, you're Irish, we're all Irish' can serve as an unwitting smoke screen for scholarly charlatanism, quackery and general Tom O'foolery. By drawing upon the saints and scholars, hibernian twilight, literary heritage myth and using Ireland's staggering cultural achievements as a false passport to poetic licence, it is possible for unscrupulous social scientists to claim exemption from normal evaluative criteria, to argue in effect that the academic rules don't apply, or shouldn't be applied, to them. As works of 'literature', their papers and publications are exempt, above criticism, a law unto themselves. Indeed, I can almost imagine a situation where an unethical marketing academic might attempt to write in para-literary style and, by claiming the poetic immunity accorded to the Irish, endeavour to pass his or her ramblings off as works of scholarship. Nah, you're right, they'd never be allowed to get away with it . . .

Will the wolf survive?

Before denouncing the discipline-defiling actions of a few deluded dunderheads, it is necessary to recognize that, like any walk of life, marketing has its fair share of shysters, charlatans and con-men. The conference and short-course circuit is literally awash with purveyors of marketing pabulum and company-sized carboys of snake oil (and which, if consumed – especially the ones with 'Drink Me' on the label – can give rise to the dreaded honey-I-shrunk-the-SBUs situation). The bookshops are knee-deep in transformational marketing tracts, with their day-glo covers, stop-me-and-buy-one exclamation marks and appropriately ambiguous pseudo-endorsements on the back cover ('his finest work to date', 'suitable for insomniacs'). It has even been suggested, though I find this hard to believe, that marketing per se is a den of iniquity and that its academic apologists are nothing but stool pigeons, a front, a kind of concept-laundering operation for the capitalistic, customer-gouging godfathers of the Marketing Mafiosi. In this respect, it is perhaps not surprising that there are one or two rogue literary theorists on the loose. True, the thought of a couple of academic marketing mobsters with sawn-off copies of *The Dialogic Imagination* or *Art and Answerability* in their violin cases is not exactly in the lock-your-doors, keep-away-from-the-windows, horse's-head-in-the-bed league. Yet, as we have seen, literary scams, if not the numbers racket, have much to contribute to marketing research, whether it be in the well-greased palms of advertising and promotion or the hitherto underexploited saps of services marketing, retailing and distribution, not-for-profit, public sector, strategic marketing planning and many more besides.

Important though the latter are, it is arguable that the most pressing task at present is to turn our literary hand to marketing literature itself. In other words, to examine the corpus of marketing theory and thought from a lit-crit perspective. After all, the vast majority of academic marketing output consists of works of literature. The companies, institutions, organizations, managers, salespersons, agents, households, shoppers, consumers, samples, surveys, interviews, attitudes, intentions, behaviours, concepts, models and theories that we encounter are *entirely textually mediated*. While they may ultimately correspond to some phenomena in the 'real' world – though even that is debatable – they only exist for us through several by no means transparent layers of textual tissue (published papers, submitted papers, data analyses, interview protocols, respondent representations, methodological guidelines, existing literature etc.). This is equally true of the pedagogic context, where much of what we do – and the metaphysics of presence notwithstanding – is essentially textual (handouts, overheads, lecture notes, textbooks and so on). Some, admittedly eccentric, academic marketers still like to think of themselves as scientists manqués, as the backroom boys behind the achievements of their managerial brethren, as a sort of scholarly pit-stop crew for Team Marketing, Formula One (gives a whole new meaning to Brands Hatch, I agree), but the brutal fact of the matter is that we are writers, authors, hacks, literary types, the chattering classes – albeit with a severe speech defect.

It follows, then, that adopting an expressly literary approach to our own literary endeavours may prove worthwhile, or a refreshing change at least. Indeed, a number of pioneering contributions to this reflexive perspective have already been made. As noted earlier, B. B. Stern (1990d) has taken a lit-crit squint at marketing's 1950s predilection for motivation theory, thereby accounting for the rise and demise of Ernest Dichter, its principal proponent. Heilbrunn (1996a), likewise, has adopted a narratological approach to consumer behaviour theory and demonstrated how the standard information-processing, stage-type models are compatible with the 'actantial' framework of Greimas, the French semiologist and literary theorist. C. J. Thompson (1993), furthermore, has not only offered a cogent hermeneutic deconstruction of the celebrated realism versus relativism debate, but he also succeeds in exposing the specious, if persuasive, rhetorical strategy espoused by one of the main protagonists (guess who?). Meamber and Venkatesh (1995), in a singularly heroic study that goes far beyond the call of postmodern duty, have waded their way through the back editions of Kotler's corpus in order to, well, *suffer*, I suppose. And, drawing upon the apocalyptic literary tradition, S. Brown *et al.* (1996) have demonstrated how its tripartite crisis–judgement–redemption schema inheres in numerous works of marketing literature (contrary to popular belief, and the vernacular use of the term, 'apocalypse' is a literary genre that is 'revelatory' – as in the Book of Revelation – in intent).

Although this line of thought can be described as postmodern navel-gazing at its most narcissistic – and the charge of undue self-obsession sticks to some extent – it can also be contended that a modicum of marketing reflexivity would not go amiss. For good or ill, academic marketers have produced a huge body of literature, but as a consequence of our obsolescent (albeit obstinate) 'make it new', 'onward and upward', 'more scientific than science' mentality, the discipline has paid too little attention to its own literariness. That's the bad news. The good news is that the scope for close reading, deconstructive analyses, textual explication and so forth remains (literally) enormous. You don't have to be an expert in Lacanian literary theory, for example, to identify the disciplinary psychosis that underpins Kerin's (1996) recent review paper in *JM* (like Lady Macbeth's inveterate hand-washing, its constant 'advancement of science' refrain speaks volumes about marketing's complete 'lack' of scientific achievement). Nor, for that matter, do you need to be deeply grounded in feminist literary theory to recognize that marketing's rigorous, objective, hard-science, comprehensive model, general theory – in short, macho – academic ethos, is a deep-seated denial of the fact that it is, and always has been, regarded as an essentially feminized domain (i.e. selling, shopping, consumption and so on, as opposed to manly activities like production and ops management). In this respect, incidentally, marketing is analogous to English Literature, another feminized area of the academy – compared, say, to mechanical engineering – that has long been characterized by a 'masculine' orientation (see Simpson 1995).

However, lest I am accused of picking easy targets or indulging in *ad-hominem* diatribe, let me attempt to demonstrate the utility of a literary slant on marketing literature by concentrating on a single sub-field of marketing thought, a sub-field that is highly contemporary, very fast growing, widely regarded as the most important conceptual contribution of recent years and, not least, occasionally associated with the *soi-disant* postmodern turn.

Relationship Marketing (RM), according to its manifold adepts, is the marketing equivalent of Luther's ninety-five theses, the Declaration of Independence and the Communist Manifesto, all rolled into one. Defined as 'a customer centred approach whereby a firm seeks long-term business relations with prospective and existing customers' (Evans and Laskin 1994: 440), relationship marketing has variously been described as 'a paradigm shift' (Gummesson 1996b: 15), 'a paradigm shift' (Grönroos 1994: 347), 'a paradigm shift' (Sheth and Parvatiyar 1993: 1), 'a paradigm shift' (Aijo 1996: 8) and – brace yourself – 'a genuine paradigm shift' (R. M. Morgan and Hunt 1994: 20), although some of us are wondering when there is going to be a paradigm shift in the 'paradigm shift' terminology used to describe, er, paradigm shifts.

From its origins in the business-to-business and services marketing arenas, RM has rapidly colonized the entire marketing discipline. It has been applied to all manner of inter- and intra-organisational settings – supply-chain relationships (Davies 1996), principal-agent relationships (Carruthers 1996), company–consumer relationships (R. A. Peterson 1995) and so on – and a veritable host of industrial sectors from airlines (D. Gilbert 1996) and advertising agencies (Michell 1996) to textile manufacturers and tyre distributors (R. M. Morgan and Hunt 1994). General models of RM's domain have been developed (Wilson 1995); stage-type theories of its implementation are in circulation (Nevin 1995); dedicated conferences, journals, chairs and centres of excellence have been established (Cravens 1995; Sheth and Grönroos 1996); specialist volumes are hitting the bookstands with monotonous regularity (McKenna 1992; Håkansson and Snehota 1995; Gummesson 1996c; Buttle 1996a; Iacobucci 1996); and I have been reliably informed that publishers now demand a relationship marketing angle – a very steep angle, let it be said – in all introductory marketing textbooks. RM, furthermore, has not only been blessed by the leading lights in our field – Kotler, Sheth, Hunt, Webster, etc. – but the concept has also served to elevate certain peripheral figures to positions of disciplinary power and influence (Berry, Gummesson). There are, admittedly, a number of dissenting voices (e.g. M. J. Baker 1994; Arnould 1995; Blois 1996). Nevertheless, it is fair to conclude that the relationship marketing charabanc, bandwagon, wagon train, – no, make that *logo*motive – is getting up a real head of steam. Academics are leaping on board with lemming-like abandon. Proprietorial 'I thought of it first' disputes are breaking out over who rides in the observatory car, let alone who occupies the prestigious positions of chief engineer and footplateman (Berry's (1995) shameless self-citation is perhaps the most blatant bid for glory.) And, it seems that the whole caboose, the whole kit and caboodle, the great RM Express, is rapidly picking up momentum as it glides out of Root Metaphor Central en route to Hegemony Halt and the Stations of the Cross.

Faced with the prospect of missing the last train to scientific respectability, many marketing academics, most notably Bagozzi (1995), are desperately rummaging through their past publications and rejected manuscripts in a frantic search for the magic word, the word which will enable them to announce that they have been relationship marketers all along and are thus entitled to a seat on board. I too could count myself among the Markonauts of the Pacific Western – in a third-class carriage, admittedly, hanging on to a ceiling strap and hoping against hope that the conductor won't check my invalid ticket – since relationship marketing and the postmodern condition are often closely linked. If, as some people proclaim, postmodernism is characterized by *chronology, fragmentation, de-differentiation, hyperreality, pastiche, anti-authoritarianism* and *apocalypticism* (S. Brown 1995a; S. Brown, Bell and Carson 1996), then RM unquestionably fits the postmodern marketing bill. Its emphasis upon retaining existing rather than attracting new customers is very much in keeping with postmodernism's *chronological* fondness for the old, the established, the retro, as opposed to the new and improved. Its eschewal of mass, undifferentiated marketing in favour of individualized, customized and client-specific marketing strategies is compatible with the *fragmentation* that typifies the postmodern moment. *De-differentiation* is apparent in RM's blurring of formerly sacrosanct boundaries between and within marketing organizations, their suppliers, their customers and what have you. Indeed, in extreme cases, such as the much-lauded hollow companies, boundaryless corporations and virtual companies, relationship marketing is teetering on the brink of the paradigmatic postmodern state of *hyperreality*. What's more, its propensity to pick 'n' mix elements from various propinquitous specialisms – TQM, HRM, re-engineering, transaction-cost analysis, the social exchange/interpersonal relationships literatures, etc. – is very close to the postmodern notion of *pastiche* and it can be contended that RM is *anti-authoritarian* in more ways than one. Obviously, it represents an anti-authoritarian challenge to the hegemony of the discredited, take-the-money-and-run transactional methods of marketing management. Yet it is also anti-authoritarian in the sense that it opposes the old antagonistic, repressive, domineering approach to, say, channel relationships and its recognition, *à la* Foucault, that power is not only extremely diffuse and non-despotic but can serve as a force for the good. Relationship marketing, finally, is even compatible with the *apocalyptic* postmodern propensity which expresses itself in what Showalter (1991) describes as 'endism' (the end of history, philosophy, work, nature, ethnography, to name but a few). The very existence of RM, remember, is a testimony to the complete failure – the end – of the original marketing concept. After all, if the original concept had delivered on its promises there would be no unsatisfied-cum-defecting customers for relationship marketing to attend to.

As you can no doubt imagine, innumerable academic benefits are liable to flow from this hypothesized strategic alliance between Relationship Marketing and the postmodern (let's call it RoMo). Association with RM, a lightly armoured but highly effective fighting machine, may help secure the postmodern marketing salient, a heavyweight intellectual 'push' liable to get bogged down in the tangled, disorienting, anti-empiricist terrain of the Franco-German marches. RoMo, conversely, supplies a prominent but somewhat undertheorized marketing conceptualization with the philosophical munitions and cerebral big battalions that it manifestly and sorely lacks. Indeed, by its ability to lay down an intellectual barrage dense enough to disconcert even the most battle-hardened pragmatist, postmodernism enables the fighting men of RM – the Royal Marines of marketing scholarship – to concentrate on the things they do best, such as drawing boxes-and-arrows diagrams of pseudo-marketing strategies, formulating stage-type models of advance and retreat, writing books bandoleered in bullet points, all of which turn out to be blanks, and berating marketing practitioners for insubordination, failing to follow orders and cowardice in the face of the enemy (accountants, human resource managers and analogous barbarian hoards). However, by far the most important benefit flowing from RoMo (moreso, even, than the fun that can be had applying a militaristic metaphor to a construct that is totally opposed to marketing warfare) is the fact that it permits me to describe Shelby Hunt, Phil Kotler, Jag Sheth, Fred Webster and the rest of the RM crew as postmodernists. Repeat, postmodernists. All together now, *postmodernists*. The prodigal sons have returned to daddy. Break out the barbie, boys and girls, the fatted calf is frying tonight!

Notwithstanding the attraction of outing Shelby Hunt as a postmodernist, and despite the personal-reputation-enhancing benefits that could flow from RoMo (whaddya want from me, integrity?), literary theory suggests that this potentially happy fusion of RM and the postmodern is more hyper than real. A brief Bakhtinian interrogation of the relationship marketing paradigm raises all sorts of *heteroglossian*, *chronotopical* and, especially, *carnivalesque* issues, which lead to the inevitable conclusion that RM has more to do with hot air, inflated egos and sibling rivalry than improving the everyday lot of practising marketing managers. In terms of heteroglossia, for example, the frequently recycled notion that RM is the answer to marketing's manifold ills, yet another upward step on the ladder of disciplinary progress, a cure-all for the 'end of marketing' malaise into which the field has sunk is revealed to be over-optimistic at best and cloud cuckoo land at worst. Relationship marketing is not a giant leap forward for *mar*kind, let alone one small step-dance, but a site of struggle where a cacophony of competing voices is audible beneath the beguiling susurrus of paradigm shifts. There is the voice of industrial or business-to-business marketing, a disciplinary sub-field long overshadowed by consumer goods marketing and which has at last been given an opportunity to occupy the spotlight. There are the voices of European academics, a group hitherto studiously ignored by American marketing associates, but as the biological parents, so to speak, of RM, they suddenly and somewhat disconcertingly find themselves acknowledged and even, on occasion, cited by their pre-post-colonialist oppressors. (To be sure, most American exordia on relationship marketing still fail to pay due obeisance to the concept's European antecedents, though it is also true to say that the standing of RM in Europe has been considerably enhanced by the great seal of belated US approval.) In a similar vein, the dialogic voices of old and new, male and female, large and small, and strong and weak can be recognized within the debating chamber that is Relationship Marketing. For some commentators, RM represents nothing more than an attempt to teach a new dog old tricks (M. J. Baker 1994); others regard it as a reinscription of marketing's inherent phallocentrism under the 'new man' disguise of cooperation, equality and the marriage metaphor (Fischer and Bristor 1994); yet others consider the talk of trust, commitment and partnership between (typically) large companies and small suppliers – and still smaller consumers – little more than a linguistic smoke screen for the continued coercion, exploitation and manipulation of the weak by the strong (Chen *et al.* 1992; Imrie and Morris 1992; Butler 1996). It is, in effect, nothing less than a latter-day version of changing the sign on the departmental door from 'sales' to 'marketing'.

If heteroglossia helps highlight some of the tensions that lurk below the seemingly placid surface of the relationship marketing paradigm shift, the Bakhtinian chronotope provides a way of conceptualizing them. Although the proponents of the RM *jihad* may find it politically and professionally necessary to suggest that it represents a radical departure from the transactional perspective – and thereby create a space for themselves in the scholarly scheme of things – the fact of the matter is that RM was always already anticipated in the original marketing concept (problematic though that was and is). To insinuate, as some weird and wonderful teRMites are wont to do, that establishing trust and commitment, or retaining customer loyalty, or tackling cross-functional integration was *not* a component part of the original marketing concept is arrant nonsense. In fairness, many of the converts to the RM cause acknowledge that it involves *re-emphasizing* certain *neglected* aspects of the marketing concept, although supporting evidence is conspicuous by its absence.

A somewhat superior way of interpreting the RM shift is to accept that its content is no different from the original marketing concept but that the chronotope has changed. When we re-examine the initial explications of the marketing concept, the most striking thing about them is their overwhelmingly temporal orientation (production/sales/marketing eras of Keith, Levitt's rise and fall of companies, etc.), whereas the RM paradigm is strongly spatial in ethos (as the innumerable 'star-burst' diagrams – see Figure 1.1 – clearly demonstrate). Admittedly, the spatial side of the original marketing concept was introduced quite quickly (McCarthy 1960; Borden 1964) and temporal elements of RM have latterly been articulated (Wilson 1995; Hutt 1995); nevertheless it is arguable that, in keeping with the prevailing worldview of the times (modern progress versus postmodern stasis), the basic chronotope of the marketing and relationship marketing concepts is where the *essential* difference lies. In this respect, it should be added that Bakhtin's (1981b) explication of the chronotope was strongly progressivist, in so far as the evolution of novelistic chronotopes was believed to exhibit a trajectory of ever increasing realism. The same could be – and is – said of RM (i.e. that it is a 'superior' representation of marketing 'reality'), although it is probably best to conclude that it is no better than the original marketing concept, just more in keeping with our sated postmodern times.

Given the earnestness and enthusiasm with which the RM paradigm is being promulgated at present – Murphy (1996) informs us that we *must* adopt a relational approach – associating it with the carnivalesque may seem somewhat misplaced. The Bakhtinian carnival, surely, involves irreverence, parody, iconoclasm, paradox, transgression, madness and all sorts of other happy-go-lucky, couldn't-care-less attributes that are rarely, if ever, found in academic explications of relationship marketing. However, closer examination reveals that, while RM can hardly be described as the conceptual equivalent of a false nose, rotating bow tie and water-squirting buttonhole, it does indeed contain many elements of the carnivalesque. Apart from the fairly obvious point that it is predicated on the idea of inversion, of antithesis, of overturning the existing transactional orthodoxy, relationship marketing contains a very strong element of carnality. The RM literature is replete with sexual metaphor and allusion, whether it be Gummesson's (1996c) reference to one-night stands, Buttle's (1996b) suggestion of extra-marital dalliances, Christy *et al.*'s (1996) supercilious comparison with Mills & Boon-style romantic fiction, Worthington and Horne's (1996) distinction between arranged marriages and love matches or the frequently drawn parallel between RM and the stages of a love affair – admiration, consummation, recrimination and dissolution (Dwyer *et al.* 1987; Heide 1994; Weitz and Jap 1995).

In addition to this omnipresent 'make love not war' ethos, it can be contended that relationship marketing is profoundly transgressive, not to say a little bit mad (Buttimer and Kavanagh 1996). R.M. Morgan and Hunt (1994) make the point that RM is inherently contradictory (aptly named or what), in so far as it emphasizes the need for cooperation in order to compete. It is also often said that relationship marketing helps transcend the tyranny of 'departmentalization' thanks to its ability to diffuse marketing throughout the entire organization (Gummesson 1991; Sheth and Parvatiyar 1995). A laudable aspiration perhaps, but since the other functional areas have hitherto successfully resisted marketing's periodic incursions – and are likely to continue to do so (G. Morgan 1992; Alvesson and Willmott 1996) – it seems that this scholarly espousal of de-departmentalization has merely served to legitimize the large-scale closure of marketing departments as part of company downsizing exercises, without any concomitant commitment to the marketing cause (and they call me a nihilist!). Indeed, RM even denies us our traditional fall-back position of castigating companies for failing fully to implement the marketing concept, for adopting the trappings rather than the substance of marketing, etc. As the teRMites openly admit that the original marketing concept was mistaken – and, hence, the non-adopters were quite right to resist full implementation – we cannot now demand that they take their RM medicine like a man (hey, you academics got it wrong last time, remember?).

In fact, the more one looks at relationship marketing, the more obvious it is that the whole thing is an elaborate postmodern joke played by European marketing academics on their credulous American cousins. After suffering under the US yolk for years, after listening to countless condescending remarks, and after being treated as third-class marketing citizens, the worm has finally turned, the Trojan Horse of relationship marketing has been slipped through the gates of the US academy and, at the risk of further mixing my metaphors, we promise to try not to laugh when the distended boiler of the great American marketing express finally bursts, the wheels come off the wagons and the guards suddenly realize that the points were switched when their attention was temporarily distracted. Just as we Europeans swallowed but failed to digest Uncle Sam's, 1950s-style McMarketing concept, so too our transatlantic twins are likely to find that when it comes to the RM Whopper, they have bitten off more than they can chew[1].

Break like the wind

Not everyone, admittedly, will accept that RM is the Piltdown Man, the Hitler Diaries, the Sokal Hoax of postmodern marketing scholarship – though I suspect that many more will be incensed by my premature revelation of the RM ruse – yet

---

1 Incidentally, we're thinking of producing an 'Americanized' version of this text. Any takers out there in the land of *sap*portunity? Nasty, I hear you say, but not much of a footnote. So, a three-liner isn't good enough for you anymore?

Right, then, let me take this opportunity to deal with the biggest purported 'shortcoming' of marketing aesthetics, the fact that, unlike marketing science, it cannot render the future predictable. Not true, and to prove it I will hereby predict the *entire* scholarly trajectory of the Relationship Marketing paradigm shift. As we've already had the equivalent of 'Broadening the Concept of Relationship Marketing' and 'Towards a General Theory of Relationship Marketing', the subdisciplinary adaptations can't be far behind (Relationship Marketing Strategy, International Relationship Marketing, Relationship Marketing for SMEs, Retail Relationship Marketing, Relationship Marketing Research, Relationship Marketing Communications, Relationship Marketing Management, Relationship Marketing Plans, Cases in Relationship Marketing, Relationship Marketing for Fish Farmers, etc.). Before too long we'll start to see evidence of that winning combination of arrogance (Relationship Marketing Science, Is Science Relationship Marketing?, Macro-relationship Marketing), anxiety (Implementing Relationship Marketing, Making Relationship Marketing Work, Integrative Relationship Marketing) and practioner-oriented pseudo-pragmitism (Maxi-relationship Marketing, Turbo-relationship Marketing, Relationship Marketing Warfare), as well as introductory volumes for the dullards who can't quite grasp the profundity of the RM paradigm (Relationship Marketing for Beginners, Relationship Marketing by Matrix, Dick and Dora's Illustrated Guide to Relationship Marketing). Then, of course, the Big Fat Books About Relationship Marketing will hove into view, quickly followed by the Even Bigger and Fatter Books About Relationship Marketing (complete with Test Bank, Instructor's Manual, Transparency Masters, Video Tapes, CD-Rom and cyanide tablet). After that, there's no place left to go, so the revivalists kick in (Neo-relationship Marketing, Rediscovering Relationship Marketing, Retro-relationship Marketing) and the right-on, do-gooding, radical-chic buzzards, who kept well out of sight when the concept was in its pomp, start to circle overhead (Critical Relationship Marketing). Last of all, the gravediggers of the discipline have their wicked way of the carcass (Relationship Marketing Relationships, Reflexive Relationship Marketing, Postmodern Relationship Marketing), though by that stage someone is sure to have come up with another concept – a mutant melding of old and new – that'll take on a life of its own (Translationship Marketing). Translationship marketing? Now *that*'s got a ring to it. A combination of transactions and relationships, with just a hint of post-structural linguistics. We could be on to a winner here, but the market's not quite ready for it. It has to be launched at the very moment the RM moment has passed. How do we know when that is? Easy-peasy. Whenever Shelby Hunt pedantically points out that he *didn't actually say* there had been a relationship marketing paradigm shift. He was only *quoting* someone who said there had been a relationship marketing paradigm shift. Off the hook again, eh, Shelbs?

the available evidence is incontrovertible. You only have to peruse the publications of Evert Gummesson, the founding father of relationships, to realize that he writes with tongue planted firmly in cheek (beats the hell out of a Biro, believe me). Some of the statements made by the teRMites are so fatuous that they *must* be parodic. Consider Tjosvold and Wong's (1994: 308) assertion that 'the successful relational marketer appears to convince clients that he or she has their interest at heart, yet at the same time pursues the company's agenda' (*translation*: if you can fake sincerity . . .). Or, what about Bitner's (1995: 246) contention that 'service relationships are built and promises are kept one encounter at a time'? As this is an academic equivalent of 'we take every match as it comes, Brian', can 'over the moon', 'sick as a parrot' and 'funny old game, innit' be far behind? Best of all, however, is the evidence cited by Heskett *et al.* (1994) concerning the value of establishing lifelong relationships with customers: namely, a potential revenue stream of $8,000 from a loyal pizza customer. Ask yourself, what company in its right mind would want to establish a relationship with someone who's prepared to spend $8,000 on pizza? Can you imagine the fetid brute? – pustular, corpulent, fire-breathing, malodorous cheese 'n' tomato-stained T-shirt, receding forehead, semi-erect posture and, like the dyslexic he undoubtedly is, with VOLE and HEAT tattooed on his pavement-skimming knuckles (my undergraduates are bad, I grant you, but this is . . . uncanny!).

Conversely, consider the question from another angle: what customer in their right mind would want to establish a *relationship* with a marketing organization? Do marketers *really* believe that today's consumers – today's increasingly sceptical consumers (Lansley 1994; Berry 1995) – have come to the conclusion that, after shafting them for years, marketers en masse have finally got the message, turned over a new leaf, and really, *really* care about their customers' welfare? Do marketers *actually* imagine that consumers are convinced by our declarations of undying love, emollient endearments and assurances of honourable intent? Something tells me that they have probably concluded that our sobbing on their shoulders and dulcet promises to be a better boy in future are little more than pathetic attempts to elicit sympathy prior to picking their pockets. Something tells me that they might just see through us, especially when our concern is as contrived as the above quotation from Tjovold and Wong suggests. Something tells me that marketers would be far better off being open about their commercial intent. We don't love you, we just want your money – and lots of it! Why pretend otherwise? I suspect it is time to be honest about our dishonesty, although as today's cynical consumers are likely to surmise that we are being dishonest about our honest dishonesty, we may have to be honestly dishonest about our honest dishonesty. It's time, I say, for the real RM –

Rip-off Marketing – to stand up and be counted (just don't expect it to add up). While you may not agree with such sentiments, you can at least trust the fact that you can't trust me. Can you trust those who can't say that? Take a look at the academics who are flogging the RM horse – Kotler, Sheth, Webster, Hunt, etc. – the exact same academics who flogged us the original, now broken-winded, bow-legged, next-stop-the-glue-factory transactional marketing plater. Would you buy a used paradigm from these people, these Melmottes of marketing?

If, of course, RM is not a huge postmodern marketing prank and we really are expected to enter into a relationship with relationship marketing (I'll stick with the transaction transaction, thanks all the same), then we have to conclude that it is deeply, irredeemably pernicious. It is the intellectual equivalent of a telephone sex line and just about as satisfying (so they tell me). You've heard of the hidden hand of the market? Well, RM is the hidden hand-job. It is a con-artist manifesto, the South Sea Bubble of marketing research, a stiff in sheep's clothing that not even a necrophiliac Welshman could warm to. RM, in fact, is the scrapie of scholarship, a sort of mad concept disease that, as a consequence of consuming reconstituted ideas, has infected the entire marketing herd. Recognizable in its later stages by pomposity, arrogance, delusions of grandeur and all-round intellectual inconti-nence, mad concept disease commenced in the lower life forms of services and business-to-business marketing, and gradually spread up through the higher dis-ciplinary orders like retailing and distribution, domains populated by individuals with an exoskeleton and cerebral cortex. True, some sub-fields have yet to be infected – international marketing, for instance – but this is probably attributable to the fact that, as a notoriously brain-dead arena, there's nothing in international marketing worth infecting. Much as I hate to alarm you, it has been rumoured that even our own field of consumer research has been touched by the affliction, though we really only have to worry when someone certifiable suggests a melding of relationship marketing and postmodernism. Incineration is the only solution, I say. A cull is called for! But, in the meantime – and just to be on the safe side – don't read anything written by Alan Smithee or, er, Stephen Brown.

Chapter 5
I've got a rocket in my pocket

The moving finger writes; and, having writ, moves on. Which is to say that had that resonant line been writ today, and had its encompassing poem been as successful as it was yesterday, then Edward Fitzgerald's finger would immediately have moved on to nationwide chains of Khayyam Kutprice Karpet warehouses, Khayyam Kosy Karavanserai motels, and Khayyam InKar Kwiksnax outlets, where the peckish driver could enjoy a drive-in flask of wine and loaf of bread without even getting out from behind the wheel.

For literature itself has moved on, and if, in 1996, a book is to be worth writing, it has to end up as far more than a mere half-pound of assorted syllables gummed down one edge. It has to be the fulcrum of a hundred lucrative spin-offs, and not simply films or television series or Lloyd Webber musicals and their Original Cast Albums either, it has to do everything it commercially can, from launching itself at Christmas as a hilarious board game for funlovers from nine to ninety, to endorsing a fabulous range of pret à porter cocktail frocks for the fashionable bibliophile . . .

And now, as we heard yesterday, to a fragrance. For the great French parfumier Frangonard – no relation to the painter as far as I know, but you can't be sure of anything these days, art may be just the same as literature, you can probably buy Van Gogh earplugs – has just launched a scent called A Year in Provence, endorsed from New York, where he now shrewdly lives, by Mr Mayle, to whom numerous smells were flown for his approval, possibly, I'm only guessing, with a little input from his accountant, too. Niffed, it apparently evokes Provence, and I say OK, fine, goodbye and good luck to it; for I now have other fish to fry.

In order to incorporate them into my own forthcoming perfume. For I, those with uneven piano legs may recall, once wrote a book called A Year in Cricklewood. *It did not, sadly, generate any spin-offs at all: no tabloid offered Weekend Cricklewood Breaks or Dream Cricklewood Cottages, there were no glossy Cricklewood Calendars or Traditional Cricklewood Recipe Cards, no ranges of Authentic Cricklewood Peasant Smocks, no Extra Virgin Cricklewood Olive Oil – nothing but a book in a window waiting stoically to be reduced from £12.95.*

I now know where we both went wrong. For while, I have to concede, there might be the odd promotional headache when it comes to pushing Cricklewood cuisine, or Cricklewood couture, or Cricklewood wines, or even romantic holidays on the sunsoaked Cricklewood Riviera, there is no question but that Cricklewood exudes an irresistible fragrance all its own: a subtle blend of cod-batter and diesel, of teeming skip and doggy verge, of squattered walkway and shredded tyre, of sun-dried lager and cloven binliner, of a thousand other more elusive constituents of that peripolitan perfume which few can sniff without the tears coming to their eyes, especially if the wind is blowing off Kilburn.

I shall ring Frangonard forthwith. I may become a literary giant yet.

(Coren 1996: 16)

It's too late to stop now

Mikhail Bakhtin, according to the renowned literary theorist-cum-gunslinger Terry Eagleton (1989), doesn't have a leg to stand on. Although his work has proved enormously influential in a host of academic disciplines, from cultural to organization studies (e.g. Cave 1990; Gardiner 1993; Hazen 1993; Thornton 1994; Gergen and Whitney 1996), the concept of 'carnival' remains deeply suspect. For Eagleton, its espousal may well provide 'a certain pleasurable grossness, a plebeian crudity, knockabout iconoclasm and orgiastic delight' (1989: 178), but looked at in another light, it 'may be little more than the intellectual's guilty dues to the populace, the soul's blood money to the body' (1989: 178–9). The scholarly appeal of the carnivalesque resides entirely in its promise of parodies and subversions in thought that academics would not contemplate for a moment in real life. 'What is truly unseemly, he concludes, 'is the apparent eagerness of deans, chaired professors and presidents of learned societies to tumble from their offices into the streets, monstrous papier mache phalluses fixed in place' (Eagleton 1989: 179).

While Eagleton's scabrous comments are doubtless designed to further his reputation as the Frank Rich/Joe Queenan/A.A. Gill of contemporary literary criticism, and while there is more than a modicum of truth in his remarks (let's be honest, there's nothing more mortifying than white, male, middle-aged academics professing the joys of orgiastic abandon), it is arguable that more not less of the carnivalesque is needed in marketing. Despite the latter-day triumph of postmodernism – and the Rabelais-rousing endeavours of your good selves – it has to be acknowledged that much of the published marketing literature remains depressingly staid and unadventurous. True, we have succeeded in banishing the Lisrelites (you remember, that strange sect with the hieroglyphics, the ones that believe they're the chosen people and the sea parts in front of them) to the wilderness where they belong and, with any luck, will be wandering for the next forty years or so. We have, what is more, petitioned for the release of our loveable rogue literary theorists and successfully forestalled attempts to rescind their poetic licences. We have actually found people prepared to work against the RM grain, the risks to their reputations notwithstanding, in order to highlight its manifold, manifest absurdities. Yet, as a glance at the journals amply testifies, much of what passes for marketing scholarship is both safe and sorry. Ten years on from Sherry's call to insouciant arms, his desire for 'ragamuffin, barefoot irreverence . . . and . . . fine disregard for the rules' (1987: 370), too much of what we do is not worth doing. It is already done to death – and deserves to be. Even the much-touted exponents of the so-called interpretive turn are often sadly deficient in the 'marketing-as-literature' stakes. Thus, we have papers on rhetoric that are all but devoid of rhetorical power (McQuarrie and Mick 1992); discussions of metaphor that lack any semblance of metaphorical reasoning (Hunt and Menon 1995); analyses of creativity that exhibit little or no evidence of creative thinking (Hackley 1996); and, incredible though it seems, celebrations of 'liberatory' postmodernism in prose that signally fails to take flight (Firat and Venkatesh 1995). None of us would disagree with the authors' emancipatory sentiments, but stylistically their paper is the Spruce Goose of postmodern marketing discourse.

Now, this is not to suggest that the above articles are poor, inadequate or substandard in any way. Quite the reverse. It's just that when we read a paper on, say, the need for a more literary approach to marketing scholarship, we expect it to exhibit literary qualities of its own. When we peruse a piece on the potential utility of narratology, our immediate response should not be 'so what?', as is often the case; it should be, 'so what happens next?' When we encounter works of marketing literature, we hope against hope that 'the manner reflects the matter' (Holbrook 1995a: 265). Just as we are inclined to assume that accountants are capable of managing their personal finances, doctors will live a fairly healthy lifestyle, fashion editors are well, if idiosyncratically, dressed, interior designers reside in tastefully appointed dwellings and librarians possess a passing interest in books (although Murphy's Law, the *only* axiom of our postmodern age, suggests that the complete reverse invariably holds true), so too we presuppose that our poetic champions can compose, that rhetoricians can walk the talk, that metaphor-mongers can flog a dead hearse and that creatives can, er, um, well, let me see . . . sorry, I can't think of anything right now.

Set against this, it can of course be argued that there is no compelling reason why form should match or complement the content, since such expectations are little more than 'imitative fallacies' in any event (Alexander 1992). Yet, whenever we encounter this counterargument our inclinations are to assume ulterior motives of the 'do as I say, not as I do' variety or, alternatively, to reach for some variation on the immortal Shavian put-down: 'those who can, do; those who can't, teach; those who can't teach, teach marketing; and those who can't teach marketing, write books on postmodernism'. Naïvely or not, inappropriately or not, unreasonably or not, we expect exponents of a stated intellectual position to be able to 'show', as Wayne Booth (1983) suggests, as well as 'tell'. In the dark days of marketing science, now thankfully behind us, we whipped ourselves into a self-flagellating frenzy over our ability to demonstrate – not simply describe – the scientific norms of rigour, objectivity, reliability and so on. Much the same applies in our aestheticized postmodern marketing world, except that where we once emphasized the representativeness of our samples, we now offer samples of our representations; where we once sought statistical significance, we now seek significant significations; where we once experimented laboratorically, we now experiment linguistically (even when it produces horrible neologisms like 'laboratorically').

If this is rock 'n' roll, I want my old job back

It almost goes without saying that postmodernists like ourselves don't need to be reminded of the manifold benefits of the 'marketing-as-literature' approach. However, I have found in my unceasing, unstinting and utterly unselfish missionary work among the hitherto unenlightened, that arguing for more 'literary' modes of marketing scholarship tends to prompt an immediate response of 'why bother?' As no-nonsense, down-to-earth, beer-swilling, para-practitioners; as horny-handed, hairy-arsed, big-bollocked sons of intellectual toil; as the Iron Johns of the academy (well, the john at least), 'real' marketers have better things to do with their time than lounge around in common rooms composing sonnets, spouting iambic pentameters and, bawdy limericks excepted, generally waxing lyrical. The marketing crusade, whatever that is, still has to be waged against the bean counters of accounts, the headhunters in human resources and the underdeveloped, undernourished and, let's be honest, underendowed denizens of R&D. The modern marketing gospel, furthermore, remains to be disseminated in far-flung lands, like Germany and Japan, which have suffered grievous economic duress whilst waiting for the cargo cult-style arrival of the holy writ (the Kotler Cults as they're sometimes known). The marketing academic's job is to contribute to this process, no more, no less.

No shit.

Of course, the irony of these antediluvian beliefs is that the single most important benefit to be gained from embracing the literary-stroke-carnivalesque perspective is a long-overdue realignment with marketing managers, many of whom have long since abandoned academics as a bad job. This is not to suggest that practitioners spend their time penning blank verse below the loading bays, though some doubtless do and good luck to them. Nor does it seek to imply that marketing practice is entirely unplanned, unsystematic and intuitive, though we all know that it is much less planned, systematic and, well, tuitive than the textbooks suggest. Nor, for that matter, does this poetics-lubricated convergence of academics and practitioners necessarily mean that decades of exemplary marketing scholarship – the models, the frameworks, the hypotheses, the matrices, the checklists, the flowcharts – are rendered redundant and Lethewards have sunk (well, it does, but modernist zealots require some sort of scientistic straw to clutch at and who am I to deprive them?). It reminds us, rather, of an all too frequently forgotten fact: that marketing practice always has been and always will be characterized by an element of the carnivalesque, by hyperbole, by showmanship, by excess, by exaggeration, by buffoonery, by blarney, by Barnum and Bailey, by buy-one-get-one-free, by now-you-see-it-now-you-don't, by hands-that-do-dishes, by it-could-be-you, by I-can't-believe-it's-not-butter, by I-feel-like-chicken-tonight, by refreshing-the-parts-that-other-beers-can't-reach, by the-crumbliest-flakiest-milk-chocolate-in-the-world, by I-bet-he-drinks-Carling-Black-Label, by swapping-two-packets-of-ordinary-powder-for-one-packet-of-Daz, by you-know-when-you've-been-Tango'd, by, believe it or not, free-flights-to-the-United-States-for-the-price-of-a-vacuum-cleaner. *That's* what people associate with marketing, that's what people expect from marketing, that's what people *want* from marketing (why do we assume that consumers *always* object to being taken for a ride – sometimes the ride is part of the fun). To contend, as academics often do, that marketing is, or should be, whiter than white merely alienates practitioners, invites ridicule and leads to the inevitable conclusion that we are trying – in a contemporary version of coals to Newcastle, refrigerators to Inuits or sand to Bedouins – to argue that black is white after all. Marketing practice, in sum, is about the carnivalesque selling of pups and lemons, it is about seeing them coming, it is about exploiting the much-vaunted markets of one (as in, born every minute). Marketing scholarship should celebrate these facts, not disguise them.

Before we go any further (and you can't go much further than endorsing exploitation, though I haven't finished yet), let me immediately acknowledge that there is a school of marketing thought implacably opposed to the realignment of academics and practitioners. I cannot deny that a number of prominent marketing intellectuals have long campaigned against managerial accountability, arguing that association with a particular interest group in society compromises our desire to be accepted as a legitimate social science (Holbrook 1985b; Belk 1986b; Hirschman 1987). The fact that most of these secessionists are leading lights of the latter-day literary turn merely adds an touch of piquancy, shall we say, to the position being adumbrated herein. In response, I can only say that, much as I admire the work of Holbrook *et al.* and much as this book owes to their pioneering postmodern endeavours, their precipitate attempt to decouple the practitioner connection is mistaken. It is predicated on the erroneous premise that *any* dealings with marketing practitioners are automatically tarnished, not to say unspeakably corrupt. While disinterested and objective analysis is unattainable in our cynical, debased and decadent postmodern times, we don't have to be in thrall to marketing managers in order to study or comment on them – as the growing number of investigations by sociologists bears eloquent witness. The idea that marketing intellectuals can abandon their links with marketers is manifestly absurd (and declaring sub-disciplinary UDI doesn't stack up either, since most 'consumer researchers' are based in business schools). For outsiders, it is the lunatic equivalent of, say, academic educationalists attempting to cut themselves off from educators, medical researchers from practitioners of medicine, legal studies from lawyers, the architectural academy from architects or scholars of journalism from journalists. We may not like some of the things marketing practitioners do, but short of locating to another discipline, academic marketers are, and always will be, indissolubly associated with their managerial brethren.

Indeed, the marketing literati's misplaced attempt to distance themselves from practitioners is doubly ironic, in so far as it was motivated by aspirations of academic legitimacy, of being accepted as fully paid-up members of the Ivory Tower Country Club rather than being occasionally signed in, as at present. However, in the sardonic, sceptical, doubting and degraded socio-cultural milieux that obtain in postmodernity, scholarly respectability is more likely to come from *disrespect*, from modes of intellectual discourse that are in tune with the carnivalesque of the marketplace rather than the generic abstractions and generalizing ambitions of traditional social science. The brutal fact of the matter is that while marketing has been arguing the toss over realism versus relativism, positivism or post-positivism, idiographic versus nomothetic, pure or applied and, that most profound of philosophical paradoxes, transactions versus relationships (eat your heart out, Zeno), many contiguous disciplines have taken to tossing the argument, examining rhetorical strategies and exploring alternative forms of academic expression. This propensity is apparent in economics (McClosky 1985, 1990, 1994), education (Eisner 1985; Hammersly 1992), sociology (R. H. Brown 1987; Atkinson 1990), organization studies (Jeffcutt 1993; Boje *et al.* 1996; Burrell 1996), geography (Barnes and Duncan 1992; Cresswell 1993; McDowell 1996), history (Joyce 1991; Schama 1992; L. Stone 1992), women's studies (Wolf 1990; Richardson 1993, 1995), politics (Lukes 1995), cultural studies (Docker 1994; Walcott 1995) and the physical sciences (Gross 1990; Locke 1992), to name but a few.

Although it is not unusual nowadays to give philosophical treatises the novelistic treatment (Gaarder 1995; Krell 1996) or compose para-platonic dialogues and playlets on the sociology of scientific knowledge (Mulkay 1985; Pinch and Pinch 1988), this process of textual introspection is perhaps furthest advanced in anthropology, where a combination of decolonialism, deconstruction and deontological disciplinary detumescence has precipitated a period of deep de-depersonalization. In other words, increasing doubts about the scientific integrity of the ethnographic method, combined with growing apprehension over the ethnographer's ability to speak for, or about, those whom he or she sought to represent and, not least, the sheer conventionality of 'conventional' ethnographic accounts, led to widespread disillusion with traditional, distanced, depersonalized styles of ethnographic exposition (Tyler 1987; Clifford 1988; Geertz 1988; Rosaldo 1993; Fontana 1994; Marcus 1994). Faced with this 'crisis of representation', Marcus and Fischer (1986) declared an 'experimental moment' where what counted as ethnographic writing was up for grabs. Some responded with more poetic, highly literary, anti-realist forms of postmodern expression, which teetered, as often as not, on the brink of obscurantism (Tyler's 'neither the scientific illusion of reality nor the religious reality of illusion is congruent with the reality of fantasy in the fantasy reality of the post-modern world' (1986: 135), being a classic case in point). Others sought to eliminate, in archetypal postmodern style, the author from the text by foregrounding the voices of the represented in a dialogic or polysemous manner, even though authors always have the final, final say in the textual selection process (Crapanzano 1992). And, yet others, in time-honoured academic fashion, sat on the fence by passing comment on, and developing classifications of, the textual proclivities of their peers. Thus, van Maanen (1988) famously distinguished between 'realist', 'confessional' and 'impressionistic' ethnographic tales, and he has since added several others, including 'dramatic', 'critical', 'self', 'comedy', 'hip-hop' and 'fictional' ethnographies (van Maanen 1995). Such typologies, of course, are works of literature in themselves, and, since they are usually written in the timeless – now time-worn – realist manner, an unsympathetic taxonomist may be inclined to dismiss them as attempts to tell it like it is about the impossibility of telling it like it is.

The self-critical textual turn of contemporary ethnography – the propensity to look *at* the text rather than through it – is highly relevant to marketing. It is relevant, not simply because ethnographic methods are now in widespread academic use (Arnould and Price 1993; Arnold and Wallendorf 1994; Groves and Belk 1995; M. C. Martin and Baker 1996), nor because it is aligned with the linguistic inclination that is apparent throughout the social sciences (Rosenau 1992; Doherty *et al.* 1992; Hollinger 1994; Geertz 1995). It is relevant because it requires us to attend to the rhetorical nature of *all* published marketing discourse (Holbrook 1995a). It reminds us that the 'correct' mode of academic address – third person, past tense, passive voice, sparsely written, devoid of literary pretension – is a rhetorical convention in itself. It is, admittedly, a styleless style, an artless art, an anti-rhetoric rhetoric, an attempt to plane plain prose that bespeaks rigour, objectivity and methodological rectitude, and whose very flatness flatters to deceive by the illusion of allusionlessness. It remains, nevertheless, a mode – *one mode* – of academic exposition, a perpetual illustration of the fact that, with an intertextual nod to Kotler and Levy (1969), the choice is not whether to rhetorize or not to rhetorize, for none of us can avoid rhetoric; the choice is whether to do it well or poorly. As Geertz so cogently observes:

> To argue . . . that the writing of ethnography involves telling stories, making pictures, concocting symbolisms and deploying tropes is commonly resisted, often fiercely, because of a confusion, endemic in the west since Plato at least, of the imagined with the imaginary, the fictional with the false, making things out with making them up. The strange idea that reality has an idiom in which it prefers to be described, that its very nature demands we talk about it without fuss – a spade is a spade, a rose is a rose – on pain of illusion, trumpery, and self-bewitchment, leads on to the even stranger idea that, if literalism is lost, so is fact . . . This can't be right.
>
> (Geertz 1988: 140)

Everybody else is doing it, so why can't we?

Few among us would gainsay the fact that very real benefits flow from adopting a more expressive approach to marketing scholarship – realignment with practitioners, academic respectability and rhetorical self-awareness. However, I have found in my missionary work among the dispossessed of marketing science (it's pathetic to see them huddled in doorways, with that desperate-for-a-fix-of-factor-analysis look in their addled eyes, surrounded by discarded, cheap and dirty data syringes . . .) that the old 'we are not worthy' objection tends to rear its ugly head. As mere marketing academics, they counter, we can't possibly write as well as literary types and to try to do so inevitably invites unflattering comparisons. Just as we are deeply embarrassed by regional television and cinema advertisements when viewed alongside the glossy products of Charlotte Square or Madison Avenue (you know, for the local restaurant/night club/massage parlour only a few minutes walk from this movie theatre, which we immediately vow never, *ever* to patronize), so too our literary endeavours are bound to be deemed doggerel at best and catastrophic at worst. The most sensible strategy in these circumstances is to stick to our unpretentious, uncontentious, inoffensive lasts, to seek safety in numbers, to attain visibility through invisibility and to aspire to the dizzy heights of mediocrity, the pedestrian peaks, even though we know – and know we know – that the author function can't be obviated or circumvented. As postmodernists, of course, we can attempt to play our personal get-out-of-jail-free card (where would we be without the death of the author?), thereby avoiding responsibility for what we write, temporarily at least, but whichever way you look at it, no matter how much of a gloss we put on it, and with the very best will in the world, we simply can't avoid or evade the burden of authorship, heavy though it is in our writerly postmodern times.

There is no doubt that, when it comes to writing, the majority of marketing academics aren't in the same league as 'real' authors. One only has to compare D. Rose's (1995) recent 35–page meditation on a shampoo bottle with Alan Coren's scintillating 800-word summary of his perplexing Saturday morning shopping trip to Boots the Chemist (S. Brown 1995a: 100) to appreciate that the former, by any other name, would still not smell as sweet as the Sage of Cricklewood. Is there a single paper in the entire marketing literature to compare with Gilbert Adair's (1993) paean to Polos, Crunchies, Toblerones and the metaphorical whirl of confectionery? I think not. Can any academic history of advertising and branding compete with Bill Bryson's (1995) wonderfully witty and worldly-wise synopsis? The answer, I suspect, is no. Insightful though they are, however, the problem with 'proper' authors is that they can't be relied upon to deal with issues that we marketing academics find interesting. Sadly, the stages theory of internationalization, Ansoff's product–market matrix, the marketing planning process and the perils of penetration pricing have not inspired works of literature that call down the years. And, when they do – as in the case of Jeffery Archer's (1991) spin on the wheel of retailing – you rather wish they hadn't, since not every 'proper' author can comment meaningfully upon marketplace phenomena.

By the same token, not every marketing academic is automatically inferior to his or her 'literary' counterparts. On the contrary, there are a number of superb stylists in the marketing community, authors whose work stands comparison with any creative writer. I would submit, for example, that Belk's (1996b) imaginative excursus public holidays in the twenty-first century (St Johnny Walker Day, Feast of the Seven-Eleven, etc.) is not only as good as, but more tautly written than, David Foster Wallace's (1996) recent, highly acclaimed novel *Infinite Jest*, in which the calendar is sponsored by participating organizations. Ted Levitt's (1960) deathless exordium on the marketing concept may be utterly abrogated – not least by the teRMites, for whom it must now represent a transactional heresy of monstrous proportions – but, from its opening allusion to time's cycle to its concluding neo-Nietzschean peroration to the *Übermensch* of marketing, it remains a truly astounding work of literature. When Morris Holbrook eschews his normal inclination to explain *everything* (just in case some of the sluggards among the readership don't get it) or overpower the unconvinced with an unnecessary blizzard of argument-bolstering citations, he reveals himself to be a writer of quite extraordinary ability. His piece on 'loving and hating New York' – clearly one from the heart – is staggering in its brilliance (Holbrook 1994b), a worthy postmodern successor to Levitt's modern marketing classic. Even Shelby Hunt, for all his faults (Yes, I know I described Motto as a modernist in Chapter 3 – what do you expect from me, consistency?), has a certain stylistic *je ne sais quoi*. It is, I grant you, an uncouth, lumpen and – how can I put this? – somewhat Wild-Westian *je ne sais quoi*. Yet, like the cheap music of legend, it is undeniably potent. Best of all, however, is Bob Grafton Small (1993, 1995, 1997), whose elegant little essays on the detritus of consumer culture are the nearest thing to poetry in the marketing canon (as opposed, that is, to the braggadocio of the 'here's a haiku I wrote earlier' mob). True, his take-it-or-leave-it-I'm-not-going-to-explain-the-message-to-you approach means that Grafton Small is perhaps the most unsung exponent of the latter-day literary turn; but he remains the Clifford Geertz of marketing scholarship.

If it's not lack of ability that prevents marketers from abandoning their aesthetic self-abasement and adopting a more stylish mode of academic expression, then what is it? Why, to paraphrase the literary theorist Mary Louise Pratt (1986: 33), do such interesting people, doing such interesting things, in such an interesting domain, produce such dull books and articles? For many leading authorities, the answer is that they are impeded by the iniquities of the peer review process. While some might say that this I-would-do-it-if-I-could-but-I-can't-because-they-won't-let-me excuse is pretty feeble, nothing less than a classic case of bad workers blaming their tools, there is no doubt that few issues in academic life generate as much discussion, debate and, let's be honest, rancour as peer review. It constantly impinges on our day-to-day activities and, in its manifold manifestations, looms large over our career aspirations – job references, grant applications, promotion prospects or, most frequently of all, in the judgement that is passed on our research output. We are all familiar with the palpitations induced by a glimpse of the journal's distinctive 'decision' envelope; the temporary loss of motor functions we experience on attempting to unsheathe the letter that seals our fate; the bitter tears of disappointment as our superhuman efforts are swept aside in a few acerbic and ill-informed sentences; and, on occasion, the overwhelming sense of relief, swiftly followed by punch-the-air euphoria, when we have been anointed by the wise and perspicacious reviewers of our chosen communication channel, the scholarly standing of which has suddenly been elevated to a level beyond the journal editor's wildest dreams (S. Brown 1995f).

When the emotions of the moment have subsided, however, most of us have paused to reflect on the arbitrary charade that is the peer review process. After all, we *know* that reviewers are capricious, inconsistent and motivated by personal animosity, professional jealousy and a narrow-minded conviction that their preferred research approach is incontestable (Table 5.1). What's more we have a pretty good idea who they are and, by Christ, we'll make them pay for it! We also *know* that journal editors are a repellent bunch of self-serving, self-satisfied self-abusers who, despite all our attempts at insinuation, are hopelessly biased towards submissions from their own institution and the old-boy, mutual back-scratching, motley crew of fellow editors. They simply don't have room for papers from uninfluential nonentities, the likes of you and me, and they conspire to send our manuscripts to the reviewers most inclined to kill them off or – mixed metaphor ahoy – kick them safely into touch whilst plagiarizing our insights and beating us to the punch. Most importantly perhaps, our convictions concerning the peer review farrago are confirmed by the fact that our *very best work* is inexplicably but invariably rejected, whereas our second-rate knock-offs, the iffy papers we consider unworthy of publication but thought we'd try our luck because you never can tell, proceed to sail through the refereeing procedure with nary an adverse remark!

Table 5.1 Hey, Joe, where you goin' with that gun in your hand?

Lesson One: *War is Hell*. The first and by far the most important thing to realise about reviewing for journals, is that it is a battle to the death. There's a lot of stuff and nonsense talked about collegiality, mutual support, self-sacrifice, the community of scholars, 'it's a far, far better thing I do' and the like. Indeed, it has actually been said, though I find it much too improbable to be true, that some naive researchers have been taken in by – they actually *believe* – this tissue of misinformation and propaganda, which has been put about by generations of unscrupulous academics. They probably also believe in Father Christmas, the

Table 5.1 Contd.

---

tooth fairy and that if you wish upon a star your dreams come true. Tempting though it is to exploit such touching credulity – though, as you know, I'm not that sort of person – it is time to grow up and get real. Academic life in general and the peer review process in particular is a battlefield, a theatre of war, where the objective is to win, to humiliate your opponents, to destroy everything that stands in your path and to put everyone, even your closest colleagues (especially your closest colleagues!) to the sword. Show no mercy, grant no quarter, brook no opposition, take no prisoners. Wage total war. Do or die. Exterminate, exterminate, exterminate. And remember at all times the three golden rules of reviewing: (1) if in doubt about the academic worth of a manuscript – reject; (2) if in no doubt about the academic worth of a manuscript – reject; and (3) if absolutely certain about the academic worth of a manuscript – reject. Get it?, got it?, good!

Lesson Two: *Railway Timetables*. Just as certain gullible individuals still subscribe to the egalitarian and congenial ideals of the Academy – we call them 'cannon fodder' in the peer reviewing trenches – so too some rookie researchers imagine that success in the art of academic warfare depends on brute strength, the big battalions, heavy intellectual weapons or copious cerebral resources. Not a bit of it. Victorious scholarly campaigning boils down to logistics, to railway timetables, to getting access to the journals, to being appointed as a reviewer and to exploiting this strategic position with extreme prejudice. Journal editors, as a rule, are an 'orrible shower, a sorry bunch of losers, who in normal circumstances wouldn't be permitted to clean, let alone enter, the officers' mess. They are, however, contractually committed to producing a certain number of issues per year and, as a consequence, they need papers, they need reviewers and, above all, they are desperate for *prompt* reviewers. Response time, in short, is the key to victory. Most academics groan when another batch of long-winded manuscripts hits the desk and the offending material is ignored until such times as the editor's pathetic begging letters start to arrive. An immediate response, by contrast, endears you to the greasy deadbeats, who are eternally grateful for not having to debase themselves for once, and they invariably come back for more, and more . . . and more. Eventually, you are elevated to star reviewer status, they become totally dependent upon you and, not least, the slimy reptiles boast about you to the other denizens of the editorial snake pit. Then the next nonentity gets in touch, and the next, and then, before you know it, you are ready for war. The scent of victory – the smell of napalm in the morning – is already in your nostrils. The battle is over before it has begun.

Lesson Three: *Forging Alliances*. Clearly, the long-term aim of the peer reviewing campaign is to win outright, to be the last academic left standing on the battlefield. However, in order to attain this ultimate objective, it is necessary to

Table 5.1 Contd.

appreciate that it can't be achieved immediately and, more to the point, that you can't do it on your own. Editors may be the most inept generals this side of the Great War, but forging and maintaining alliances with them is imperative if you wish to deny your enemies access to the journals. Now, whereas you and I know that most editors deserve to be court-martialled for dereliction of duty, they like to think of themselves as sagacious and prescient leaders in their field, who are open new ideas and radical experimentation. Hence, if you succumb to your perfectly natural inclination to torpedo every paper in sight, they pigeon-hole you as a 'hard reviewer' and the flow of manuscripts slowly but inexorably dries up. The scenario planning and ballistics people inform me that the best way of dealing with this situation is a calibrated rejection ratio, where you endeavour to be quite generous and supportive – to begin with. As the editors become increasingly reliant on your expeditious reviews, you progressively increase the rejection ratio until you have pushed them as far as they will go. In this regard, watch out for the subtle warning signs, such as a little note which laughably asks you to go easy on a paper by an academic newcomer. When this happens, make a tactical withdrawal, collaborate with them for a while and then continue the build-up, the preparations for war.

Lesson Four: *Basic Training*. Some people are born sadistic and others have sadism thrust upon them. Regardless of whether you are one of the lucky few 'naturals' or, like most of us, find your reviewing skills forged in the crucible of battle, preparation and training remain of paramount importance. I'm sure you don't need to be reminded of the manuscript reviewing basics, but the key to survival is very, very simple – never, repeat never, read the paper. To do so not only wastes valuable time, which can be better spent 'reviewing' all the other manuscripts in your bulging pending tray, but it also runs the risk that you might actually like what you see and, in your misplaced enthusiasm, recommend immediate acceptance without alteration. True, such is the vapidity of most marketing research that this is only the most remote of outside possibilities, but even if the manuscript *is* readable and, perish the thought, publishable, why deny yourself the pleasure of tormenting your antagonists with a few gratuitous insults and cavalier amendments? Take every opportunity to sap their strength, weaken their resolve, undermine their morale or, at the very least, frustrate and irritate them with every delaying tactic you can muster. That said, it is necessary to give the editor and, on certain occasions, the author, the *impression* that you have read the paper, though this is easily achieved with a quick scan to pick up a few misplaced commas, minor grammatical errors or, manna from Heaven, a missing reference or two. If the worst comes to the worst, read the abstract and possibly the concluding paragraph, but try not to make a habit of it.

Table 5.1 Contd.

Lesson Five: *Discipline and Punish*. Having mastered the art of ignoring the content whilst retaining the support of the editor, another important psychological issue often raises its ugly head – an extremely dangerous amalgam of arrogance, boastfulness and overconfidence. As you advance rapidly through the academic ranks and your enemies are as chaff beneath your chariot wheels, it is easy to become slothful, self-important and erroneously convinced of your invulnerability. Remember at all times that the mighty are forever falling, that you are dealing with devious individuals, many of whom are highly skilled in the art of war and are more than capable of slipping a surreptitious paper through your 'impregnable' defences, if you're not careful. Beware, therefore, of all references to your own work (that means they have worked out in advance who the referee is likely to be, or, after reading your first set of remarks, who in fact you are). Don't fall for their asinine compliments, most notably acknowledging the 'helpful comments' of anonymous referees (this means that they can't quite decide who it is). And, above all, laugh in the face of any transparently obvious attempts at ingratiation (return unsolicited manuscripts unopened and ignore all pleas for assistance, especially from first-time authors, PhD students or analogous parasites). If you find your resolve weakening and your iron discipline starting to rust, do as I do and revert to a regime of solitary confinement, cold baths, bread and water, bed of nails, electrodes on the testicles and a hand-cranked battery. Remember, however, that it is possible to have too much of a good thing; so, no more than a few days furlough before returning to the fray.

Lesson Six: *Strategy and Tactics*. After establishing an alliance with that mob of unspeakables in pursuit of the unpublishable and having gone through the agonies and ecstasies of basic training, the next, and by any reckoning one of the most crucial lessons, concerns battlefield strategy and tactics. The all-important rule – the absolute and guaranteed secret of success – is knowing your enemy. The question, in short, of whether you are facing new recruits or battle-hardened veterans. It almost goes without saying that new recruits with freshly minted PhDs are comparatively easily dispatched. As they have invariably lived fairly sheltered lives, often subscribe to idealistic nonsense concerning the community of scholars and have absolutely no notion that war is hell, a review consisting of several savage sentences unfailingly saps their very will to live. They don't like it up 'em and a swift rattle of the bayonets, coupled with a rebel yell or two, is usually sufficient to have them begging for mercy and running from the field in disarray. Frontal assaults of this kind, however, do *not* work with battle-hardened veterans. On the contrary, if you go over the top by expressing extreme hostility to their endeavours, they invariably cry foul to the editor and, disastrously, may succeed in switching his or her allegiance. Lily-livered renegades to a man,

Table 5.1 Contd.

editorial cowardice in the face of the enemy is only to be expected, but if they decide to change sides the long-term implications can be disastrous. Particular care must also be taken when fighting on unfamiliar terrain, since the slightest slip-up in your referee's report – such as misattributing a key reference – allows the author to challenge your authority by complaining to the editor about unknowledgeable reviewers. The upshot is that you have not only lost the battle, you may well have lost the war in that particular theatre of operations.

Lesson Seven: *Feints and Manoeuvres*. When forced into a head-to-head confrontation with individuals skilled in the art of academic warfare or find yourself campaigning in uncharted intellectual territory, the trick is to feint and manoeuvre. One option is to suggest that while the manuscript under review contains much of merit, it fails to refer to a highly pertinent body of literature. Cite a couple of obscurantist French philosophers – Jacques Lacan is always good value – and if your opponent is foolhardy enough to track the material down or, even better, seeks to understand or incorporate it, you can rest assured that you're unlikely to see a revised version of the manuscript before 1999 at the earliest. Another possibility is to play the psychological warfare card by disrupting the author's culturally engrained expectations. Thus, for example, as most American academics are used to receiving long, detailed and broadly supportive referees' comments, a short, sharp shock to the system can prove extremely effective. British academics, by contrast, are perfectly familiar with a few surly paragraphs and the sight of scholarly blood. Therefore, give them five pages of hell, a bombardment so heavy that they will be too shell-shocked ever to contemplate anything other than raising the white flag of surrender. Yet another possibility is to fight dirty by scrutinising and criticising every tiny detail of the research and, after the authors have written a thirty page letter explaining the rationale behind their twenty page manuscript, concoct a completely different set of concerns. String them along like this for a couple of 'rounds' and, when they have successfully responded to everything you asked for and more, simply conclude that, on reflection, the paper's subject matter is inappropriate for the journal. So traumatic is the impact of this particular tactic that grown men have been known to burst into tears and apply for a immediate medical discharge. Meanwhile, you can revel in the realisation that yet more of your mortal enemies have unceremoniously bitten the dust.

Lesson Eight: *Early Warning Systems*. Now, some might argue that while any number of feints and manoeuvres are available, the double blind review process serves as an effective smoke-screen between our adversaries and ourselves. If we don't know who they are, how can we possibly decide on the most appropriate tactics to deploy? The answer to this is perfectly obvious – careful reconnaissance. Indeed, if you are capable of recognising the tell-tale signs,

Table 5.1 Contd.

---

everything you need to know about an author is contained in the manuscript concerned. An effective rule of thumb is that the longer the list of references, the less experienced the researcher (tyro academics have to demonstrate their credentials, after all). A list with a lot of self-citation – i.e. the least well-known name has the greatest single number of references – is invariably an assistant professor (no one else mentions their papers, so they have to do it themselves). Be on your guard, however, whenever you encounter a short list of references with no obvious signs of self-promotion. You're dealing with a lean, mean, fighting machine and, unless you're feeling lucky or want to make someone's day, simply let them pass. If, on the other hand, you discover that a disciplinary heavyweight is serving as reviewer for one of your own manuscripts, do everything in your power to flush them out of the undergrowth. Goading them into a comment and rejoinder exchange practically guarantees victory since, in time-honoured David versus Goliath tradition, the onlookers are automatically on your side. Not only do the giants of the discipline have more to lose, but the very fact that they deign to descend to your level goes some way towards elevating you to theirs.

Lesson Nine: *Defensive Emplacements*. Constant vigilance, it must be emphasised, is not confined to offensive situations or opportunist guerrilla raids on the great and good. Certain defensive positions necessitate guard duty of the highest calibre. Prominent among these is the conference circuit, where it often proves necessary to 'circle the wagons'. You will find that as your reviewing star rises, journal editors will attempt to grab your attention and, as often as not, impose upon you with their conscientious objector propaganda. The golden rule of these admittedly loathsome personal encounters is always to agree with what they say. Under no circumstances contradict any opinion they express about papers presented at the conference. To do so suggests that you fail to share the editor's impeccable intellectual taste, precipitates the conclusion that he or she was wrong about you all along and word soon gets out that you are not 'one of us'. Remember: careless talk costs lives. Another extremely dangerous situation is the ambush, the almost inevitable invitation to act as guest editor, or even editor, of an academic journal. Make no mistake, this bait is extremely tempting, not least because it raises the prospect of offloading some of your own unpublishable pieces (naturally, you'll say, my own manuscript went through the full rigours of the refereeing procedure – of course it did!), but the upshot of entering such a valley of academic death is that, mixed metaphor notwithstanding, the tables are irrevocably turned. As *you* now require contributors, reviewers and the like, *you* are hopelessly dependent upon other academics, the very combatants *you* set out to destroy. Incidently, if you do get entrapped in this manner, do *not* seek the support of colleagues at your own institution. Never, as they say, end up fighting on two fronts.

Table 5.1 Contd.

Lesson Ten: *Covert Operations*. If you have absorbed all of the foregoing lessons, you have nothing or no one to fear. As a finely honed exponent of the art of academic warfare, you are perfectly capable of developing all manner of personalised manoeuvres that should stand you in very good stead when the pounding is heavy and the hand-to-hand combat is at its most ferocious. My own signature stratagem is a sort of intellectual enfilade (raking fire from end to end) which involves returning the (unreviewed) manuscript with a short comment to the effect that, although it is a worthy albeit imperfect contribution, the paper may not cohere with the overall objectives of the journal. This effectively kills four birds with the one stone in that it (a) sends a subtle 'reject' message which even the dullest of editors can decode; (b) means that I didn't actually spurn the manuscript myself, thereby adversely affecting my carefully calibrated rejection ratio; (c) implies that by my refusal to pass judgement I am a worthy scholarly citizen interested solely in the disinterested pursuit of marketing knowledge; and (d) it flatters the editor – thereby adding to my reviewing duties – by suggesting that his filthy rag actually has a set of overall objectives in the first place. In conclusion, however, let me just mention that I have several other deadly arrows in my peer reviewing quiver, not least the possibility that this entire table is a tissue of misinformation and which, if acted upon, is liable to alienate you from journal editors everywhere, thereby denying you access to positions of influence and leaving more manuscripts for me. But, hey, what sort of marketing academic do you take me for? I wouldn't do that to you! You can trust me . . . honest.

Source: S. Brown 1995f: 702–6

Given the prominent place peer review occupies in the academic imagination, it is not surprising that the issue has attracted an enormous amount of research attention. Since its inception in the seventeenth century this regulatory mechanism has been subject to periodic scrutiny, though, thanks largely to the pioneering analyses of R. K. Merton, a flourishing subdiscipline devoted to the study of peer review now exists (Chubin and Hackett 1990; Rennie 1990; Daniel 1993; Cummings and Frost 1995). Conducted in scientific fields as diverse as economics, criminology, astrophysics and biochemistry, the results of these investigations are remarkably consistent. They reveal that referees are unreliable, in so far as the degree of agreement between different reviewers of the same manuscript is very low indeed (Marsh and Ball 1989). By highlighting, moreover, that manuscripts rejected by the leading journals often turn out to be the ones with the greatest long–term influence, such exercises demonstrate that reviewers' judgements are both invalid and unsound (Bornstein 1991). More disconcertingly still, they have served to expose the manifold biases that inhere in and taint this supposedly objective procedure. These include the author's rank (professors do better than postdocs), gender (patriarchy prevails), nationality (non-nationals and, especially, third-world authors need not apply), institutional affiliation (striking 'in-house' concentrations have been observed), the nature of their findings (those that support the preconceived opinions of the reviewers are more favourably treated) and, above all, his or her professional standing (well-known academics are much more likely to be published than the mediocrities). The last of these biases is known as the Matthew Effect, after the famous passage in the Gospel According to St Matthew, 'for whosoever hath, to him shall be given, and he shall have more abundance; but whosoever hath not, from him shall be taken away, even that he hath' (Merton 1968, 1988).

In light of such devastating findings it seems reasonable to conclude that the whole reviewing process is hopelessly compromised and should be dispensed with entirely. Not only is the so-called 'double-blind' review process a transparent veil – almost 80 per cent of reviewers, for example, claim to be able to recognize the authors' identity – but this pseudo-anonymity also prompts reviewers to be *more* critical than they would otherwise be (Ceci and Peters 1984). The system, as Daniel (quoting Kornhuber) points out, is 'unreliable, invalid and harmful to the best type of research – that which is innovative' (Daniel 1993: 3). Indeed, some commentators have called for its complete abandonment (Mahoney 1985) and several reputable academic periodicals have eschewed blind review or opted for a battery of potential-bias-reducing procedures – formalizing the reviewing instrument, involving authors in reviewer selection, eliminating reviewer anonymity, increasing the number of reviewers, establishing a right of appeal and so on (S. Brown 1995f).

Although the irredeemably tainted peer review system has been responsible for much weeping, wailing and gnashing of teeth within the academic marketing community (e.g. Holbrook 1986b, 1994c, 1995c; AMA Task Force 1988; Churchill 1988; Hubbard 1995; McDonagh 1995b), and although all manner of improvements have been suggested – signed reviews, editorial leadership, explicit statements concerning innovation and, my personal favourite, the triple-blind review, where the author closes his or her eyes before attaching their name to the paper, thereby ensuring that they too are ignorant of the source (Belk 1996c) – I am not entirely convinced that tinkering at the edges will make a great deal of difference. As Foucault (1980b) explains, every discipline disciplines the discourses within it, out of fear that new or aberrant discourses might disrupt the contours of the subject area.

It is just as if prohibitions, barriers, thresholds and limits had been set up in order to master, at least partly, the great proliferation of discourse, in order to remove from its richness the most dangerous part, and in order to organize its disorder according to figures which dodge what is most uncontrollable about it.

(Foucault 1970: 66)

Hence, the peer review system, adversarial, iniquitous and sado-masochistic though it undoubtedly is, is as much a symptom of the styleless-style problem as a cause of it. Peer review and the associated tenure-tracking process (which encourages people to produce 'publishable' output) merely exaggerate, perpetuate and, to some extent, codify the fact that the academic paper is a distinctive literary genre and, like all genres, is characterized by certain norms, forms, rules, expectations, customs, practices, devices, procedures – discursive formations, if you will – which are very difficult to modify, let alone revolutionize.

Genre, according to Palmer, 'is the French term commonly used to indicate that texts can be sorted into groups which have common characteristics' (1992: 112). As exemplified by the standard shelf-markings in most bookshops – crime, romance, war, fantasy, travel, etc. – we are all conscious of and familiar with literary genres even though the majority of us give them very little thought (Figures 5.1 and 5.2). After all, the bulk of our mass-mediated experiences come wrapped in some form of generic packaging – television game shows, soap operas and situation comedies; cowboy, spy and horror films; country and western, heavy metal and acid house music; and, lookalike advertisements for beer, shampoo and washing powder. Although the study of genre is often dated to Aristotle's *Poetics*, with its tripartite distinction between tragedy, comedy and epic literary forms, it is only within the past forty years, and the clision of the traditional division between élite and popular culture, that genre has emerged as a separate field of academic study (Perloff 1989; Todorov 1990; Berger 1992). Like most academic specialisms, genre studies is beset by all manner of competing conceptual frameworks. Distinctions, for example, are often made between 'theoretical' and 'historical' genres (Todorov 1970), 'enunciative situation' and 'subject matter' (Schaeffer 1989) and the manifold loci of literary meaning – the unconscious, capitalism, reader response and the like (see Frye 1971; Cawelti 1976; Palmer 1992).

For our present purposes, however, it is sufficient to note that genres work in two closely related ways, described by Berger (1992) as being akin to figure and ground. First, they provide a 'horizon of expectations', a framework or schema within which individual works are placed and interpreted. Thus, if we recognize a text

Figure 5.1 Simply the Beth, better than all the rest

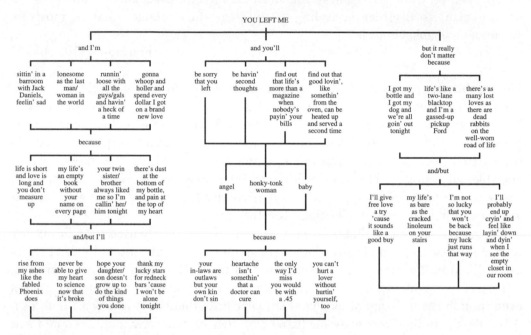

Source: Berger 1992; original by Larry Tritten

as belonging to the category 'situation comedy', 'film noir', 'sword and sorcery novel' or whatever, we come to it with certain pre-formed expectations derived from our previous experiences with the category in question. Second, genre functions as a norm, a set of unwritten and ill-defined rules which apply to individual works and which, if flouted, result in confusion and rejection. Radway's (1987) renowned study of romantic fiction readers, for example, found that the novels deemed disappointing or unrewarding were invariably those that failed to adhere to the norms of the form. Similarly, a blues song which follows 'well I woke up this morning' with 'in my 36-bedroom mansion' or 'and I'd won the National Lottery' is likely to be less appealing to aficionados of the genre than 'with a hell-hound on my trail' or 'and my baby done left me'.

Set against the need to provide readers with a sense of the familiar, genre theory emphasizes that it is necessary to introduce sufficient variety and innovation to maintain the audience's interest. In this respect, Cawelti (1971) distinguishes between the need for 'convention' and 'invention'. The former ensures than an

Figure 5.2   Ba·ba·ba·ba·Bagozzi

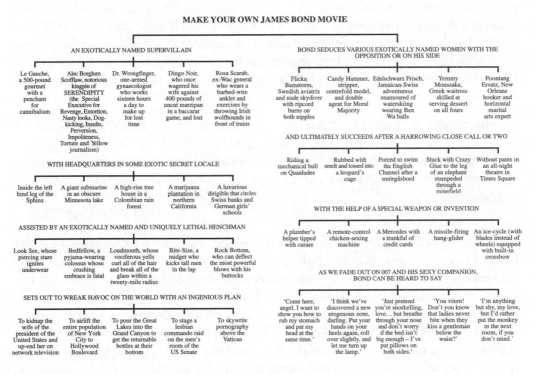

MAKE YOUR OWN JAMES BOND MOVIE

AN EXOTICALLY NAMED SUPERVILLAIN

Le Gauche, a 500-pound gourmet with a penchant for cannibalism	Alec Borglum Scofflaw, notorious kingpin of SERENDIPITY (the Special Executive for Revenge, Extortion, Nasty looks, Dog-kicking, Insults, Perversion, Impoliteness, Torture and Yellow journalism)	Dr. Wrongfinger, one-armed gynaecologist who works sixteen hours a day to make up for lost time	Dingo Noir, who once wagered his wife against 400 pounds of uncut marzipan in a baccarat game, and lost	Rosa Scarab, ex-Wac general who wears a barbed-wire anklet and exercises by throwing Irish wolfhounds in front of trains

BOND SEDUCES VARIOUS EXOTICALLY NAMED WOMEN WITH THE OPPOSITION OR ON HIS SIDE

Flicka Bamstorm, Swedish aviatrix and nude skydiver with ripcord burns on both nipples	Candy Hammer, stripper, centrefold model, and double agent for Moral Majority	Edelschwarz Frisch, Jamaican-Swiss adventuress enamoured of waterskiing wearing Ben Wa balls	Yemmy Moussaka, Greek waitress skilled at serving dessert on all fours	Poontang Ersatz, New Orleans hooker and horizontal marital arts expert

WITH HEADQUARTERS IN SOME EXOTIC SECRET LOCALE

Inside the left hind leg of the Sphinx	A giant submarine in an obscure Minnesota lake	A high-rise tree house in a Colombian rain forest	A marijuana plantation in northern California	A luxurious dirigible that circles Swiss banks and German girls' schools

AND ULTIMATELY SUCCEEDS AFTER A HARROWING CLOSE CALL OR TWO

Riding a mechanical bull on Quaaludes	Rubbed with smelt and tossed into a leopard's cage	Forced to swim the English Channel after a smörgåsbord	Stuck with Crazy Glue to the leg of an elephant stampeded through a minefield	Without pants in an all-night theatre in Times Square

ASSISTED BY AN EXOTICALLY NAMED AND UNIQUELY LETHAL HENCHMAN

Look See, whose piercing stare ignites underwear	Bedfellow, a pyjama-wearing colossus whose crushing embrace is fatal	Loudmouth, whose vociferous yells curl all of the hair and break all of the glass within a twenty-mile radius	Bite-Size, a midget who kicks tall men in the lap	Rock Bottom, who can deflect the most powerful blows with his buttocks

WITH THE HELP OF A SPECIAL WEAPON OR INVENTION

A plumber's helper tipped with curare	A remote-control chicken-sexing machine	A Mercedes with a trunkful of credit cards	A missile-firing hang-glider	An ice-cycle (with blades instead of wheels) equipped with built-in crossbow

SETS OUT TO WREAK HAVOC ON THE WORLD WITH AN INGENIOUS PLAN

To kidnap the wife of the president of the United States and up-end her on network television	To airlift the entire population of New York City to Hollywood Boulevard	To pour the Great Lakes into the Grand Canyon to get the returnable bottles at their bottom	To stage a lesbian commando raid on the men's room of the US Senate	To skywrite pornography above the Vatican

AS WE FADE OUT ON 007 AND HIS SEXY COMPANION, BOND CAN BE HEARD TO SAY

'Come here, angel. I want to show you how to rub my stomach and pat my head at the same time.'	'I think we've discovered a new erogenous zone, darling. Put your hands on your heels again, roll over slightly, and let me turn up the lamp.'	'Just pretend you're snorkelling, love... but breathe through your nose and don't worry if the bed isn't big enough – I've put pillows on both sides.'	'You vixen! Don't you know that ladies never bite when they kiss a gentleman below the waist?'	'I'm anything but shy, my love, but I'd rather put the monkey in the next room, if you don't mind.'

Source: Berger 1992, original by Larry Tritten

individual text falls into a familiar and recognizable category, while the latter provides the surprise, whether it be in terms of form or content (or both), which elevates a particularly successful text above its copious competitors, the also-rans of the genre. These inventions, in turn, serve to shape the readership's extant horizon of expectations – the rules of the game – which is explored and tested by subsequent textual contributions, and so the genre evolves. To be sure, works of high culture are usually associated with the 'invention' end of the literary spectrum, whereas works of low culture are often dismissed as 'convention'-bound. However, as Palmer (1992) observes, even prior to the postmodern elision of high and low, a dialectic of order and novelty, similarity and difference, identity and opposition was discernible in numerous artistic fields, both élite and popular (Lotman 1975).

In light of the foregoing, it takes a very small leap of the imagination to appreciate that the academic paper is also a very distinctive literary genre and can be studied accordingly. Thus, a recent close reading of the published output of physical scientists reveals how they make full and frequent use of ostensibly 'literary' devices, from irony and cacophony to metaphor and parody (Locke 1992). In fact, a number of longitudinal literary analyses of scientific journals have been undertaken, including several informed by the principles of genre theory (Bazerman 1988; Selzer 1993; Halliday and Martin 1993), leading Locke to conclude that:

> the papers of the scientist are the most formulaic of writings; their rigidly prescribed patterns put the generic conventions of the western or the detective story to shame. A glance through a scientific journal reveals paper after paper with identical patterns of organisation, often precisely the same headings.

(Locke 1992: 168)

If the published output of the physical sciences has proved amenable to genre-based interpretations, and the published record of 'hard' social sciences, such as economics, has proved equally susceptible (e.g. McCloskey 1985, 1990, 1994), it seems reasonable to conclude that the endeavours of marketing academics are ripe for analyses predicated on genre theory. True, as postmodernists, you may prefer to examine the genre of genre theory – the extent to which explications of genre theory are themselves genre-bound – but one only has to peruse a few back issues of any of our discipline's principal journals to appreciate that the papers adhere to a clearly discernible set of conventions concerning content, form, sequencing, language and protocol. Most of us, for example, can recite the 'typical' structure of an academic marketing paper in our sleep (indeed, many of us have been put to sleep by authors' rigid adherence to the 'rules'). We all know, as noted earlier, that writing in a neutral, disinterested, pseudo-scientific fashion is *de rigueur*, that it is necessary to bolster our claims with an appreciation of the existing body of literature and the positioning of our contributions therein, and, not least, that it is imperative to conclude with some suitably vague allusion to 'managerial implications', even though no manager in their right mind is ever likely to read our pearls of wisdom or, heaven forfend, proceed to act upon our recommendations.

There is more to genre theory, however, than the application of its principles to myriad modes of marketing literature – textbooks, working papers, literature reviews, monographs, consultancy reports, PhD theses – and the differences that exist among various sub-fields of the discipline. Genre theory contains some very important lessons for marketing scholarship in general and the peer review circus in particular. Perhaps the most obvious of these is that failure to conform to the norms of the form invites immediate, unceremonious rejection. The expectations of the readership, shaped by their prior experiences with the genre, are extremely difficult to violate successfully. Indeed, as these are reinforced, not to say 'policed', by the associated institutional apparatus – peer review, tenure-tracking, self-censure (safety first), publishers who expect marketing textbooks to look like marketing textbooks, students taught to recognize certain types of work as works of marketing scholarship and, not least, the conventions of 'normal science' – the forces ranged against radical change are very great, almost insurmountable. This does not mean that iconoclastic papers or heretical opinions are unpublishable – far from it – but they are well-nigh unpublishable in the most prestigious outlets and tend to be relegated to the disciplinary badlands (edited volumes, conference proceedings, book reviews and anything by Haworth Press). As the very existence of these vehicles serves to vent some aggression, thereby sustaining the conservatism of mainstream journals, all the huffing and puffing by editors (we need more innovative papers), maltreated authors (especially when the most vocal critics, such as Morris Holbrook, are among the most published figures in the field) and attempts to modify the peer review system, are unlikely to have much of an impact.

Another, closely related but often overlooked, point is that there is a positive side to formulaic works of marketing scholarship. It is easy to be dismissive of 'lookalike' papers, but the conventions of the genre play an important function, in so far as they provide a frame of reference. The existence of guidelines, however tacit or ill defined, makes the writing task much less demanding than it already is, particularly for inexperienced researchers. Few of us, after all, spring fully armed from the scholarly soil, and it is only reasonable to expect that our intellectual apprenticeships will result in hackneyed and derivative manuscripts. We all have experience of trying to explain to our students 'what a dissertation should look like' and, when that fails, of steering them towards the voluminous literature on 'how to write up a research project'. Even as seasoned academics, what is more, we prefer to write within a comparatively stable generic context, in the belief that what we write continues to qualify as academic writing, that the rules of the game haven't changed while we were conducting our five-year programme of longitudinal research. For many people, then, the costs of radical change are greater than the benefits, even though this results in tedious, derivative, unimaginative, incrementalist – call them what you will – papers, serves to stifle progress, ossifies the discipline, perpetuates the pedestrian and gives rise to a widespread sense of disillusionment and ennui. It has often been said, for example, that the secret of academic success is *not* to pick an important problem; *not* to challenge existing beliefs; *not* to obtain surprising results; *not* to use simple methods; *not* to provide full disclosure; and, an axiom I try to abide by at all times, *not* to write clearly (Armstrong 1995; Hubbard 1995).

Set against this, however, radical change can and does take place. Genres are mutable. The rules of the writing game can be and are broken. Invention *is* as important as convention. Periods of radical change, admittedly, tend to be very short-lived – the unorthodox quickly becomes the orthodox, generic conventions rapidly cohere around the new format and, you-know-what's-coming-next-but-if-I-don't-say-it-your-expectations-are-bound-to-be-confounded, the pursuit of 'normal science' soon reasserts itself after the, er, paradigm shift. Yet you only have to look through the back issues of *JM*, *JMR*, *JCR*, *JAMS* or whatever – or examine one of the many longitudinal studies of scientific journals (e.g. Bazerman 1988) – to appreciate that the contents of Category One marketing publications are markedly different from those of fifteen, thirty or forty-five years ago. As Brown so artfully observes in that spare, elegant, unadorned style we have come to know, love and occasionally comprehend:

> it is no exaggeration to state that many marketing 'classics', as they are referred to in the anthologies, would simply be unpublishable today. Although the quality of latter-day academic rhetoric may be no better – possibly worse – than that of a generation ago, the standards of marketing scholarship have increased so much in the interim that the *Journal of Marketing* no longer appears to have room for papers, like Kotler and Levy's (1969) prize-winner, of six pages and four references.
>
> (S. Brown 1995f: 691)

In these circumstances, the question has to be asked: how does change take place? If genres are rule-bound and would-be heretics or non-conformists are routinely excommunicated (literally, in that they are denied the opportunity to communicate their views), how can we account for the academic transubstantiation that manifestly transpires? Clearly, some of these changes are attributable to developments in the broader socio-economic and intellectual environments, as illustrated in Figure 5.3 (sorry about the boxes and arrows, but I wasn't responsible for them). Others, as we have noted, are undoubtedly the result of sheer boredom, a feeling that the existing formula is becoming stale and unrewarding (Skinner 1985). And yet others are due to generational effects – a thirty-year cycle in intellectual life has often been reported (Kassarjian 1994; Levy 1994b; S. Brown 1995g) – and the career trajectories of individual researchers who wish to make a meaningful mark on their field. It seems that whereas the key to academic *acceptance* is writing to the formula, the secret of *prominence* is related to writing in a radical or

Figure 5.3 Howard rain's gonna fall

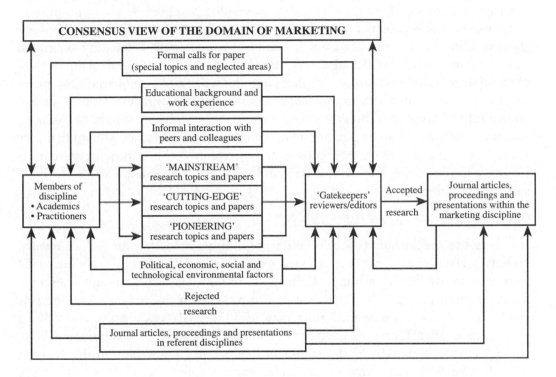

Source: adapted from Meinert *et al.* 1993

unconventional manner. Studies of seminal scientific papers, the real paradigm-displacing milestones by the likes of Crick and Watson, Einstein, Darwin or Newton, reveal that they invariably adopt a rhetorical approach that sets them apart, that differs from the prevailing norms. Indeed, one of the reasons for the initial failure of Mendel's innovative approach to genetics was on account of his decidedly conventional account of the discovery (Locke 1992). This is not to suggest that rhetoric is the be-all and end-all of intellectual innovation (nor to imply that rhetoric is confined to the written word), but it is imperative to appreciate that it is not 'mere' rhetoric either.

Nevermind

By this stage in the 'marketing-as-literature' proceedings, some of the more credulous among you may be under the impression that I have painted myself into an expositional corner. Having berated academic marketers for failing to adopt a more poetic mode of expression, having contended that peer review is a symptom not cause of this problem, and having hinted that there is an ineffable link between stylistic idiosyncrasy and academic accomplishment, surely I am duty bound to disburse some much-needed advice on best writing practice. Most of us doubt your credentials and ability to do so, Stephen, and, let's be frank, there aren't too many practitioners beating a path to your door, let alone your postmodern mousetrap, but you've told us what we should be doing, you've told us why we should be doing it, now show us *how* to do it. No, Stephen, we don't enjoy watching you squirm, we are only interested in the greater good of the discipline at this critical juncture in its history and improving our writing skills in line with your recommendations. Show and tell, remember?

Bastards!

If I were the melancholy type, I'd be deeply disappointed by your lack of loyalty, especially after what we've been through over the past 203 pages. What's more, if I were true to my literary leanings, I'd respond to your laughable attempt at entrapment by engineering a *Boy's Own*-style escape – 'with one mighty leap, he was free', kind of thing. However, I am a man of integrity (I am, *I am!*), and while I cannot deny that I have inadvertently committed myself to dispensing creative writing advice, the truth of the matter is that I don't know how to do it. I can provide you with some tips on academic paper content, most of which you're already aware of (Table 5.2). I've got a couple of spare 'peel me a grape, Philip' catch phrases, which you're more than welcome to (anyone for 'beam me up, Shelby', 'Life is a boxes and arrows diagram', *'Il n'y a pas de hors-Kotler'*?). And if you're *really* stuck you could always resort to writing about writing. Morris Holbrook, for example, has published more papers on the problems of getting published than the rest of us have publications. But apart from that I am completely bereft when it comes to creative writing. Honest.

Look folks, if I knew the secret of successful composition, I'd tell you, believe me. I can't give advice on writing better academic papers because I'm still learning myself and I'm a pretty slow pupil, remedial in fact. It's not a question of superstition – I don't imagine that if I tell *you* how to write *I'll* never be able to write again – though I do have a healthy respect for hubris, the idea that pride comes before a fall. I'm not so proud of my penmanship, such as it is, that I consider myself qualified to pontificate about best paper-writing practice. And, anyway, there are any number of published guidelines on how to unleash your literary talents, how to become a creative-cum-original thinker and the like. Holbrook

Table 5.2 That's the way the girls are from Texas (or, the ten times multi-publication table)

---

1   Your title *must* contain a colon (semi-colons are for wimps – real men eat semi-colons for breakfast – whereas full stops connote incipient megalomania).

2   Introductory paragraphs normally employ some kind of spatial or positioning metaphor ('gap in the literature', 'strange lacunae', 'open up', 'situate', 'lack', 'silence', 'clear a space', 'add to growing stream of research', etc.). If you're feeling confident, try 'caesura'.

3   Your theoretical framework, and you must have a theoretical framework, should comprise not five, not four, not two, but precisely *three* stages or elements (Kotler's three stages of marketing consciousness, Hunt's three calamities model, Bagozzi's three types of exchange and, er, have you noticed anything vaguely trichotomous about this text?).

4   A few hypotheses are nice, though it's rare in these post-Popper times to state them in the formal, 'negative' manner (i.e. H1: there is no relationship between stating hypotheses and publication in *JMR*). You should realize, however, that some of the wild men of marketing science have abandoned hypotheses for 'propositions'. Radical, or what? (Incidentally, *never* state more than ten hypotheses. Not only is it unseemly, but it's indicative of serious cerebral softening.)

5   It's always prudent to include a diagram of a *pyramid*. (Matrices are passé, molecular-type things risible and boxes and arrows the graphic equivalent of polyester tank tops. Fortunately in our X-Filesque times, pyramids are still acceptable, though, for God's sake, don't draw a *pentagram* by mistake. That's a green light for the green ink brigade.)

6   A couple of tables add a much-needed touch of class, but as no one ever reads them, you can fill them up with any old rubbish (household accounts, articles from *Hello* and *National Enquirer*, erotic fantasies, lists of all-time favourite albums, movies, books, guidelines for getting marketing papers published, etc.).

7   There's a lot of stuff and nonsense talked about survey response rates. The old idea that a low response rate (say, less than 20 per cent) compromises the integrity of the research, has been completely abandoned. Thanks to the decisive intervention of Shelby Hunt (1990b), poor response rates are now perfectly acceptable. The fact that 90 per cent of your sample binned your incomprehensible questionnaire is neither here nor there. Remember at all times, the lower the response rate the better (it implies that 'challenging' questions were posed and we can't expect cretinous marketing practitioners to understand our challenging questions, now can we?). If, by some terrible accident, you end up with a 100 per cent response rate, don't even try to publish your worthless findings.

Table 5.2 Contd.

---

8 Always, but *always*, refer to the 'exploratory' nature of the research, since this gets you off all sorts of methodological, epistemological, ontological, axiological and any other 'logical' hooks you can mention. (These days, by the way, they call it 'discovery-oriented' research, but it means the same thing.)

9 It's sensible to concoct a few concluding 'limitations', because this gives you an opportunity to add the old reliable rider 'additional research is urgently/ sorely/undoubtedly/obviously (delete as necessary) needed'. This 'need' for additional research can then be cited in your next paper, and the next and, hey presto, one successful academic career is made. However, too much self-citation makes you go blind, so it helps if you can organize some kind of secret citation 'ring' with your cronies. If the worst comes to the worst, change your name to that of somebody famous (but *not* 'Alan Smithee', there are dozens of them already).

10 Finally, avoid the following like the plague: big words (pretentious), big foreign words (even more pretentious), philosophical epigraphs in Latin (excuse me, while I stick two fingers down my throat), bullet points (yeuch, practitioners!) and, above all, numbered lists of the (1), (2), (3) variety (too much like Shelby Hunt for safety).

(1986b), for example, advises authors to be clear, succinct, poetic and humble. Daft recommends that we tell a story, pay due attention to the overall structure of the argument and, above all, listen to the reviewers, who 'are on your side [and] enjoy helping transform a good paper into an excellent one' (1985: 180) (stop laughing at the back – he can't help his name!). Indeed, none other than that monument to the pursuit of scholarship before profit, MCB Press, has issued a set of guidelines and position papers on writing management research (Literati Club 1995).

Like everyone else, I enjoy reading such compositional commandments. In affording us the vicarious thrill of comparing our own untutored habits against those of the 'expert', they are the academic equivalent of quasi-questionnaires and pseudo sex surveys in glossy magazines and offer almost as much insight into the realities of the publishing game. It is, admittedly, interesting to note how many of these authorities emphasize the importance of aesthetics; in other words, the style of the manuscript rather than its content (textual analyses of reviewer comments, for example, reveal that accepted scientific papers are often referred to in aesthetic terms – 'attractive', 'charming', 'elegant', 'appealing', etc.). Nevertheless, it seems to me that while such best-practice blueprints may assist us to get published in the first place, they are less than helpful when it comes to creativity, to writing in a more innovative, experimental fashion. For that, I suggest, we can turn with some profit – and not a little humility – to the copious literature on greatness, genius and outstanding personal achievement (e.g. Battersby 1989; Henry 1991a; Freeman 1993; Buzan and Keene 1994; Eysenck 1995; Ford and Gioia 1995).

According to one of the world's leading literary theorists, Harold Bloom, the key to greatness in literature, or any walk of intellectual life, is nothing less than *strangeness*, defined as 'a mode of originality that either cannot be assimilated, or that so assimilates us that we cease to see it as strange' (1995: 3). When you experience their work for the first time, he continues, 'you encounter a stranger, an uncanny startlement rather than a fulfilment of expectations' (Bloom 1995: 3). In many ways, Bloom's means to greatness is reminiscent of Victor Shklovsky's notion of 'defamiliarization', the ability of works of literature (or art generally) to focus attention on and problematize the mundane, the accepted, the everyday, the habitual; that is, to make the familiar strange or the strange *stranger*. By informing us, as Steiner so eloquently puts it, 'of the inviolate enigma of the otherness in things and in animate presences, serious painting, music, literature or sculpture make palpable to us, as do no other means of communication, the unassuaged, unhoused instability and estrangement of our condition' (1989: 139). In this respect, it is entirely appropriate that Gane summarizes Jean Baudrillard's post-modern 'project' as an attempt, 'to render the world more mysterious, more enigmatic than he encounters it' (1995: 119).

This air of peculiarity or abnormality (Lincoln and Denzin 1994; Marcus 1994), which in its extreme manifestations can prompt shock, outrage and outright dismissal (Baudrillard, again, is a perfect case in point), is largely attributable to the fact that *genuine* innovations in art or science are often so different from what has gone before that the existing rules no longer appear to apply. They 'violate prescribed conventions' (Richardson 1994: 520). There are, in effect, no criteria by which to judge the worth of the contribution. It is perhaps not surprising, then, that in addition to extensive domain-specific knowledge – ten years of in-depth study/practice/experience is often cited as the preparatory minimum (Henry 1991b) – creative people in general and geniuses in particular are invariably characterized by persistence, self-reliance and an unquenchable conviction in the 'rightness' of their accomplishments. Contrary to the popular belief that such individuals are indolent, precocious, eccentric, absent-minded, scatter-brained, super-intelligent sociopaths, studies of the highly gifted demonstrate that they tend to be energetic, obstinate, hard-working, risk-taking, reasonably intelligent, mildly introverted and somewhat rebellious, with considerable social presence, if not poise (Buzan and Keene 1994; Eysenck 1995). There's something else as well;

now, what is it? Oh yes, they have phenomenal memories. Sorry about that moment of forgetfulness, folks, it's not like me to let something slip my mind, because I have a memory like an, um, what do you call the big grey thing with a trunk that's afraid of mice?

('Stephen?'
'Francesca, just the person I'm looking for. What do you call the big, grey thing, with enormous floppy ears and huge tusks?'
'Stephen Brown?'
'Very funny. Come on, the animal, I need it for the book.'
'It's a silly question I know, but why are you writing about elephants in a book on postmodern marketing? You're not resorting to the old blind men feeling an elephant cliché, are you? I was hoping you'd be a bit more original than that.'
'Please, Francesca, what do you take me for? Give me some credit. Do you think I would use that hoary old chestnut?'
'Or the hoary old chestnut about hoary old chestnuts.'
'Quite. You know, I once gave a conference paper on that, er, old elephant chestnut.'
'You did?'
'Yeah, it was called "The elephant's tale: who the hell are these guys and why do they keep feeling me up?"'
'I'm sure it was the highlight of the conference, Stephen.'
'No, no, it wasn't. Just the opposite, in fact.'
'Tell me about it.'
'Well, I hit them with my opening line, as you do.'
'Which was?'
'Some of you may think it's fun to have eight people fumbling around your private parts. Take it from me, it is fun to have eight people . . ."
'I don't think I want to hear any more of this.'
'That's exactly what the chairman said, Francesca, before he called the session to a halt. Would you believe it?'
'So, Stephen, you're still suffering from a touch of the – how can I put this? – the Oscar Wildes then?'
'No, no, no. That was just a temporary aberration. I'm fully recovered now. Everything's going well. The book's almost finished. I'll have it on your desk before long.'
'That's what I want to talk to you about, Stephen.'
'Oh yes?'
'I've decided to leave my job. At the end of the month. I need a change; you know how it is. Career move and all that.'

'You've got to be joking.'

'No joke.'

'Stop messing around, Francesca.'

'I'm deadly serious, Stephen.'

'Tell me something, did you jump or were you pushed?'

'Funny you should say that, because a jumping, um, incident sort of brought things to a head.'

'Are you telling me that our, er, negotiations cost you your job? Jesus, that's terrible!'

'Well . . ., look, I really appreciate your concern on my behalf. Don't worry about me, Stephen. I'll be all right. I was getting pretty fed up with the academic publishing game. The job market's pretty tough just now and there's the rent to pay and the family to feed. But I'll find something else. Don't concern yourself. Really.'

'But what about my book? What's going to happen when I deliver it? We had an agreement. Has this affected my contract in any way?'

'You're a real charmer, Stephen. A real smooth talker. A true friend. Anyway, the bottom line is that your book, subject to acceptance, has been transferred to ITBP.'

'ITBP? That's a practitioner-oriented imprint, isn't it? Practitioners?*'*

'Yes, 'fraid so. I hear you've been spouting about the academic–practitioner interface. Now's your big chance, buddy.'

'But, but, but, but . . .'

'Your bluff's been called, buster.'

'. . . practitioners? Please, I beg you Francesca, anything but practitioners.'

'Sorry, Stephen, it's a done deal.'

'But, but . . . that's just not fair.'

'All's fair in marketing warfare, don't you know.'

'Relationships, Francesca, it's all about relationships these days. Love, peace, understanding. I'm a relationship marketer, Francesca. Always have been, always will . . .)

As with most academic arenas, the study of creativity is subject to vigorous debate (see Eysenck 1995). Apart from interminable terminological disputation over the precise nature of, and relationships between, 'genius', 'innovation', 'intuition', 'intelligence' and so on, the relative importance of psychosis, playfulness and perseverance are periodically pondered, as are issues like nature versus nurture, individuality or *Zeitgeistianism*, ethnic and religious influences, gender, situational factors, handedness, time of birth and the influence, or otherwise, of sunspot cycles. It is widely accepted, however, that the creative process itself involves a form of analogical or metaphorical reasoning, seeing one thing in terms of another. Variously described as 'bisociation' (Koestler 1964), 'Janusian' (Rothenberg 1976),

'Dionysian' (Martindale 1990), 'right-brained' (Mintzberg 1991), and 'upside-down' (Handy 1989) thinking, this analogical facility, this ability to associate two domains of knowledge previously deemed unrelated or incompatible, not only is the essence of creativity, but also 'pervades all our thinking, our everyday speech and our trivial conclusions as well as artistic ways of expression and the highest scientific achievements' (Holyoak and Thagard 1995: 13).

Given its overwhelming importance, analogy occupies a prominent place in the manifold techniques designed – and reputed – to increase our innate creativity. Assessed by checklists akin to Figure 5.4, these include 'brainstorming', 'synectics', 'lateral thinking', 'mind mapping', 'morphological analysis' and 'imaginization', to name but a few (Majaro 1992; G. Morgan 1993; Buzan and Keene 1994). Although different in their details, such procedures are as one in their attempts to stimulate our metaphorical reasoning capacity. (Incidentally, my own score on Figure 5.4 falls, as you might expect, into the 'lock them up' category.) Analogy, furthermore, is an integral part of post-structuralism, where knowledge claims are held to be inherently metaphorical, tropes are deemed to lie at the very heart of our under-standing of the world and figurative thinking is considered central to discursive formations, regimes of truth and the process of theory articulation (S. Brown 1995a). Most importantly for our present purposes, councillors on creative writing invariably emphasize the importance of metaphorical experimentation, extra-polation, emancipation, expression, extraction, edification, expansion, extrusion, elimination, extension, exacerbation, ejaculation, exaggeration, explication, encap-sulation, extirpation, exhortation, enunciation, explanation, examination, epistemo-logicalization (what?) and enumeration – well, scrub enumeration (Lomax 1983; Hills 1987; Metzger 1993). Metaphor, as Richardson metaphorically avers, 'is the backbone of social science writing. Like the spine, it bears weight, permits move-ment, is buried beneath the surface, and links parts together into a functional, coherent whole' (1994: 519). Metaphors, she concludes, are everywhere.

It appears, then, that if we want to improve our creative writing skills we should seek to coin new metaphors or, conversely, tickle the fancy of established metaphors rather than leave them standing like wallflowers at the edge of the dance floor (untangle that one, if you're brave enough to bite the hand that lays the golden egg!). Marketing, fortunately, is not exactly short of metaphors and discussions about metaphor (Zaltman *et al.* 1982; van den Bulte 1994; Hunt and Menon 1995). The former, as sticking a figurative pin in a figurative textbook readily reveals, includes such familiar conceptual frameworks as – *yawn* – the marketing mix, the product life-cycle, marketing warfare, stages theory of internationalization and marketing myopia, youropia, theiropia, nohopia; whereas the best-known example

Figure 5.4 Belk, I need somebody, Belk not just anybody

	0	1	2	3	4	5	6	7	8	9	10
Conceptual fluency											
Mental flexibility											
Originality											
Suspension of judgement											
Impulse acceptance											
Attitude towards authority											
Tolerance											

Over 60	A rare species. Almost too good to be true.
51–60	Very creative person. Grab him/her.
41–50	Useful to have around during creativity work.
31–40	An acceptable average.
21–30	Worth working on, but will not invent the wheel.
under 20	Lock them up when creative groups are at work.

Source: adapted from Majaro 1992

of the latter is arguably Zaltman's metaphor elicitation technique (see Zaltman and Coulter 1995; Zaltman 1996; Ramocki 1996).

Encouraging though this tropeography is, it seems to me that our metaphorical bearing is somewhat misdirected at present – we are P-ing into the wind, as it were – in so far as it is instrumentalist, instead of essentially aesthetic, in orientation. In other words, we search for, agonize over and gnash our teeth about generating new or alternative metaphors for marketing phenomena – and there's nothing more certain to inhibit creativity than the dread injunction, 'think of a metaphor for . . .' – yet fail to appreciate the metaphor-manufacturing role of creative writing. Our evident and continuing fondness for an impersonal, unadorned, 'scientific' mode of marketing expression, reinforced as it is by the rules of genre and peer review, serves to reduce our trope-production capacity generally. Many of the metaphors created in this way may well collapse like soufflés in the fan-assisted oven of academic debate, but if the literature on creativity teaches us anything it teaches us that sheer output is integral to outstanding intellectual achievement (if 95 per cent of what we produce is complete dross, 5 per cent of lots of ideas may still comprise a considerable number). Thus, on a personal note, in my faltering and admittedly amateur attempt to write this text in a non-traditional fashion – you noticed? I'm so pleased – I have filled a notebook with turns of phrase, tropes, aphorisms and ideas, most of which don't quite 'fit' or are too extravagant for what I'm trying to convey (yes, friends, you're reading the restrained version). The key point is that writing in a creative manner is not mere affectation, though it can of course be just that, but it is potentially 'creative' in a broader, non-pejorative, discipline-affirming, discipline-enhancing, discipline-rejuvenating sense.

Let me put it to you another way: how many times have you been shocked – genuinely *shocked* – by something you've read in a marketing journal? Sure, we've all been 'defamiliarized' on occasion; you know, responding to a paper with a, 'gee, that's really interesting, I've never thought of it like that before'. In this respect, I still recall with enormous pleasure my first intoxicating encounter with a marketing textbook. It occurred when, as an undergraduate geography student browsing in the library between lectures, I came across Engel, Kollat and Blackwell (1978) and suddenly realized the amazing, career-determining fact that some people *actually studied* shops and shoppers. For what it's worth, moreover, my own personal pantheon of 'defamiliarizing' academic experiences would include Peter and Olson's (1983) 'Is science marketing?', Holbrook's (1986b) 'I hate when that happens', Belk *et al.*'s (1989) 'Sacred and profane' and, although it pains me deeply to confess it, Hunt's (1976) seminal 'Nature and scope of marketing'. However, I can honestly say that I have only once been shocked – that is, shocked as in 'the shock of the new', as in 'what on earth is this?' – by a work of marketing scholarship. Indeed, the more I think about it, the more I am convinced that Steve Gould's (1991) paper on self-manipulation is the only authentic work of genius in the entire marketing canon. An introspective account of his sexual proclivities and their perceived relationship to product use, Gould's paper has been condemned, derided, dismissed, belittled, mocked and held up as an exemplar of how *not* to write up a research project (Wallendorf and Brucks 1993). Yet, it is clear in retrospect that Gould shattered the academic marketing taboo on eroticism. Practitioners, of course, have been pressing the flesh into marketing service from time immemorial, each and every one of us knows that 'sex sells', and carnality has pervaded western art forms from the very dawn of civilization, if not before (Lucie-Smith 1991). But were we prepared to talk about sex in all its sweaty detail prior to Gould? We are now. There is no shortage of researchers lining up to grasp the erotic – tempting, but I'll play safe – nettle (e.g. Deighton and Greyson 1995; Belk *et al.* 1996; Elliott and Ritson 1995; Elliott 1996b). Steve Gould, however, paid a very heavy price for this breakthrough (I understand his paper all but cost him tenure). What's more, he didn't have the opportunity to defend his work against a critique that was not only hostile and ill-informed (Wallendorf and Brucks 1993), but actually predicated on researcher introspection, the very procedure it ruled out of court (see Brown and Reid 1997)! Such censoriousness does not reflect well on our discipline, although it is perfectly in keeping with the history of innovation, where creative thinkers are routinely crucified only to be resurrected and deified when it is too late.

Although we should be suitably grateful for the miraculous fact that Gould's paper managed to survive the peer review process, its author is not above criticism. In attempting to vindicate the research, he made the fatal mistake of resorting to standard 'scientific' arguments concerning the reliability, validity and trustworthiness of his introspective technique (S. J. Gould 1993, 1995). The methodology *can* be justified on these grounds, as Holbrook (1995a) explains, but the very act of doing so concedes too much to the critics. The power of personal introspection resides, not in its 'scientific' credentials, such as they are, nor in the everyday fact that it is an accepted, if not exactly standard, procedure in adjacent academic disciplines (C. Ellis 1991; Hixon and Swann 1993; Clandinin and Connelly 1994), but in its overwhelmingly aesthetic resonance. Introspective essays are works of art; they attempt to capture the world in a grain of sand; they reverberate; they dazzle; they aim to evoke an epiphanic 'A-ha, that rings true, *that*'s the way it is' response in the reader (Calvino 1986; Kundera 1988; Bachelard 1994). Introspections do not represent the 'truth' in any absolute, neo-positivistic sense (an aspiration that is unattainable in any event), but they are not necessarily unreliable, invalid or untrue either, at least not in aesthetic terms. If they were, creative writers – 'real' writers – would be in very serious trouble, because introspection is integral to literary insight and expression. As the postmodern novelist Paul Auster brilliantly observes:

> the more deeply I descended into the material, the more distanced I became from it. In order to write about myself, I had to treat myself as though I were someone else. . . . The astonishing thing, I think, is that at the moment when you are most truly alone, when you truly enter a state of solitude, that is the moment when you are not alone anymore, when you start to feel your connection with others. . . . In the process of writing or thinking about yourself, you actually become someone else.
>
> (Auster 1995: 106–7)

It is my contention, then, that introspective essays should be judged by the sorts of criteria outlined in Table 5.3. These include: *mode of representation*, poetic rather

Table 5.3 Let's rock, let's rock, let's rock, let's rock

Criteria	Science	Art
Mode of representation	Formal statements; literal language	Non-literal language; evocative statements
Appraisal criteria	Validity paramount; unbiased methods of data collection and analysis; conclusions supported by evidence	Persuasiveness paramount; seek illumination, penetration and insight; arguments supported by success in shaping concepts
Point of focus	Concentrates on overt or expressed behaviour (which can be recorded, counted and analysed)	Concentrates on experiences and meanings (observed behaviour provides springboard to understanding)
Nature of generalization	Extrapolates from particular to general; randomly drawn sample is deemed representative of universe and statistically significant inferences drawn about latter from former	Studies single cases and the idiosyncratic, but presupposes that generalizations reside in the particular, that broad (if not statistically significant) lessons can be learned from unique events
Role of form	Results reported in neutral, unembellished manner (third person, past tense) and according to a standard format (problem, literature review, sample, analysis, implications)	Avoidance of standardization; form and content interact; meaning of content determined by form in which it is expressed
Degree of licence	Factual emphasis; little scope for personal expression or flights of imaginative fancy	Subjective orientation; imaginative self-expression both permitted and expected

Table 5.3 Contd.

Criteria	Science	Art
Prediction and control	Aims to anticipate the future accurately, thus enabling or facilitating its control	Aims to explicate, thereby increasing understanding; less algorithmic than heuristic
Sources of data	Standardized instruments, such as questionnaire surveys or observation schedules, used to collect data	The investigator is the principal research instrument and his or her experiences the major source of data
Basis of knowing	Methodological monism; only formal propositions provide knowledge (affect and cognition separate)	Methodological pluralism; knowledge conveyed by successful evocation of the experience in question (affect and cognition combined)
Ultimate aims	Discovery of truth and laws of nature; propositions taken to be true when they correspond with the reality they seek to explain	Creation of meaning and generation of understanding; statements seek to alter extant perceptions about the world

Source: adapted from Eisner 1985

than literal language; *criteria for appraisal*, believability versus validity; *the nature of generalization*, inscribed in the particular not extrapolated from a sample; *the importance of form*, diversity of expression *contra* unity of approach; and *ultimate aims*, creation of meaning as opposed to the discovery of truth. In an attempt, moreover, to further Gould's introspective revolution – or, rather, atone for his sacrifice on the alter of pseudo-science – I am going to offer a little introspective essay of my own. Clearly, I wasn't going to escape from this chapter without 'showing' as well as 'telling', and if I have to show myself up I may as well do so in a good cause. Crude and unaccomplished though these reflections undoubtedly are, I would submit that they say as much about the stresses, strains and sheer emotional trauma of grocery shopping behaviour – the well-documented rise of 'trolley rage', for example (Tedre 1995; Everitt 1995; *The Sunday Times* 1996; Thorpe 1996) – as any number of more traditional research methods.

Saturday morning fever

Saturday night, according to Elton John, is all right for fighting, but Saturday morning also has its moments – in our house at least. For most families, I suppose, Saturday morning is a time of bonding, of togetherness, of rest and recuperation at the end of another hectic week. *Chez* Brown it is like the Battle of the Somme. The children, who have to be literally dragged out of bed on schooldays, are up with the proverbial lark and just about as vocal. This less than tuneful dawn chorus, more-over, quickly degenerates into the Dawn Patrol as cat and dog fights break out over breakfast cereal ('we want Coco-Pops'), portion allocation ('Sophie got more than me'), seating arrangements ('Holly's sitting in my chair'), property rights ('that's my teddy'), television programming ('Power Rangers! Power Rangers!'), fashion trends ('I don't want to wear that dress'), and the many and unbounded joys of sisterhood ('Madison's biting Holly, Daddy'). These screams of battle are counter-pointed by the siren wail of the Hoover, the distant rumble of the washer-drier and the acrid fumes of Domestos-cum-Toilet Duck, as my multi-dexterous wife single-handedly attacks all the jobs that have been ignored during the working week and which I would have to do if I hadn't already volunteered for the suicide mission that is the weekly grocery shopping.

To be honest, it is something of a blessed relief to be dispatched to Crazy Prices on Saturday mornings, to retreat temporarily from the tooth-and-nail fighting in the Brown Redoubt with my sanity comparatively intact. As often as not, however, it's not long before I'm back, having realized that I've forgotten my credit card or discovered that I don't have a £1 coin for the shopping trolley. Or, even worse, on rummaging through Linda's handbag (why do women carry so much bloody stuff around with them?), finding that she doesn't have one either. Already behind schedule, I drive off again with my wife's parting endearment still ringing in my ears: 'For God's sake, don't buy any more tins of sweetcorn.' The ringing continues as the melodic yet restrained strains of AC/DC erupt at full volume from my CD and the air slowly turns blue when I discover that I'm stuck, as ever, behind a pair of doolally pensioners out for a 29 miles per hour Saturday morning 'run'. They say it's impossible to overtake on the narrow and twisting Monkstown Road, but, as any number of stricken OAPs in the Newtownabbey area can readily testify, there is at least one road hog capable of passing at high speed whilst making rude gestures, mouthing obscenities and singing along with the choruses of 'Highway to Hell'.

Sans £1 coin, I invariably have to get some money out of the autobank and, equally invariably, find myself queueing for hours behind Mr let-me-just-check-my-balance-order-a-new-chequebook-and-try-out-a-couple-of-duff-cards Dickhead. Eventually, I make my way down the mall to Eason's, where I buy a newspaper to break the note and, thanks to the 'Don't you have anything smaller? Sorry about all the change!' syndrome that seems to afflict the shop on Saturday mornings, end up with a pocket full of £1 coins, fifty pence pieces and assorted smaller specie. After clanking back up the mall with a 'no, that enormous bulge in my pocket is not advanced elephantiasis' look on my face, I nip outside and attempt to remove a trolley from the rear end of its manifold bum-chums in the trolley park. Why is it always rutting season in the trolley park? Would a bucket of cold water help expedite the extraction process? Are trolleys heterosexual, enjoined in male–female combinations? Or is that trolley conga in the car park a grotesque act of homosexual depravity? (I've heard of troilism, but trolleyism is a new one on me.) Is there a great Queen Trolley somewhere, extruding little trolley larvae whilst being serviced by expendable soldier trolleys? Are shopping trolleys an alien life form intent on taking over the world? I think we should be told.

I don't know who was responsible for the layout of Crazy Prices' Abbeycentre store, but I can only assume that he or she has a well-developed sense of humour. The conventional wisdom of grocery store design suggests that something enticing or succulent, like exotic fruit, new-baked bread or the judiciously ducted aroma of freshly ground coffee should greet the customer on entry, endeavour to convey an impression of abundance and plenitude, and thereby seduce people into that all-important spending mood. No such sophistication is evident at the entrance to Crazy Prices, which comprises – wait for it – a sportswear concession. Now, I'm sure that this ingenious merchandising ploy induces lots of shoppers into impulse purchases of high-margin football boots and exercise equipment, yet even here the store managers have patently failed to develop the concept's full potential. I mean, why don't they just pipe the smell of athlete's foot and sweaty jockstraps around the entire store, and be done with it?

Disconcerting though the entry phase of the Crazy Prices 'experience' undoubtedly is, there's much, much worse to come. The first aisle proper is like a throwback to the 1940s, or, rather, to the 1940s of my imagination – air raids, rationing, powdered eggs and monosodium glutamate. Yes friends, all those products you thought had gone to the great brand graveyard in the sky are alive, well, barcoded and, heaven help us, best before datestamped in Crazy Prices. Tins of spam, Libby's corned beef, processed peas, packets of dates, Vesta curries, black pudding, vegetable roll, Daddies sauce, Brylcream, Omo washing powder, packets of jelly and lard, instant cake mix, Crosse & Blackwell soups, Paris buns, custard creams, huge plastic bottles of own-brand bleach and rolls of corrugated iron purporting to be toilet paper, all vie for your attention, whilst the E-numbers literally scream at you from the top-gallants of the industrial-style shelving. I suppose the management think this represents some sort of value-for-money or 'power' aisle. Perhaps it's a parodic postmodernist attempt to create a retro-retailing environment. But to me it bespeaks social security, single parenthood, hyperactive children with rickets, teen-age delinquency, high-rise flats, council estates, noisy neighbours, dog shit on the pavement, standing at bus stops in the rain, broad working-class accents and there but for the grace of God (and the eleven-plus) go I.

Although it is too early in the morning – and too late in the day – to start reflecting on my lucky escape from the fate of the underclass, it is not too soon to be disconcerted by the next section of the store. The sight of freshly plucked, shrink-wrapped chicken breasts and bright-red beefburgers may instil confidence in certain categories of shopper, or provide the basis of all manner of tasty and nutritious recipes, but it puts the wind up me. Fortunately, this disquiet soon passes since I'm usually shopping on automatic pilot by this stage, following the same route I always follow and employing the store as an *aide-mémoir* for my mental shopping list. Yoghurts for the girls, ham and cheese slices for their lunches, extra pint of milk, 2-litre container of Tropicana orange juice, soured cream and tin of sweetcorn for the dish I never quite get round to making (and for which my wife is eternally grateful), packets of crisps, pot of strawberry jam, Baxter's carrot and butterbean soup, giant jar of Maxwell House coffee, fresh bread, Ballygowan water, oven-ready southern-fried chips, Goodfella's pizza, Ariel automatic and, naturally, a selection from the store's impressive display of bruised apples, bruised oranges, bruised potatoes, bruised bananas and bruised grapes. I used to wonder why Crazy Prices' fruit was so awful, then I saw them replenishing the shelves one morning. Well, I think they were replenishing the shelves. It was either that or an energetic practice session for the staff's annual 'throw a bag of peaches' competition.

Although invariant, my shopping routine is always liable to interruption. These interruptions are of three types, all of them extremely irritating. Why, oh why, oh why do retailers insist on moving merchandise around the store, on relocating goods from hither to yon, on shifting me from soporific to splenetic? Is it their little power-crazy attempt to show us who's boss? Do they really think that rearranging the layout somehow stimulates the shopper, helps maintain consumer interest or tickles our collective fancy? Are they indulging in a private dispute with their suppliers to which we, the customers, aren't invited but have to suffer the collateral spatial consequences? I don't know what the rationale is for relocating merchandise categories; all I do know is that it drives me up the wall when I turn into an aisle expecting to find the usual display of breakfast cereals or kitchen rolls, only to find that I'm facing serried ranks of dog food, cat litter and all-purpose worming tablets. If I could get my hands on the store manager at that moment, I'd ram my freshly baked baguette so far up his you-know-where that he'd never need to take another worming tablet, believe me.

The second irritant is other people. Every so often, you run into a friend or colleague from work and are forced to exchange early-morning, non-university-related pleasantries, even though you know (and they know you know) that any delay can have serious downstream consequences at the seething maelstrom of human immiseration colloquially known as the checkouts. Worse still are the Crazy Prices regulars, the bunch of cretinous sluggards, incompetents and Neanderthals who also shop at the same time every Saturday morning and do everything in their power to slow me down. I am a reasonable man, an easy-going dude, some would say moderation personified, but there's one particular couple the very sight of whom sends me into orbit (or bananas if you prefer). They shop together. They are in love with being in love and want everyone to know it. They have a shopping list. She calls out the next item to him; he bounds off to fetch the avocado dip, or whatever, and returns wagging his tail with a stupid, lovestruck look on his cross-bred face and terms of endearment lolling on the excited tip of his extended tongue. One of these days I'm going to grab Lassie by the throat and demand to know if he's a man or a mongrel.

There is, of course, an important exception to the 'other people' rule, and that is the Dean. By coincidence, the Dean of the Faculty – my boss – also shops at Crazy Prices on a Saturday morning. While I am reluctant to impose upon him with my university-related concerns, I rarely get to see him during the week, and have occasionally found it necessary to raise faculty matters whilst he is attempting to select the least bruised cucumber on display. Thanks, however, to my ready wit, laid-back manner and, if I say so myself, justifiably renowned interpersonal skills, these encounters usually pass off pleasantly enough. True, I did once berate him, at length, about certain disagreeable aspects of faculty policy, and threatening to get medieval on his ass with a distressed cucumber was perhaps not the most circumspect career decision I've ever made, but he assures me that this unfortunate incident has been completely forgotten about and that my future at UU is totally secure. Strangely enough, I haven't seen the Dean in Crazy Prices for quite a while now, though I occasionally catch a glimpse of someone who looks just like him skulking behind the freezer cabinets. Must be a trick of the light.

The final and by far the most annoying form of disruption involves merchandise that lies outside my normal Saturday morning repertoire. Once in a while, I am instructed to acquire certain unusual, not to say idiosyncratic, items, such as a new bag for the vacuum cleaner, wooden-floor polish, something that removes ink stains from school uniforms, bayonet-mounted, tulip-style 100-watt lightbulbs and – I kid you not – a square bucket. The pursuit of these figments of my wife's febrile imagination invariably has me hunting fruitlessly up and down aisles that I never knew existed or staring in impotent rage at a vast selection of products, all ever so slightly different, and only one of which is precisely what I'm looking for (have you *any* idea just how many variants of vacuum cleaner bag there are?). Such time-wasting futilities, however, pale by comparison with the excruciating embarrassment that is sanitary protection. Every so often, my wife asks me to buy some sanitary towels and provides me with very detailed instructions about the brand and type she requires. I know it's immature; I know it's irrational; I know it's merely an instantiation of the primordial menstruation taboo beloved by anthropologists; I know a Freudian psychoanalyst would have a field day with my disquiet. But, I can't pretend that I'm anything other than very uncomfortable in the sanitary protection aisle. I feel like I should be wearing a sign that says 'my other coat is a dirty macintosh' or 'yes, I'm a fetishist and proud of it'. My discomfort is compounded when there are women in the aisle, redoubled by the fact that I can never quite find my wife's specified brand (which invariably makes me wonder about the consequences of returning empty-handed – perhaps she won't ask me again) and culminates – oh God – with the ultimate nightmare of having to take the bloody things through the checkouts.

Ah, the checkout. Checkout, checkout, checkout. Doesn't that word just resonate? Doesn't that word just conjure up visions of examination and achievement, incarceration and escape, death and resurrection? Superstore checkouts are the Pearly Gates of the late twentieth century, where the St Peters of the Barcode scrutinize your shopping accomplishments one-by-one, assess your overall creditworthiness and, having weighed you in the commercial balance, permit you to pass to the Elysium that lies beyond. In theory at least. In practice, of course, checkouts are the nearest things to Hell this side of the grave. Crazy Prices has thirty-odd checkouts, only one of which seems to be open when I round the final aisle. After marching up and down the line, hoping to find another that is *about* to open and glaring at the herd of checkout operators, dozens of whom are gathered round receiving instructions from their supervisor or checking their floats prior to opening, I reluctantly join the queue for the only lane in operation. There are hundreds of trolleys ahead of mine, all filled to the gunnels, all the property of wizened old ladies, all of whom remove the items at a rate of one per hour, pay in five pence pieces and, as a long-lost acquaintance of the checkout girl, proceed to bring them up to date about the past fifty years of extended family affairs. I bite my lip. 'Give that granny a Prozac', 'HRT is available on the NHS, missus' or, come to think of it, 'for fuck's sake get a move on', is not the sort of expression one expects to hear in mixed company at 9.30 on Saturday morning.

Bad as the old biddies are, there's one denizen of the checkout lane that's even worse. I am a reasonable man, an easy-going dude, some would say moderation personified. Indeed, as most of my friends – if I had any friends – would willingly testify, I am full of the milk of human kindness. But, when someone ahead of me in the queue pulls out a chequebook and proceeds to go through the elaborate, time-consuming gavotte of paying by personal cheque, the proverbial red mist descends. It is all I can do to restrain myself from picking up the jumbo-sized tin of sweetcorn from my trolley and flinging it at the miscreant. In fact, it seems to me that this perfectly reasonable reaction in the face of extreme provocation presents yet another profitable merchandising opportunity, which, as ever, the management of Crazy Prices is just too obtuse to appreciate. I believe that the impulse-purchase display racks adjacent to the checkouts should be replaced, as a matter of urgency, by a reasonably priced selection of rotten fruit, stale bread, cracked eggs and damaged vegetables, especially those big knobbly potatoes that fit snugly into the palm of the hand, with which we could pelt anyone or anything that is holding up the queue. Yeah, you're right, they've probably tried it already (ever wondered why there are so many dented cans?), only to find that their suppliers of seconds couldn't keep up with the demand. Instead, we're stuck with the ubiquitous racks of Mars bars and – I swear – razor blades in case we decide to slit our throats, or gorge ourselves into Weightwatchers Anonymous, while we wait to meet our maker at the head of the queue.

Many people, I know, don't particularly enjoy the so-called service encounter, that fleeting face-to-face exchange with someone forcing a smile, faking sincerity and asking asinine questions about innocuous topics. Having to put up with all that whilst trying to operate a bar-code scanner must be a nightmare for most checkout operators. Personally, I always endeavour to manufacture a modicum of till-side bonhomie, not least because checkout people are often a very useful source of information on company strategy, consumer behaviour, new product launches and so on. To be honest, I find it difficult to maintain this engaging demeanour, although not, as you might think, on account of my reputation as the Victor Meldrew of Marketing, but simply due to the fact that my patience is often very sorely tried. There's one particular checkout operator, for example, who *always* makes a comment about the vestigial warmth of my baguette even when the thing is approximately three weeks old and sporting a luxurious beard (perhaps its encounter with the store manager warmed it up a trifle). Still, she's very pretty and obviously fancies me like mad, so I usually respond to her conversational gambit with a 'Yeah, it must be really fresh' or one of my other equally infallible chat-up lines (a silver-tongued devil, or what?).

When it comes to the checkout system itself, however, I am much less amenable. In the old days, this used to comprise a simple trolley-in, trolley-out arrangement. As you unloaded the goods from one trolley, they were scanned and placed in another. Nothing could be simpler or speedier. Now, as a consequence of Crazy Prices' continuing commitment to – get this – 'improving customer service', it consists of a single-trolley system, whereby you deposit *all* of your purchases on to a conveyor belt, then manoeuvre your shopping chariot to the far end where the scanned and ready-bagged merchandise is waiting to be reloaded. Unfortunately, the conveyer belt can't accommodate a full trolley's worth, it is highly unstable, with a propensity to 'convey' bottles and packages in the general direction of the floor rather than the pick-up spot, and invariably precipitates a mad dash to the far side, swiftly followed by a load-the-trolley-at-speed-and-to-hell-with-the-broken-eggs frenzy, whilst bagging the items that, for some strange, unexplained reason the checkout operator has chosen not to pack. Talk about slow. Talk about irritating. Talk about the checkout manufacturing company that sold Crazy Prices a pup. Don't talk to me about 'improving customer service'.

Despite the one-lane catatonia, hyperreal conversations and simulacra of customer service that characterize the Saturday morning till-side experience, there is nevertheless a genuine sense of euphoria associated with reaching the head of the checkout queue. For a start, it gives you a chance to whip out your chequebook and waggle it at the sad bastards further down the line. The audible groan that goes up, coupled with the sight of grown men fighting over the razor blades, is really quite invigorating, as is the subsequent howl of indignation when you ostentatiously repocket the chequebook – I never pay by cheque – and pull out a credit card. To many neophytes of checkout psychology, the credit card may seem like a much faster method of payment than personal cheque, but in Crazy Prices at least, it's actually a lot slower. They only have three on-line credit terminals, which must have been at the cutting edge of EPOS technology sometime around 1950, and as the operator has to close her till to make her way to these steamdriven machines, it takes an awfully long time from swipe to signature, so to speak. Meanwhile, you can gaze down the queue with a wistful 'sorry about this delay folks, but it really isn't my fault' look in your eyes, whilst revelling in their anguish and the thought of their burgeoning blood pressures.

Unfortunately, this coronary-inducing ploy can come very seriously unstuck if you're not careful. Last Christmas, on a day when the store was absolutely heaving with queues stretching back to the delivery bays, I thought I'd play my trusty credit card trick. Well, it was the season of peace and goodwill, after all. I was still smirking at the hatchet-faced psychopaths down the line when the checkout operator returned to tell me that my card had been rejected. Upping the stakes, I demanded that she try another machine, and by the time she came back with the bad news, I was not only soaked in sweat and expecting a jumbo-sized can of sweetcorn to come whistling past my ear at any second, but there were people literally *barking* at me from the back of the queue. Fearing for my life, I was escorted from the store, frogmarched to the nearest autobank, where, after pausing only to ring my wife and whisper a few sweet nothings about her failure to pay our Access bill, I withdrew enough money to cover the price of the goods, if not the cost to my dignity. For weeks afterwards I had this recurring nightmare about my grocery shopping mortification making the Sunday papers (I mean, a Professor of Retailing in a retailing-related incident) and, to this day, ensure that on entering Crazy Prices I carry sufficient cash to cover every possible checkoutcome.

Traumatic though my 'don't ask for credit as a refusal often offends' farrago undoubtedly was, I have actually had worse experiences in Crazy Prices (whose singularly appropriate television advertising soundtrack is BTO's 'You ain't seen nothing yet'). Once I was actually within hailing distance of the checkout operator when the computer system crashed, and until it was up and running there was no way to get out. Cast adrift in a sea of fully laden shopping trolleys, becalmed in an ocean of mutinous consumers, drowning in a pool of queue-engendered panic, I could see my past life flashing before me, felt like screaming 'women and children first' before self-preservation prevailed, and was coming up for the third time when the system was fortuitously rebooted. The following Saturday, I arrived at 9.05 a.m. to find that the store-front shutters had not been retracted. Fifteen minutes later they were still in place and by this stage a substantial crowd had built up outside, circling like great white sharks, peering angrily into the fully lit and staffed establishment beyond. I was advocating the construction of a massive battering ram made up of our combined shopping trolleys, and which, with the run-up afforded by the main mall, would have been sufficient to effect entry, when a sacrificial lamb appeared from behind the screens to announce that the system had failed again and would take at least two hours to restore. Laugh? I almost had an embolism.

I am, as you know, a reasonable man, an easy-going dude, some would say moderation personified. But in light of my Crazy Prices-occasioned paranoia –

it's not known as Crazies for nothing – you will appreciate why I always need a little post-grocery shopping therapy. After unloading the laden carrier bags into the back of my car, examining the freshly gouged scratch on its side (doubtless perpetrated by one of the affable old dears in the queue), and ramming my frisky shopping trolley into the inviting posterior of its fellows, I usually return to the centre and make my way to Our Price music. Their selection, admittedly, is terrible – so much so that I have occasionally been reduced to buying those revolting 'Greatest Rock CD Ever!' compilations – but I need something to restore my retailing equilibrium and, in the absence of a good bookstore, a record shop is the next best thing. Now and then, I confess, I glance into the off-licence, tempted by the prospect of a few relaxing beers for later. However, the thought of walking down the mall carrying a carry-out, with all its connotations of fecklessness, over-indulgence and loss of self-control, is usually sufficient to erect an invisible barrier between me and the establishment. If, of course, things have proved particularly stressful, I get in my car, drive into town and make straight for Dillons, Waterstones and Virgin Mega-store. But that, as they say, is another story . . .

Chapter 6
Hey ho, let's go!

It was a time for crumpets. The first frost had lain upon the lawn all day, pocked by squirrels scuttling to garner their hibernal tucker and blackbirds bravely drilling the adamantine sod for one last worm, and, as the misty gloaming settled upon Cricklewood, I too felt the old need come on for that little winter something which has been, for centuries, the Englishman's exclusive treat. So I wrapped up warm, and I jogged up the hill through my own pluming breath to Quality Family Foods, where I inquired, and he pointed.

'No,' I said from beside the shelf, 'what I want is crumpets.'

'Those are *crumpets,' he insisted, from the till.*

I looked at the packet. I picked it up. I brought it into the brighter light beside the till. The nine things inside the packet were oblong, roughly five inches by one.

'Crumpets?' I said. You'll guess my tone.

'Finger crumpets,' *he said, with, if I judge aright, a tactical hint of embarrassment shrewdly calculated to ensure that I did not henceforth take my business elsewhere. 'They are new from Mother's Pride.'*

'I'm sure they are,' I said. 'Have you got any round ones?'

'No,' he said.

Time passed. I could hear his cat scratching in some further aisle.

'The thing about a round crumpet,' he said after a bit, 'is that the butter runs down your chin. Down your arm sometimes.'

'Yes,' I said, 'that is exactly the thing about a round crumpet. Butter from a round crumpet has been doing that for several hundred years.'

'But the thing about these,' he said, gamely, 'is that they fit the mouth. You bite from one end. No mess.'

'Do they, perhaps,' I said, 'conform to some new EC standard or other? Has Mother been compelled to knuckle under before some bloody Brussels directive? Is what we are looking at nothing more nor less, in fact, than a Eurocrumpet?'

'I don't think so,' he said. 'I think it's more a matter of marketing progress. They have always moved with the times, up Mother's Pride.'

'Oh, have they?' I said. 'Oh good. And the times are clamouring for oblong crumpets, are they?'

He shrugged.

'All I know is,' he said, 'they're selling like . . .'

'Don't say it,' I warned. He looked disappointed, and my heart went out to him: as a toiler in that same waggish vineyard I know how rare such opportunities are. So I bought a packet, and left, and walked down the hill again, wondering if, perhaps, Gibraltar's apes might not be chucking their bits and bobs into suitcases, now, or the Tower's ravens revving their wings for exile; because there was a new straw in the November wind, and it might just be the last one.

Back home, I wrestled with the packet, and a little later I toasted the oblongs, and then I ate them, spotlessly . . .

(Coren 1995b: 32–3)

Strange days

What are the four most horrifying words in marketing, apart, of course, from 'written by Malcolm McDonald'? As creative intellectuals one and all, as post-modernists through and through, you can doubtless think of dozens of contenders: 'relationship marketing paradigm shift', *Journal of Marketing Research*, 'top grade British beef', 'you paid *how* much?', 'general theory of marketing', 'according to Philip Kotler', 'looks perfect on you', 'ten items or less', 'product, place, price, promotion', 'the marketing concept says', 'I've written a poem', 'it's on the Web', 'overdrawn on your account', 'board of examiners' meeting', 'substantial revisions are necessary', 'stages theory of internationalization', 'production-, sales-, market-ing-oriented', 'she's in a meeting', 'just out of stock', 'Marketing Science Institute Report', 'Shelby Hunt clearly states', 'hold the line please', 'do you take cheques?' and, it almost goes without saying, *Postmodern Marketing Two* (yes, I know that's one word short of a mouthful, but what else do you expect from a postmodernist?).

After pondering this conundrum for some considerable time, and notwithstanding the very stiff competition from 'gave me your name' (which is swiftly followed by 'little bit of consultancy', 'no money to spend' and some combination of, or variation on, 'university', 'taxpayer', 'rip-off' and 'outrageous'), my considered opinion is that the four most blood-curdling words in the marketing lexicon are 'I have a model'. Granted, the words themselves are fairly innocuous – beguiling even – but they are invariably announced with an tone of absolute assurance and accompanied by a look of such grim, gimlet-eyed conviction that you instantly know you are in the presence of a marketing fundamentalist. No matter what you try to say – and, if you want to live, don't argue with them or mention their model's manifest shortcomings – these people *know* that their model is *right*. They have spent years developing the thing, which unfailingly looks like the bastard child of Buckminster Fuller and Heath Robinson. They have agonized long into the night over the precise placement of boxes and arrows or the number of cells in their matrix. They have boldly gone where no marketer has gone before and, by God, they are going to tell us all about it. They are totally, utterly, completely certain that their model will set the marketing world on fire, transform our understanding of marketing understanding and elevate them to a justly deserved place in the academic marketing firmament.

Faced with such resolute implacability, it is tempting to tell the so-and-sos that there are thousands of marketing models just like theirs, that library bookshelves the world over are lined with PhD theses, every one of which boasts a model or two. It is difficult to avoid pointing out that the last post for modern marketing scholarship has long since sounded and that reveille was played some time back in a place called Postmodernity. It is hard to resist misinforming them that there is a great graveyard – a Marlington Cemetery – of marketing models that have fallen in battle, or spinning them a yarn about the existence of a land beyond time – Mavalon – where the once and future King Kotler and his Knights of the Profound Table await our heartfelt call and remain ever ready to smite villainous model-mockers with the Excaliber of Exchange. Indeed, it is all we can do to stop ourselves confessing that in 99.9 per cent of cases we would rather have our teeth pulled by a rusty, gripless socket wrench or pizzles nibbled by a frenzied pitbull (hey, don't knock it 'til you've tried it) than have anything to do with their me-too model. But, these people are convinced that their recently coined concept is the exception to the rule, that theirs is the one that's going to make all the difference and show us the error of our epistemological ways.

To put it in a nutshell (and I mean nutshell), model-builders are the Moonies of the marketing academy. Or, to be more precise, they are the Scientologists, because it seems to me that this infestation of model-mongers, this claque of modeliacs, this appalling waste of intellectual resources in what can only be described as conspicuous cerebration, is a direct result of marketing's failure fully to straighten out our unfashionable, archaic and, frankly, absurd scientific bent. We all know marketing science is superstitious nonsense – nonsense scientifically disproved on many occasions – but it still has a disconcertingly large number of adherents. What's more, its devotees continue to try to corrupt our offspring and the less discerning among us with their cabalistic talk of axioms, laws and, most incorrigibly of all, general models of marketing. Thus, despite my earlier, admittedly overconfident, insistence that we had exorcized the evil scientific spirit and thereby ushered in a paradisiacal era of postmodern marketing scholarship, it is clear that such deep rooted forms of demonic possession are not so easily extirpated.

In these increasingly desperate times, when marketing Scientologists openly stalk the streets preaching their pagan, model-building heresies, pushing their scientific hallucinogens among the young and innocent, and generally terrorizing the law-abiding citizens of the postmodern marketing community, we have no alternative but to get tough, fight fire with fire and develop our own model-crushing model (MCM). Illustrated in Figure 6.1, this meta-model – or should that be meta-your-maker model? – consists of three separate but sequential stages termed shake, rattle and roll. Exhausted, abandoned and even unheard of marketing models are sucked into the hopper at the top, disassembled by a state-of-the-art, computer-controlled, laser-guided atom-smasher in stage two and eventually extruded as enigmatic epigrams, apposite aphorisms, local narratives, telling tales and all-purpose, pre-packaged, environment-friendly, biodegradable postmodern marketing mulch.

Obviously, this is only a prototype, and comprehensive testing is necessary before it is safe to operate on the distinguished corpus of twentieth-century marketing scholarship. We need to determine, for example, whether MCM runs most efficiently on the low-grade fuel found in undistinguished and indistinguishable PhD theses, the supposedly high-grade theoretical seams running through the premier journals (fool's gold, if you ask me) or indeed the much recycled conceptual canker of the marketing management textbooks. For what it's worth, I recommend we experiment on the hierarchy of needs framework, as we don't really need it any more, and thereafter sacrifice the three calamities model, since its loss is not exactly calamitous. There is, admittedly, an outside possibility – a very remote outside possibility, it must be stressed, almost infinitesimal – that the MCM will overheat, go critical and proceed to crush every good, bad or indifferent marketing model from time immemorial. But, that nightmare scenario will only ever happen if someone reads *Postmodern Marketing Two* and takes it seriously. I mean, surely no one would ever believe all that stuff on Rip-off Marketing, sex 'n' shopping novels, Coca-Kotlerization, marketing aesthetics and so on, would they? Hold on, what's happening here? The dials have gone crazy. They're into the red. The machine's out of control. A reader must have fallen for it. It's you! You fool! Marketing is finished and it's all your fault. The thing can't be stopped, not even by the intellectual firebreak – the wasteland – that is international marketing. Whoops, there goes the PLC, dead as a PoMo Dodo. Cripes, the marketing mix has just been

Figure 6.1 Tybout yellow ribbon Calder old oak tree

swallowed whole. Jeez, it's munching it's way through *Postmodern Marketing* – that won't hold it up for long. Watch out, it's behind you!!

When the music's over, turn out the lights.

Fisherman's blues

For many marketing researchers, I suppose, the foregoing flight of fancy represents the sorts of 'anarchy of self-indulgence and paroxysms of self-expression' that Calder and Tybout (1987, 1989) warned us about. Along with the present author's uncorroborated, unwarranted, unproved and well-nigh unconstitutional suggestion that postmodernism has taken over the marketing academy, it epitomizes the nihilistic void that our discipline is certain to sink into unless we keep our passions under control, undertake programmatic research in a rigorous, disinterested, objective fashion and, at all times, endeavour to resist the temptation to stray from the straight and narrow of scientific discourse. Personally, I wouldn't describe the above confection, or any of the others in this particular book, as paroxysms of self-expression. As someone who aspires to paroxysms of self-expression, who sees nothing wrong with paroxysms of self-expression, who feels that academic market-ing could do with a few more paroxysms of self-expression, I don't for a moment imagine that I've actually achieved my ultimate aesthetic objective. The best I can hope for is to have my work described as proto-paroxysms of self-expression. Maybe one day I'll manage the real thing.

Nor, for that matter, does it bother me to be described as a nihilist, an anarchist or, my personal favourite, a marketing maverick. Pejorative labels of this kind, according to Hunt's (1990a, 1991, 1992, 1993) cogent and learned disquisitions on academic terms of abuse, such as 'positivist', invariably conceal the accuser's profound ignorance of the disparaged position. (Hold on a minute, I hear you say, surely Shelby Hunt routinely deploys pejorative terms like 'nihilist' and 'anarchist'. Really? Are you telling me that Professor Hunt engages in the very actions he rails against? I find that very hard to credit!) Nihilism, like positivism, is a highly variegated intellectual movement – Romantic Nihilism, Left Hegelianism, New Left Hegelianism, Nietzschean Nihilism, Revolutionary Nihilism, etc. (see Devine 1989; Vattimo 1991; Gillespie 1995; Löwith 1995) – and, despite appear-ances to the contrary, it is important to appreciate that there is a *positive* side to nihilism. There are real benefits to be gained from, in effect, wiping the slate clean and starting again, albeit the decision to abandon our academic birthright, to admit that we made a serious mistake, to acknowledge that we got it wrong, is actually *harder* to take than the comparatively easy option of continuing as if nothing were amiss, of mistakenly assuming that everything in the garden of marketing delights is rosy. As Feuerbach, a New Left Hegelian and one of the progenitors of European nihilism, rightly reminds us, 'no-one without the courage to be absolutely negative has the strength to create anything new' (quoted in Hayman 1982: 99).

You know, the thing that *really* gets me about Calder and Tybout-style witch-hunts, their authoritarian desire to discipline the discipline, is not their paroxysms pronouncement nor the pejorative appellations, but the dictat that we must aspire to scientific status and report our research in an appropriately emotionless scientific idiom. It is my belief that marketing's current malaise, whilst partly attributable to trends in the socio-economic environment, the *fin-de-siècle* effect and seismic shifts in the tectonic plates of scholarship, is primarily due to the discipline's ill-advised, post-war pursuit of scientific respectability. Notwithstanding Kerin's (1996) recent, high-profile pronouncements on the 'science of marketing', I would submit that marketing's scientific aspirations are manifestly absurd, an unattained and unattainable fantasy, a bad joke (and, as you can readily testify, I know all there is to know about bad jokes). More fundamentally perhaps, I would submit that marketing's fruitless quest for scientific status has served only to drive a wedge between academics and practitioners. Not everyone, as we have seen, accepts the contention that marketing is essentially an applied discipline. Many putative 'scientists' unthinkingly turn to Tucker's (1974) tired trope that marketers study consumers as fishermen study fish (rather than as dispassionate marine biologists), thereby overlooking the blindingly obvious truism that experienced fishermen often know as much, if not more, about piscine habits and behaviour than a shoal of marine biologists (S. Brown 1995b). Yet, whatever way you look at it, the fact of the matter is that thirty-something years ago many of the most enthusiastic contributors to academic marketing journals were practitioners. Today, it is almost inconceivable that a paper by a marketing manager would appear in the premier American and, increasingly, European academic fora, though possibly not as inconceivable as the notion of practising managers turning to these journals for guidance. Be honest, how many of us really *want* managers to implement our pseudo-suggestions, especially if we are held (financially) responsible, despite all the standard caveats and get-out clauses, when things go awry?

Pretty hate machine

In an attempt to demonstrate that there is an alternative – a meaningful alternative – to marketing science, this book has sought to highlight the potential of marketing aesthetics in general and the world of literature in particular. It has argued that important marketing insights can be derived from works of literature, that the tools and techniques of literary criticism can be applied to all manner of marketing artifacts and, not least, that marketers should seek to adopt more literary modes of academic expression. In Chapter 3, the contents of two bestselling sex and shopping novels were examined at length and related to the extant literature in the fields of retailing and consumer research. In Chapter 4, the manifold schools of literary theory were noted and a Bakhtinian interrogation of three contrasting disciplinary domains (marketing communications, services marketing and marketing thought) conducted. Chapter 5, furthermore, contended that the preponderant form of academic address – neutral, dispassionate, unadorned, 'scientific', etc. – is a *choice* not a requirement and drew upon studies of creativity, innovation and metaphor to suggest that other options are available – marrative, markography, markriture, call them what you will.

Exhausting though they were in some cases, the exercises presented in this volume do not claim to be exhaustive. On the contrary, they comprise merely a foretaste, a sample, a *soupçon*, a suggestion, an indicator of the sorts of studies that could be undertaken, of the opportunities for future research. As the merest fraction of the literary canon has been culled thus far, the 'marketing-in-literature' approach is ripe for further exploitation. To cite but a single example: contemporary marketing-cum-consumer research is devoting much time and effort to 'misbehaviour' or 'dark side' issues – drug addiction, alcoholism, prostitution, homelessness and so on (Holbrook 1987; Hirschman 1992, 1996; Hill 1991, 1996). These are topics that have spawned innumerable novels, short stories and various forms of creative writing, yet there have been comparatively few attempts by the academic community to combine literary theory and dark-side studies (S. Brown 1995h). True, Hirschman's (1993b) analogous interpretations of various motion pictures, Holbrook's (1991) scholarly discourse on the sorrows of consumption, and Belk's (1985, 1987b, 1989) acknowledgement of the adverse effects of untrammelled materialism as portrayed in comic books are very significant indicators of the applicability of the 'marketing-in-literature' approach to consumer misbehaviour. Nevertheless, in light of the innumerable depictions of 'dark-side' activities in works of popular fiction, additional research may prove particularly fruitful.

Although, as Belk rightly notes, 'art may often suggest innovative hypotheses that are unlikely to occur to the analytical scientist' (1986a: 24), it is equally important to stress that works of literature are not simply the source of potentially testable propositions. They are not mere canon fodder, as it were, for academic marketing researchers. Part of the thesis of this book is that creative writers and artists can provide insights into marketing phenomena that are as good, *if not better*, than those obtainable from more conventional means. I would suggest, for example, that Toby Litt's (1996b) extraordinary excursus on Mr. Kipling, the long-established, much-loved 'trade character' of a leading manufacturer of cakes and pastries (Table 6.1), says as much about the nature of the consumer-product relationship as any number of worthy but dull academic disquisitions (Callcott and Lee 1995; Mizerski 1995). In a similar vein, the columnist-cum-novelist Gilbert Adair (1995) offers an interpretative reading of a Silk Cut cigarette advertisement that is more subtle, more suggestive and more succinct than the vast majority of our sub-scientific scholarly scratchings (Table 6.2, Figure 6.2). And, when it comes to the so-called 'schemer schema' (P. Wright 1986), moreover, is there a better encapsulation of the process than Alan Coren's sublime skit on the Euro-crumpet? The essential point is not that most of our academic endeavours are worthless – whoa, what's happening to my nose? – but that we have much to learn from creative writers and artists. They are not our subordinates; they are our instructors (or our insubordinates, if you prefer).

Table 6.1 Objects in the rear view mirror may appear closer than they are

Mr Kipling, as you no doubt already know, makes *exceedingly* good cakes; and has done so now for about as long as most of us can remember, though it was, in fact, only in 1967 that he first came to public notice. What I would not expect you to know is that Mr Kipling is the best friend I have in the world. We correspond. I write to him, almost daily now, telling him of the small travails of my small life, and he replies, under a pseudonym, politely denying that he exists. He is so kind. He claims that he is merely the invention of an advertising executive, established in order to humanize a rather soggy line of cakes and biscuits. He only admitted this after a very long while; before then, he thanked me for my letters, and was afraid that he couldn't help, but was glad that I enjoyed his products. He sometimes even sent me a token. I have them, framed, up above my desk. It is a 'quiet country retreat' I have here. In fact, there is an orchard out back not dissimilar to the one in which the apples for Mr Kipling's Bramley Apple Pies are picked. There is a village postmistress, who is the 'bane' of my life. She looks like a rabid wolf and, I am sure, steams open my letters. Her name is Miss Blood. My neighbours, on the left side, dress their children in Christmas jumpers and, during the summer, walk around in rather less than was considered proper in Mr Kipling's day; on the right side, I have the dairy farm: Mrs Jones is constantly threatening but never delivering children. I live alone and am trying to get some money from the National Trust to repair the roof. It is thatched, but has not been redone since the Jubilee, when a rather shoddy job was made of it. Thatched roofs have never done particularly well under Labour governments. At four o'clock every afternoon, just as Noël Coward would have it, everything 'stops' for tea. Mr Kipling is with me in spirit. I always pour him a cup and put a little treat on his plate. Some people would say that surely by now Mr Kipling must be rather tired of eating his own cakes, but I believe that – given the prestigious circumstance (the oaken walls, the cheery log fire, the sympathetic company) – Mr Kipling could always be prevailed upon to partake. If not, then he is a different man from the one I take him for. Yesterday, it was his Battenberg Treats that I did justice to; today, Saturday, the Glazed Fruit Tartlets; tomorrow, I have not yet decided. Perhaps the Lemon Slices or perhaps the Almond. They know me of 'old' in the Village Shop, and tell me whenever Mr Kipling is preparing an innovation. 'Oh, he's harmless enough,' I heard Mrs Poon say, as I left the other day. I wonder how anyone could ever think Mr Kipling capable of harm? There was a new girl. Miss Ogbuku. I think she may diminish the pleasures of shopping. Mrs Poon anticipates me in everything, and I hope she is not thinking of retiring. Mrs Poon is only middle-aged. She does not attend church. Mr Kipling does. Mr Kipling is a High Anglican, like myself. I suspect, though, that he has more of an inclination towards Rome than I do. The occasional overuse of cinnamon in his Mince Pies tells me so. Who cannot be sensible of the lure of further incense and plusher robes? A more august tradition and a bloodier roll of honour? But I will not desert the church of Betjeman and Larkin. And Mr Kipling will never, I trust, go to Rome. I have in my letters warned him off Jesuitical dinner parties and other Popish dabblings. I believe I have made him fully aware of their dangerous allure. Such a distinguished convert, no doubt, has great attractions for them. In a way, if Mr Kipling were suborned, it would undermine the constitutional position of the Church of England. I don't quite know how, but it would. Mr Kipling does not take Earl Grey tea, being more desirous of robuster flavours; and to take, as he does, 'Three sugars, please,' in that Queen of Teas would inevitably lead to suspicions of effeminacy and, indeed, of Sodomism. No, Mr Kipling has his three heaped teaspoons in a small china cup of fine but strong Assam. I can't stand the stuff myself. We pipe smokers have a phrase for what happens when the accumulated tobacco finds its noxious way into the mouth, we call it Arab's Armpit: that is how Assam tastes to me. Mr Kipling does not smoke a pipe; he likes a long cool cigar, and I always make sure to have some in. Mr Kipling is a widower, totally devoted to his culinary craft. Mrs Kipling, sadly, died a number of years ago. They met during the Blitz, when she was the prettiest girl in the shelter, and he the dashingest man. They were happily married for 30 years. She supported him through his early struggles. She never cooked. It was a great grief to him when she passed away. He went through one of his darker periods. I like to think that the Rich Chocolate Tart is his posthumous tribute to a passion whose strength he hardly realized until it was too late. There is certainly something mournful and even gothic about this creation. A 'requiem'

Table 6.1 Contd.

---

in chocolate. Mrs Kipling is with the angels now, looking down upon Mr Kipling and blessing him and his work. I often pray to Mrs Kipling to intercede for me when, as it does, temptation overtakes me. The Own Brand Devils dance before my eyes and the Discount Demons whisper. Of course Mr Kipling's cakes are more expensive; it is because they contain love and compassion and, even, grief. I believe Mr Kipling would be the ideal man to provide flavoured wafers for the Mass, if such a measure were ever introduced to encourage new worshippers into our churches. His every recipe is a homily, his every baking, a prayer. That he makes Angel Cakes is hardly surprising. It is a great joy to him that his many nephews come to visit him at Christmas. He sometimes can be prevailed upon to put on his Santa Claus costume. The Mince Pies which he proffers during the festive season are his own humble offering to the Lamb of God. How integral they are to so many people's celebrations! On Christmas Eve, I always raise a glass of sherry to Mr Kipling, for his sterling efforts yet again in providing the larger part of the nation with their Yuletide fare. It is an heroic yet humble achievement, recalling his experiences during the Blitz. I believe we may even have fire-watched together, once or twice.

Source: Litt 1996b: 27–30
Adventures in Capitalism © Toby Litt. (1996) London: Secker & Warburg. Reproduced by kind permission of the author

Table 6.2 They asked me how I knew

Against a dark curtained background, the index finger of a svelte white-gloved hand taps, with faintly sinister aplomb, the cradle of an old-fashioned black telephone. The image is such that the casual observer could be forgiven for supposing it to be a still from an old movie whodunit (Hitchcock's *Dial M For Murder*, perhaps), but it is in fact an advertisement for cigarettes. Given, however, that there is no packet of cigarettes visible in the image and no brand name emblazoned on it, how do I know that?

By the first paradox of what is an extremely paradoxical advertisement, I know because it carries the statutory health warning from the Chief Medical Officer: Smoking Kills. That, in itself, strikes me as rather amazing – that my attention be drawn to an advertised product by virtue of the one element likely to deter me from ever purchasing it. But even if it is tempting to attribute such a perverse stratagem to the disrepute in which cigarettes are currently held, it is worth recalling that this is by no means the only case in point. In the nineteen eighties, for example, Porsche successfully revived its thirty-year-old Speedster model, whose main claim to notoriety – and, by extension, main selling point – was that

Table 6.2 Contd.

---

it was the automobile in which James Dean killed himself. Worth recalling, too, that just such brutal candour is the (equally successful) marketing tactic of the self-styled Death brand of cigarettes.

But I also know that the image is an advertisement for Silk Cut. How come? Mainly because it reminds me of the earlier ads in the same series. Initially perplexed by its obscurity, I find myself subliminally ruling out a number of other well-known brands, Marlboro, Benson & Hedges, Peter Stuyvesant and the like, with whose advertising styles I am vaguely familiar – and am left, in consequence, with Silk Cut. The advertisement has therefore entrusted the charge of driving home brand-name recognition, surely the ultimate objective of all publicity, to a convoluted process of elimination. 'This has to be for Silk Cut,' it seems to be saying to me, 'because it cannot conceivably be for anything else.'

That, anyway, is how I interpreted the ad when I originally saw it on a billboard. I subsequently came across it in a magazine and realised that the brand name is present in the image after all. Except that, as in a rebus or an acrostic, its presence actually has to be *deciphered*, an unexpected mental obstacle in publicity material, whose effectiveness one has always supposed to be predicated on instant comprehension. If one takes a close look at it, closer than is possible with a billboard, one sees that the glove, of so transparently fine a sheen as to render perceptible the outline of its wearer's fingernails, is made of white silk. And, of course, what the outstretched finger is doing is cutting the telephone connection. *Ergo*, Silk Cut.

(If I may permit myself a digression here, I have always found puzzling the fact that, in the movies, and specifically in old movies, when a character is cut off in the middle of a crucial phone call, he will always agitatedly jiggle the hook with his finger, crying, 'Hello? Hello? Are you still there?' But why on earth does he do this – since the effect is automatically to break the connection? Or has not this always been so? *Mystère*, as the French say.)

To return to Silk Cut I may seem to be making heavy weather out of what is merely an advertisement for cigarettes. But its perversity does raise a wider issue: that of Britain's increasing indifference, when not outright hostility, to advertising. Indeed, a recent poll revealed that more than half of this country's television viewers will do *anything* to avoid having to watch commercials, regarding them as a nuisance on a par with insurance salesmen and Jehovah's Witnesses. When, at the end of the first half of ITN's *News At Ten*, Trevor McDonald murmurs, 'After the break . . . ', the idea is that only the news, not the viewer, is about to take a break. Yet a commercial break tends to be considered at worst an irksome interruption and at best an intermission, except by very small children.

How, then, can advertisers continue to persuade us to purchase something

Table 6.2 Contd.

when our distaste for the medium of persuasion risks overriding our potential interest in what is on offer? Paradoxically, in Britain at least they do so by seeking to disguise the basic mercantile nature of the exercise, winning us over to their side by giving us the impression that they actually share our own growing contempt for the whole business of advertising.

For many advertisers, the product is becoming not much more than a MacGuffin, as Hitchcock called it, a narrative factor of no especial significance except in so far as it generates a brief fragment of fiction (the most famously Gold Blend ads). And the most ingenious of all are those who, as Hitchcock himself did, appear to enjoy setting themselves self-referential challenges, often (as with the Silk Cut television commercial) at the expense of the product itself. Thus the Munchies ad ridicules the very brand name which it is supposed to be promoting. That for First Direct telephone banking makes humorous play out of its own lack of production values. Boddington's Beer parodies rival commercials. And the John Smith Beer ads with Jack Dee mock, even as they exploit, the codified language of publicity. The more disrespectfully a product is treated, the more appealing, apparently, we start to find it.

It is, when you think about it, an extraordinarily sophisticated approach to the question of selling something and one which, as yet, has remained a local speciality. Certainly, anyone who has ever been exposed to American commercials will have noted how positively prehistoric their methods are by comparison with ours. Here, then, is one area where it is possible to refer to real old British knowhow – and also, for once, to real old American don't knowhow.

Source: Adair 1995: 4

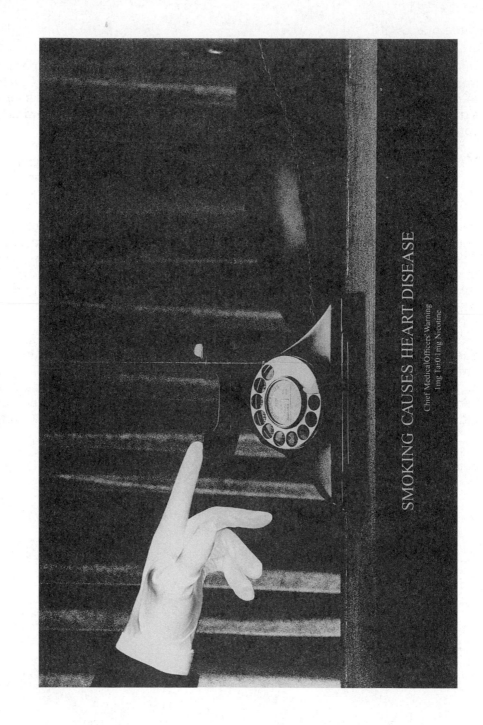

Figure 6.2 No Bettman, no cry

Another, and perhaps the most important, point to be made about marketing aesthetics is that works of art go beyond mere description. At their best, they are capable of unveiling the hitherto veiled, of rendering the intangible tangible, of giving form to the unformed, of making the incoherent cohere, of not just telling but *compelling* the truth. Granted, the very act of discussing these issues leaves us open to the charge of pretentiousness (*nous?*), but as Ernst Bloch (1988) maintains, great works of art exhibit *Vor-Schein* ('anticipatory illumination'), a kind of fore-glow of future possibilities. They provide a means of bringing the not-yet-conscious into (sudden, seemingly miraculous) consciousness. In this respect, it is surely no accident that the foremost American philosopher Richard Rorty (1980, 1989) cleaves to the view that in the absence of timeless, indisputable Truth we must turn away from exhausted positivistic philosophies and, by drawing upon imaginative literary genres like ethnography, journalism, comic books, docudramas and, above all, the novel, endeavour to position ourselves as 'auxiliary to the poet rather than to the physicist' (Rorty 1989: 9). Analogously, Umberto Eco aphoristically notes that 'the fundamental question of philosophy (like that of psychoanalysis) is the same as the question of the detective novel: who is guilty?' (1985: 54). For Young and Caveney, furthermore, 'fiction is now the closest we're likely to come to truth and as such it should be loved and cherished' (1992: viii).

Fiction, in actual fact, is truer that truth because, unlike Truth, it does not pretend to be true.

Just as there is ample scope for additional study of 'marketing in literature', so too the 'literature-in-marketing' tradition possesses enormous potential. Apart from the application of lit-crit procedures beyond the by now familiar arena of advertising and promotion – the service encounter, new product development, retailing and distribution, marketing relationships, etc. – it is clear that the academic marketing literature itself is in sore need of critical interrogation. To some extent this is already happening, what with C. J. Thompson's (1993) timely reading of the tumultuous 'realism versus relativism' contretemps, Stern's (1996c) studies of writing strategies in consumer research, Marion's (1993) revelation of Levitt and Keith's rhetorical sleights of hand, and Heilbrunn's (1996b) narratological explication of the classic cognition–affect–conation model. But more and more detailed investigations are necessary. Again, to cite a couple of illustrative examples, an application of David Lodge's (1977) celebrated metaphor–metonymy dialectic may prove very pertinent to the development of marketing thought. Derived from the work of Roman Jakobson, co-founder of both the Moscow and Prague Linguistic Circles, Lodge contends that the history of the novel is characterized by a cyclical trajectory, by periods when metaphor is predominant and eras when metonymy holds centre stage. Applied to marketing constructs, this dialectic helps illuminate the process whereby innovative metaphors (e.g. the wheel of retailing) are subject to metonymical extension (multiple wheels, reversed wheels, broken wheels, slowing wheels, speeding wheels, spare wheels, wheels within wheels, wheels on fire, wheel you give me a break) until such times as a new metaphor bursts on to the scene, only to undergo the same metonymical accretion process (cf. the retail life-cycle).

Likewise, it doesn't take a stroke of genius to appreciate that Northrop Frye's (1971) five-stage model of the evolution of the novel or Harold Bloom's (1973) thesis on the 'anxiety of influence' are applicable to the trajectory of marketing thought. The latter states that poets (and ambitious intellectuals generally) position themselves against, are antithetical to and 'write against' the achievements of their forebears. This essentially oedipal interpretation of the contest for aesthetic ascendancy is acknowledged by many leading writers (Calvino 1986; Kundera 1988; Barth 1990; Said 1995) and, applied to our own domain, this Markipus Complex provides a means of conceptualizing, if not explaining, the art/science debate, the realist/relativist tussle or, more recently, the transactions/relationships transition. In complete contrast to Bloom's dialectical procedure, Frye identifies five (recursive) phases in the history of the novel: *myth*, where the hero is superior in kind; *romance*, where the hero is superior in degree; *high mimetic*, where the hero is still superior but subject to the same constraints as ourselves; *low mimetic*, where the hero is one of us; and *ironic*, where the hero is inferior to ourselves. Once again, the evolution of marketing thought can be viewed in terms of this framework. In the mythical era of the 1950s, giants like Levitt, Alderson and Drucker bestrode the scene, expounding their visions of a perfect marketing world. The romantic era of the 1960s witnessed the heroic struggle of Kotler, Levy and the like to broaden marketing's scope, despite the reservations of the little people. In the 1970s, high mimetic predominated in the form of social, societal and macro-marketing, when the constraints of the environment impinged increasingly upon our disciplinary consciousness, whereas the low mimetic era of the 1980s saw the rise of the everyday – interpretivism, relativism and quotidian concerns like implementation. As for the advent of irony in the 1990s, it is clear that Frye's framework breaks down completely at this point. Marketing, fortunately, is an irony-free zone. It has no time for insouciance, irreverence or buffoonery and subscribes to David Ogilvy's uncompromising (possibly ironic?) credo that 'no one buys from a joker'. Most importantly of all perhaps, if irony *did* obtain, if parody prevailed, if mockery abounded, then the dominant concept of the present decade, relationship marketing, would surely be exposed as an hopelessly ironic endeavour, a huge joke, a straight-faced scholarly spoof. As we noted in Chapter 4, that simply isn't the case. Thank goodness.

Appealing though it is, not least on account of its suggestion that an upsurge of irony is a harbinger of significant change, Frye's framework is possibly too structuralist for contemporary postmodern tastes, as indeed are Bloom's and Lodge's. Hence, a more fruitful line of future research inquiry may well be found in the 'marketing-as-literature' approach; that is, in a deliberate attempt to write (right?) academic discourse in a creative, non-scientific, unashamedly 'literary' fashion. Although they are something of a commonplace in contiguous disciplines, new literary forms (NLF) remain conspicuous by their absence in marketing and consumer research. As we have seen, some gifted scholars have championed and, moreover, demonstrated the utility of such approaches, but a combination of factors has been sufficient to staunch the flow of creative juices and ensure that demonstrations of academic literary virtuosity remain regrettably few and far between. These include inertia, tenurism, the peer review process, the extant horizons of generic expectations, an ineradicable residue of the marketing science mind set, a lack of familiarity with the appropriate (aesthetic) criteria by which to assess the 'worth' of any individual contribution, and, above all I suspect, an old-fashioned fear of failure, of being deemed uppity, unstable, untrustworthy, unacceptable; in a word, unpublishable.

If there is a single message contained in this book, apart of course from the subtle subliminal embeds designed to increase your appetite for the works of Stephen Brown, it is that marketing academics should seek to adopt more expressive modes of expression. Despite appearances to the contrary, there are real, tangible, discipline-enhancing benefits to be gained from such literary endeavours, not least a long-overdue realignment with marketing practitioners and elevated standing in the eyes of propinquitous scholarly specialisms. To this end, the introspective process of critical self-examination, what Kundera terms 'meditative interrogation' (1988: 31), is of paramount importance. By reflecting on our own marketing-related behaviours and trying to capture them in poetic, aesthetic, creative prose, we can succeed in saying the unsaid, grasping the ungraspable, and by bringing into consciousness the hitherto hidden, the inchoate, the unformed, generate meaningful, original and important insights into marketplace phenomena. Granted, personal subjective introspection is procedure *non grata* at present, though I suspect that Wallendorf and Brucks' (1993) critique will be remembered as the marketing counterpart of the record labels that rejected the Beatles or the aesthetic establishmentarians who excoriated Van Gogh, the Brontë sisters, John Keats, Thomas Hardy, Friedrich Nietzsche *et al.* Yet, one only has to read the flat, drab, uninspired prose of the typical ethnographic account – positivistic papers aren't worth reading at all – to appreciate that, by comparison, even moderately well-written introspective essays literally leap off the page (well, okay, leap meta-phorically) and make you feel *part* of the experience. Although they are first-class, well-conducted, perfectly competent examples of the ethnographic genre, Holt's (1995b) cub-reportage from Wrigley Field or Schouten and McAlexander's (1995) hogtied description of the Harley Davidson subculture, to mention but two, manifestly do not communicate the inherent excitement – the *rapture* – of the subject matter (although the authors occasionally exhibit real flashes of literary sensibility, as in Schouten and McAlexander's (1995: 49) wonderful allusion to 'riding highly customised Harleys down the backroads of mid-life crises').

Indeed, and at the risk of being excoriated out of hand, I would contend that Table 6.3, an introspective account written by one of my undergraduate students, is more the sort of thing we should be striving for (Lyttle 1996). This particular shopping expedition may not resonate or reverberate with you as an individual, though it most certainly did with me? nevertheless the introspective procedure itself comes through the experience unscathed. As the commanding intellectual heavyweight and polymath about town George Steiner, magisterially observes:

> More than ordinary men and women, the significant painter, sculptor, musician or poet relates the raw material, the anarchic prodigalities of consciousness and sub-consciousness to the latencies, often unperceived, untapped before him, of articulation. This translation out of the inarticulate and the private into the general matter of human recognition requires the utmost crystallisation and investment of introspection and control.
>
> (Steiner 1989: 12)

We may well be ordinary marketing men and women, incapable of the utmost introspective investment, but surely we can strive to write in a manner than has 'implosive powers within the echo chambers of the self' (Steiner 1989: 10).

Table 6.3 Should I stay or should I go?

'Do we really have to go to this bloody wedding?' was my first question, when I arrived at the front door of my girlfriend's (now ex-girlfriend) house, who had been nagging me for weeks to take her shopping in Belfast to look for a dress for her and a suit for myself so we could look the part at a wedding we had been invited to. Up to that point I had made every excuse not to go, but in the end I had

Table 6.3 Contd.

---

to give in and get used to the idea of walking from one end of Belfast to the other in search of a long black dress for my girlfriend and a suit for myself which I didn't think I needed as I had a suit in my wardrobe at home that I had only worn once or twice. This shopping expedition to most people would seem quite a simple task, but in hindsight I think it was the beginning of the end of a beautiful relationship.

As we drove down the M1 motorway towards Belfast I was still trying to come up with excuses why we shouldn't bother going to the wedding. From the first day that the invitation came through the letterbox I did not want to go considering I had only met the happy couple once before and even that seemed like a distant memory. The bride to be had worked with my girlfriend as a hotel receptionist some two years earlier and decided that we should attend the wedding. We arranged to meet at a bar on the Lisburn Road in order to get acquainted. I thought I would give myself a head start and arrived at the pub an hour before the time we had arranged and started sinking a few pints of the old blonde with the black dress (Guinness). The rest of the night went quite well from what I remembered, as I went from the stage of being slightly tipsy to extremely drunk in double quick time. But I still didn't want to go to the wedding.

We arrived in Belfast, parked the car, and started to get on with the task in hand of looking for the long black dress. I don't mind going shopping as long as I'm going shopping for myself. I can happily wander around on my own as I know exactly what I want before I start. But I hate going shopping with my girlfriend who has to get into every ladies shop – and more.

Things started off quite well that day. I followed her around the various shops, wading through the rails of clothing, stopping every now and then for her to pick something off a rail, hold it up to herself, and then look to me for some sort of sign of approval. This ritual would go on until she had an armful of clothes, then it was off to the changing rooms while I waited for her to appear every five minutes to ask me what I thought. I would try and look interested, complimenting her on how well she looked in the outfit, but after half an dozen more shops I was trying to sound more convincing in the hope that she would take my word for it and buy the bloody thing, but she wasn't to be fooled. Saying that the outfit didn't feel right on her and that she knew another shop that she could try.

So off we headed again, hand in hand, with me trying to reassure her that I really did like the last outfit that she had tried on, only to be told to put out the cigarette I had just lit. I wouldn't have minded that much, only it was the first one I had smoked since we left home.

We walked for what seemed like hours from shop to shop and then back again, and I hadn't had a chance to look for a suit for myself but that didn't seem to matter. My girlfriend then dropped the bombshell. When she had found the dress

Table 6.3 Contd.

---

that she wanted she would need a pair of shoes to match. 'Shit!' We would have to walk from one of Belfast to the other again. I started to realize how my dog, Ben must feel when I drag him along on the lead when he doesn't really want to go.

We entered another ladies boutique and went through the same procedure of looking through the rails of clothes with me nodding approval like one of those miniature dogs you sometimes see in the back window of a car. Then it was off to the changing rooms with me standing like a sentry outside waiting while she tried on the various outfits.

The changing rooms in this particular store just happened to be positioned right at the back of the store smack in the middle of the lingerie department. I wouldn't have minded, only, where I was standing there were ladies parading in and out past me with handfuls of knickers and bras giving me funny sideways glances. The sight of ladies with their underwear in their hands didn't annoy me as I had a business of my own which stocked among other things the same type of ladies underwear, and I was used to them asking me for all shapes, colours and sizes. But standing in the middle of these ladies I started to feel very uncomfortable and imagined that all eyes were fixed on me as if I was some sort of Peeping Tom. I said to myself that this was it. I wasn't going into any more shops to stand around like a wet lettuce while my girlfriend tried on clothes that she seemed to have no intention of buying. When she emerged from the changing room with that look on her face that meant that we would have a look elsewhere for the long black dress, I gave one of those eyes-half-closed, teeth-gritted looks that you give when you are extremely pissed off with someone, and she duly gave me one back. I knew from that moment that the rest of the day was going to be a disaster, and that is exactly what it turned out to be.

I suggested that maybe we could get a cup of coffee and something to eat, but that was the wrong suggestion. We would have to get the dress before we did anything else. At this stage in the proceedings I was walking about ten paces behind my girlfriend, who had broken into what can only be described as a gallop. When I eventually caught up with her she had a face like a bulldog chewing a wasp and started to give me my second public warning of the day. At this point I didn't care about getting myself a suit. I just wanted her to get the dress so that we could get the hell out of Belfast.

And so, with total disinterest I followed my girlfriend around a few more shops until eventually she had satisfied herself that every shop that could possibly have done what she wanted had been visited, and so we headed back to one of the first that we had been in at the start of the day. At this point our conversation consisted of two words, yes and no, but I was prepared to give it one last go as we entered through the front door of Jigsaw for the second time. Our first visit had been a friendly shopping experience with very friendly staff greeting us with a

Table 6.3 Contd.

---

smile and asking if they could be of assistance.

This time around the reaction seemed to be quite the opposite. The staff didn't smile or ask us if they could help. They were more interested in standing around talking among themselves and sniggering. When my girlfriend had made her choice and asked if they would have it in her size the assistant looked directly at the clock on the wall which showed the time as being ten past five, twenty minutes before closing time. I made a comment to my girlfriend that maybe we should let them keep the dress and look elsewhere, just as the assistant came back from looking for the correct size and informed us that that particular dress had sold really well and that there were only two left, and neither was the size that my girlfriend wanted. We were just about to leave the store when my girlfriend spotted the dress among other clothes on a rail, and upon closer inspection found it to be the correct size. I immediately looked around at the assistant, who turned and started to make herself busy tidying the clothes on a rail. At this point I really wanted to let rip with a well-rehearsed string of verbal abuse, but decided that it wouldn't read that well on a charge-sheet if the worst came to the worst and the assistant decided that she needed the help of the 'boys in blue' to calm the situation. And so, I thought the best course of action would be for my girlfriend and myself to leave the shop minus the dress. But no! My girlfriend had other ideas. As I headed for the door expecting her to follow, she made a beeline for the changing room with the dress slung over her arm. At this point I was outside in the street mouthing obscenities to myself and feeling a real prick, convincing myself that I would definitely not be going to the wedding. When my girlfriend appeared from the changing room kitted out in the long black dress, she wagged me to come in and take a look, but there was no chance. I shouted to her that I would meet her back at the car, turned on my heels and walked off.

I was sitting in the car for about ten minutes thinking just how fast our relationship was going downhill when she arrived holding a Jigsaw carrier bag smiling from ear to ear. She jumped into the car and proceeded to tell me how well the dress had looked on and that she would have to get a pair of shoes to match. I couldn't believe it. Gone was the bulldog, and the wasp features had been replaced by a butter wouldn't melt in the mouth look. I pointed out that we had spent so much time looking for the bloody dress I hadn't had a chance to look for a suit for myself. This didn't seem a real problem to her, and she suggested that we could come down to Belfast another day and look for a suit. At this point the shit really hit the fan. I told her that the wedding invitation was worse than getting a bloody summons, and that I definitely wouldn't be going, so she may make other arrangements.

As we headed out of the car park towards the NCP attendant in his little booth, I realized that I didn't have any change, and I wasn't going to ask her. When I

Table 6.3 Contd.

---

handed over the ticket to the attendant and was duly asked to pay the amount I handed over a ten pound note, at which the attendant took a look and proceeded to tear strips off me, shouting about the correct fucking change, and how I was holding up the rest of the motorists behind me. At this point I replied with a stream of equally colourful language, while my girlfriend sat beside me telling me to shut up, instead of at least backing me up or producing the correct change. When we eventually left the car park with wheels spinning, my temper had moved into the red face with busting headache stage and stayed like that until we were halfway down the motorway.

The hairs on the back of my neck had just settled down when up behind me in the fast lane came a car with its headlights flashing. I instinctively took a look at the speedometer as this type of thing has happened to me before. It was reading 78 MPH and my fear soon became reality when the sound of a siren and a uniformed arm out of the window of the following car indicated that I should pull over. A very polite conversation ensued on my behalf and I was allowed to continue my journey after a stern warning. We continued in the direction of home with not a word spoken between either of us until we had reached my girlfriend's house. It was then that I started to relate in detail the day's shopping experience, and why we would not be doing it again in the near future.

Needless to say, I went back on my word and attended the wedding, and surprisingly enough we had a really good day. My girlfriend in her new black dress and me in my nearly new suit. But at the end of the day we would never go through a nightmare shopping experience again like it, or at least not together anyway, as we decided shortly after that to go our separate ways.

Appetite for destruction

According to the celebrated literary theorist Wayne Booth (1983), writers should seek to show as well as tell and, in keeping with this credo, the present volume has endeavoured to make its case in a 'showy' manner. Irrespective of whether this ambition has been successfully or unsuccessfully realized, it seems to me that several contrasting reactions are likely to be prompted by my attempted postmodern fusion of literature and marketing. The first of these is simply to dismiss the project *in toto*, to treat it as an aberration, an embarrassment, a mistake, a grotesque deviation from the norms of the discipline and, not to mince words, a singularly inappropriate experiment that has served not only to bring marketing into serious academic disrepute, but also to subvert our long-cherished desire to be regarded as a worthy incumbent of the ivy-clad ivory tower. It represents, frankly, a ridiculous attempt to rationalize the irrational, legitimize the illegitimate, justify the unjustifiable and, by means of its smart-ass posturing and self-serving iconoclasm, permit the impermissible. Risibly, moreover, it merely conforms to the non-conformist cliché, the unconventional convention, the stereotyped, the hackneyed, the standardized all too standardized rebel without applause (Seal 1996). It is, in sum, the unacceptable face of postmodernism.

If that is your reaction, so be it. But before you send me into intellectual exile, let me just ask you one question: what *exactly* is being put at risk by books such as this? Our academic ambitions and credibility, perhaps? (Have you actually *read* what other disciplines say about us?) Our position at the top of the scholarly tree? (I can only surmise we got there while most of us were otherwise engaged.) The respect and admiration of adjacent subject areas? (Don't kid yourself; even org. studies looks down on us.) Or, what about the undying support of practising managers, prospective managers, policy-makers and the general public? (Do I *really* have to answer that one?) But, then again, we're just an emergent subject area, aren't we? Marketing's still developing, isn't it? Nascent, don't you know. Finding its intellectual feet, a veritable academic babe in arms; great things will happen in the fullness of time. Now, how could I possibly have forgotten that old saw? I'm sorry, folks, but we really should start to face up to the fact that marketing scholarship is more than 100 years old. There are newer kids on the academic block – genetics, sociology of scientific knowledge (SSK), cultural studies, etc. – that have *already* achieved more than us. Time's up for the 'give us time' excuse, I'm afraid.

Irrespective of your irritation at, distaste for, or hostility towards my approach, if you have managed to read this far you must by now appreciate that every time you put pen to paper you are *choosing* to write the way you do. Every time you express yourself in what Agger (1989) terms the 'midwestern empiricist' mode of enunciation, you are reinforcing its 'rightness' and literally sentencing marketing to the lowest levels of the intellectual hierarchy. Every time you crank out a paper according to the 'normal', 'usual' or 'standard' formula, you are perpetuating the hegemonic (in a Gramscian sense) character of academic marketing discourse; you are – with apologies to Althusser – sustaining extant ISAs (Ideological Scholarly Apparatuses) and RSAs (Repressive Scholarly Apparatuses). This book, for all its faults, has tried to demonstrate that there is an alternative, a sustainable alternative, to the academic marketing argot of lifeless, desiccated, disinterested and indeed uninteresting prose. Granted, it is harder to get published when you write in a 'literary' manner. Granted, your bridges are irrevocably burned when you cross the Rubicon and decide to mix with metaphors. Granted, the risks are greater, as Holbrook regularly reminds us. But only in the short term; only until such times as the mainstream opens its eyes to what's happening in adjoining disciplines; only until marketing's absurd infatuation with 'science' is deposited in the non-recyclable bottle bank of history (and metaphors don't come much more mixed than that). Next time you sit down at your desk, remember that third-person, passive-voice, unadorned modes of expression are a custom not a command, a convention not a condition, a choice not a covenant. And if you don't believe me – why should you after all the tall tales I've told you? – I recommend you read Agger's (1989) outstanding critique of the sociological literature, virtually every word of which is applicable to contemporary marketing scholarship.

Another, somewhat different, objection that can be levelled at this particular volume is that it doesn't go far enough, it's not sufficiently postmodern, it only regurgitates what has already been said by other – and better – marketing researchers. As unreasonable criticisms go, this one is perfectly reasonable and not one I would try to repudiate. Yes, I could have devoted the present essay to a lengthy discussion of the latest thoughts of the leading lights of postmodernism, not to mention dealing with the ones I didn't cover in the first volume, and related their latter-day reflections to the theory and practice of marketing. I yield to no one in my undying admiration for Jean Baudrillard (to mention but one among many postmodernist possibilities). We have much to learn, as marketers, from his often staggeringly brilliant *aperçus*. Consider, for instance, his recent revelation: 'At Disneyworld in Florida they are building a giant mock-up of Hollywood, with the boulevards, studios etc. One more spiral in the simulacrum. One day they will rebuild Disneyland at Disneyworld' (Baudrillard 1996: 42). Or, what about his suggestion that:

> In the southern hemisphere, tornadoes and cyclones, like the water in the sinks, spin in the opposite direction from the northern hemisphere. It would be nice for the same to be true of social phenomena. And, in fact, it is. Marketing analysts have shown that the human flows in Australian supermarkets also move in the opposite direction.
>
> (Baudrillard 1996: 53)

These cogitations may or may not be true – who cares? – but they are wonderful examples of a creative marketing imagination at work and an inspiration to us all.

Yet despite the undeniable attractions of the 'sceptical' strand of postmodern thought, my suspicion is that this nihilistic, essentially continental European perspective – although wonderfully refreshing to imbibe on occasion – is incapable of sustaining a programme of empirical research. By its own anti-representational criteria, it cannot do so because empiricism is ruled out of postmodern court

(Rosenau 1992; Bonnycastle 1996). Thus, it is always susceptible to the rejoinder: 'Ok, you have told us that our existing models, theories, concepts and suchlike are wrongheaded, mistaken, unsustainable, old-fashioned and so on, but unless you have something better to put in their place we'll stick with the imperfect devils we know.' Postmodernism of the Baudrillardian or Derridean variety is impotent against this kind of critique, and it follows that the 'affirmative', the storytelling, the anecdotal, the autobiographical, the conversational, the confessional, the narrative-based, the less extreme school of Anglo-American postmodernism possesses greater revolutionary potential, paradoxical though it at first appears.

To be sure, the espousal of a storytelling stance is not new and proponents of such an approach are condemned to labour in the immense shadow cast by Morris Holbrook, arguably the foremost exponent of marketing's latter-day literary turn. To be honest, I'd be delighted to have my third-rate, second-hand thoughts described as Holbrookian, as Holbrook-babble, as I-can't-believe-it's-not-Morris. If this volume helps further Holbrook's intellectual agenda, so much the better. There is no doubt that Morris Holbrook is one of the finest literary stylists in the marketing academy, although his perennial complaints about maltreatment at the hands of the Odyssians (who portrayed him as a 'big game hunter') are wearing somewhat thin. Holbrook may not be a big game hunter in any literal sense, but his inordinate fondness for animalistic tropes clearly reveals that he is a big game *metaphunter*. As he has ruthlessly exploited the entire animal kingdom in his pursuit of expositional figures – cats, dogs, fish, birds, turtles, wolves, gorillas and, heaven help us, *roaches* – Holbrook will doubtless go down in history as the Buffalo Bill, the Tom-cat Cody, the Kitty Carson of marketing scholarship.

Notwithstanding my overall support for Holbrook's aesthetic quest and his robust defence of personal subjective introspection, I would contend that, aside from the respective emphases on high and low culture, there is one all-important difference between the literary agendas of Morris the Cat and myself. Whereas Holbrook has long opposed the academic–executive connection in pursuit of his characteristically romantic vision of intellectual purity, I am not concerned about consorting with managers, since studying marketing practitioners is not necessarily the same as serving their interests. Whereas Holbrook considers aesthetics to be a means of breaking free from our banausic bindings, I regard them as a way of restoring the sadly sundered link between practitioner and pedagogue. Whereas, furthermore, Holbrook writes to convince fellow intellectuals of the rightness of his cause, I hope against hope (and the advance on my royalties) that marketing managers will read, enjoy and get something useful from this text, if only a chuckle or two.

Lest there is any misunderstanding, however, let me make it absolutely clear that, although I am sympathetic to the managerial cause, I don't consider it necessary to dance to the practitioners' tune. On the contrary, I would argue than my kind of (im)pure research – conducted for its own sake, driven by curiosity, unfettered by 'pragmatic' considerations – is actually *more relevant* to today's marketing managers than the brainless, bullet-pointed, model-building, customer-hugging, here's-a-matrix-I-prepared-earlier garbage that passes for 'practitioner-oriented' marketing scholarship. Ironic, or what? Postmodern, or what? Hail, hail rock and roll!

The final line of attack[1] likely to be taken against the present text lies somewhere between the total antipathy of the first and the insufficiently postmodern of the second, though it may appear, on the surface at least, to be the most depredatory of all. Proponents of this position are broadly sympathetic to the 'affirmative' post-modern cause, recognize the academic benefits that may accrue from literary analyses and appreciate that it is not enough to advocate creative marketing writing, it must also be demonstrated. Poems, tropes, conceits and figures of speech are grist to their metaphorical mills. 'Marketing in literature', 'literature in marketing' and 'marketing as literature' are as mother's milk to new born babes (yeah I know, I'm really scraping the metaphorical bottom of my metaphor barrel, but, as my use of the barrel-scraping metaphor indicates, I'm just about troped out by this stage – forgive me). They don't have the slightest problem with the argument advanced herein. Their objections, rather, concern the *tone* of my thesis – the parody, the punning, the wisecracks, the ridicule, the irreverence, the insincerity, the mockery, the effrontery, the cruelty, the quips, the guru-baiting, the abuse, the

---

1 Yes, I appreciate that there are likely to be several other critiques, but as these are certain to come from the nit-picking, it's-my-paradigm-and-I'll-pry-if-I-want-to crowd, there's no real point in responding, since it only encourages them. You know the sort of people I mean. They'll say, 'Science is defined as "disciplined inquiry", therefore your art/science dichotomy is a gross caricature.' I know it is. It's meant to be (just go and read Bloom's (1975) *A Map of Misreading*, will you?). And, anyway, it's ill-disciplined inquiry I'm advocating! Others will complain about my narrow focus on literature – 'aesthetics are much more than books, you understand' – or gripe about my failure to make more of the muscial metaphor (marketing as rock band – elements working in harmony, role of improvization, audience participation, etc.). Yeah, yeah, yeah. I know. Fiddle with the trope if you want to. Do I have to do everything for you? Then, of course, there are the *real* pedants. 'Surely,' they'll smirk, 'Adam Smith described the *invisible* – not the *hidden* – hand of the market.' I know, but 'hidden' is also used and it suited my purposes better. Worst of all are the do-gooding pluralists. 'Why can't we all be friends?' 'Why can't we all show a little toleration toward each other's preferred research approaches?' (*Translation*: 'please allow my work to be published and I promise not to complain about your papers full of meaningless structural equations.') What's wrong with conflict?, I say. As Nietzsche points out in *The Genealogy of Morals*, 'If a temple is to be erected, *a temple must be destroyed*: that is the law' (1956, 2: 24).

slang, the effing, the blinding, the incessant crudity, the unremitting carnality, the coitus uninterruptus. That sort of language, that sort of behaviour, that sort of treatment doubtless has its place, but that place is not in works of marketing scholarship.

Look, I can fully appreciate that many marketers may find my expositional strategy distasteful, even though such forms of expression are routine in everyday life, numerous cultural spheres (films, books, magazines, television), certain academic domains (women's studies and gay studies, for instance) and, not least, contemporary marketing practices (cf. the notorious 'Beaver-España' campaign for Club 18–30). I am well aware, moreover, that lowering the literary tone is a dangerous rhetorical manoeuvre and I didn't embrace it lightly, believe me (ssshhh, keep it down, I'm pretending to be sincere here). There are, nevertheless, several perfectly legitimate, eminently defensible reasons for adopting the strategy I did, not least its defamiliarizing function, its above-mentioned ability to throw the 'conventionality' of the conventional academic approach into sharp relief and thereby indicate the existence of alternative expositional options. More importantly perhaps, the parody, the playfulness, the profanity, the all-pervasive priapism are very much in keeping with postmodernism. Parody, as numerous academic authorities make perfectly clear, is the postmodern mode of expression *par excellence* (Hutcheon 1989; Haraway 1990; McHale 1992; Waugh 1992b; McRobbie 1994; Gane 1995). It never ceases to amaze me that people continue to take seriously – and fulminate at length about – the manifestly ironic, sarcastic, tongue-in-cheek comments of Baudrillard, Derrida, Foucault and the like. Baudrillard's espousal of 'pataphysics', for example, is predicated on the work of Alfred Jarry (1873–1907), a renowned practical joker. Is it any wonder, when he is excoriated by right-on, left-wing zealots, that Baudrillard is moved to retort, 'What is being destroyed more quickly than the ozone layer is the subtle layer of irony that protects us from the radiation of stupidity' (1996: 34)? Likewise, Derrida's deconstruction is almost entirely playful in spirit – at one stage he asks himself, 'what am I going to be able to come up with this time?' (Derrida 1992: 311) – although the procedure has been systematized, routinized, asceticized, diluted and, yes, emasculated by its more high-minded administrators, the Yale School in particular. Foucault, furthermore, famously opens his breakthrough text *The Order of Things* with a brief explanation that:

> This book first arose out of a passage from Borges, out of the laughter that shattered, as I read the passage, all the familiar landmarks of my thought – *our* thought, the thought that bears the stamp of our age and our geography

> – breaking up all the ordered surfaces and all the planes with which we are accustomed to tame the wild profusion of existing things, and continuing long afterwards to disturb and threaten with collapse our age-old distinction between the Same and the Other.
>
> (Foucault 1972: xv)

In a similar vein, the sexual–textual connection is made again and again by postmodern thinkers, whether it be Barthes' (1990a, 1990b) '*jouissance*' and *A Lover's Discourse*, Foucault's (1979, 1986, 1990) histories of sexuality, Kristeva's (1982) 'desire in language', Baudrillard's (1990) 'seduction', Lyotard's (1993c) 'libidinal economy', Deleuze and Guattari's (1984) 'micropolitics of desire', Bakhtin's (1984) 'grotesque body' or Derrida's veritable deluge of sex-text terms: 'dissemination' (1981a), 'invagination' (1979), 'hymen' (1981b), 'phallogocentrism' (1982), etc. So prevalent, indeed, is this propensity that the postmodern condition can reasonably be described as a textually transmitted disease, as a license for textual promiscuity, textual intercourse, textual deviation, textual liberation, textual abandon, textual perversion, textual politics, textual congress, textual fantasy, textual energy, textual frenzy, textual awakenings, bitextuality, homotextuality, heterotextuality and textual emissions, secretions, lucubrations, juices, fluids, flows, flux (see also Belsey 1994; Rhiel and Suchoff 1996; Simon 1996).

There is, however, yet another reason for the rhetorical effusions/excesses/excrescences of *Postmodern Marketing Two* and that is its espousal – its attempted embodiment – of the carnivalesque. As we found in Chapter 4, carnival is characterized by inversion, by exaggeration, by transgression, by liminality, by perversity, by impiety, by grotesquerie, by debauchery, by reflexivity, by cheek, by jowl, by genitalia. For Bakhtin (1984), moreover, carnival is not just a temporary transposition, an amusing sideshow, or spectacle, designed to reinforce the rules by breaking them (the allow'd fool of *Twelfth Night*). It is a fundamental correlate of the human condition, a means of societal and intellectual transformation, a long-established propensity – *a propensity associated, above all, with the marketplace* – that cannot be restrained or repressed, at least not for long. The carnivalesque is always liable to erupt unexpectedly, in unusual locales, and sweep the prevailing status quo, the doxa, the Establishment, aside in a gale of ribald and irreverent laughter. Whereas rational critique is almost certain to fail – both 'sides' merely rehearse incommensurable arguments and talk past one another – the carnivalesque modes of parody, irony, scatology and satire, its extravagant dialectic of high praise and low abuse, can prove to be very powerful political weapons when used successfully

(R. H. Brown 1989, 1995; Powell and Paton 1988; Griffin 1994; Palmer 1994; Fine and Martin 1995).

Carnival can be, and often is, condemned as mere froth, mildly diverting, an irrelevance at best and at worst a sop to the proletariat. Conversely, it can be considered a means of control through decontrol, a moment of authorized madness, which sustains rather than subverts the existing order. However, the long and distinguished history of carnivalesque literature – Aristophanes, Sterne, Swift, Cervantes, Balzac, Wilde, Dostoyevsky, Waugh, etc. – suggests that, by undermining and helping break up discursive and epistemological formations, it helps create conditions conducive to the possibility of change (Belk 1994). The real power of the carnivalesque, therefore, resides in its ability to suspend the present, to step outside the extant, to intimate that alternative arrangements, be they social, political, cultural, scholarly or whatever, are indeed attainable. Just as jokes are often regarded as the epitome of metaphorical thinking (Palmer 1994), and playfulness the essence of creativity (J.N.T. Martin 1991), so too carnival provides a cornucopia of choices, options, prospects, imaginings, possibilities. Carnival, for Bakhtin, is essentially *utopian*, an escape from the official way of life, a communal expression of belief in a future time in which fear, authority and repression are vanquished.

> Carnival is not a spectacle seen by the people; they live in it, and everyone participates because its very idea embraces all the people. While carnival lasts, there is no other life outside it. During carnival time life is subject only to its laws, that is, the laws of its own freedom. It has a universal spirit; it is the special condition of the entire world, of the world's revival and renewal, in which all take part. Such is the essence of carnival . . . the second life of the people, who for a time entered the utopian realm of community, freedom, equality and abundance.
>
> (Bakhtin 1984: 6–7)

Now 'utopian', I grant you, is a word that is infrequently encountered in a marketing context (but see Floch 1988; C. J. Thompson *et al.* 1994; C. J. Thompson and Holt 1996). It carries connotations of impractical, unrealistic, otherworldly daydreamers, accusations that are rarely, if ever, levelled at marketing practitioners or, postmodernists excepted, the vast majority of marketing academics. What is more, the long history of literary utopias, which commenced in 1516 when Sir Thomas More conflated the Greek terms *outopia* (no place) and *eutopia* (good place) to describe his blessed isle (although the concept of a perfect world – Eden, Arcadia, Paradise and so on – long predates More), reveals that their authors are implacably opposed, as a rule, to the marketing system (Brown, Maclaran and Stevens 1996). Commercial life, in all its myriad manifestations, is considered inimical to the good life, the perfect society, the ideal world that utopian writers and commentators typically portray. Yet, the briefest acquaintance with utopian precepts indicates not only that marketing practice is deeply, irredeemably utopian, but that the *creation* of utopias, or utopian surrogates, is nothing less than marketing's *raison d'être*. True, the archetypal marketing utopias of fresh breath, clean clothing, shiny hair, safe sex and instant credit may be less grandiose than the visions of universal societal transformation propounded by the great nineteenth-century utopian prophets like Saint-Simon, Comte and Marx, but marketing more than any other contemporary cultural institution is the keeper of the late-twentieth-century utopian flame.

Just as the practices of marketing involve the creation, stimulation and exploitation of our utopian appetites – all the way from the 'dream worlds' of the department store or theme park, through the sale of products with an impeccable utopian pedigree (such as Oneida furniture or Kellogg's corn flakes), to the evanescent anal epiphany promised by manufacturers of extra-soft toilet tissue – so too marketing theory and thought has a decidedly Arcadian aspect. The very notion of a marketing orientation, with its ambition of perfectly satisfied customers whose every conceivable want or need is anticipated, investigated and accommodated by perennially profitable companies which are fully integrated around the marketing function and where careful analysis, planning, implementation and control is the order of the day, is nothing less than an utopian fantasy that is preposterous, some would say lunatic, in its ambition and scope. Equally utopian are those ubiquitous textbook diagrams of marketing functions or marketing's coordinating role within the firm (Figure 2.1). Circular, concentric and symmetrical, sometimes with radial elements, these are an almost exact replica of utopian illustrations of the Ideal City, most notably Campenella's city of the sun. (In their modern marketing equivalent, of course, that which is most sacred – the customer – occupies the very centre of the circle and this holy of holies is surrounded by functionally subdivided zones of steadily decreasing significance, over which control is less easily exercised or exercisable.) Perhaps the most striking example of this propensity, however, is found in the burgeoning relationship marketing paradigm, the omnipresent representations of which comprise a very distinctive spatial layout around the hub of the network. As Figure 1.1 indicates, this arrangement carries clear paradisal connotations, since it patently resembles the radiating rays of numinous celestial light that have for centuries signified heaven, saints, angels and spiritual enlightenment in countless artistic representations of the Godhead.

Marketing, then, is inherently utopian in ethos; it is inherently carnivalesque (cf. the legendary land of Cockaygne, a sort of hedonistic people's paradise where the marketing system succeeds in meeting every conceivable human need). Indeed, it can be contended that the current travails of marketing scholarship, as outlined in Chapter 1, are part of the characteristic, late-twentieth-century 'retreat from utopia' (Kumar 1995a). Yet, it can also be argued that the marketing academy's problems derive from its eschewal of carnival, from its desire for analysis, planning, implementation and control, from abandoning its ecstatic Dionysian side in favour of essentially Apollonian forms of understanding. The utopias that marketing has been pursuing for the past fifty years – marketing orientation, general theories, quantification, and, above all, marketing science – are quite simply the wrong utopias. As Steiner, yet again, so artfully avers, 'Observe an historian or sociologist resorting to equations and you will, well-nigh inevitably, witness a retreat from thought' (1989: 79). How true. How true of marketing. How come we keep retreating towards the thoughtless utopia of marketing science?

The last record album

In conclusion, then, it is my belief that if academic marketing is to move forward intellectually, if it is to attract practitioners back into the fold, if it is to transcend its current crisis of representation, if it is to face the twenty-first century with renewed confidence, it must abandon its futile fixation with Science and it must abandon it forthwith. It must set aside the naïve belief that a Galileo, Newton or Mendel of marketing science will eventually materialize and somehow manage to unravel the underlying laws and principles of the marketplace. It must accept that, our ever larger data sets, ever faster computing facilities and ever more sophisticated mathematical models notwithstanding, we are not going to break through to the bright uplands of absolute marketing understanding. We will not be descending in triumph bearing our tablets of marketing stone, the iron, inviolate, universal laws of the marketplace. We are never going to attain the ultimate fruit of our labours, the bright and shining Science of Marketing. It is important, indeed imperative, to appreciate that we have been pursuing an impossible dream, a vision of plenitude that can never be realized, no matter how hard we try. It is time to join Markaholics Anonymous, to confess our hopeless addiction to the academic narcotic known as Science and, having acknowledged our dependency, to set out on the rough and rocky road to recovery. It is then that we will be able to come to terms with the side of ourselves that we have tried to suppress – the fact, the glorious fact, that marketing is an Art, it always has been an Art, it always will be an Art. And the sooner academic marketers acquaint themselves with the tools and techniques of aesthetic appreciation, the sooner marketing scholarship will make a quantum leap forward (if you'll pardon the scientific expression).

To my mind, the first step on this markaholics recovery programme involves challenging the scientistic dictat that we must rein in our passions, undertake disinterested research and report it in emotionless idiom. Call me eccentric, call me iconoclastic, call me the Syd Barrett of scholarship, but I reckon we need more passion in marketing, not less. If academic marketing is uninteresting, it's because all emotion has been systematically eliminated. I don't know about you, but I'm passionate about marketing. I love marketing and I'm not ashamed to say so. In fact, I'll say it again, *I love marketing.*

Make no mistake, I am very well aware of the fact that it is deeply unfashionable to make such a confession. The critical theorists, who like to think that they see through the pretence of the marketplace (even though we can see through their holier-than-thou seeings-through), are certain to be scandalized by my seemingly indiscriminate endorsement of the sometimes exploitative, often iniquitous and always anti-emancipatory marketing system. Look, I know it is imperfect, pernicious and in sore need of improvement. But, as far as I am concerned, you can scream false consciousness, or any other chic cliché from the creased and dog-eared Marxian catechism, till you're blue (sorry, red) in the face. I *still* love marketing. I *love* it when I see a brilliant new cinema or television advert (the first time I saw Guinness's 'art gallery', the one where Rutger Hauer makes his way through tableaux of artistic masterpieces, I wanted to jump out of my cinema seat and cheer this truly sublime advertising achievement). I *love* it when a marketing practitioner pulls off an outrageous promotional stunt (a small businessman in our area, the owner-manager of a motor-car silencer centre, once stood for parliament on a noise abatement ticket and took full marketing advantage of his free electoral publicity entitlement, not to mention the ensuing media attention). And I *love* it when I witness an expert salesperson at work (should we ever meet, I'm the one with the purple polka-dot shirt, emerald bowtie, tartan stay-pressed, bri-nylon slacks, mismatched socks, two left spats, comprehensive life insurance and an empty wallet – but at least I've got a smile on my face).

However, and this is a very big however (we're talking 48-point bold and caps, here), I *don't* love it when I read about marketing in the principal academic journals. True, my double-glazed, light-sensitive, high-fashion, bifocal, designer-framed, *faux*-plastic reading glasses might have something to do with this – especially since my eyesight is perfect or it was prior to the sex 'n' shopping study – and it's not easy to get to a good business library when you live in a one-bedroom, no-bathroom, unelectrified, luxury time-share apartment in a prestigious development, picturesquely situated amid the miasmic swamps of Northern Ireland. Yet I for one believe it is time we banished banishing passion from works of marketing scholarship, as indeed some creative researchers are attempting to do in propinquitous academic domains (see, for example, Game and Metcalfe's (1996) superb new book on *Passionate Sociology*). I, for one, believe it is time to object to objectivity, neutralize neutrality, falsify falsification, invalidate validity and authorize anti-authoritarianism. I, for one, believe it is time to detach ourselves from detachment, cease to rely on reliability, become partial to impartiality, accept the truthlessness of truth and make the heterodox orthodox. I, for one, believe it is time to be unequivocal in our search for equivocation, unambiguous in our espousal of ambiguity, to agree on the need for disagreement and at all times be certain about uncertainty, determined about indeterminacy, consistent about inconsistency. I, for one, believe it is time to recognize that our postmodern propensity for paradox is not paradoxical, to appreciate that we should be singular in our espousal of pluralism and, having divested ourselves of positivists and analogous scholarly low-lifes, to acknowledge our abandonment of I'm-better-than-you-are academic hierarchies and élites. I, for one, believe it is time to give it a rest, to wrap up wrapping up, to stop torturing you with my convoluted syntax, contrived juxtapositions and metaphorical manglings. (And so say all of us.)

OK, then, let me leave you with one last postmodern thought (just for old times' sake). More than anything else in the world, I believe it is time to sweep aside marketing's self-appointed academic authorities, the big brothers, the thought police, the brains trust of our discipline. These people have destroyed academic marketing with their Ur-scholarship, Ur-objectivity, Ur-rigour, Ur-quantification, Ur-models, Ur-relationships, Ur-paradigm shifts, Ur-science. Urs-holes, if you ask me.

(Damn, I can't finish on Urs-holes. People might get the wrong idea. We need some sort of resonant rallying cry. Let me see. How's about marketing for marketing's sake? The market is the message? I've got it. Brace yourself. Marketomanes of the world unite, you have nothing to lose but your pains!)

Epilogue
I rock, therefore I am

'No.'

'Yes.'

'No!'

'But why not?'

'Jules, how many times do I have to tell you? The answer is no.'

'Come on, Stephen, it's a great idea for a book and you know it.'

'It may well be, Jules, but I don't do that sort of thing. I'm sorry.'

'Well, I'll just take my idea to another author, then.'

'From what I hear, you've already done the academic round without success and now seem to think you can come crawling back to me. Read my lips, Jules, the answer is no, N-O spells no!'

'But think of your public.'

'My public?'

'Yes, your public. Just think how disappointed they'll be.'

'My disappointed public?'

'Yeah, what's wrong with that?'

'I'm sorry, Jules, I can't go on with this. I've had this conversation before. On more than one occasion.'

'Well, if you won't do it, Stephen, we have a very serious problem.'

'What do you mean, we have a very serious problem. I delivered the manuscript on time, as per our contract.'

'Contract? Don't make me laugh, mate. Your contract isn't worth the paper . . . '

'Hold on a minute here. What exactly are you saying, Jules?'

'I'm saying, Stephen, you either revise the book in line with my suggestions or we don't publish it at all. We'll simply sit on your manuscript. It'll never see the light of day. What's more, we'll let it be known how awful it is. Unpublishable, don't you know. How long did it take you to write? Five years, wasn't it?'

'You can't do that.'

'*I think you'll find, in the small print of our contract, that we can. And will, believe me.*'

'*I thought your contracts aren't worth the paper they're written on.*'

'*No, no, no, no, no.* Your *contract is worth zilch.* Ours *is perfectly legit, my son.*'

'*We'll see about that.*'

'*Stephen, if you think you can afford an expensive lawsuit, go ahead; make my legal department's day. Academics, we usually find, don't have the wherewithal . . .* '

'*What? You've done this sort of thing before?*'

'*Oh yeah. All the time. Obviously, I can't discuss specific cases, but have you ever heard of a book called* Marketing by Matrix?'

'*Yes, I seem to recall it.*'

'*That was all my idea.*'

'*It was? I don't know what to say.*'

'*You should've seen the original manuscript, mate. Complete crap. All sorts of pseudo-philosophical stuff. Episte-something or other. Episte-off, I said.*'

'*And you came up with the matrix idea.*'

'*Got it in one, sunshine.*'

'*But what have you got against the, er, episte-stuff, Jules? My own manuscript is suffused with erudition and philosophical insight, if I say so myself.*'

'*Yeah, right. Look, Stephen, I've got nothing against erudition. If people want to ponder apriorism, root around for distributed middles or cogitate on mind–body dualism, good luck to them. What they do in the privacy of their own homes is no concern of mine. So long as they don't expect ITBP to publish their so-called philosophical insights.*'

'*You're a Philistine, Jules. A complete Philistine.*'

'*Catford, Steve, Catford born and bred. Never been near the Middle East.*'

'*Quite. I must say, it's comforting to know that marketing scholarship is in safe hands.*'

'*Scholarship? Don't make me laugh, mate. Since when has marketing had anything to do with scholarship?*'

'*How can you suggest such a thing? Marketing is a sophisticated academic discipline with a long and illustrious pedigree. Rigorous. Learned. Profound. Scholarly.*'

'*Scholarly, is it?*'

'*Well, it would be if ill-informed publishers refrained from interfering with academic texts.*'

'*Let me tell you something about scholarship, mate. Marketing managers aren't the least bit interested in all that episte-malarky. Students haven't got a baldy notion what you're on about. So, who do you think you're writing for? Other academics, is it? They're no good to us. Cheapskate bastards that they are, academics don't buy books. They order free inspection copies for courses they don't intend to run. And you try getting the books back from them. In a word, im-bloody-possible. Even when they do return them, you should see the state of the things – dog-eared, teethmarks, strange stains, the lot. Don't talk to me about scholarship.'*

'Do you feel better now that you've got that off your chest, Jules?'

'Well, I did once work in Dispatches. You've no idea. Some of the things I've seen would . . .'

'Jules, I think you underestimate marketing managers. The old fire-a-few-bullet-points-at-them-and-they'll-all-fall-over days are long gone. Most of them are graduates – not necessarily business studies graduates, I grant you – but they expect more than the simple-minded monosyllables they had in the past.'

'Don't agree with you, my son. Managers may be graduates, as you say, but these days graduates can hardly read or write. And, as for 'rithmetic . . .'

'Perhaps we shouldn't go into the quantification debate just now, Julian.'

'This marketing scholarship stuff. It's just a dream you know. That's the way you and your cronies would like it to be, Stephen. Time to get real. Time for bullet points, mate. Time for boxes and arrows diagrams. You can't go far wrong with a couple of matrices, as my old Uncle Malcolm used to say. Bless his heart.'

'That's a gross and, if I may say so, filthy slur on the intellectual endeavours of the marketing academy. You should be ashamed of yourself.'

'It's not just me, Steve. You know what they're saying up at Oxford?'

'Spank me harder, Tarquin? Cover me in Jell-O, fellow? Once more into the breeches?'

'Well, that too. Obviously. But I was thinking more of the comments of Director of Oxford's new Management Centre.'

'Don't tell me. Let me through, I'm an Oxonian? Step aside, cretin, Oxford's finally on the Management case? Marketing Warfare a speciality (with arms dealing option)?'

'Well, that too. Allegedly. But he also said that most management research is complete crap.'

'That's a very scholarly turn of phrase. Did he really say that?'

'Well, Steve, that's what the papers said he said. He also said that management research needed a good old-fashioned dose of micro-economics to stiffen it up.'

'Now, that's complete crap.'

'Couldn't agree more, Steve.'

'At least we agree on something, Jules. You know I've heard that Oxford's English Literature and Business Studies departments are working together on a production of Arms and the Man-agement Centre, or was it Armani and the Man?'

'Not with you mate. But, I'm sure we can thrash something out here. We're both reasonable men, after all.'

'Absolutely.'

'Let me ask you a question, Steve. Do you want to be rich?'

'Not really, though a few extra sheckles would be nice.'

'Do you want to be famous?'

'No, not really, though a few extra people at my conference papers would be nice. It gets rather lonely at times.'

'Do you want to be idolized? Do you want to be — er, what's the polite word? — importuned, by lovestruck admirers?'

'The thought's never occurred to me, Jules.'

'Come on, Steve, you're a good-looking guy.'

'I am?'

'Well, nothing that £20,000 worth of plastic surgery wouldn't fix.'

'I've already had extensive, um, cosmetic enhancement . . . treatment . . . you know . . . '

'Jesus Christ. Did you complain? Sue? Ask for your money back?'

'I don't like to talk about it, Julian.'

'Not even a credit note for the rhinoplasty?'

'I'm sorry, but what has all this got to do with my manuscript?'

'Look, Steve, I'm trying to help you here. I am.'

'I'm sure you are.'

'But the bottom line is that we won't be publishing your manuscript. There's no market for that sort of stuff anymore. It's old-fashioned, mate. I'm sorry.'

'It's a work of marketing scholarship, Jules. How can it possibly be old-fashioned? Intellectual life doesn't have fashions. It involves the gradual accretion of robust, reliable and replicable constructs.'

'You think so?'

'Slow but steady progress is the order of the day.'

'No good to us, my son.'

'I am, of course, prepared to make a few minor adjustments if you think it will increase sales. One doesn't want to be dogmatic, after all.'

'It's a dog all right. Look at your title for a start.'

'What's wrong with Marketing Theory? It describes the contents perfectly.'

'What's wrong with Marketing Theory? What's wrong with Marketing Theory? Lead balloon, mate. Remainder bins, sunshine. May as well ship the stuff straight to the paper recycling plant, Steve. Bog roll in waiting, that's all it is.'

'Well, there is a touch of the oxymoronic about it, I grant you.'

'What did you call me? I'll send for my editorial assistants, if there's any more of that language. They can do serious damage with bulldog clips and a staple gun, take it from me.'

'Sorry, Jules, you misunderstand. I simply meant that my title is a bit of a contradiction in terms.'

'Contradiction in terms? You're telling me. We find that the word 'theory' goes down like a fart in the space shuttle.'

'Quite.'

'And you want to stick "marketing" in front of it? They'll think you're trying to flog them theories, for God's sake. How much am I bid for "don't ask for credit as a refusal often offends"? I mean, come on, mate.'

'Actually, you could put it like that, Jules. We do try to sell, to persuade other academics to purchase our concepts, after all.'

'Not exactly back-of-a-lorry-don't-ask-no-questions-quick-respray-and-plates job, is it?'

'No, indeed not.'

'Tell me, Steve, how does Postmodern Marketing grab you? Sexy title. Fashionable. Sell like Vaseline up at Oxford. Guaranteed.'

'Yes, there is a touch of the lock-up-your-daughters-or-your-livestock-at-least about it, but I think someone has used the title already.'

'Oh yeah? We'll give him a bung. My editorial assistants will go round and have a friendly chat with him. Make him an offer he can't, you know. He's sorted.'

'I'll take your word for it. There's just one problem.'

'What is it Steve?'

'Postmodern. What does it mean, exactly?'

'You don't need to know, my boy. All you gotta do is stick it on the front cover and if anyone asks about it, tell them it's postmodern.'

'So, you're saying it's postmodern to put "postmodern" in the title even though the text is about something else completely?'

'Basically, yes.'

'Sounds unethical to me. Marketing didn't get where it is today by being unethical, Jules. Marketing scholars wouldn't put up with that sort of unscrupulous behaviour; nor would practitioners and students, I'm sure.'

'Marketing academics are pretty big on scruples, are they?'

'Well, yes. Some of my best friends have devoted their entire careers to writing about scruples. But, my point is that most marketers expect a book to be about what it says it's about. You, of all people, must know that.'

'You could be right, Stevie. We may have to do something with the text too.'

'Sorry, Julian, absolutely not. I'm prepared to change the title if it helps sell a few extra copies. The content is sacrosanct. Minor adjustments aside, of course. There's nothing more to say on the matter. I fear we're wasting each other's time.'

'Now don't get excited. Just hear me out. You know, Stephen, your manuscript was *great. Best I've ever read. I don't normally like that onto-episte-type stuff, but your's was something else.'*

'You're very kind.'

'As soon as I picked it up, I knew it was a classic.'

'A minor classic, perhaps.'

'Oh no, it's the real thing, mate. You can always tell.'

'Thank you, Julian.'

'If we were in the business of publishing books on marketing theory, Stephen, there's no book I'd rather publish, believe me.'

'I'm flattered.'

'But all this stuff about hypothetico-deductive reasoning, verification theory of meaning, the KKK thesis . . . '

'K-K, I think you'll find.'

'Whatever. It's just not on, Steve. I'm sorry. Nobody cares any more. No one wants to know. And I think you know no one wants to know.'

'It took five years to write, Jules.'

'I know. I know it did.'

'Blood, sweat, toil and tears went into that manuscript.'

'That's exactly how I felt when I read it. However, I'm sure you appreciate that a book with "postmodern" in the title must have some postmodern content.'

'Must it?'

'Strictly speaking, no. But, as you just said, marketing expects . . . '

'I did, didn't I?'

'You did, Steve.'

'So, what do you suggest, Jules?'

'Well, I wouldn't dream of imposing my ideas on you, but have you thought of playing the rebel card?'

'I'm afraid I'm not quite with you.'

'You know, the Johnny Rotten-, Sid Vicious-, Billy Idol-type pose.'

'Who, pray, are Rotten, Vicious and Idle? Sociologists? Economists? Not psychologists, surely. Anthropologists, I suspect. Yes, they definitely sound like ethnographers to me. Am I right?'

'The names aren't important, Steve. The point is that you set out to attack orthodoxy, subvert the establishment, undermine the taken-for-granted, challenge the unchallenged. You see what I'm getting at?'

'Only too well. I'm afraid we don't go in for that sort of thing in the marketing academy. That type of behaviour wouldn't be tolerated.'

'*Let me put it to you another way. What's the biggest thing in marketing at the moment?*'

'*The relationship marketing paradigm shift, I suppose.*'

'*What do you make of it?*'

'*Well, between you and I, Jules, I do have some concerns about the concept.*'

'*OK, that's a start. Express your concerns, Stephen. That's all I want you to do.*'

'*That's all?*'

'*That's all.*'

'*In a suitably scholarly manner?*'

'*Scholarly as you like, sunshine.*'

'*Is this postmodern, then?*'

'*Barthes is rotating as we speak.*'

'*Pardon?*'

'*Never mind, Steve. In joke. Will you do it?*'

'*I suppose I could stretch that far. Yes, Jules, I'll do it. I'll go the extra mile if it means getting my book published.*'

'*Good man. I knew we could sort something out to our mutual satisfaction.*'

'*Indeed.*'

'*As a matter of interest, Steve, do you have any other, er, minor worries about the state of the marketing academy?*'

'*To be honest, Jules, I'm ever so slightly anxious about our obsession with Science.*'

'*Marketing Science? Is that a joke? You're having me on, right? Are you seriously telling me there's marketing academics who think they're scientists?*'

'*Yes, of course. What's wrong with that?*'

'*Is* everyone *a marketing scientist?*'

'*Well, no, there are a few deluded fellows who advocate a form of, what's it called now? Marketing aesthetics. But, you can rest assured, anyone who is anyone is a marketing scientist.*'

'*Really? That's amazing, Steve.*'

'*It* is *amazing, Jules. Major breakthroughs are imminent, I'm told, though they've been saying that for some time now. It does seem to be dragging on somewhat.*'

'*Would you be prepared to say so, Stephen? In a suitably scholarly way, of course.*'

'*I'm not so sure. It's a very touchy subject. Career decision. Pecking order. Ex-communication. You do understand, don't you?*'

'*Perfectly.*'

'*Jules, I'm a reasonable man . . .*'

'*An easy-going dude. Some would say moderation personified?*'

'*How on earth do you know that?*'

'*Dunno. Something just told me. I can sense these things. Look, Stephen, I'm not asking you to tell lies or betray your colleagues in any way . . . '*

'*I'm sorry Jules, the answer is no. It's not just about Science. All the big American names are marketing scientists. An attack on scientific marketing could be misconstrued as anti-Americanism.'*

'*What's America got to do with it?'*

'*The journals . . . the associations . . . academic reputation . . . I'd rather not talk about it.'*

'*So, if you slighted truth, justice and the American way of marketing scholarship, you could really cause a rumpus?'*

'*That's quite enough. I'm not listening to any more of this. I know what you're trying to do to me with your soft-soap tactics. I shan't let down my academic peers. I'd rather my manuscript wasn't published at all than be party to this outrage. Good day to you, sir.'*

'*All the best, bozo.'*

'*How dare you! A lesson in manners is what you need, young man.'*

'*A lesson in negotiation is what you need, matey. Call yourself a marketing man?'*

'*What on earth do you mean?'*

'*Well, sunshine, you've just told me everything I need to know. We'll bring out a book along the lines you just suggested. We'll rubbish relationship marketing. We'll ridicule marketing science. We'll make it an anti-American diatribe, for good measure. And I don't know, maybe we'll try to do something with marketing aesthetics, isn't that what you called it?'*

'*Good luck to you. Good day.'*

'*You haven't heard the best bit, Stevie boy.'*

'*Make it brief. I have another appointment.'*

'*We're going to bring it out under your name.'*

'*Monstrous! Outrageous! You can't do that.'*

'*We can. We will. We fully intend to. We'll scandalize them, believe me. When we've finished with you, you won't be able to show your face in your precious marketing academy. Not for a very long time.'*

'*You'll never get someone to write it, sir. You're bluffing.'*

'*That's where you're wrong, my son. We have a guy on retainer. Alan Smithee, he's called. Rewrites all our stuff. You name it, he'll imitate it. Even better than the real thing.'*

'*Alan Smithee doesn't exist. He's a* nom du cinéma. *He's a flag of convenience for film directors who don't want their name on the credits.'*

'*He does exist, you know. And* you *brought him into existence.'*

'*What* are *you talking about? Utter nonsense. Yes, I referred to him, to this non-existent person, in one of my books. As a joke. No one got it. End of story.'*

'*Not quite, Stevie baby. If you read Steven King's* The Dark Half, *or Eco's* Foucault's

Pendulum, *or Borges'* Labyriths, *or even* Fly Fishing *by J. R. Hartley, you'd realize that the very act of writing about someone or something can call it into existence.'*

'They're just novels, books, stories, vignettes. No one pays any attention to such absurd tales. Has no one ever explained this to you Julian?'

'No interest in tales, you say?'

'You're telling me.'

'I've got news for you, mate. Alan Smithee does *exist*. Hollywood's making a major bio-pic of him at this very moment. He'll be writing your book and telling it in storytelling mode.'

'Really. Don't forget the gratituous sex scenes, Jules.'

'Sex, of course. Perfect! I hadn't thought of that, Steve. Lots of sex. Yes, there'll be stacks of sex.'

'Why stop there, Jules? What about drugs and rock 'n' roll? Isn't that what they say: sex, drugs and rock 'n' roll?'

'You've got some great ideas, Stevie baby. Are you sure you don't want in on this? It's gonna be hot, hot, hot.'

'Jules, you forgot something.'

'What's that, me old mucker?'

'How's about a catch phrase to round the whole thing off? Wouldn't that just be perfect?'

'Now you're talkin'. Got any up your sleeve, sunshine?'

'Oh, let me see . . . what about "Ich bin ein marketer"?'

'Nah, old hat, mate. You can do better than that.'

'May the 4Ps be with you?'

'You gotta personalize it, Steve. Sorry. Try again.'

'Well, why mess around? Let's go all the way. "Peel me a grape, Philip." How's about that?'

'Jeez. If that's what you want, sunshine. Even I know that's a bit of an affront. It'll slay then in Northwestern, that's for sure. You'd have to have balls like an elephant to get away with that one. Could be the end of your career, mate. Finish. Kaput. Nada.'

'If you publish like you say, my career will be over anyway. I hope you're satisfied with yourself, Julian. I hope you sleep well at night. Goodbye.'

'Look, Stephen, let's not quarrel over this. We can come to an arrangement. There must be some common ground.'

'No, I'm afraid not. I think your whole scheme is despicable.'

'What if we kept the citations? To give it a scholarly look.'

'You're planning to remove the references? Heavens above.'

'I'll chuck in a couple of footnotes, how does that grab you?'

'How many?'

'*Two.*'

'*Eight.*'

'*Four.*'

'*Six.*'

'*Five and we have a deal, Steve.*'

'*Are these going to be proper footnotes?*'

'*The real thing, mate. Bottom of the page. None of your back-of-the-book rubbish.*'

'*Your offer's very tempting, Julian, but I'm afraid the answer is still no.*'

'*I tell you what. I'll let you keep your pretentious philosophical epigraph.*'

'*Really?*'

'*Amor fati. What the hell does it mean anyhow? Something to do with your, er, fondness for, um, big girls? Know what I'm saying?*'

'*God help us. It's from Nietzsche, you ignoramus.*'

'*Was Nietzsche a red-hot mommas man too?*'

'*I don't really know. He was unlucky, shall we say, in love.*'

'*Remind me, what was his big idea? Will to pork, wasn't it?*'

'*Will to power, Julian, will to power. Anyway, to answer your question,* amor fati *means love of fate. Nietzsche says that we should accept that everything is as it is and always will be, again and again in perpetuity.*'

'*So, you accept that we're going to bring out this book in your name?*'

'*Well . . . I suppose so.*'

'*And that you are duty bound to embrace it wholeheartedly?*'

'*If you put it like that, yes. But I'm still not very happy.*'

'*Can we get round this another way, Steve? I don't know, a framing device of some sort? A way to distance you from the scurrilous content of the book while still reaping the rewards.*'

'*Representation without taxation, as it were, Jules?*'

'*Yeah, something like that. You could discuss our discussion, couldn't you? Pin all the blame on me.*'

'*That might be possible, I suppose. No, let's be sensible here. No one would believe a book containing imaginary conversations between author and commissioning editor.*'

'*They will, Steve, trust me. If marketing academics could fall for Science, they'll certainly fall for Fiction. Science fiction, Stephen. Sexy science fiction. We could even call it* The Sex-Files*!*'

'*Streuth!*'

'*The streuth is out there, Stephen.*'

'*It's just too bizarre. It'll never work. I'm ruined.*'

'It'll work. I know it will work. Tell you what, mate, go with this and I'll let you keep your acknowledgements. That's my final offer.'

'You mean, I can thank everyone who helped me along the way? Francesca Weaver at Routledge? Julian Thomas from ITBP? Sharon Dornan, Tony Feenan and Pat Ibbotson of the University of Ulster for all their technical backup?'

'Go for it, Steve.'

'What about the people and companies who allowed me to reproduce copyright material – Abhann Productions, Gilbert Adair, Bloomsbury Publishing, Chartered Institute of Marketing, Alan Coren, Crown Publishing, Gallagher's, MCB Press, McGraw-Hill, Moët & Chandon, Secker and Warburg?'

'If you must.'

'Some colleagues read through the draft manuscript. They wouldn't speak to me afterwards, for some strange reason, but I suppose I ought to acknowledge their assistance.'

'What draft is this we're talking about? Not Smithee's I take it.'

'No, the one read by Russ Belk, Anne Marie Doherty, Bob Grafton Small, Pauline Maclaran, Barbara Stern and Lorna Stevens.'

'Are these the same people you compliment in the text.'

'Yes, the very same. What's wrong with that, Jules?'

'Don't you think the readers will suspect something? Logrolling. Porkbarrelling. You scratch my back catalogue and I'll scratch yours, kind of thing.'

'Absolutely not. Marketing academics don't think like that. It's all perfectly legitimate, perfectly scholarly, perfectly above board.'

'I'm not so sure, Steve, I reckon you should cut them out completely. Don't even mention them. Just to be on the safe side.'

'Okay, but in return I think I should be allowed to say a few kind words of acknowledgement to my wife, Linda, and the girls, Madison, Holly and Sophie.'

'I'm sure you should, though I suspect they'd prefer to hear it from you personally and maybe see you from time to time. Maybe not, come to think of it.'

'Quite.'

'Any more, Stephen? Are you sure you wouldn't like to namecheck your goldfish, bank manager, football team, plastic surgeon . . . ?'

'Well, there is the Dean . . .'

'I don't think a namecheck'll help you there, sunshine.'

'Should I say something about Alan Smithee?'

'No more. That's your lot mate. You drive a had bargain, Brown, you old marketing bastard.'

'Right, Jules, we're agreed then. I'll do it. I'll go along with your plan. Just so long as the rebellious stuff is done tastefully. Criticism is fine, but it must be scholarly criticism.'

'*You can trust me, Steve. All we need now is to reposition you a little.*'

'*What?*'

'*A few minor adjustments to your biography. A bit of poetic licence in your background. It can do wonders for sales, mate.*'

'*What sort of* repositioning *do you have in mind, Jules?*'

'*I was thinking of making you Irish. How does that sound?*'

'*Irish? Irish? Anything but Irish. Please.*'

'*I dunno, Steve. Cultural heritage. Saints and scholars. Literary tradition. All that stuff. Might help. You're gonna need all the help you can get, you know.*'

'*Yes, I see what you mean. Only trouble is; I'm not Irish.*'

'*You don't have to be. Jack Charlton sorted that one out. Do you have any Irish connections, Stephen?*'

'*Not really.*'

'*No aunts, uncles, grandparents? Do you own an Irish Setter? A Van Morrison album?*'

'*Terribly sorry, Jules. Tunbridge Wells, through and through. No dogs. No guru, no method, no teacher.*'

'*Jeez. This is tough. Have you ever, um, kissed the Blarney Stone?*'

'*No, but I once made a pass at a Stonehenge Sarsen. Blarney's carboniferous limestone, you see. Not really my type.*'

'*Very good, Steve. I reckon you have a flair for this kinda thing. You and Smithee should get together sometime. Could be quite a partnership.*'

'*I don't think so, Jules. I prefer to work alone.*'

'*Yeah, I can see why.*'

'*Well, I'd better be off.*'

'*Before you go, Steve, what do you make of this proposal? I found it in a pile of rejects the other day. It seems to be a book about marketing theory. Written in the form of a murder mystery. Has potential, I think. And right up your street.*'

'*What's it called?*'

'Kotler is Dead!'

'*Outrageous!*'

'*Great!*'

'*Don't call us, Jules.*'

'*We'll call you, Stephen.*'

How can a poor man stand such times and live?

Aaker, D. A. and Stayman, D. M. (1992) 'Implementing the concept of transformational advertising', *Psychology and Marketing* 9(3): 237–53.

Abhann Productions (1996) *Riverdance the Show*, Cork: Abhann Productions.

Adair, G. (1992) *The Postmodernist Always Rings Twice*, London: Fourth Estate.

—— (1993) 'Sweet dreams', *The Sunday Times*, 14 March, Section 9: 8; reprinted in S. Brown (1995a) *Postmodern Marketing*, London: Routledge, p. 135.

—— (1995) 'The glove that need not speak its name', *The Sunday Times*, 4 June, Section 10: 4.

Adam, B. and Allan, S. (eds) (1995) *Theorizing Culture: An Interdisciplinary Critique After Postmodernism*, London: UCL Press.

Adam, I. and Tiffin, H. (eds) (1991) *Past the Last Post: Theorising Post-colonialism and Post-modernism*, Hemel Hempsted: Harvester Wheatsheaf.

Agger, B. (1989) *Reading Science: A Literary, Political and Sociological Analysis*, Dix Hills: General Hall.

Aijo, T. S. (1996) 'The theoretical and philosophical underpinnings of relationship marketing: environmental factors behind the changing marketing paradigm', *European Journal of Marketing* 30(2): 8–18.

Alba, J. W., Hutchinson, J. W. and Lynch, J. G. (1991) 'Memory and decision making', in T. S. Robertson and H. H. Kassarjian (eds) *Handbook of Consumer Behaviour*, Englewood Cliffs: Prentice Hall, pp. 1–49.

Alderson, W. and Cox, R. (1948) 'Towards a theory of marketing', *Journal of Marketing* 13 (October): 137–52.

Alexander, J. (1992) 'General theory in the postpositivist mode: the "epistemological dilemma" and the search for present reason', in S. Seidman and D. G. Wagner (eds) *Postmodern and Social Theory: The Debate Over General Theory*, Cambridge, MA: Blackwell, pp. 322–68.

Alvesson, M. (1994), 'Critical theory and consumer marketing', *Scandinavian Journal of Management* 10(3): 291–313.

—— and Willmott, H. (1992), 'Critical Theory and management studies: an introduction', in M. Alvesson and H. Willmott (eds) *Critical Management Studies*, London: Sage, pp. 1–20.

—— and —— (1996), *Making Sense of Management*, London: Sage.

AMA Task Force (1988) 'Developing, disseminating and utilizing marketing knowledge', *Journal of Marketing* 52 (October): 1–25.

Amin, A. (ed.) (1994) *Post-Fordism: A Reader*, Oxford: Blackwell.

Amis, M. (1994) *Money*, Harmondsworth: Penguin.

Anderson, L. McT. (1994) 'Marketing science: where's the beef?', *Business Horizons* 37(1): 8–16.

Anderson, P. F. (1983) 'Marketing, scientific progress and scientific method', *Journal of Marketing* 47 (Fall): 18–31.

—— (1986) 'On method in consumer research: a critical relativist perspective', *Journal of Consumer Research* 13 (September): 155–73.

—— (1989) 'On relativism and interpretivism – with a prolegomenon to the "why" question', in E.C. Hirschman (ed.) *Interpretive Consumer Research*, Provo: Association for Consumer Research, pp. 10–23.

Appignanesi, R. and Garratt, C. (1995) *Postmodernism for Beginners*, Cambridge: Icon.

Apple, M. (1984) *Free Agents*, New York: Harper & Row; reprinted in B. McHale (1992) *Constructing Postmodernism*, London: Routledge, pp. 38–41.

Appleby, J., Covington, E., Hoyt, D., Latham, M. and Sneider, A. (eds) (1996) *Knowledge and Postmodernism in Historical Perspective*, London: Routledge.

Appleyard, B. (1992) *Understanding the Present: Science and the Soul of Modern Man*, London: Picador.

Archer, G. (1991) *As the Crow Flies*, New York: HarperCollins.

Armstrong, J. S. (1995) 'Quality control versus innovation in the development of marketing knowledge', *Journal of Marketing Management*, 11(7): 655–60.

Arnold M. J. and Fisher, J. E. (1996) 'Counterculture, criticisms and crisis: assessing the effect of the sixties on marketing thought', *Journal of Macromarketing* 16(1): 118–33.

Arnold, S. J. and Fischer, E. (1994) 'Hermeneutics and consumer research', *Journal of Consumer Research*, 21 (June): 55–70.

Arnould, E. J. (1995) 'West African marketing channels: environmental duress, relationship management, and implications for western marketing', in J. F. Sherry (ed.) *Contemporary Marketing and Consumer Behavior: An Anthropological Sourcebook*, Thousand Oaks: Sage, pp. 109–68.

—— and Price L. L. (1993), 'River magic: extraordinary experience and the extended service encounter', *Journal of Consumer Research*, 20 (June): 24–45.

—— and Wallendorf, M. (1994) 'Market-oriented ethnography: interpretation building and marketing strategy formulation', *Journal of Marketing Research*, 31 (November): 484–504.

Ashcroft, B., Griffiths, G. and Tiffin, H. (1989) *The Empire Writes Back: Theory and Practice in Post-colonial Literatures*, London: Routledge.

Atkinson, P. (1990) *The Ethnographic Imagination: Textual Constructions of Reality*, London: Routledge.

Austen, A. (1983) 'The marketing concept – is it obsolete?', *Quarterly Review of Marketing*, 9 (Autumn): 6–8.

Auster, P. (1995) *The Red Notebook and Other Writings*, London: Faber & Faber.

Babbes, G. S. (1996) 'The necessity of metaphorical reasoning and its effect on knowledge representation and decision making', in K. P. Corfman and J. G. Lynch (eds) *Advances in Consumer Research, vol. XXIII*, Provo: Association for Consumer Research, p. 454.

Babin, B. J., Darden, W. R. and Griffin, M. (1994) 'Work and/or fun: measuring hedonic and utilitarian shopping value', *Journal of Consumer Research*, 20 (March): 644–56.

Bachelard, G. (1994 [1958]) *The Poetics of Space*, trans. M. Jolas, Boston: Beacon Press.

Baddeley, A. (1990) *Human Memory: Theory and Practice*, Hillsdale: Lawrence Erlbaum Associates.

Bagozzi, R. P. (1995) 'Reflections on relationship marketing in consumer markets', *Journal of the Academy of Marketing Science*, 23(4): 272–7.

Baker, M. J. (1994) 'Research myopia: recency, relevance, reinvention and renaissance (the 4Rs of marketing?)', Department of Marketing, Working Paper Series 94/2, Glasgow: University of Strathclyde.

—— (1995) 'The future of marketing', in M. J. Baker (ed.) *Companion Encyclopedia of Marketing*, London: Routledge, pp. 1003–18.

Baker, N. (1989) *The Mezzanine*, Cambridge: Granta.

Baker, T. (1996) 'The PoMo dance', in D. Jones (ed.) *Sex, Power and Travel: Ten Years of* Arena, London: Virgin Publishing, pp. 38–40.

Bakhtin, M. (1981a [1934–5]) 'Discourse in the novel', in M. Bakhtin *The Dialogic Imagination: Four Essays*, trans. C. Emerson and M. Holquist, Austin: University of Texas Press, pp. 259–422.

—— (1981b [1937–8]) 'Forms of time and chronotope in the novel', in M. Bakhtin

The Dialogic Imagination: Four Essays, trans. C. Emerson and M. Holquist, Austin: University of Texas Press, pp. 84–258.

—— (1984 [1965]) *Rabelais and his World*, trans. H. Iswolsky, Bloomington: Indiana University Press.

Balsamo, A. (1996) *Technologies of the Gendered Body: Reading Cyborg Women*, Durham: Duke University Press.

Banes, S. (1987) *Terpsichore in Sneakers: Post-modern Dance*, Hanover: Wesleyan University Press.

Barnes, T. J. and Duncan, J. S. (eds) (1992) *Writing Worlds: Discourse, Text and Metaphor in the Representation of Landscape*, London: Routledge.

Barry, P. (1995) *Beginning Theory: An Introduction to Literary and Cultural Theory*, Manchester: Manchester University Press.

Bartels, R. (1951) 'Can marketing be a science?', *Journal of Marketing*, 16 (January): 319–28.

—— (1968) 'The general theory of marketing', *Journal of Marketing* 32 (Janaury): 29–33.

Barth, J. (1980) 'The literature of replenishment: postmodernist fiction', *The Atlantic*, 245(1): 65–71; reprinted in C. Jencks (1992) *The Postmodern Reader*, London: Academy Editions, pp. 172–80.

—— (1990) 'The literature of exhaustion', in M. Bradbury (ed.) *The Novel Today: Contemporary Writers on Modern Fiction*, London: Fontana, pp. 71–85.

Barthes, R. (1973 [1957]) 'Myth today', in R. Barthes *Mythologies*, trans. A. Lavers, London: Paladin, pp. 117–74.

—— (1977a [1968]) 'The death of the author', in R. Barthes *Image Music Text*, trans. S. Heath, London: Fontana, pp. 142–8.

—— (1977b [1966]) 'Introduction to the structural analysis of narratives', in R. Barthes *Image Music Text*, trans. S. Heath, London: Fontana, pp. 79–124.

—— (1990a [1973]) *The Pleasure of the Text*, trans. R. Miller, Oxford: Blackwell.

—— (1990b [1977]) *A Lover's Discourse: Fragments*, trans. R. Howard, Harmondsworth: Penguin.

Barwise, P. (1995) 'Good empirical generalisations', *Marketing Science*, 14(3): G29–G35.

Bass, F. M. (1993) 'The future of research in marketing: marketing science', *Journal of Marketing Research*, 30 (February): 1–6.

—— (1995) 'Empirical generalisations and marketing science: a personal view', *Marketing Science*, 14(3): G6–G19.

—— and Wind, J. (1995) 'Introduction to the special issue: empirical generalisations in marketing', *Marketing Science*, 14(3): G1–G5.

Battersby, C. (1989) *Gender and Genius: Towards a Feminist Aesthetics*, London: Women's Press.

Baudrillard, J. (1983 [1981]) *Simulations*, trans. P. Foss, P. Patton and P. Beitchman, New York: Semiotext(e).

—— (1990 [1979]) *Seduction*, trans. B. Singer, Montreal: New World Perspectives.

—— (1994a [1992]) *The Illusion of the End*, trans. C. Turner, Cambridge: Polity.

—— (1994b [1981]) *Simulacra and Simulation*, trans. S. F. Glaser, Ann Arbor: University of Michigan Press.

—— (1996 [1990]) *Cool Memories II*, trans. C. Turner, Cambridge: Polity.

Bauman, Z. (1987) *Legislators and Interpreters: On Modernity, Postmodernity and Intellectuals*, Cambridge: Polity Press.

Bazerman, C. (1988) *Shaping Written Knowledge: The Genre and Activity of the Experimental Article in Science*, Madison: University of Wisconsin Press.

Becker, U. (ed.) (1994) *The Element Encyclopedia of Symbols*, trans. L. W. Garmer, Shaftesbury: Element.

Belk, R. W. (1976), 'It's the thought that counts: a signed digraph analysis of gift-giving', *Journal of Consumer Research*, 3 (December): 155–62.

—— (1979) 'Gift-giving behavior' in J. N. Sheth (ed.) *Research in Marketing*, vol. 2, Greenwich: JAI Press, pp. 95–126.

—— (1985) 'Materialism: trait aspects of living in the material world', *Journal of Consumer Research*, 12 (December): 265–80.

—— (1986a) 'Art versus science as ways of generating knowledge about materialism', in D. Brinberg and R. J. Lutz (eds) *Perspectives on Methodology in Consumer Research*, New York: Springer-Verlag, pp. 3–36.

—— (1986b) 'What should ACR want to be when it grows up?', in R. L. Lutz (ed.) *Advances in Consumer Research, vol. XIII*, Provo: Association for Consumer Research, pp. 423–4.

—— (1987a) 'A modest proposal for creating verisimilitude in consumer-information-processing models and some suggestions for establishing a discipline to study consumer behavior', in A. F. Firat, N. Dholakia and R. P. Bagozzi (eds) *Philosophical and Radical Thought in Marketing*, Lexington: Lexington Books, pp. 361–72.

—— (1987b) 'Material values in the comics: a content analysis of comic books featuring themes of wealth', *Journal of Consumer Research*, 14 (June): 26–42.

—— (1988) 'Possessions and the extended self', *Journal of Consumer Research*, 15 (September): 139–68.

—— (1989) 'Materialism and the modern US Christmas', in E. C. Hirschman (ed.)

Interpretive Consumer Research, Provo: Association for Consumer Research, pp. 115–35.

—— (1990) 'The role of possessions in constructing and maintaining a sense of the past', in M. E. Goldberg, G. Gorn and R. W. Pollay (eds) *Advances in Consumer Research, vol. XVII*, Provo: Association for Consumer Research, pp. 669–76.

—— (1991) 'Epilogue: lessons learned', in R. W. Belk (ed.) *Highways and Buyways: Naturalistic Research From the Consumer Behaviour Odyssey*, Provo: Association for Consumer Research, pp. 234–8.

—— (1994) 'Carnival, control and corporate culture in contemporary Halloween celebrations', in J. Santino (ed.) *Halloween and Other Festivals of Life and Death*, Knoxville: University of Tennessee Press, pp. 105–32.

—— (1995) *Collecting in a Consumer Society*, London: Routledge.

—— (1996a) 'On aura, illusion, escape and hope in apocalyptic consumption: the apotheosis of Las Vegas', in S. Brown, J. Bell and D. Carson (eds) *Marketing Apocalypse: Eschatology, Escapology and the Illusion of the End*, Routledge: London, pp. 87–107.

—— (1996b) 'Hyperreality and globalisation: culture in the age of Ronald McDonald', *Journal of International Consumer Marketing*, 8(3/4): 23–37.

—— (1996c), personal communication.

—— and Coon, G. S. (1993) 'Gift giving as agapic love: an alternative to the exchange paradigm based on dating experiences', *Journal of Consumer Research*, 20 (December): 393–417.

—— and Pollay, R. W. (1985) 'Images of ourselves: the good life in twentieth century advertising', *Journal of Consumer Research*, 11 (March): 887–97.

——, Ger, G. and Askegaard, S. (1996) 'Metaphors of consumer desire', in K. P. Corfman and J. G. Lynch (eds) *Advances in Consumer Research, vol. XXIII*, Provo: Association for Consumer Research, pp. 368–73.

——, Wallendorf, M. and Sherry, J. F. (1989) 'The sacred and profane in consumer behavior: theodicy on the Odyssey', *Journal of Consumer Research* 16 (June): 1–38.

——, ——, —— and Holbrook, M. B. (1991) 'Collecting in a consumer culture', in R. W. Belk (ed.) *Highways and Buyways: Naturalistic Research From the Consumer Behavior Odyssey*, Provo: Association for Consumer Research, pp. 178–215.

——, ——, ——, —— and Roberts, S. (1988) 'Collectors and collecting', in M. J. Houston (ed.) *Advances in Consumer Research, vol. XV*, Provo: Association for Consumer Research, pp. 548–53.

Bell, A. O. and McNeillie, A. (eds) (1980) *The Diary of Virginia Woolf, 1925–1930*, vol. III, London: Hogarth Press.

Bell, E. (1996) 'Persil stops the soap opera', *The Observer*, Sunday 5 May: 16.

Bell, J. and Young, S. (1995) 'Internationalisation stage theories: are we still worshipping golden calves', in S. Brown, J. Bell and D. Carson (eds) *Proceedings of the Marketing Eschatology Retreat*, Belfast: University of Ulster, pp. 132–44.

Bellenger, D. N. and Korgaonkar, P. K. (1980) 'Profiling the recreational shopper', *Journal of Retailing*, 53(2): 29–38.

——, Robertson, D. H. and Greenberg, B. A. (1977) 'Shopping center patronage motives', *Journal of Retailing*, 56(3): 77–92.

Belsey, C. (1994) *Desire: Love Stories in Western Culture*, Oxford: Blackwell.

Bennett, A. and Royle, N. (1995) *An Introduction to Literature, Criticism and Theory: Key Critical Concepts*, Hemel Hempsted: Harvester Wheatsheaf.

Benson, P. (ed.) (1993) *Anthropology and Literature*, Urbana: University of Illinois Press.

Berger, A. A. (1992) *Popular Culture Genres: Theories and Texts*, Newbury Park: Sage.

Berry, L. L. (1995) 'Relationship marketing of services – growing interest, emerging perspectives', *Journal of the Academy of Marketing Science*, 23(4): 236–45.

Bertens, H. (1995) *The Idea of the Postmodern: A History*, London: Routledge.

Best, S. and Kellner, D. (1991) *Postmodern Theory: Critical Interrogations*, Basingstoke: Macmillan.

Bhabha, H. K. (ed.) (1990) *Nation and Narration*, London: Routledge.

Bitner, M. J. (1995) 'Building service relationships: it's all about promises', *Journal of the Academy of Marketing Science*, 23(4): 246–51.

——, Booms, B. H. and Mohr, L. A. (1994) 'Critical service encounters: the employee's viewpoint', *Journal of Marketing*, 58 (October): 95–106.

——, —— and Tetreault, M. S. (1990) 'The service encounter: diagnosing favorable and unfavorable incidents', *Journal of Marketing*, 54 (January): 71–84.

Blattberg, R., Buesing, T., Peacock, P. and Sen, S. (1978) 'Identifying the deal prone segment', *Journal of Marketing Research*, 15(3): 369–77.

Bloch, E. (1988 [1974]) *The Utopian Function of Art and Literature: Selected Essays*, trans. J. Zipes and F. Mecklenburg, Cambridge, MA: MIT Press.

Bloch, P. H. and Richins, M. L. (1983) 'Shopping without purchase: an investigation of consumer browsing behavior', in R. P. Bagozzi and A. M. Tybout (eds) *Advances in Consumer Research*, *vol. X*, Provo: Association for Consumer Research, pp. 389–93.

——, Ridgway, N. M. and Sherrell, D. L. (1989) 'Extending the concept of shopping: an investigation of browsing activity', *Journal of the Academy of Marketing Science*, 17(1): 13–21.

Blois, K. J. (1996) 'Relationship marketing in organisational markets: when is it appropriate?', *Journal of Marketing Management* 12(1–3): 161–73.

Bloom, H. (1973) *The Anxiety of Influence: A Theory of Poetry*, Oxford: Oxford University Press.

—— (1975) *A Map of Misreading*, New York: Oxford University Press.

—— (1995) *The Western Canon: The Books and School of the Ages*, Basingstoke: Papermac.

—— (1996) *Omens of Millennium: The Gnosis of Angels, Dreams and Resurrection*, London: Fourth Estate.

Boehmer, E. (1995) *Colonial and Postcolonial Literature: Migrant Metaphors*, Oxford: Oxford University Press.

Bogart, M. H. (1995) *Artists, Advertising, and the Borders of Art*, Chicago: University of Chicago Press.

Boje, D. M. (1991) 'The storytelling organisation: a study of story performance in an office-supply firm', *Administrative Science Quarterly* 36(1): 106–26.

—— (1994) 'Organisational storytelling: the struggles of pre-modern, modern and postmodern organisational learning discourses', *Management Learning* 25(3): 433–61.

—— (1995) 'Stories of the storytelling organisation: a postmodern analysis of Disney as "*Tamara*-Land"', *Academy of Management Journal* 38(4): 997–1035.

——, Gephart, R. P. and Thatchenkery, T. J. (eds) (1996) *Postmodern Management and Organization Theory*, Thousand Oaks: Sage.

Bolz, N. and Bosshart, D. (1995) *Kult-Marketing: Die neuen Götter des Marktes*, Düsseldorf: ECON.

Bonnycastle, S. (1996) *In Search of Authority: An Introductory Guide to Literary Theory*, Peterborough, Ontario: Broadview.

Booth, W. C. (1983) *The Rhetoric of Fiction*, 2nd edn, Harmondsworth: Penguin.

Borden, N. H. (1964) 'The concept of the marketing mix', *Journal of Advertising Research*, 4 (June): 2–7.

—— (1965) 'The concept of the marketing mix', in G. Schwartz (ed.) *Science in Marketing*, New York: Wiley, pp. 386–97.

Bornstein, R. F. (1991) 'The predictive validity of peer review: a neglected issue', *Behavioural and Brain Sciences*, 14(1): 138–9.

Bottomore, T. (1984) *The Frankfurt School*, London: Routledge.

Bouchet, D. (1994) 'Rails without ties. The social imaginary and postmodern culture. Can postmodern consumption replace modern questioning?', *International Journal of Research in Marketing* 11(4): 405–22.

—— (1995) 'Marketing and the redefinition of ethnicity', in J. A. Costa and G. J.

Bamossy (eds) *Marketing in a Multicultural World: Ethnicity, Nationalism and Cultural Identity*, Thousand Oaks: Sage, pp. 68–104.

—— (1996) 'The return of superfluousness and utility, and consumption in the postmodern culture: a comment on "postmodern perspectives on consumption"', in R. Belk, N. Dholakia and A. Venkatesh (eds) *Consumption and Marketing: Macro Dimensions*, Cincinnati: South-Western, pp. 275–81.

Boyce, D. G. and O'Day, A. (eds) (1996) *The Making of Modern Irish History: Revisionism and the Revisionist Controversy*, London: Routledge.

Brady, J. and Davis, I. (1993) 'Marketing's mid-life crisis', *McKinsey Quarterly* 2: 17–28.

Brandist, C. (1996) 'The official and the popular in Gramsci and Bakhtin', *Theory, Culture and Society* 13(2): 59–74.

Briggs, A. and Snowman, D. (eds) (1996) Fins de Siècle: *How Centuries End 1400–2000*, New Haven: Yale University Press.

Brinson P. (1991) *Dance as Education: Towards a National Dance Culture*, London: Falmer Press.

Bristor, J. and Fischer, E. (1993) 'Feminist thought: implications for consumer research', *Journal of Consumer Research* 19(March): 518–36.

Bronner, S. E. (1994) *Of Critical Theory and its Theorists*, Oxford: Blackwell.

Brophy, E. (1996) 'Beyond words – the story of Riverdance', *Riverdance the Show*, Cork: Abhann Productions, pp. 6–7.

Brosseau, M. (1994) 'Geography's literature', *Progress in Human Geography*, 18(2): 333–53.

Brown, L. O. (1948) 'Toward a profession of marketing', *Journal of Marketing*, 13(July): 27–31.

Brown, R. (1987) 'Marketing – a function and a philosophy', *Quarterly Review of Marketing* 13 (Spring–Summer): 25–30.

Brown, R. H. (1987) *Society as Text: Essays on Rhetoric, Reason and Reality*, Chicago: University of Chicago Press.

—— (1989) *A Poetic for Sociology: Toward a Logic of Discovery for the Human Sciences*, 2nd edn, Chicago: University of Chicago Press.

—— (1995) 'Postmodern representation, postmodern affirmation', in R. H. Brown (ed.) *Postmodern Representations: Truth, Power and Mimesis in the Human Sciences and Public Culture*, Urbana: University of Illinois Press, pp. 1–19.

Brown, S. (1988) 'The wheel of the wheel of retailing', *International Journal of Retailing* 3(1): 16–37.

—— (1991) 'Variations on a marketing enigma: the wheel of retailing theory', *Journal of Marketing Management* 7(2): 131–55.

—— (1992) 'The wheel of retailing: still rollin' after all these years', in C. R. Taylor, S. W. Kopp, T. Nevett and S. C. Hollander (eds) *Marketing History – Its Many Dimensions*, East Lansing: Michigan State University, pp. 179–98.

—— (1994) 'Marketing and postmodernism: opportunity or aporia?', in M. J. Baker (ed.) *Perspectives on Marketing Management*, vol. 4, Chichester: Wiley, pp. 73–96.

—— (1995a) *Postmodern Marketing*, London: Routledge.

—— (1995b) 'Life begins at 40? Further thoughts on marketing's mid-life crisis', *Marketing Intelligence and Planning*, 13(1): 4–17.

—— (1995c) 'Postmodernism, the wheel of retailing and will to power', *International Review of Retail, Distribution and Consumer Research* 5(3): 287–310.

—— (1995d) 'Postmodern marketing research: no representation without taxation', *Journal of the Market Research Society* 37(3): 287–310.

—— (1995e) 'Sex 'n' shopping: a "novel" approach to consumer research', *Journal of Marketing Management* 11(8): 769–83.

—— (1995f) 'The eunuch's tale: reviewing reviewed', *Journal of Marketing Management* 11(7): 681–706.

—— (1995g) 'Christaller knew my father: recycling central place theory', *Journal of Macromarketing*, 15 (Spring): 60–73.

—— (1995h) 'Psycho shopper: a comparative literary analysis of the "dark side"', in F. Hansen (ed.) *European Advances in Consumer Research*, vol. 2, Provo: Association for Consumer Research, pp. 96–103.

—— (1995i) 'Nightmare on IMR Street', *Irish Marketing Review* 8: 157–60.

—— (1995j) 'Coca-Kotler: over-wrought, over-rated and over here', *Irish Marketing Review* 8: 134–9.

—— (1996a), 'Art or science?: fifty years of marketing debate', *Journal of Marketing Management*, 12(4): 243–67.

—— (1996b) 'Trinitarianism, the Eternal Evangel and the three eras schema', in S. Brown, J. Bell and D. Carson (eds) *Marketing Apocalypse: Eschatology, Escapology and the Illusion of the End*, London: Routledge, pp. 23–43.

—— (1996c) 'Consumption behavior in the sex 'n' shopping novels of Judith Krantz: a post-structuralist perspective', in K. P. Corfman and J. G. Lynch (eds) *Advances in Consumer Research*, vol. XXIII, Provo: Association for Consumer Research, pp. 43–8.

—— (1997a) *Postmodern Marketing Two: Telling Tales*, London: ITBP (the old ones are best, don't you agree?!).

—— (1997b) 'Sex 'n' shopping: consumption behavior in the Scruples novels of

Judith Krantz', in R.W. Belk and J.A. Costa (eds) *Research in Consumer Behavior vol. 7*, Greenwich: JAI Press, 1.46.

—— (1997c) 'Marketing science in a postmodern world', *European Journal of Marketing*, 31(3/4), pp. 167–82.

——, Bell, J. and Carson, D. (1996) 'Apocaholics anonymous: looking back on the end of marketing', in S. Brown, J. Bell and D. Carson (eds) *Marketing Apocalypse: Eschatology, Escapology and the Illusion of the End*, London: Routledge, pp. 1–20.

——, Maclaran, P. and Stevens, L. (1996) 'Marcadia postponed: marketing, utopia and the millennium', *Journal of Marketing Management* 12(7): 671–83.

——, —— and —— (1997) 'Mucha do about nothing: literary theory, the Bakhtin Circle and postmodern marketing communications', paper presented at American Marketing Association conference, Dublin, June.

—— and Quinn, B. (1993) 'Re-inventing the retailing wheel: a postmodern morality tale', in P. McGoldrick (ed.) *Cases in Retail Management*, London: Pitman, pp. 26–39.

—— and Reid, R. (1997) 'Shoppers on the verge of a nervous breakdown: chronicle, composition and confabulation in consumer research', in S. Brown and D. Turley (eds) *Consumer Research: Postcards From the Edge*, London: Routledge, pp. 79–149.

Brownlie, D. (1997) 'Beyond ethnography: towards writerly account of organising in marketing', *European Journal of Marketing* 31(3/4), pp. 263–82.

—— and Desmond, J. (1996) 'Apocalyptus interruptus: a tale by parables, apostles and epistles', in S. Brown, J. Bell and D. Carson (eds) *Marketing Apocalypse: Eschatology, Escapology and the Illusion of the End*, London: Routledge, pp. 66–86.

—— and Saren, M. (1992) 'The four Ps of the marketing concept: prescriptive, polemical, permanent and problematical', *European Journal of Marketing* 26(4): 34–47.

—— and —— (1995) 'On the commodification of marketing knowledge: opening themes', *Journal of Marketing Management* 11(7): 619–27.

——, ——, Whittington, R. and Wensley, R. (1994) 'The new marketing myopia: critical perspectives on theory and research in marketing – introduction', *European Journal of Marketing* 28(3): 6–12.

Bryson, B. (1995) *Made in America*, London: Minerva.

Bull, M. (1995) 'On making ends meet', in M. Bull (ed.) *Apocalypse Theory and the Ends of the World*, Oxford: Blackwell, pp. 1–17.

Burnham, C. (1995) *The Jamesonian Unconscious: The Aesthetics of Marxist Theory*, Durham: Duke University Press.

Burrell, G. (1997) *Pandemonium*, London: Sage.

Butler, P. (1996) 'Industry analysis and relational exchange', Dublin: Trinity College School of Business Studies, unpublished paper.

Buttimer, C. G. and Kavanagh, D. (1996) 'Markets, exchange and the extreme', in S. Brown, D. Carson and J. Bell (eds) *Marketing Apocalypse: Eschatology, Escapology and the Illusion of the End*, London: Routledge, pp. 145–70.

Buttle, F. (1994) 'Editorial: new paradigm research in marketing', *European Journal of Marketing* 28(8/9): 8–11.

—— (ed.) (1996a) *Relationship Marketing: Theory and Practice*, London: Paul Chapman Publishing.

—— (1996b) 'Relationship marketing', in F. Buttle (ed.) *Relationship Marketing: Theory and Practice*, London: Paul Chapman, pp. 1–16.

Buzan, T. and Keene, R. (1994) *Buzan's Book of Genius and How to Unleash Your Own*, London: Stanley Paul.

Buzzell, R. D. (1963) 'Is marketing a science?', *Harvard Business Review* 41(1): 32–40, 166–70.

—— (1984) 'Preface to – is marketing a science?', in S. W. Brown and R. P. Fisk (eds) *Marketing Theory: Distinguished Contributions*, New York: John Wiley, p. 66.

Byatt, A. S. (1990) *Possession: A Romance*, London: Vintage.

Cahoone, L. E. (1995) *The Ends of Philosophy*, Albany: State University of New York Press.

—— (ed.) (1996) *From Modernism to Postmodernism: An Anthology*, Oxford: Blackwell.

Calder, B. J. and Tybout, A. M. (1987) 'What consumer research is', *Journal of Consumer Research* 14 (June): 136–40.

—— and —— (1989) 'Interpretive, qualitative and traditional scientific empirical consumer behavior research', in E. C. Hirschman (ed.) *Interpretive Consumer Research*, Provo: Association for Consumer Research, pp. 199–208.

Callcott, M. F. and Lee, W-N. (1995) 'Establishing the spokes-character in academic inquiry: historical overview and framework for definition', in F.R. Kardes and M. Sujan (eds) *Advances in Consumer Research, vol. XXII*, Provo: Association for Consumer Research, pp. 144–51.

Callinicos, A. (1995a) 'Postmodernism as normal science', *British Journal of Sociology* 46 (December): 134–9.

—— (1995b) *Theories and Narratives: Reflections on the Philosophy of History*, Cambridge: Polity.

Calvet, L. -J. (1994 [1990]) *Roland Barthes: A Biography*, trans. S. Wykes, Cambridge: Polity.

Calvino, I. (1986 [1982]) *The Uses of Literature*, trans. P. Creagh, San Diego: Harcourt Brace and Company.

Campbell, C. (1987) *The Romantic Ethic and the Spirit of Modern Consumerism*, Oxford: Blackwell.

Campion, N. (1994) *The Great Year: Astrology, Millenarianism and History in the Western Tradition*, Harmondsworth: Arkana.

Carey, J. (1995) 'Introduction', in J. Carey (ed.) *The Faber Book of Science*, London: Faber & Faber, pp. xiii–xxvii.

Carruthers, N. (1996) 'Principal-agent relationships', in F. Buttle (ed.) *Relationship Marketing: Theory and Practice*, London: Paul Chapman, pp. 29–39.

Catterall, M., Maclaran, P. and Stevens, L. (1996) 'The pathetic phallusies of St Thomas Aquinas and why marketing should give Eve a break', in S. Brown, J. Bell and D. Carson (eds) *Marketing Apocalypse: Eschatology, Escapology and the Illusion of the End*, London: Routledge, pp. 223–36.

——, —— and —— (1997) 'The "Glasshouse Effect": women in marketing management', *Marketing Intelligence and Planning* 15, in press.

Cave, M. (1990) 'Bakhtin and feminism: the chronotopic female imagination', *Women's Studies* 18(2): 117–27.

Cawelti, J. G. (1971) *The Six-Gun Mystique*, Bowling Green: Bowling Green Popular Press.

—— (1976) *Adventure, Mystery and Romance: Formula Stories as Art and Popular Culture*, Chicago: University of Chicago Press.

Ceci, S. J. and Peters, D. (1984) 'How blind is blind review?', *American Psychologist* 39(2): 1491–4.

Chaplin, E. (1994) *Sociology and Visual Representation*, London: Routledge.

Chen, I. J., Calantone, R. J. and Chung, C.-H. (1992) 'The marketing–manufacturing interface and manufacturing flexibility', *OMEGA* 20(4): 431–43.

Chia, R. (1996) 'Teaching paradigm shifting in management education: university business schools and the entrepreneurial imagination', *Journal of Management Studies* 33(4): 409–28.

Christy, R., Oliver, G. and Penn, J. (1996) 'Relationship marketing in consumer markets', *Journal of Marketing Management* 12(1–3): 175–87.

Chubin, D. E. and Hackett, E. J. (1990) *Peerless Science: Peer Review and US Science Policy*, Albany: State University of New York Press.

Churchill, G. A. (1988) 'Comments on the AMA Task Force study', *Journal of Marketing* 52 (October): 26–31.

Clandinin, D. J. and Connelly, F. M. (1994) 'Personal experience methods', in N. K. Denzin and Y. S. Lincoln (eds) *Handbook of Qualitative Research*, Thousand Oaks: Sage, pp. 413–27.

Clegg, S. R. and Gray, J. T. (1996) 'Metaphors of globalisation', in D. M. Boje, R. P. Gephart and T. J. Thatchenkary (eds) *Postmodern Management and Organization Theory*, Thousand Oaks: Sage, pp. 293–307.

Clifford, J. (1988) *The Predicament of Culture: Twentieth-century Ethnography, Literature and Art*, Cambridge: Harvard University Press.

Coles, R. (1989) *The Call of Stories: Teaching and the Moral Imagination*, Boston: Houghton Mifflin.

Connor, S. (1989) *Postmodernist Culture: An Introduction to Theories of the Contemporary*, Oxford: Blackwell.

Converse, P. D. (1945) 'The development of the science of marketing – an exploratory survey', *Journal of Marketing* 10 (July): 14–23.

Cooper, D. E. (1996) *Thinkers of our Time: Heidegger*, London: Claridge Press.

Coopers and Lybrand (1994) *Marketing at the Crossroads: A Survey on the Role of Marketing*, London: Coopers and Lybrand.

Copeland, R. (1993) 'Postmodern dance and the repudiation of primitivism', *Partisan Review* 150: 101–21.

Coren, A. (1991) 'Avon calling', *A Year in Cricklewood*, London: Robson Books, pp. 32–34.

—— (1994) 'A reminder on a tub of Flora of one's mortality is an intrusion at breakfast'. *The Times*, Wednesday 14 September: 14.

—— (1995a) 'Serving us right', *A Bit on the Side*, London: Robson Books, pp. 113–5.

—— (1995b) 'Crumpet involuntary', *A Bit on the Side*, London: Robson Books, pp. 31–3.

—— (1996a) 'Camcorders as jailbird bait, eh? It's the end of the free gift as we know it', *The Times*, 6 March.

—— (1996b) 'Do I scent, at long last, a whiff of literary celebrity?', *The Times*, Wednesday 17 July: 16.

Costa, J. A. (ed.) (1993) *Gender and Consumer Behavior: Second Conference Proceedings*, Salt Lake City: University of Utah Printing Service.

—— (ed.) (1994a) *Gender Issues and Consumer Behavior*, Thousand Oaks: Sage.

—— (1994b) 'Gender issues: gender as a cultural construct', in C. T. Allen and D. R. John (eds) *Advances in Consumer Research, vol. XXI*, Provo: Association for Consumer Research, pp. 372–3.

—— (ed.) (1996) *Gender, Marketing and Consumer Behavior: Third Conference Proceedings*, Salt Lake City: University of Utah Printing Service.

—— and Belk, R. W. (1990) 'Nouveaux riches as quintessential Americans: case studies of consumption in an extended family', in R. W. Belk (ed.) *Advances in Nonprofit Marketing, vol. 3*, Greenwich: JAI Press, pp. 83–140.

Cova, B. (1996) 'What postmodernism means to marketing managers', *European Management Journal* 14(5): 494–9.

—— (1997) 'Community and consumption: towards a definition of the "linking value" of product or services', *European Journal of Marketing* 31(3/4): 295–314.

—— and Badot, O. (1995) 'Marketing theory and practice in a postmodern era', in M. J. Baker (ed.) *Marketing Theory and Practice*, Basingstoke: Macmillan, pp. 416–31.

—— and Svanfeldt, C. (1993) 'Societal innovations and the aestheticisation of everyday life', *International Journal of Research in Marketing* 10(3): 297–310.

Cox, R. and Alderson, W. (1950) *Theory in Marketing*, Chicago: Richard D. Irwin.

Crapanzano, V. (1992) *Hermes' Dilemma and Hamlet's Desire: On the Epistemology of Interpretation*, Cambridge: Harvard University Press.

Cravens, D. W. (1995) 'Introduction to the special issue', *Journal of the Academy of Marketing Science* 23(4): 235.

Cresswell, T. (1993) 'Mobility as resistance: a geographical reading of Kerouac's *On the Road*', *Transactions of the Institute of British Geographers* 18(2): 249–62.

Cummings L. L. and Frost, P. J. (eds) (1995) *Publishing in the Organisational Sciences*, 2nd edn, Thousand Oaks: Sage.

Cunningham, V. (1994) *In the Reading Gaol*, Oxford: Blackwell.

Czepiel, J. A. (1990) 'Service encounters and service relationships: implications for research', *Journal of Business Research* 20(1): 13–21.

d'Astous, A. (1990) 'An inquiry into the compulsive side of "normal" consumers', *Journal of Consumer Policy* 13(1): 15–31.

Daft, R. L. (1995) 'Why I recommend that your manuscript be rejected and what you can do about it', in L. L. Cummings and P. J. Frost (eds) *Publishing in the Organisational Sciences*, Thousand Oaks: Sage, pp. 164–82.

Daniel, H. -D. (1993) *Guardians of Science: Fairness and Reliability of Peer Review*, Weinheim: VCH Press.

Danto, A. (1987) *The State of the Art*, New York: Prentice Hall.

Darden, W. R. and Reynolds, F. D. (1971) 'Shopping orientations and product usage rates', *Journal of Marketing Research* 8 (November): 505–8.

Davidson, M. (1992) *The Consumerist Manifesto: Advertising in Postmodern Times*, London: Routledge.

Davies, G. (1996) 'Supply-chain relationships', in F. Buttle (ed.) *Relationship Marketing: Theory and Practice*, London: Paul Chapman, pp. 17–28.

Dawson, L. M. (1971) 'Marketing science in the Age of Aquarius', *Journal of Marketing* 35 (July): 66–72.

Day, E. (1989) 'Share of heart: what is it and how can it be measured?', *Journal of Consumer Marketing* 6 (1): 5–12.

Day, G. S. (1996) 'Using the past as a guide to the future: reflections on the history of the *Journal of Marketing*', *Journal of Marketing* 60 (January): 14–16.

Debord, G. (1990 [1988]) *Comments on the Society of the Spectacle*, trans. M. Imrie, Verso: London.

—— (1994 [1967]) *The Society of the Spectacle*, trans. D. Nicholson-Smith, New York: Zone Books.

Deighton, J. (1992) 'The consumption of performance', *Journal of Consumer Research* 19(December): 362–72.

—— and Grayson, K. (1995) 'Marketing and seduction: building exchange relationships by managing social consensus', *Journal of Consumer Research* 21(March): 660–76.

Deleuze, G. and Guattari, F. (1984 [1972]) *Anti-Oedipus: Capitalism and Schizophrenia*, trans. R. Hurley, M. Seem and H. R. Lane, London: Athlone Press.

—— (1988 [1980]) *A Thousand Plateaus: Capitalism and Schizophrenia*, trans. B. Massumi, London: Athlone Press.

Dellamora, R. (ed.) (1995) *Postmodern Apocalypse: Theory and Cultural Practice at the End*, Philadelphia: University of Pennsylvania Press.

Denison, T. and McDonald, M. (1995) 'The role of marketing past, present and future', *Journal of Marketing Practice: Applied Marketing Science* 1(1): 54–76.

Dentith, S. (1995) *Bakhtinian Thought: An Introductory Reader*, London: Routledge.

Derrida, J. (1979) 'Living on: border lines', in H. Bloom (ed.) *Deconstruction and Criticism*, New York: Seabury Press, pp. 75–175.

—— (1981a [1969]) 'Dissemination', in *Dissemination*, trans. B. Johnson, London: Athlone Press, pp. 287–366.

—— (1981b [1970]) 'The double session', in *Dissemination*, trans. B. Johnson, London: Athlone Press, pp. 173–285.

—— (1982 [1972]) *Margins of Philosophy*, trans. A. Bass, Hemel Hempstead: Harvester Wheatsheaf.

—— (1992 [1984]) 'Psyche: invention of the other', in D. Attridge (ed.) *Acts of Literature*, New York: Routledge, pp. 310–43.

Desmond, J. (1993) 'Marketing: the split subject', in D. Brownlie *et al.* (eds)

Rethinking Marketing, Coventry: Warwick Business School Research Bureau, pp. 259–69.

—— (1995) 'Reclaiming the subject: decommodifying marketing knowledge', *Journal of Marketing Management* 11(7): 721–46.

Despande, R. (1983) 'Paradigms lost: on theory and method in research in marketing', *Journal of Marketing* 47 (Fall): 101–10.

Devine, P. E. (1989) *Relativism, Nihilism and God*, Notre Dame: University of Notre Dame Press.

Dibb, S., Simkin, L., Pride, W. M. and Ferrell, O. C. (1994) *Marketing Concepts and Strategies*, Boston: Houghton Mifflin.

Dicken, P. (1992) *Global Shift: The Internationalisation of Economic Activity*, London: Paul Chapman.

Dickens, D. R. and Fontana, A. (eds) (1994a) *Postmodernism and Social Inquiry*, London: UCL Press.

—— (1994b) 'Postmodernism in the social sciences', in D. R. Dickens and A. Fontana (eds) *Postmodernism and Social Inquiry*, London: UCL Press, pp. 1–22.

Dittmar, H. (1992) *The Social Psychology of Material Possessions: To Have Is To Be*, Hemel Hempstead: Harvester Wheatsheaf.

Docker, J. (1994) *Postmodernism and Popular Culture: A Cultural History*, Cambridge: Cambridge University Press.

Dodson, K. and Belk, R. W. (1996) 'Gender in children's birthday stories', in J. A. Costa (ed.) *Gender, Marketing and Consumer Behavior, Third Conference Proceedings*, Salt Lake City: University of Utah Printing Service, pp. 96–108.

Doherty, J., Graham, E. and Malek, M. (eds) (1992) *Postmodernism and the Social Sciences*, Basingstoke: Macmillan.

Donnelly, R. (1996) '*Riverdance*: the replay', *The Irish Times*, 23 August: 9.

Dougill, D. (1996) 'Ceili caper', *The Sunday Times*, 21 July, Section 10: 21.

Douglas, A. (1980) 'Soft-porn culture', *New Republic*, 30 August: 25–9.

Dowling, L. (1986) *Language and Decadence in the Victorian* Fin de Siècle, Princeton: Princeton University Press.

Doyle, P. (1995) 'Marketing in the new millennium', *European Journal of Marketing* 29(13): 23–41.

Drucker, P. F. (1994) 'The theory of the business', *Harvard Business Review* 72(5): 95–104.

Duncan, A. (1994) *Art Nouveau*, London: Thames & Hudson.

Duncker, P. (1996) *Hallucinating Foucault*, London: Serpent's Tail.

Dunning, J. H. (1993) *The Globalisation of Business*, London: Routledge.

Durant, J. (1996) 'Jury out in the cold on science', *The Times Higher*, 19 January: 16.

Durgee, J. F. (1988) 'Interpreting consumer mythology: a literary criticism approach to Odyssey informant stories', in M. J. Houston (ed.) *Advances in Consumer Research, vol. XV*, Provo: Association for Consumer Research, pp. 531–6.

—— (1991) 'Interpreting Dichter's interpretations: an analysis of consumption symbolism in "The Handbook of Consumer Motivations"', in H. H. Larsen, D. G. Mick and C. Alsted (eds) *Marketing and Semiotics: Selected Papers from the Copenhagen Symposium*, Copenhagen: Nyt Nordisk Forlag Arnold Busck, pp. 52–74.

Dwyer, F. R., Schurr, P. H. and Oh, S. (1987) 'Developing buyer–seller relationships', *Journal of Marketing* 51 (April): 11–27.

Eagleton, T. (1984) *The Function of Criticism: From the Spectator to Post-structuralism*, London: Verso.

—— (1989) 'Bakhtin, Schopenhauer, Kundera', in K. Hirschkop and D. Shepherd (eds) *Bakhtin and Cultural Theory*, Manchester: Manchester University Press, pp. 178–88.

—— (1995) 'The flight to the real', in S. Ledger and S. McCracken (eds) *Cultural Politics at the* Fin de Siècle, Cambridge: Cambridge University Press, pp. 11–21.

—— (1996a) *The Illusions of Postmodernism*, Oxford: Blackwell.

—— (1996b) *Literary Theory: An Introduction*, 2nd edn, Oxford: Blackwell.

Ebert, T. L. (1996) *Ludic Feminism and After: Postmodernism, Desire and Labor in Late Capitalism*, Ann Arbor: University of Michigan Press.

Eco, U. (1985) *Reflections on the Name of the Rose*, London: Minerva.

—— (1986 [1973]) *Travels in Hyper-reality*, trans. W. Weaver, London: Picador.

The Economist (1994) 'Death of the brand manager', *The Economist*, 9 April: 79–80.

Ehrenberg, A. S. C. (1995), 'Empirical generalisations: theory and method', *Marketing Science* 14(3): G20–G28.

Eisner, E. (1985) *The Art of Educational Evaluation: A Personal View*, London: Falmer Press.

Eldridge, R. (ed.) (1996) *Beyond Representation: Philosophy and Poetic Imagination*, Cambridge: Cambridge University Press.

Eliade, M. (1996 [1958]) *Patterns in Comparative Religion*, trans. R. Sheed, Lincoln: Bison Books.

Elias, N. and Scotson, J.L. (1994) *The Established and the Outsiders*, London: Sage.

Elliott, R. (1993) 'Marketing and the meaning of postmodern consumer culture', in

D. Brownlie *et al.* (eds) *Rethinking Marketing*, Coventry: Warwick Business School Research Bureau, pp. 134–42.

—— (1994) 'Addictive consumption: function and fragmentation in postmodernity', *Journal of Consumer Policy* 17(2): 157–79.

—— (1996a) 'Review of *Consumer Research: Introspective Essays on the Study of Consumption*, by M. B. Holbrook', *Irish Marketing Review* 9: 140–1.

—— (1996b) 'The discourse of advertising and the construction of consumer desire', paper presented at Association for Consumer Research Annual Conference, Tucson, October.

—— (1997) 'Existential consumption and irrational desire', *European Journal of Marketing* 31(3/4): 283–94.

——, Eccles, S. and Hodgson, M. (1993) 'Pe-coding gender representations: women, cleaning products and advertising's "new man"', *International Journal of Research in Marketing* 10(3): 311–24.

——, Jones, A., Benfield, A. and Barlow, M. (1995) 'Overt sexuality in advertising: a discourse analysis of gender responses', *Journal of Consumer Policy* 18(2): 187–217.

—— and Ritson, M. (1995) 'Practising existential consumption: the lived meaning of sexuality in advertising', in F. R. Kardes and M. Sujan (eds) *Advances in Consumer Research, vol. XXII*, Provo: Association for Consumer Research, pp. 740–5.

Ellis, B. E. (1991) *American Psycho*, London: Pan.

Ellis, C. (1991) 'Sociological introspection and emotional experience', *Symbolic Interaction* 14(1): 23–50.

Elsner, J. and Cardinal, R. (eds) (1994) *The Cultures of Collecting*, London: Reaktion Books.

Engel, J. F., Kollat, D. T. and Blackwell, R. D. (1978) *Consumer Behavior*, Chicago: Dryden.

Estés, C.P. (1993) *Women Who Run With the Wolves: Contacting the Power of the Wild Woman*, London: Rider.

Evans, J. R. and Laskin, R. L. (1994) 'The relationship marketing process: a conceptualisation and application', *Industrial Marketing Management* 23(1): 439–52.

Everitt, A. (1995) 'It's shopping rage! Don't get mown down or beaten up in the rush – know thine enemy', *Sunday Mirror Magazine*, 10 December: 22.

Ewen, S. (1988) *All Consuming Images: The Politics of Style in Contemporary Culture*, New York: Basic Books.

Eysenck, H. (1995) *Genius: The Natural History of Creativity*, Cambridge: Cambridge University Press.

Farganis, S. (1994) 'Postmodernism and feminism', in D. R. Dickens and A. Fontana (eds) *Postmodernism and Social Inquiry*, London: UCL Press, pp. 101–26.

Featherstone, M. (1991) *Consumer Culture and Postmodernism*, London: Sage.

—— (1995) *Undoing Culture: Globalisation, Postmodernism and Identity*, London: Sage.

—— and Burrows, R. (eds) (1995) *Cyberspace/Cyberbodies/Cyberpunk: Cultures of Technological Embodiment*, London: Sage.

Fine, G. A. and Martin, D. D. (1995) 'Humor in ethnographic writing: sarcasm, satire and irony as voices in Erving Goffman's *Asylums*', in J. van Maanen (ed.) *Representation in Ethnography*, Thousand Oaks: Sage, pp. 165–97.

Firat, A. F. (1994) 'Gender and consumption: transcending the feminine?', in J. A. Costa (ed.) *Gender Issues and Consumer Behavior*, Thousand Oaks: Sage, pp. 205–28.

—— (1995) 'Consumer culture or culture consumed?', in J. A. Costa and G. J. Bamossy (eds) *Marketing in a Multicultural World: Ethnicity, Nationalism and Cultural Identity*, Thousand Oaks: Sage, pp. 105–25.

——, Dholakia, N. and Venkatesh, A. (1995a) 'Consumption culture – modern and postmodern: implications for international marketing', unpublished manuscript.

—— (1995b) 'Marketing in a postmodern world', *European Journal of Marketing* 29(1): 40–56.

—— and Schultz, C. J. (1997) 'From segmentation to fragmentation: markets and marketing strategy in the postmodern era', *European Journal of Marketing* 31(3/4): 182–206.

—— and Venkatesh, A. (1993) 'Postmodernity: the age of marketing', *International Journal of Research in Marketing*, 10(3): 227–49.

—— and —— (1995) 'Liberatory postmodernism and the reenchantment of consumption', *Journal of Consumer Research* 22 (December): 239–67.

—— and —— (1996) 'Postmodern perspectives on consumption', in R. W. Belk, N. Dholakia and A. Venkatesh (eds) *Consumption and Marketing: Macro Dimensions*, Cincinnati: South-Western, pp. 234–65.

Firestone, S. (1971) *The Dialectic of Sex: The Case for Feminist Revolution*, London: Women's Press.

Fischer, E. and Arnold, S. J. (1990) 'More than a labor of love: gender roles and Christmas gift shopping', *Journal of Consumer Research* 17(December): 333–45.

—— and Bristor, J. (1994) 'A feminist poststructuralist analysis of the rhetoric of marketing relationships', *Inernational Journal of Research in Marketing* 11(4): 317–31.

Fisk, G. (1971) 'The role of marketing theory', in G. Fisk (ed.) *New Essays in Marketing Theory*, Boston: Allyn and Bacon, pp. 1–5.

—— (1995) 'Questioning eschatological questions about marketing', in S. Brown, J. Bell and D. Carson (eds) *Proceedings of the Marketing Eschatology Retreat*, Belfast: University of Ulster, pp. 289–97.

Fisk, R. P. and Grove, S. J. (1996) 'Applications of impression management and the drama metaphor in marketing: an introduction', *European Journal of Marketing* 30(9): 6–12.

Floch, J. -M. (1988) 'The contribution of structural semiotics to the design of a hypermarket', *International Journal of Research in Marketing* 4(2): 233–52.

Flynn, E. A. and Schweikart, P. P. (eds) (1986) *Gender and Reading: Essays on Readers, Texts and Contexts*, Baltimore: Johns Hopkins University Press.

Fontana, A. (1994) 'Ethnographic trends in the postmodern era', in D. R. Dickens and A. Fontana (eds) *Postmodernism and Social Inquiry*, London: UCL Press, pp. 203–23.

Ford, C. M. and Gioia, D. A. (eds) (1995) *Creative Action in Organisations: Ivory Tower Visions and Real World Voices*, Thousand Oaks: Sage.

Forth, I. (1995) *The Chaos of Meaning: Communicating in the Postmodern World*, London: BMP DDB Needham.

Foster, R. (1996) 'The poet of the coming times', *Times Literary Supplement*, 27 September: 9–10.

Foucault, M. (1972 [1966]) *The Order of Things: An Archaeology of the Human Sciences*, trans. A. Sheridan, London: Routledge.

—— (1977 [1975]) *Discipline and Punish: The Birth of the Prison*, trans. A. Sheridan, Harmondsworth: Penguin.

—— (1979 [1976]) *The History of Sexuality Volume 1: An Introduction*, trans. R. Hurley, Harmondsworth: Penguin.

—— (1980a) *Power/Knowledge: Selected Interviews and Other Writings 1972–1977*, C. Gordon (ed.), Hemel Hempstead: Harvester Wheatsheaf.

—— (1980b) 'The order of discourse', in R. Young (ed.) *Untying the Text: A Post-structuralist Reader*, London: Routledge, pp. 48–78.

—— (1986 [1984]) *The Use of Pleasure: The History of Sexuality Volume Two*, trans. R. Hurley, Harmondsworth: Penguin.

—— (1990 [1984]) *The Care of the Self: The History of Sexuality Volume Three*, trans. R. Hurley, Harmondsworth: Penguin.

Fournier, S. and Guiry, M. (1993) 'An emerald green Jaguar, a house on Nantucket and an African safari: wish lists and consumption dreams', in L. McAlister and M. L. Rothschild (eds) *Advances in Consumer Research, vol. XX*, Provo: Association for Consumer Research, pp. 352–8.

Fowles, J. (1996) *Advertising and Popular Culture*, Thousand Oaks: Sage.

Freeman, M. (1993) *Finding the Muse: A Sociopsychological Inquiry into the Conditions of Artistic Creativity*, Cambridge: Cambridge University Press.

Friedman, M. (1985) 'The changing language of a consumer society: brand name usage in popular American novels in the post-war era', *Journal of Consumer Research* 11 (March): 927–38.

—— (1987) 'Word-of-author advertising and the consumer: an empirical analysis of the quality of product brands noted by authors of popular cultural works', *Journal of Consumer Policy* 10(3): 307–18.

—— (1991) *A 'Brand' New Language: Commercial Influences in Literature and Culture*, Westport: Greenwood Press.

Frisby, D. (1994) 'The *flâneur* in social theory', in K. Tester (ed.) *The Flaneur*, London: Routledge, pp. 81–110.

Frye, N. (1971) *Anatomy of Criticism: Four Essays*, Princeton: Princeton University Press.

Fukuyama, F. (1992) *The End of History and the Last Man*, London: Hamish Hamilton.

Fullerton, R. (1994) 'Marketing action and the transformation of western consciousness: the examples of pulp literature and department stores', in R. A. Fullerton (ed.) *Research in Marketing Supplement 6: Explorations in the History of Marketing*, Greenwich: JAI Press, pp. 237–54.

Gaarder, J. (1995) *Sophie's World: A Novel About the History of Philosophy*, London: Phoenix House.

Game, A. and Metcalfe, A. (1996) *Passionate Sociology*, London: Sage.

Gane, M. (1995) 'Radical theory: Baudrillard and vulnerability', *Theory, Culture and Society* 12(4): 109–23.

Gardiner, M. (1993) 'Ecology and carnival: traces of a "green" social theory in the writings of M. M. Bakhtin', *Theory and Society* 22(6): 765–812.

Geertz, C. (1983) *Local Knowledge: Further Essays in Interpretive Anthropology*, London: Fontana Press.

—— (1988) *Works and Lives: The Anthropologist as Author*, Stanford: Stanford University Press.

—— (1995) *After the Fact: Two Countries, Four Decades, One Anthropologist*, Cambridge: Harvard University Press.

Gephart, R. P., Boje, D. M. and Thatchenkery, T. J. (1996) 'Postmodern management and the coming crises of organisational analysis', in D. M. Boje, R. P. Gephart, and T. J. Thatchenkery (eds) *Postmodern Management and Organisation Theory*, Thousand Oaks: Sage, pp. 1–18.

Gergen, K. J. and Whitney, D. (1996) 'Technologies of representation in the global corporation: power and polyphony', in D. M. Boje, R. P. Gephart and T. J. Thatchenkery (eds) *Postmodern Management and Organisation Theory*, Thousand Oaks: Sage, pp. 331–57.

Gilbert, D. (1996) 'Airlines', in F. Buttle (ed.) *Relationship Marketing: Theory and Practice*, London: Paul Chapman, pp. 131–44.

Gilbert, S. M. (1996) 'Rider Haggard's heart of darkness', in L. Pykett (ed.) *Reading* Fin de Siècle *Fictions*, Harlow: Longman, pp. 39–46.

Gillespie, M. A. (1995) *Nihilism Before Nietzsche*, Chicago: University of Chicago Press.

Gillott, J. and Kumar, M. (1995) *Science and the Retreat From Reason*, London: Merlin Press.

Goldman, R. and Papson, S. (1994a) 'The postmodernism that failed', in D. R. Dickens and A. Fontana (eds) *Postmodernism and Social Theory*, London: UCL Press.

—— (1994b) 'Advertising in the age of hypersignification', *Theory, Culture and Society* 11(1): 23–53.

Goodwin, C. (1992) 'Good guys don't wear polyester: consumption ideology in a detective series', in J. F. Sherry and B. Sternthal (eds) *Advances in Consumer Research, vol. XIX*, Provo: Association for Consumer Research, pp. 739–45.

Gould, S. J. (1991) 'The self-manipulation of my pervasive, perceived vital energy through product use: an introspective-praxis perspective', *Journal of Consumer Research* 18 (September): 194–207.

—— (1993) 'The circle of projection and introjection: an investigation of a proposed paradigm involving the mind as "consuming organ", in R. W. Belk and J. A. Costa (eds) *Research in Consumer Behavior, vol. 6*, Greenwich: JAI Press, pp. 185–230.

—— (1995) 'Researcher introspection as a method in consumer research: applications, issues and implications', *Journal of Consumer Research* 21(March): 719–22.

Gould, S. Jay (1991) *Bully for Brontosaurus: Reflections in Natural History*, London: Hutchinson Radius.

—— (1996) *Dinosaur in a Haystack: Reflections in Natural History*, London: Jonathan Cape.

Grafton Small, R. (1993) 'Consumption and significance: everyday life in a brand new second-hand bow tie', *European Journal of Marketing* 27(8): 38–45.

—— (1995) 'From goods to beast: consumer interpretations of order and excess', in F. Hansen (ed.) *European Advances in Consumer Research, vol. 2*, Provo: Association for Consumer Research, pp. 92–5.

—— (1997) 'Trading partners: everyday intercourse in words and things', *European Journal of Marketing* 31(3/4): 207–12.

—— and Linstead, S. A. (1989) 'Advertisements as artefacts: everyday understanding and the creative consumer', *International Journal of Advertising* 8(3): 205–18.

Grayson, K. and Shulman, D. (1996) 'The genuine article: product authenticity and its value to consumers', in K. P. Corfman and J. G. Lynch (eds) *Advances in Consumer Research, vol. XXIII*, Provo: Association for Consumer Research, pp. 391–2.

Greer, G. (1971) *The Female Eunuch*, London: Paladin.

Grenz, S. J. (1995) *A Primer on Postmodernism*, Cambridge: William B. Eerdmans.

Greyser, S. (1976) 'Foreword', in M. P. McNair and E. G. May, *The Evolution of Retail Institutions in the United States*, Cambridge: Marketing Science Institute, pp. iii–iv.

Griffin, D. (1994) *Satire: A Critical Reintroduction*, Lexington: University Press of Kentucky.

Gripsrud, G. (1986) 'Market structure, perceived competition and expected competitor reactions in retailing', in L. P. Bucklin and J. M. Carman (eds) *Research in Marketing, vol. 8*, Greenwich: JAI Press, pp. 251–71.

Grönroos, C. (1989) 'Defining marketing: a market orientated approach', *European Journal of Marketing* 23(1): 52–60.

—— (1990) 'Relationship approach to marketing in service contexts: the marketing and organisational behavior interface', *Journal of Business Research* 20(1): 3–11.

—— (1991) 'The marketing strategy continuum: a marketing concept for the 1990s', *Management Decision* 29(1): 7–13.

—— (1994) 'Quo vadis, marketing? Toward a relationship marketing paradigm', *Journal of Marketing Management* 10(5): 347–60.

—— (1995) 'Relationship marketing: the strategy continuum', *Journal of the Academy of Marketing Science* 23(4): 252–4.

Gross, A. G. (1990) *The Rhetoric of Science*, Cambridge, MA: Harvard University Press.

Grosso, M. (1995) *Millennium Myth: Love and Death at the End of Time*, Wheaton: Quest Books.

Groves, R. and Belk, R. W. (1995) 'The Odyssey Downunder: a qualitative study of

Aboriginal consumers', in F. R. Kardes, and M. Sujan, (eds) *Advances in Consumer Research*, *vol. XXII*, Provo: Association for Consumer Research, pp. 303–5.

Gummesson, E. (1987) 'The new marketing – developing long-term interactive relationships', *Long Range Planning* 20(4): 10–20.

—— (1991) 'Marketing-orientation revisited: the crucial role of the part-time marketer', *European Journal of Marketing* 25(2): 60–75.

—— (1993) 'Marketing according to textbooks: six objections', in D. Brownlie *et al.*, (eds) *Rethinking Marketing: New Perspectives on the Discipline and Profession*, Coventry: Warwick Business School Research Bureau, pp. 248–58.

—— (1996a) 'Relationship marketing and imaginary organisations: a synthesis', *European Journal of Marketing* 30(2): 31–44.

—— (1996b) 'Mega and nano relationships in relationship marketing', *Irish Marketing Review* 9: 9–16.

—— (1996c) *Relationship Marketing: From 4Ps to 30Rs*, in press.

Habermas, J. (1985) 'Modernity – an incomplete project', in H. Foster (ed.) *Postmodern Culture*, London: Pluto Press, pp. 3–15.

Hackley, C. (1996) 'Unravelling the happy enigma of creative expertise in marketing management – a psychological view', in M. J. Baker (ed.) *2021 – A Vision for the Next 25 Years*, Marketing Education Group Conference Proceedings, Glasgow: University of Strathclyde, Track 8, Session F, pp. 1–11.

Hague, H. (1996) 'Drama on the shop floor', *The Sunday Times*, 7 January, Section 10: 22.

Håkansson, H. and Snehota, I. (eds) (1995) *Developing Relationships in Business Networks*, London: Routledge.

Halbert, M. (1965) *The Meaning and Sources of Marketing Theory*, New York: McGraw-Hill.

Halliday, M. A. K. and Martin, J. R. (1993) *Writing Science: Literacy and Discursive Power*, London: Falmer Press.

Hammersley, M. (1992) *What's Wrong With Ethnography? Methodological Explorations*, London: Routledge.

Handy, C. (1989) *The Age of Unreason*, London: Business Books.

—— (1994) *The Empty Raincoat: Making Sense of the Future*, London: Hutchinson.

—— (1995) *Beyond Certainty: The Changing Worlds of Organisations*, London: Hutchinson.

Haraway, D. J. (1990) 'A manifesto for cyborgs: science, technology and socialist feminism in the 1980s, in L. J. Nicholson (ed.) *Feminism/Postmodernism*, New York: Routledge, pp. 190–233.

—— (1991) *Simians, Cyborgs and Women: The Reinvention of Nature*, London: Free Association.

Harlow, J. (1996) 'Dirty dancing', *The Sunday Times*, 28 July, Section 1: 12.

Harvey, D. (1989) *The Condition of Postmodernity*, Oxford: Blackwell.

Hassan, I. (1985) 'The culture of postmodernism', *Theory, Culture and Society* 2(2): 119–31.

Hassay, D. N. and Smith, M. C. (1996) 'Fauna, foraging and shopping motives', in K. P. Corfman and J. G. Lynch (eds) *Advances in Consumer Research, vol. XXIII*, Provo: Association for Consumer Research, pp. 510–15.

Haug, W. (1987) *Critique of Commodity Aesthetics: Appearance, Sexuality and Advertising in Capitalist Society*, Cambridge: Polity.

Hayman, R. (1982) *Nietzsche: A Critical Life*, Harmondsworth: Penguin.

Haynes, R. D. (1994) *From Faust to Strangelove: Representations of the Scientist in Western Literature*, Baltimore: Johns Hopkins University Press.

Hazen, M. A. (1993) 'Towards polyphonic organisation', *Journal of Organisation Change Management* 6(5): 15–26.

Heide, J. (1994) 'Interorganisational governance in marketing channels', *Journal of Marketing* 58 (January): 70–85.

Heidegger, M. (1975 [1936–60]) *Poetry, Language, Thought*, trans. A. Hofstadter, New York: Harper & Row.

—— (1993) *Basic Writings*, D. F. Krell (ed.), London: Routledge.

Heilbrunn, B. (1996a) 'In search of the hidden Go(o)d: a philosophical deconstruction and narratological revisitation of the eschatological metaphor in marketing', in S. Brown, J. Bell and D. Carson (eds) *Marketing Apocalypse: Eschatology, Escapology and the Illusion of the End*, London: Routledge, pp. 111–32.

—— (1996b) 'My brand the hero? a semiotic analysis of the consumer–brand relationship', in M. Lambkin *et al.* (eds) *European Perspectives in Consumer Behavior*, Hemel Hempstead: Prentice Hall, in press.

Henry, J. (ed.) (1991a) *Creative Management*, London: Sage.

—— (1991b) 'Making sense of creativity', in J. Henry (ed.) *Creative Management*, London: Sage, pp. 1–11.

Heskett, J. L., Jones, T. O., Loveman, G. W., Sasser, W. E. and Schlesinger, L. A. (1994) 'Putting the service-profit chain to work', *Harvard Business Review* 72(March–April): 164–74.

Hetrick, W. P. and Lozada, H. R. (1993) 'From marketing theory to marketing anti-theory: implications of ethical critique within the (post)modern experience', in D. Brownlie *et al.* (eds) *Rethinking Marketing*, Coventry: Warwick Business School Research Bureau, pp. 279–90.

—— and —— (1994) 'Construing the critical imagination: comments and necessary diversions', *Journal of Consumer Research* 21(December): 548–58.

—— and —— (1995) 'Feminism, postmodernism and consumer research: critique and (re)construction', in B. B. Stern and G. M. Zinkhan (eds) *Enhancing Knowledge Development in Marketing*, vol. 6, Chicago: American Marketing Association, pp. 254–5.

Hetzel, P. (1996) 'The fall and rise of marketing fundamentalism: the case of the "Nature et Découvertes" distribution concept', in S. Brown, J. Bell and D. Carson (eds) *Marketing Apocalypse: Eschatology, Escapology and the Illusion of the End*, London: Routledge, pp. 171–86.

Hewison, R. (1995) 'Out to change the message on a bottle', *The Sunday Times*, 28 May, Section 10: 10–11.

Hill, R. P. (1991) 'Homeless women, special possessions and the meaning of "home": an ethnographic case study', *Journal of Consumer Research* 18 (December): 298–310.

—— (1993) 'Ethnography and marketing research: a postmodern perspective', in D. W. Cravens and P. R. Dickson (eds) *Enhancing Knowledge Development in Marketing*, vol. 4, Chicago: American Marketing Association, pp. 257–61.

—— (1995) 'Critical ethnography: a postpositivist method for social/public policy research in marketing', in B. B. Stern and G. M. Zinkhan (eds) *Enhancing Knowledge Development in Marketing*, vol. 6, Chicago: American Marketing Association, pp. 456–61.

—— (ed.) (1996) *Marketing and Consumer Research in the Public Interest*, Thousand Oaks: Sage.

Hills, R. (1987) *Writing in General and the Short Story in Particular*, Boston: Houghton Mifflin.

Hirschkop, K. (1989) 'Introduction: Bakhtin and cultural theory', in K. Hirschkop and D. Shepherd (eds) *Bakhtin and Cultural Theory*, Manchester: Manchester University Press, pp. 1–38.

Hirschman, E. C. (1986) 'Humanistic inquiry in marketing research: philosophy, method and criteria', *Journal of Marketing Research* 23 (August): 237–49.

—— (1987) 'Marketing research: to serve what purpose?', in R. W. Belk *et al.* (eds) *Marketing Theory: Proceedings of the AMA Winter Educators' Conference*, Chicago: American Marketing Association, pp. 204–8.

—— (1990) 'Secular immortality and the American ideology of affluence', *Journal of Consumer Research* 17 (June): 31–42.

—— (1991) 'Secular mortality and the dark side of consumer behavior; or, how semiotics saved my life', in R. H. Holman and M. R. Solomon (eds) *Advances in*

Consumer Research, vol. *XVIII*, Provo: Association for Consumer Research, pp. 1–4.

—— (1992) 'The consciousness of addiction: toward a general theory of compulsive consumption', *Journal of Consumer Research* 19 (September): 155–79.

—— (1993a) 'Ideology in consumer research, 1890 and 1990: a Marxist and feminist critique', *Journal of Consumer Research* 19 (March): 537–55.

—— (1993b) 'Consumer behavior meets the nouvelle femme: feminist consumption in the movies', L. McAlister and M. L. Rothschild (eds) *Advances in Consumer Research*, vol. *XX*, Provo: Association for Consumer Research, pp. 41–7.

—— (1996) 'Professional, personal and popular culture perspectives on addiction', in R. P. Hill (ed.) *Marketing and Consumer Research in the Public Interest*, Thousand Oaks: Sage, pp. 33–53.

—— and Holbrook, M. B. (1982) 'Hedonic consumption: emerging concepts, methods and propositions', *Journal of Marketing* 46 (Summer): 92–101.

—— and —— (1992) *Postmodern Consumer Research: The Study of Consumption as Text*, Newbury Park: Sage.

—— and Stampfl, R. W. (1980) 'Retail research: problems, potential and priorities', in R. W. Stampfl and E. C. Hirschman (eds) *Competitive Structure in Retail Markets: The Department Store Perspective*, Chicago: American Marketing Association, pp. 68–77.

—— and Stern, B. B. (1994) 'Women as commodities: prostitution as depicted in *The Blue Angel*, *Pretty Baby* and *Pretty Woman*', in C. T. Allen and D. R. John (eds) *Advances in Consumer Research*, vol. *XXI*, Provo: Association for Consumer Research, pp. 576–81.

Hirst, P. and Thompson, G. (1996) *Globalisation in Question*, Cambridge: Polity.

Hixon, J. G. and Swann, W. B. (1993) 'When does introspection bear fruit? Self-reflection, self-insight and interpersonal choices', *Journal of Personality and Social Psychology* 64(1): 35–43.

Hobsbawm, E. (1983) 'Mass producing traditions: Europe, 1870–1914', in E. Hobsbawm and T. Ranger (eds) *The Invention of Tradition*, Cambridge: Cambridge University Press, pp. 263–307.

Hoch, S. J. and Loewenstein, G. F. (1991) 'Time-inconsistent preferences and consumer self-control', *Journal of Consumer Research* 17(March): 492–507.

Holbrook, M. B. (1985a) 'The consumer researcher visits Radio City: dancing in the dark', in E. C. Hirschman and M. B. Holbrook (eds) *Advances in Consumer Research*, vol. *XII*, Provo: Association for Consumer Research, pp. 28–31.

—— (1985b) 'Why business is bad for consumer research: the Three Bears revisited', in E. C. Hirschman and M. B. Holbrook (eds) *Advances in Consumer Research*, *vol. XII*, Provo: Association for Consumer Research, pp. 145–56.

—— (1986a), 'I'm hip: an autobiographical account of some musical consumption experiences', in R. J. Lutz (ed.) *Advances in Consumer Research*, *vol. XIII*, Provo: Association for Consumer Research, pp. 614–18.

—— (1986b) 'A note on sado-masochism in the review process: I hate when that happens', *Journal of Marketing* 50 (July): 104–8.

—— (1987) 'What is consumer research?', *Journal of Consumer Research* 14 (June): 128–32.

—— (1988) 'The psychoanalytical interpretation of consumer research: I am an Animal', in E. C. Hirschman and J. N. Sheth (eds) *Research in Consumer Behavior*, *vol. 3*, Greenwich: JAI Press, pp. 149–78.

—— (1990) 'The role of lyricism in research on consumer emotions: Skylark, have you anything to say to me?', in M. Goldberg, G. Gorn and R. Pollay (eds) *Advances in Consumer Research*, *vol. XVII*, Provo: Association for Consumer Research, pp. 1–18.

—— (1991) 'Romanticism and sentimentality in consumer behavior: a literary approach to the joys and sorrows of consumption', in E. C. Hirschman (ed.), *Research in Consumer Behavior*, *vol. 5*, Greenwich: JAI Press, pp. 105–80.

—— (1993) *Daytime Television Gameshows and the Celebration of Merchandise: The Price is Right*, Bowling Green: Bowling Green State University Popular Press.

—— (1994a) 'Postmodernism and social theory', *Journal of Macromarketing* 13 (Fall): 69–75.

—— (1994b) 'Loving and hating New York: some reflections on the Big Apple', *International Journal of Research in Marketing* 11(4): 381–5.

—— (1994c) 'Ethics in consumer research: an overview and prospectus', in C. T. Allen and D. R. John (eds) *Advances in Consumer Research*, *vol. XXI*, Provo: Association for Consumer Research, pp. 566–71.

—— (1995a) *Consumer Research: Introspective Essays on the Study of Consumption*, Thousand Oaks: Sage.

—— (1995b) 'The three faces of elitism: postmodernism, political correctness and popular culture', *Journal of Macromarketing* 15(2): 128–65.

—— (1995c) 'The four faces of commodification in the development of marketing knowledge', *Journal of Marketing Management* 11(7): 641–54.

—— (1996a) 'Consumption as communication in the world of *Mrs. Cage*', *Journal of Marketing* 60 (April): 139–42.

—— (1996b) 'Romanticism, introspection and the roots of experiential consumption: Morris the epicurean', in R. W. Belk, N. Dholakia and A. Venkatesh (eds)

Consumption and Marketing: Macro Dimensions, Cincinnati: South-Western, pp. 20–82.

——, Bell, S. and Grayson, M. W. (1989) 'The role of the humanities in consumer research: close encounters and coastal disturbances', in E.C. Hirschman (ed.) *Interpretive Consumer Research*, Provo: Association for Consumer Research, pp. 29–47.

—— and Day, E. (1994) 'Reflections on jazz and teaching: Benny, Woody and we', *European Journal of Marketing* 28(8/9): 133–44.

—— and Grayson, M. (1986) 'Cinematic consumption: symbolic consumer behavior in *Out of Africa*', *Journal of Consumer Research* 13 (December): 374–81.

—— and Hirschman, E. C. (1982) 'The experiential aspects of consumption: consumer fantasies, feelings and fun', *Journal of Consumer Research* 9 (September): 132–40.

—— and —— (1993) *The Semiotics of Consumption: Interpreting Symbolic Consumer Behavior in Popular Culture and Works of Art*, Berlin: de Gruyter.

Hollander, S. C. (1960) 'The wheel of retailing', *Journal of Marketing* 24 (July): 37–42.

—— (1966) 'Notes on the retail accordion', *Journal of Retailing* 42 (Summer): 29–40, 54.

Hollinger, R. (1994) *Postmodernism and the Social Sciences: A Thematic Approach*, Thousand Oaks: Sage.

Holquist, M. (1990) *Dialogism: Bakhtin and his World*, London: Routledge.

Holt, D. R. (1995a) 'Consumption and society: will marketing join the conversation?', *Journal of Marketing Research* 31 (November): 487–93.

—— (1995b) 'How consumers consume: a typology of consumption practices', *Journal of Consumer Research* 22 (June): 1–16.

—— (1997) 'Poststructuralist lifestyle analysis: conceptualising the social patterning of consumption in postmodernity', *Journal of Consumer Research* 23 (March): 326–50.

Holyoak, K. J. and Thagard, P. (1995) *Mental Leaps: Analogy in Creative Thought*, Cambridge, MA: MIT Press.

Horgan, J. (1996) *The End of Science*, New York: Addison-Wesley.

Hornby, N. (1995) *High Fidelity*, London: Indigo.

Horrocks, C. and Jevtic, Z. (1996) *Baudrillard for Beginners*, Cambridge: Icon.

Horton, J. and Baumeister, A. T. (eds) (1996) *Literature and the Political Imagination*, London: Routledge.

Hoy, D. C. (1985) 'Jacques Derrida', in Q. Skinner (ed.) *The Return of Grand Theory in the Human Sciences*, Cambridge: Cambridge University Press, pp. 41–64.

—— and McCarthy, T. (1994) *Critical Theory*, Oxford: Blackwell.

Hubbard, R. (1995) 'The commodification of marketing knowledge: it's not enough to count the numbers', *Journal of Marketing Management* 11(7): 671–3.

Hudson, L. A. and Murray, J. B. (1986) 'Methodological limitations of the hedonic consumption paradigm and a possible alternative: a subjectivist approach', in R. J. Lutz (ed.) *Advances in Consumer Research, vol. XIII*, Provo: Association for Consumer Research, pp. 343–8.

Hunt, S. D. (1976) 'The nature and scope of marketing', *Journal of Marketing* 40 (July): 17–28.

—— (1984) 'Should marketing adopt relativism?', in P. F. Anderson and M. J. Ryan (eds) *Scientific Method in Marketing*, Chicago: American Marketing Association, pp. 30–4.

—— (1989) 'Naturalistic, humanistic and interpretive inquiry: challenges and ultimate potential', in E. C. Hirschman (ed.) *Interpretive Consumer Research*, Provo: Association for Consumer Research, pp. 185–98.

—— (1990a) 'Truth in marketing theory and research', *Journal of Marketing* 54 (July): 1–15.

—— (1990b) 'A commentary on an empirical investigation of a general theory of marketing ethics', *Journal of the Academy of Marketing Science* 18 (Spring): 173–7.

—— (1991) 'Positivism and paradigm dominance in consumer research: toward critical pluralism and rapprochement', *Journal of Consumer Research* 18 (June): 32–44.

—— (1992) 'For reason and realism in marketing', *Journal of Marketing* 56 (April): 89–102.

—— (1993) 'Objectivity in marketing theory and research', *Journal of Marketing* 57(2): 76–91.

—— (1994) 'On rethinking marketing: our discipline, our practice, our methods', *European Journal of Marketing* 28(3): 13–25.

—— and Edison, S. (1995) 'On the marketing of marketing knowledge', *Journal of Marketing Management* 11 (October): 635–9.

—— and Menon, A. (1995) 'Metaphors and competitive advantage: evaluating the use of metaphors in theories of competitive advantage', *Journal of Business Research* 33(1): 81–90.

—— and Morgan, R. M. (1995) 'Relationship marketing in the era of network competition', *Marketing Management* 3(1): 19–28.

Hutcheon, L. (1988) *A Poetics of Postmodernism: History, Theory, Fiction*, London: Routledge.

—— (1989) *The Politics of Postmodernism*, London: Routledge.

Hutchinson, K. D. (1952) 'Marketing as a science: an appraisal', *Journal of Marketing* 16 (January): 286–93.

Hutt, M. D. (1995) 'Cross-functional working relationships in marketing', *Journal of the Academy of Marketing Science* 23(4): 351–7.

Iacobucci, I. (ed.) (1996) *Networks in Marketing*, Thousand Oaks: Sage.

Iley, C. (1996) 'Genius on tap', *The Sunday Times Magazine*, 9 June: 30–5.

Imrie, R. and Morris, J. (1992) 'A review of recent changes in buyer–supplier relationships', *OMEGA* 20(5/6): 641–52.

Jacques, M. (1993) 'The rest is science', *The Sunday Times*, 25 April, Section 9: 24–5.

Jameson, F. (1981) *The Political Unconscious: Narrative as a Socially Symbolic Act*, London: Methuen.

—— (1985) 'Postmodernism and consumer society', in H. Foster (ed.) *Postmodern Culture*, London: Pluto Press, pp. 111–25.

—— (1991) *Postmodernism, or, The Cultural Logic of Late Capitalism*, London: Verso.

Jeffcutt, P. (1993) 'From interpretation to representation', in J. Hassard and M. Parker (eds) *Postmodernism and Organisations*, London: Sage, pp. 25–48.

Jefferson, A. and Robey, D. (eds) (1986) *Modern Literary Theory: A Comparative Introduction*, 2nd edn, London: Batsford.

Jencks, C. (1989) *What is Postmodernism?*, London: Academy Editions.

—— (1995) *The Architecture of the Jumping Universe. A Polemic: How Complexity Science is Changing Architecture and Culture*, London: Academy Editions.

Jenkins, K. (1995) *On 'What is History?'*, London: Routledge.

Jones, P. (1996) 'Post-modernism, *Coronation Street* and retail marketing – a bit of whimsy!', *International Journal of Retail and Distribution Management* 24(4): 17–19.

Joy, A. and Venkatesh, A. (1994) 'Postmodernism, feminism and the body: the visible and invisible in consumer research', *International Journal of Research in Marketing* 11(4): 333–57.

—— and Wallendorf, M. (1996) 'The development of consumer culture in the Third World: theories of globalism and localism', in R. W. Belk, N. Dholakia and A. Venkatesh (eds) *Consumption and Marketing: Macro Dimensions*, Cincinnati: South-Western, pp. 104–42.

Joyce, P. (1991) 'History and post-modernism', *Past and Present* 133: 204–9.

Jung, C. G. (1964) *Man and his Symbols*, Basingstoke: Picador.

Kanter, R. M. (1994) 'Collaborative advantage: the art of alliances', *Harvard Business Review* 72 (July–August): 96–108.

Kassarjian, H. H. (1994) 'Scholarly traditions and European roots of American consumer research', in G. Laurent, G. L. Lilien and B. Pras (eds) *Research Traditions in Marketing*, Dordrecht: Kluwer, pp. 265–79.

Kavanagh, D. (1994) 'Hunt versus Anderson: round sixteen', *European Journal of Marketing* 28(3): 26–41.

Kell, I., Rees, P. and Clarke, I. (1996) 'If the high priests question the faith, can the noviciates believe in the catechism?', in M.J. Baker (ed.) *2021 – A Vision for the Next 25 Years*, Marketing Education Group, Glasgow: Strathclyde University 8(I): 1–2.

Kennedy, D. (1996) 'Where the grass is always greener', *The Sunday Times*, 10 November, Section 10: 4–5.

Kerin, R. A. (1996) 'In pursuit of an ideal: the editorial and literary history of the *Journal of Marketing*', *Journal of Marketing* 60(1): 1–13.

Kermode, F. (1967) *The Sense of an Ending: Studies in the Theory of Fiction*, New York: Oxford University Press.

—— (1995) 'Waiting for the end', in M. Bull (ed.) *Apocalypse Theory and the Ends of the World*, Oxford: Blackwell, pp. 250–63.

Kernan, J. B. (1973) 'Marketing's coming of age', *Journal of Marketing* 37 (October): 34–41.

Kiberd, D. (1995) *Inventing Ireland: The Literature of the Modern Nation*, London: Vintage.

Koestler, A. (1964) *The Art of Creation*, New York: Macmillan.

Kollat, D. T. and Willet, R. P. (1969) 'Is impulse purchasing really a useful concept for marketing decisions?', *Journal of Marketing* 33(1): 79–83.

Kotler, P. (1972) 'A generic concept of marketing', *Journal of Marketing* 36 (April): 46–54.

—— (1988) 'The convenience store: past developments and future prospects', in T. Nevett and R. A. Fullerton (eds) *Historical Perspectives in Marketing: Essays in Honor of Stanley C. Hollander*, Lexington: D. C. Heath, pp. 163–75.

—— (1994) 'Reconceptualising marketing: an interview with Philip Kotler', *European Management Journal* 12(4): 353–61.

——, Armstrong, A., Saunders, J. and Wong, V. (1996) *Principles of Marketing: The European Edition*, Hemel Hempstead: Prentice Hall.

—— and Levy, S. J. (1969) 'Broadening the concept of marketing', *Journal of Marketing* 33 (January): 10–15.

Krantz, J. (1978) *Scruples*, London: Warner Books.

—— (1992) *Scruples Two*, London: Bantam Books.

Krell, D. F. (1996) *Nietzsche: A Novel*, Albany: State University of New York Press.

Kristeva, J. (1982) *Desire in Language: A Semiotic Approach to Literature and Art*, trans. T. Gora *et al.*, Oxford: Blackwell.

Kroker, A. and Cook, D. (1986) *The Postmodern Scene: Excremental Culture and Hyper-aesthetics*, Montreal: New World Perspectives.

Kumar, K. (1993) 'The end of Socialism? The end of Utopia? The end of History?', in K. Kumar and S. Bann (eds) *Utopias and the Millennium*, London: Reaktion, pp. 63–80.

—— (1995a) 'Apocalypse, millennium and utopia today', in M. Bull (ed.) *Apocalypse Theory and the Ends of the World*, Oxford: Blackwell, pp. 200–24.

—— (1995b) *From Post-industrial to Post-modern Society: New Theories of the Contemporary World*, Oxford: Blackwell.

Kundera, M. (1988) *The Art of the Novel*, trans. L. Asher, London: Faber & Faber.

—— (1995) *Testaments Betrayed*, trans. L. Asher, London: Faber & Faber.

LaBarbera, P. (1988) 'The *nouveaux riches*: conspicuous consumption and the issue of self-fulfillment', in E. C. Hirschman and J. N. Sheth (eds) *Research in Consumer Behavior, vol. 3*, Greenwich: JAI Press, pp. 179–210.

Lamb, C. (1982) 'Red Riding Hood and the dirty old wolf', *The Guardian*, 18 September: 8.

Landesman, C. (1996) 'Consumed by herself', *The Sunday Times*, 25 February, Section 10: 19.

Lansley, S. (1994) *After the Gold Rush: The Trouble With Affluence 'Consumer Capitalism' and the Way Forward*, London: Century Business Press.

Larsen, V. and Wright, N. D. (1993) 'A critique of Critical Theory: response to Murray and Ozanne's "The Critical Imagination"', in L. McAlister and M. J. Rothchild (eds) *Advances in Consumer Research, vol. XX*, Provo: Association for Consumer Research, 439–43.

Lataif, L. E. (1992) 'Debate – MBA: is the traditional model doomed?', *Harvard Business Review* 70 (November–December): 128–9.

Ledger, S. and S. McCracken (1995) 'Introduction', in S. Ledger and S. McCracken (eds) *Cultural Politics at the* Fin de Siècle, Cambridge: Cambridge University Press, pp. 1–10.

Lee, C. E. (1965), 'Measurement and the development of science and marketing', *Journal of Marketing Research* 2 (February): 20–5.

Lemert, C. (1995) *Sociology After the Crisis*, Boulder: Westview.

Lesser, J. A. and Hughes, M. A. (1986) 'Towards a typology of shoppers', *Business Horizons* 29(6): 56–62.

Levin, D. M. (1990) 'Postmodernism in dance: dance, discourse, democracy', in H.

J. Silverman (ed.) *Postmodernism – Philosophy and the Arts*, New York: London, pp. 207–33.

Lévi-Strauss, C. (1968 [1958]) *Structural Anthropology*, trans. C. Jacobson and B. G. Schoepf, London: Penguin.

Levitt, T. (1960) 'Marketing myopia', *Harvard Business Review* 38 (July–August): 45–56.

—— (1983), 'The globalisation of markets', *Harvard Business Review* 61 (May–June): 92–102.

Levy, S. J. (1976) 'Marcology 101 or the domain of marketing', in K. L. Bernhardt (ed.) *Marketing 1776–1976 and Beyond*, Chicago: American Marketing Association, pp. 577–81.

—— (1981) 'Interpreting consumer mythology: a structural approach to consumer behavior', *Journal of Marketing* 45 (Summer): 49–61.

—— (1994a) 'Interpreting consumer mythology: structural approach to consumer behavior focuses on story telling', *Marketing Management* 2(4): 4–9.

—— (1994b) 'Commentary by Sidney J. Levy', in G. Laurent, G. L. Lilien and B. Pras (eds) *Research Traditions in Marketing*, Dordrecht: Kluwer, pp. 283–7.

Lincoln, Y. S. and Denzin, N. K. (1994) 'The fifth moment', in N. K. Denzin and Y. S. Lincoln (eds) *Handbook of Qualitative Research*, Thousand Oaks: Sage, pp. 575–86.

Linder, J. C. and Smith, H. J. (1992) 'The complex case of management education', *Harvard Business Review* 70 (September–October): 16–33.

Lindley, D. (1994) *The End of Physics: The Myth of a Unified Theory*, New York: Basic Books.

Linstead, S. A. and Grafton Small, R. (1990) 'Theory as artifact: artifact as theory', in P. Gagliardi (ed.) *Symbols and Artefacts: Views of the Corporate Landscape*, Berlin: de Gruyter, pp. 387–419.

Literati Club (1995) *How to Publish Management Research*, Bradford: MCB University Press.

Litt, T. (1996a) 'When I met Michel Foucault', in T. Litt, *Adventures in Capitalism*, London: Secker & Warburg, pp. 189–228.

—— (1996b) 'Mr Kipling', in T. Litt, *Adventures in Capitalism*, London: Secker & Warburg, pp. 27–30

Little, J. D. C., Lodish, L. M., Hauser, J. R. and Urban, G. L. (1994) 'Commentary', in G. Laurent, G. L. Lilien and B. Pras (eds) *Research Traditions in Marketing*, Dordrecht: Kluwer, pp. 44–51.

Locke, D. (1992) *Science as Writing*, New Haven: Yale University Press.

Lodge, D. (1977) *Modes of Modern Writing: Metaphor, Metonymy and the Typology of Modern Literature*, London: Edward Arnold.

—— (ed.) (1988) *Modern Criticism and Theory: A Reader*, London: Longman.

—— (1990) 'After Bakhtin', in D. Lodge *After Bakhtin: Essays on Fiction and Criticism*, London: Routledge, pp. 87–99.

Lomax, R. (1983) *Writing the Short Story*, London: Clarefen.

Lotman, Y. (1975) *The Structure of the Artistic Text*, Ann Arbor: Michigan Slavic Contributions.

Löwith, K. (1995 [1983/1984]) *Martin Heidegger and European Nihilism*, trans. G. Steiner, New York, Columbia University Press.

Lozada, H. and Mintu-Wimsatt, A. (1995) 'Ecofeminism and green marketing: reconciling nature and hu(man)kind', in B. B. Stern and G. M. Zinkhan (eds) *Enhancing Knowledge Development in Marketing*, vol. 6, Chicago: American Marketing Association, pp. 450–5.

Lucie-Smith, E. (1991) *Sexuality in Western Art*, London: Thames & Hudson.

Lukes, S. (1995) *The Curious Enlightenment of Professor Caritat: A Novel*, London: Verso.

Lunt, P. K. and Livingstone, S. M. (1992) *Mass Consumption and Personal Identity*, Buckingham: Open University Press.

Lynch, J. (1995) 'The end of marketing?', in O. Westall (ed.) *British Academy of Management Annual Conference Proceedings*, Lancaster: Lancaster University, pp. 322–4.

Lynch, K. (1960) *The Image of the City*, Cambridge, MA: MIT Press.

Lyotard, J. -F. (1984 [1979]) *The Postmodern Condition: A Report on Knowledge*, trans. G. Bennington and B. Massumi, Manchester: Manchester University Press.

—— (1989) 'Lessons in paganism', in A. Benjamin (ed.) *The Lyotard Reader*, Oxford: Blackwell, pp. 122–54.

—— (1993a [1986]) *The Postmodern Explained to Children: Correspondence 1982–1985*, trans. D. Barry *et al.*, London: Turnaround.

—— (1993b) *Toward the Postmodern*, R. Harvey and M. S. Roberts (eds), Atlantic Highlands: Humanities Press.

—— (1993c [1974]) *Libidinal Economy*, trans. I. H. Grant, London: Athlone.

—— (1994 [1991]) *Lessons on the Analytic of the Sublime*, trans. E. Rottenberg, Stanford: Stanford University Press.

Lyttle, J. (1996) 'It's worse than getting a summons', unpublished undergraduate essay, Coleraine: University of Ulster.

McCarthy, E. J. (1960) *Basic Marketing: A Managerial Introduction*, Homewood: Richard D. Irwin.

McCloskey, D. N. (1985) *The Rhetoric of Economics*, Madison: University of Wisconsin Press.

—— (1990) *If You're So Smart: The Narrative of Economic Expertise*, Chicago: University of Chicago Press.

—— (1994) *Knowledge and Persuasion in Economics*, Cambridge: Cambridge University Press.

McCracken, G. (1986) 'Culture and consumption: a theoretical account of the structure and movement of the cultural meaning of goods', *Journal of Consumer Research* 13 (June): 71–84.

McCreery, J. (1995) 'Malinowski, magic and advertising: on choosing metaphors', in J. F. Sherry (ed.) *Contemporary Marketing and Consumer Behavior: An Anthropological Sourcebook*, Thousand Oaks: Sage, pp. 309–29.

McDonagh, P. (1995a) 'Q: is marketing dying of consumption? A: yes, and the answer is consumption', in S. Brown, J. Bell and D. Carson (eds) *Proceedings of the Marketing Eschatology Retreat*, Belfast: University of Ulster, pp. 48–59.

—— (1995b) 'Radical change through rigorous review? A commentary on the commodification of marketing knowledge', *Journal of Marketing Management* 11(7): 675–9.

—— and Prothero, A. (1996) 'Making a drama out of a crisis: the final curtain for the marketing concept', in S. Brown, J. Bell and D. Carson (eds) *Marketing Apocalypse: Eschatology, Escapology and the Illusion of the End*, London: Routledge, pp. 44–65.

McDowell, L. (1996) 'Off the road: alternative views of rebellion, resistance and "the beats"', *Transactions of the Institute of British Geographers* 21(2): 412–19.

McGinn, B. (1995) 'The end of the world and the beginning of Christendom', in M. Bull (ed.) *Apocalypse Theory and the Ends of the World*, Oxford: Blackwell, pp. 58–89.

McHale, B. (1987) *Postmodernist Fiction*, London: Routledge.

—— (1992) *Constructing Postmodernism*, London: Routledge.

McKenna, R. (1992) *Relationship Marketing: Own the Market Through Strategic Customer Relationships*, London: Century.

Mackrell, J. (1991) 'Post-modern dance in Britain: an historical essay', *Dance Research* 9 (Spring): 40–57.

McKibben, B. (1990) *The End of Nature*, London: Viking.

McNair, B. (1996) *Mediated Sex: Pornography and Postmodern Culture*, London: Arnold.

McNair, M. P. (1958) 'Significant trends and developments in the post-war period', in A. B. Smith (ed.) *Competitive Distribution in a Free, High Level Economy and its Implications for the University*, Pittsburg: University of Pittsburg Press, pp. 1–25.

McNay, L. (1994) *Foucault: A Critical Introduction*, Cambridge: Polity.

McQuarrie, E. F. (1989) 'Advertising resonance: a semiological perspective', in E. C. Hirschman (ed.) *Interpretive Consumer Research*, Provo: Association for Consumer Research, pp. 97–114.

—— and Mick, D. G. (1992) 'On resonance: a critical pluralist inquiry', *Journal of Consumer Research* 19 (September): 180–97.

—— and —— (1996) 'Figures of advertising rhetoric', *Journal of Consumer Research* 22(March): 424–38.

McRobbie, A. (1994) *Postmodernism and Popular Culture*, London: Routledge.

Maffesoli, M. (1991) 'The ethic of aesthetics', *Theory, Culture and Society* 8(1): 7–20.

—— (1996) *The Time of the Tribes: The Decline of Individualism in Mass Society*, trans. D. Smith, London: Sage.

Mahoney, M. J. (1985) 'Open exchange and epistemic progress', *American Psychologist* 40(1): 29–39.

Mailer, N. (1991) 'Children of the pied piper', *Vanity Fair* 54 (March): 154–9, 220–1.

Majaro, S. (1992) *Managing Ideas for Profit: The Creative Gap*, Maidenhead: McGraw-Hill.

Marcus, G. E. (1994) 'What comes (just) after "post"? The case of ethnography', in N. K. Denzin and Y. S. Lincoln (eds) *Handbook of Qualitative Research*, Thousand Oaks: Sage, pp. 563–74.

—— and Fischer, M. M. J. (1986) *Anthropology as Cultural Critique: An Experimental Moment in the Human Sciences*, Chicago: University of Chicago Press.

Marion, G. (1993) 'The marketing management discourse: what's new since the 1960s?', in M. J. Baker (ed.) *Perspectives on Marketing Management*, vol. 3, Chichester: Wiley, pp. 143–68.

Marris, P. and Thornham, S. (eds) (1996) *Media Studies: A Reader*, Edinburgh: University of Edinburgh Press.

Marsh, H. W. and Ball, S. (1989) 'The peer review process used to evaluate manuscripts submitted to academic journals: interjudgemental reliability', *Journal of Experimental Education* 57(2): 151–69.

Martin, J. N. T. (1991) 'Play, reality and creativity', in J. Henry (ed.) *Creative Management*, London: Sage, pp. 34–40.

Martin, M. C. and Baker, S. M. (1996) 'An ethnography of Mick's Sports Card Show: preliminary findings from the field', in K. P. Corfman and J. G. Lynch (eds) *Advances in Consumer Research*, *vol. XXIII*, Provo: Association for Consumer Research, pp. 329–36.

—— and Kennedy, P. F. (1994) 'The measurement of social comparison to advertising models: a gender gap revealed', in J. A. Costa (ed.) *Gender Issues and Consumer Behavior*, Thousand Oaks: Sage, pp. 104–24.

Martindale, C. (1990) *The Clockwork Muse*, New York: Basic Books.

Mason, R. (1992) 'Modelling the demand for status goods', in F. Rudmin and M. Richins (eds) *Meaning, Measure and Morality of Materialism*, Provo: Association for Consumer Research, pp. 88–95.

Maupin, A. (1978) *Tales of the City*, London: Black Swan.

Maxted, A. (1996) 'Sex and shopping: the orgasmic connection', *Cosmopolitan* (December): 154–8.

Mead, R. (1994) 'Where is the culture of Thailand?', *International Journal of Research in Marketing* 11(4): 401–4.

Meamber, L. (1995) 'Symbols for self-construction: product design in postmodernity', in B. B. Stern and G. M. Zinkhan (eds) *Enhancing Knowledge Development in Marketing*, *vol. 6*, Chicago: American Marketing Association, pp. 529–34.

—— and Venkatesh, A. (1995) 'Discipline and practice: a postmodern critique of marketing as constituted by the work of Philip Kotler', in B. B. Stern and G. M. Zinkhan (eds) *Enhancing Knowledge Development in Marketing*, *vol. 6*, Chicago: American Marketing Association, pp. 248–53.

Meinert, D. B., Vitell, S. J. and Reich, R. V. (1993) 'The domain of marketing: how are the boundaries of the marketing discipline established?', *Journal of Marketing Theory and Practice* 2 (Fall): 1–12.

Merton, R. K. (1968) 'The Matthew Effect in science', *Science* 159(3810): 56–63.

—— (1988) 'The Matthew Effect in science II: cumulative advantage and the symbolism of intellectual property', *ISIS* 79: 606–23.

Meštrović, S. G. (1991) *The Coming* Fin de Siècle, London: Routledge.

Metcalf, F. (ed.) (1987) *The Penguin Dictionary of Modern Humorous Quotations*, Harmondsworth: Penguin.

Metzger, D. (1993) *Writing for Your Life: A Guide and Companion to the Inner Worlds*, New York: HarperCollins.

Michell, P. (1996) 'The advertising agency–client relationship', in F. Buttle (ed.) *Relationship Marketing: Theory and Practice*, London: Paul Chapman, pp. 159–69.

Mick, D. G. (1987) 'Toward a semiotic of advertising story grammars', in J. Umiker-Seboek (ed.) *Marketing and Semiotics: New Directions in the Study of Signs for Sale*, Berlin: de Gruyter, pp. 249–78.

—— (1992) 'Levels of subjective comprehension in advertising processing and their relations to ad perceptions, attitudes and memory', *Journal of Consumer Research* 18 (March): 411–24.

—— and Buhl, C. (1992) 'A meaning-based model of advertising experiences', *Journal of Consumer Research* 19 (December): 317–38.

—— and DeMoss, M. (1990) 'Self-gifts: phenomenological insights from four contexts', *Journal of Consumer Research* 17 (December): 322–32.

——, —— and Faber, R. J. (1992) 'A projective study of motivations and meanings of self-gifts: implications for retail management', *Journal of Retailing* 68(2): 122–44.

—— and Politi, L. G. (1989) 'Consumers' interpretations of advertising imagery; a visit to the hell of connotation', in E. C. Hirschman (ed.) *Interpretive Consumer Research*, Provo: Association for Consumer Research, pp. 85–96.

Midgley, M. (1992) *Science as Salvation: A Modern Myth and its Meaning*, London: Routledge.

Miller, D. (ed.) (1995) *Acknowledging Consumption: A Review of New Studies*, London: Routledge.

Mills, H. D. (1961) 'Marketing as a science', *Harvard Business Review* 39 (September–October): 137–42.

Mills, S. and Pearce, L. (eds) (1996) *Feminist Readings, Feminists Reading*, Hemel Hempstead: Harvester Wheatsheaf.

Mintzberg, H. (1991) 'Planning on the left side and managing on the right', in J. Henry (ed.) *Creative Management*, London: Sage, pp. 58–71.

—— (1992) 'Debate – MBA: is the traditional model doomed?', *Harvard Business Review* 70 (November–December): 129.

Mitroff, I. I. and Churchman, C. W. (1992) 'Debate – MBA: is the traditional model doomed?', *Harvard Business Review* 70 (November–December): 134–6.

Mizerski, R. (1995) 'The relationship between cartoon trade character recognition and attitude toward product category in young children', *Journal of Marketing* 59 (October): 58–70.

Moore, S. (1991) *Looking for Trouble: On Shopping, Gender and the Cinema*, London: Serpent's Tail.

Morgan, G. (1992) 'Marketing discourse and practice: towards a critical analysis', in M. Alvesson and H. Willmott (eds) *Critical Management Studies*, London: Sage, pp. 136–58.

—— (1993) *Imaginization: The Art of Creative Management*, Newbury Park: Sage.

Morgan, R. M. and Hunt, S. D. (1994) 'The commitment–trust theory of relationship marketing', *Journal of Marketing* 58 (July): 20–38.

Morley, D. and Chen, K. -H. (eds) (1996) *Stuart Hall: Critical Dialogues in Cultural Studies*, London: Routledge.

Morris, P. (ed.) (1994) *The Bakhtin Reader: Selected Writings of Bakhtin, Medvedev, Voloshinov*, London: Arnold.

Moschis, G. P. and Smith, R. B. (1985) 'Consumer socializations: origins, trends and directions for consumer research', in C. T. Tan and J. N. Sheth (eds) *Historical Perspective in Consumer Research: National and International Perspectives*, Singapore: Association for Consumer Research, pp. 275–81.

Mowen, J. C. and T. W. Leigh (1996) 'State of marketing thought and practice: a panel discussion', *Marketing Educator* 15(1): 1–3.

Muensterberger, W. (1994) *Collecting, an Unruly Passion: Psychological Perspectives*, Princeton: Princeton University Press.

Muir, F. and Brett, S. (1981), *The Third Frank Muir Goes Into . . .*, London: Robson Books.

Mulkay, M. (1985) *The Word and the World: Explorations in the Form of Sociological Knowledge*, London: Allen & Unwin.

Mun, K.-C. (1988) 'Chinese retailing in a changing environment', in E. Kaynak (ed.) *Transnational Retailing*, Berlin: de Gruyter, pp. 211–26.

Murphy, J. A. (1996) 'Retail banking', in F. Buttle (ed.) *Relationship Marketing: Theory and Practice*, London: Paul Chapman, pp. 74–90.

Murray, J. B. and Ozanne, J. (1991) 'The critical imagination: emancipatory interests in consumer research', *Journal of Consumer Research* 18 (September): 129–44.

——, —— and Shapiro, J. M. (1994) 'Revitalising the critical imagination: unleashing the crouched tiger', *Journal of Consumer Research* 21 (December): 559–65.

Murray, K. D. (1995), 'Narratology' in J. A. Smith, R. Harré and L. van Langenhove (eds) *Rethinking Psychology*, London: Sage, pp. 179–95.

Naisbitt, J. (1994) *Global Paradox: The Bigger the World Economy, the More Powerful Its Smallest Players*, London: Nicholas Brealey.

Nehamas, A. (1985) *Nietzsche: Life as Literature*, Cambridge: Harvard University Press.

Nevin, J. R. (1995) 'Relationship marketing and distribution channels: exploring fundamental issues', *Journal of the Academy of Marketing Science* 23(4): 327–34.

Nicholson, L. J. (ed.) (1990) *Feminism/Postmodernism*, New York: Routledge.

Nietzsche, F. (1956 [1887]) *The Genealogy of Morals: An Attack*, trans. F. Golffing, New York: Anchor Books.

—— (1974 [1887]) *The Gay Science: With a Prelude in Rhymes and an Appendix of Songs*, trans. W. Kaufmann, New York: Vintage.

—— (1993 [1872]) *The Birth of Tragedy Out of the Spirit of Music*, trans. S. Whiteside, Harmondsworth: Penguin.

Norris, C. (1991) *Deconstruction: Theory and Practice*, London: Routledge.

—— (1992) *Uncritical Theory: Postmodernism, Intellectuals and the Gulf War*, London: Lawrence & Wishart.

Nowotny, H. (1994) *Time: The Modern and Postmodern Experience*, Cambridge: Polity.

Ó'Cinnéide, B. (1995) *Riverdance*, Cranfield: European Case Clearing House.

—— (1996) 'IMR case study: *Riverdance*', *Irish Marketing Review* 9: 1–7.

O'Donohoe, S. (1994) 'Advertising uses and gratifications', *European Journal of Marketing* 28(8/9): 52–75.

—— (1997) 'Raiding the pantry: advertising intertextuality and the young adult audience', *European Journal of Marketing* 31(3/4): 234–53.

O'Guinn, T. C. (1996) 'The romantic arbiter: a comment on Holbrook', in R.W. Belk, N. Dholakia and A. Venkatesh (eds) *Consumption and Marketing: Macro Dimensions*, Cincinnati: South-Western, pp. 83–6.

—— and Faber, R. J. (1989) 'Compulsive buying: a phenomenological exploration', *Journal of Consumer Research* 16 (September): 147–57.

O'Reilly, L., Rucker, M., Hughes, R., Gorang, M. and Hand, S. (1984) 'The relationship of psychological and situational variables to usage of a second-order marketing system', *Journal of the Academy of Marketing Science* 12(3): 53–76.

O'Shaughnessy, J. and Ryan, M.J. (1979) 'Marketing, science and technology', in O.C. Ferrell, S.W. Brown and C.W. Lamb (eds) *Conceptual and Theoretical Developments in Marketing*, Chicago: American Marketing Association, pp. 557–89.

Ogilvy, J. (1990) 'This postmodern business', *Marketing and Research Today* 18(1): 4–21.

Ohmae, K. (1990) *The Borderless World*, London: Collins.

—— (1995) 'Putting global logic first', *Harvard Business Review* 73 (January–February): 119–25.

Ormerod, P. (1994) *The Death of Economics*, London: Faber & Faber.

Otnes, C., Lowrey, T. and Kim, Y. C. (1993) 'Christmas gift selection for easy and difficult recipients: a social roles interpretation', *Journal of Consumer Research* 20 (September): 229–44.

Ozanne, J. L. and Murray, J. B. (1996) 'Uniting Critical Theory and public policy to create the reflexively defiant consumer', in R.P. Hill (ed.) *Marketing and Consumer Research in the Public Interest*, Thousand Oaks: Sage, pp. 3–15.

Ozick, C. (1996) *Portrait of the Artist as a Bad Character: And Other Essays on Writing*, London: Pimlico.

Palmer, J. (1992) *Potboilers: Methods, Concepts and Case Studies in Popular Fiction*, London: Routledge.

—— (1994) *Taking Humour Seriously*, London: Routledge.

Pearce, L. and Stacey, J. (eds) (1995) *Romance Revisited*, London: Lawrence & Wishart.

Pearman, H. (1996) 'Postmodernism: the century in design', *The Sunday Times Style Magazine*, 7 April: 33–4.

Pearson, C. and Pope, K. (1981) *The Female Hero in American and British Literature*, New York: R. R. Bowker.

Peñaloza, L. (1994) 'Crossing boundaries/crossing lines: a look at the nature of gender boundaries and their impact on marketing research', *International Journal of Research in Marketing* 11(4): 359–79.

Pennell, G. E. (1994), 'Babes in Toyland: learning an ideology of gender', in C. T. Allen and D. R. John (eds) *Advances in Consumer Research, vol XXI*, Provo: Association for Consumer Research, pp. 359–64.

Perloff, M. (ed.) (1989) *Postmodern Genres*, Norman: University of Oklahoma Press.

Peter, J. P. and Olson, J. C. (1983) 'Is science marketing?', *Journal of Marketing* 47 (Fall): 111–25.

Petersen, C. and Toop, A. (1994) *Sales Promotion in Postmodern Marketing*, Aldershot: Gower.

Peterson, R. A. (1995) 'Relationship marketing and the consumer', *Journal of the Academy of Marketing Science* 23(4): 278–81.

Phillips, A. (1993) *On Kissing, Tickling and Being Bored*, London: Faber & Faber.

—— (1994) *On Flirtation*, London: Faber & Faber.

Pielou, A. (1996) 'There's more to this woman than fancy footwork', *You Magazine*, 21 April: 26–9.

Pinch, T. and Pinch, T. (1988) 'Reservations about reflexivity and new literary forms or why let the Devil have all the good tunes?', in S. Woolgar (ed.) *Knowledge and Reflexivity: New Frontiers in the Sociology of Knowledge*, London: Sage, pp. 178–97.

Pollay, R. W. (1985) 'The subsidising sizzle: a descriptive history of advertising 1900–1980', *Journal of Marketing* 49 (Summer): 24–37.

—— (1986) 'The distorted mirror: reflections on the unintended consequences of advertising', *Journal of Marketing* 50 (April): 18–36.

—— (1991) 'Signs and symbols in American cigarette advertising: a historical analysis of "picture of health"', in H. H. Larsen, D. G. Mick and C. Alsted (eds) *Marketing and Semiotics: Selected Papers from Copenhagen Symposium*, Copenhagen: Nyt Nordisk Forlag Arnold Busck, pp. 160–76.

Posner, R. A. (1995) *Overcoming Law*, Cambridge: Harvard University Press.

Powell, C. and Paton, G. E. C. (eds) (1988) *Humour in Society: Resistance and Control*, Basingstoke: Macmillan.

Pratt, M. L. (1986) 'Fieldwork in common places', in J. Clifford and G. E. Marcus (eds) *Writing Culture: The Poetics and Politics of Ethnography*, Berkeley: University of California Press, pp. 27–50.

Propp, V. (1958 [1928]) *Morphology of the Folktale*, trans. L. Scott, Austin: University of Texas Press.

Pykett, L. (1996) 'Introduction', in L. Pykett (ed.) *Reading* Fin de Siècle *Fictions*, Harlow: Longman, pp. 1–21.

Quantick, D. (1996), 'Thunderous: *Riverdance*, all-singing, all-dancing, alright', *Q Magazine* 120 (September): 160–1.

Radway, J. (1987) *Reading the Romance: Women, Patriarchy and Popular Culture*, London: Verso.

Ramocki, S. P. (1996) 'Developing creative marketing graduates', *Marketing Education Review* 6(1): 47–53.

Ramond, C. (1974) *The Art of Using Science in Marketing*, New York: Harper & Row.

Rau, P. A. (1996) 'Rigor, relevance, readibility and maybe some rethinking', *Marketing Educator* 15(2): 3.

Ray, L. J. (1993) *Rethinking Critical Theory: Emancipation in the Age of Global Social Movements*, London: Sage.

Readings, B. and Schaber, B. (eds) (1993) *Postmodernism Across the Ages: Essays for a Postmodernity That Wasn't Born Yesterday*, Syracuse: Syracuse University Press.

Reason, P. (1993) 'Reflections on sacred experience and sacred science', *Journal of Management Inquiry* 2(3): 273–83.

Regan, S. (1995) 'W. B. Yeats and Irish cultural politics in the 1890s', in S. Ledger and S. McCracken (eds) *Cultural Politics at the* Fin de Siècle, Cambridge: Cambridge University Press, pp. 66–84.

Rennie, D. (1990) 'Guarding the guardians – research on editorial peer review', *Journal of the American Medical Association* 263(10): 1311–441.

Rhiel, M. and Suchoff, D. (1996) *The Seductions of Biography*, New York: Routledge.

Richardson, L. (1993) 'Poetics, dramatics and transgressive validity: the case of the skipped line', *Sociological Quarterly* 34(4): 695–710.

—— (1994) 'Writing: a method of inquiry', in N. K. Denzin and Y. S. Lincoln (eds) *Handbook of Qualitative Research*, Thousand Oaks: Sage, pp. 516–29.

—— (1995) 'Narrative and sociology', in J. van Maanen (ed.) *Representation in Ethnography*, Thousand Oaks: Sage, pp. 198–221.

Richins, M. L. (1991) 'Social comparison and the idealised images of advertising', *Journal of Consumer Research* 18 (June): 71–83.

—— (1996) 'Materialism, desire and discontent: contributions of idealized advertising images and social comparison', in R.P. Hill (ed.) *Marketing and Consumer Research in the Public Interest*, Thousand Oaks: Sage, pp. 109–32.

Rifkin, J. (1995) *The End of Work: The Decline of the Global Labour Force and the Dawn of the Post-market Era*, New York: Tarcher.

Ritson, M., Elliott, R. and Eccles, S. (1996) 'Reframing Ikea: commodity-signs, consumer creativity and the social/self dialectic', in K. P. Corfman and J. G. Lynch (eds) *Advances in Consumer Research*, *vol. XXIII*, Provo: Association for Consumer Research, pp. 127–31.

Robin, D. P. (1970) 'Toward a normative science in marketing', *Journal of Marketing* 24 (October): 73–6.

Robinson, M. (1996) 'Message from President Robinson', *Riverdance the Show*, Cork: Abhann Productions: 5.

Rook, D. W. (1985) 'The ritual dimension of consumer behavior', *Journal of Consumer Research* 12 (December): 251–64.

—— (1987) 'The buying impulse', *Journal of Consumer Research* 14 (September): 189–99.

—— and Hoch, S. J. (1985) 'Consuming impulses', in M. B. Holbrook and E. C. Hirschman (eds) *Advances in Consumer Research*, *vol. XII*, Provo: Association for Consumer Research, pp. 23–7.

Rorty, R. (1980) *Philosophy and the Mirror of Nature*, Oxford: Blackwell.

—— (1989) *Contingency, Irony and Solidarity*, Cambridge: Cambridge University Press.

Rosaldo, R. (1993) *Culture and Truth: The Remaking of Social Analysis*, London: Routledge.

Rose, D. (1995) 'Active ingredients', in J. F. Sherry (ed.) *Contemporary Marketing and Consumer Behavior*, Thousand Oaks: Sage, pp. 51–85.

Rose, G. (1996) *Mourning Becomes the Law: Philosophy and Representation*, Cambridge: Cambridge University Press.

Rosenau, P. M. (1992) *Post-modernism and the Social Sciences: Insights, Inroads and Intrusions*, Princeton: Princeton University Press.

Rothenberg, A. (ed.) (1976) *The Creativity Question*, Durham: Duke University Press.

Rothman, J. (1992) 'Postmodern research and the arts', *Journal of the Market Research Society* 34(4): 419–35.

Ryan, K. (ed.) (1996) *New Historicism and Cultural Materialism: A Reader*, London: Arnold.

Rylance, R. (1994) *Roland Barthes*, Hemel Hempstead: Harvester Wheatsheaf.

Said, E. W. (1978) *Orientalism: Western Conceptions of the Orient*, Harmondsworth: Penguin.

—— (1984) *The World, the Text and the Critic*, London: Vintage.

—— (1995) 'Adorno as lateness itself', in M. Bull (ed.) *Apocalypse Theory and the Ends of the World*, Oxford: Blackwell, pp. 264–81.

Savitt, R. (1988), 'Comment: the wheel of the wheel of retailing', *International Journal of Retailing* 3(1): 38–40.

Schaeffer, J. -M. (1989) *Qu'est-ce qu'un Genre littéraire?*, Paris: Éditions du Seuil.

Schama, S. (1992) *Dead Certainties*, Harmondsworth: Granta.

Schiffman, L. G. and Schnarrs, S. P. (1981) 'The consumption of historical romance novels: consumer aesthetics in popular literature', in E. C. Hirschman and M. B. Holbrook (eds) *Symbolic Consumer Behavior*, New York: Association for Consumer Research, pp. 46–51.

Schorske, C. E. (1980) Fin de Siècle *Vienna: Politics and Culture*, New York: Knopf.

Schouten, J. W. and McAlexander, J. H. (1995) 'Subcultures of consumption: an ethnography of the new bikers', *Journal of Consumer Research* 22 (June): 43–61.

Schwartz, B. (1967) 'The social psychology of the gift', *American Journal of Sociology* 73(1): 1–11.

Schwartz, G. (1965) 'Nature and goals of marketing science', in G. Schwartz (ed.) *Science in Marketing*, New York: John Wiley, pp. 1–19.

Schweik, R. C. (1987) 'Oscar Wilde's *Salome*, the Salome theme in western art and a problem of method in cultural history', in O. M. Brack (ed.) *Twilight of Dawn: Studies in English Literature in Translation*, Tucson: University of Arizona Press, pp. 123–36.

Scott, L. M. (1990) 'Understanding jingles and needledrop: a rhetorical approach to music in advertising', *Journal of Consumer Research* 17 (September): 223–36.

—— (1992) 'Playing with pictures: postmodernism, poststructuralism and advertising visuals', in J. F. Sherry and B. Sternthal (eds) *Advances in Consumer Research*, *vol. XIX*, Provo: Association for Consumer Research, pp. 596–612.

—— (1993) 'Spectacular vernacular: literacy and commercial culture in the post-modern age', *International Journal of Research in Marketing* 10(3): 251–75.

—— (1994a) 'Images in advertising: the need for a theory of visual rhetoric', *Journal of Consumer Research* 21 (September): 252–73.

—— (1994b), 'The bridge from text to mind: adapting reader-response theory to consumer research', *Journal of Consumer Research* 21 (December): 461–80.

Scruton, R. (1990) 'Modern philosophy and the neglect of aesthetics', in R. Scruton, *The Philosopher on Dover Beach: Essays*, London: Carcanet, pp. 98–112.

Seal, G. (1996) *The Outlaw Legend: A Cultural Tradition in Britain, America and Australia*, Cambridge: Cambridge University Press.

Seidman, S. (ed.) (1994) *The Postmodern Turn: New Perspectives on Social Theory*, Cambridge: Cambridge University Press.

Selden, R. and Widdowson, P. (1993) *A Reader's Guide to Contemporary Literary Theory*, Hemel Hempstead: Harvester Wheatsheaf.

Self, W. (1995) 'Eight miles high', in W. Self, *Junk Mail*, London: Bloomsbury, 112–17.

Selzer, J. (ed.) (1993) *Understanding Scientific Prose*, Madison: University of Wisconsin Press.

Sherry, J. F. (1983) 'Gift-giving in anthropological perspective', *Journal of Consumer Research* 10 (September): 157–68.

—— (1987) 'Keeping the monkeys away from the typewriters: an anthropologist's view of the Consumer Behavior Odyssey', in M. Wallendorf and P. F. Anderson (eds) *Advances in Consumer Research*, *vol. XIV*, Provo: Association for Consumer Research, pp. 370–3.

—— (1991) 'Postmodern alternatives: the interpretive turn in consumer research', T. S. Robertson and H. H. Kassarjian (eds) *Handbook of Consumer Research*, Englewood Cliffs: Prentice-Hall, pp. 548–91.

—— (1995) 'Marketing and consumer behavior: into the field', in J.F. Sherry (ed.) *Contemporary Marketing and Consumer Behavior*, Thousand Oaks: Sage, pp. 3–44.

—— and Camargo, E. G. (1987) '"May your life be marvellous"': English language labelling and the semiotics of Japanese promotion', *Journal of Consumer Research* 14 (September): 174–88.

——, McGrath, M. A. and Levy, S. J. (1993) 'The dark side of the gift', *Journal of Business Research* 28(2): 225–44.

——, —— and —— (1995) 'Modanic giving: anatomy of gifts given to the self', in J. F. Sherry (ed.) *Contemporary Marketing and Consumer Behavior*, Thousand Oaks: Sage, pp. 399–432.

Sheth, J. N., Gardner, D. M and Garrett, D. E. (1988) *Marketing Theory: Evolution and Evaluation*, Chichester: John Wiley.

—— and Grönroos, C. (1996) 'Relationship marketing: provincial views or global vision?', call for papers and special session proposals, Chicago: American Marketing Association, Special Conference (Dublin): 2–3.

—— and Parvatiyar, A. (1993) 'The evolution of relationship marketing', paper presented at the Sixth Marketing History Conference, Atlanta, May.

—— and —— (1995) 'Relationship marketing in consumer markets: antecedents and consequences', *Journal of the Academy of Marketing Science* 23(4): 255–71.

Shoaf, F. R., Scattone, J., Morrin, M. and Maheswaran, D. (1995) 'Gender differences in adolescent compulsive consumption', in F. R. Kardes and M. Sujan (eds) *Advances in Consumer Research, vol XXII*, Provo: Association for Consumer Research, pp. 500–4.

Showalter, E. (1991) *Sexual Anarchy: Gender and Culture at the* Fin de Siècle, London: Bloomsbury.

—— (1993) 'Introduction', in E. Showalter (ed.) *Daughters of Decadence: Women Writers of the* Fin de Siècle, London: Virago, pp. vii–xx.

Shusterman, R. (1988) 'Postmodernist aestheticism: a new moral philosophy?', *Theory, Culture and Society* 5(2–3): 337–55.

Sim, S. (1996) *Jean François Lyotard*, Hemel Hempstead: Harvester Wheatsheaf.

Simon, W. (1996) *Postmodern Sexualities*, London: Routledge.

Simpson, D. (1995) *The Academic Postmodern and the Rule of Literature: A Report on Half-Knowledge*, Chicago: University of Chicago Press.

Skinner, Q. (ed.) (1985) *The Return of Grand Theory in the Human Sciences*, Cambridge: Cambridge University Press.

Smithee, A. (1997) 'Kotler is dead!', *European Journal of Marketing* 31(2/3): 315–25.

Smyth, S. (1996) *Riverdance: The Story*, London: Andre Deutsch.

Soderlund, M. (1990) 'Business intelligence in the postmodern era', *Marketing Intelligence and Planning* 8(1): 7–10.

Solomon, M. R. (1994) *Consumer Behavior: Buying, Having and Being*, Boston: Allyn & Bacon.

Sorell, T. (1991) *Scientism: Philosophy and the Infatuation with Science*, London: Routledge.

Spiggle, S. (1986) 'Measuring social values: a content analysis of Sunday comics and underground comix', *Journal of Consumer Research* 13 (June): 100–13.

Sporre, D. J. (1989) *A History of the Arts: Prehistory to Post-modernism*, London: Bloomsbury.

Springer, C. (1996) *Electronic Eros: Bodies and Desire in the Postindustrial Age*, London: Athlone.

Stafford, T. (1996) 'Paradigm's cost: the price we'll pay for relationship marketing', *Academy of Marketing Science News* 17(3): 4.

Stallabrass, J. (1996) *Gargantua: Manufactured Mass Culture*, London: Verso.

Stallybrass, P. and White, A. (1986) *The Politics and Poetics of Transgression*, London: Methuen.

Starkey, K. (1995) 'A postmodern perspective on strategy', School of Management and Finance, Discussion Papers, 95/07, Nottingham: University of Nottingham.

Steiner, G. (1989) *Real Presences: Is There Anything in What we Say?*, London: Faber & Faber.

—— (1992) *Heidegger*, London: Fontana.

Stern, B. B. (1988a) 'Literary analysis of the company *persona*: a speaker schema', in J. H. Leigh and C. R. Martin (eds) *Current Issues and Research in Advertising*, *vol. 11*, Ann Arbor: University of Michigan, pp. 3–19.

—— (1988b) 'Medieval allegory: roots of advertising strategy for the mass market', *Journal of Marketing* 52 (July): 84–94.

—— (1989) 'Literary criticism and consumer research: overview and illustrative analysis', *Journal of Consumer Research* 16 (December): 322–34.

—— (1990a) 'Humanising marketing theory: literary criticism and the art of marketing', in D. Lichtenthal *et al.* (eds) *Marketing Theory and Practice*, Chicago: American Marketing Association, pp. 24–8.

—— (1990b) '*Other-speak*: classical allegory and contemporary advertising', *Journal of Advertising* 19(3): 14–26.

—— (1990c) 'Pleasure and persuasion in advertising: rhetorical irony as a humor technique', in J. H. Leigh and C. R. Martin (eds) *Current Issues and Research in Advertising*, *vol. 12*, Ann Arbor: University of Michigan, pp. 25–42.

—— (1990d) 'Literary criticism and the history of marketing thought: a new perspective on "reading" marketing theory', *Journal of the Academy of Marketing Science* 18(4): 329–36.

—— (1991a) 'Two pornographies: a feminist view of sex in advertising', in R. H. Holman and M. R. Solomon (eds) *Advances in Consumer Research*, *vol. XVIII*, Provo: Association for Consumer Research, pp. 384–91.

—— (1991b) 'Who talks advertising? Literary theory and narrative "point of view"', *Journal of Advertising* 20(3): 9–22.

—— (1992) 'Historical and personal nostalgia in advertising text: the *fin de siècle* effect', *Journal of Advertising* 21(4): 11–22.

—— (1993) 'Feminist literary criticism and the deconstruction of ads: a postmodern view of advertising and consumer responses', *Journal of Consumer Research* 19 (March): 556–66.

—— (1994a) 'Authenticity and the textual persona: postmodern paradoxes in advertising narrative', *International Journal of Research in Marketing* 11(4): 387–400.

—— (1994b) 'Classical and vignette television advertising dramas: structural models, formal analysis and consumer effects', *Journal of Consumer Research* 20 (March): 601–15.

—— (1995) 'Consumer myths: Frye's taxonomy and the structural analysis of consumption text', *Journal of Consumer Research* 22 (September): 165–85.

—— (1996a) 'Advertising comedy in electronic drama: the construct, theory and taxonomy', *European Journal of Marketing* 30(9): 37–59.

—— (1996b) 'Deconstructive strategy and consumer research: concepts and illustrative exemplar', *Journal of Consumer Research* 23(September): 136–47.

—— (1996c) 'Postmodern consumer research narratives: problems in construct definition, structure and classification', paper presented at Association for Consumer Research Annual Conference, Tucson, October.

Stern, L. W. and El-Ansary, A. I. (1977) *Marketing Channels*, Englewood Cliffs: Prentice-Hall.

Stone, G. P. (1954) 'City shoppers and urban identification: observations on the social psychology of urban life', *American Journal of Sociology* 60(1): 36–45.

Stone, L. (1992) 'History and post-modernism', *Past and Present* 135: 189–94.

Storey, J. (1996) *Cultural Studies and the Study of Popular Culture: Theories and Methods*, Edinburgh: University of Edinburgh Press.

Sudjic, D. (1987) *Cult Objects: The Complete Guide to Having it All*, London: Paladin.

Suerdem, A. (1994) 'Social de(re)construction of mass culture: making (non) sense of consumer behavior', *International Journal of Research in Marketing* 11(4): 423–43.

—— (1996) 'The (un)(ma)king? of the postmodern consumer', in R. Belk, N. Dholakia and A. Venkatesh (eds) *Consumption and Marketing: Macro Dimensions*, Cincinnati: South-Western, pp. 266–74.

The Sunday Times (1996) '"Trolley rage" kills shopper', *The Sunday Times*, 13 October, Section 1: 28.

Taylor, M. C. and Saarinen, E. (1994) *Imagologies: Media Philosophy*, London: Routledge.

Taylor, W. J. (1965) 'Is marketing a science? Revisited', *Journal of Marketing* 29 (July): 49–53.

Tedre, R. (1995) 'Suddenly, spectacularly, losing your cool is all the rage', *The Observer*, Sunday 15 October: 14.

—— (1996) 'Is this dance taken?', *The Observer Review*, Sunday 12 May: 10.

Tester, K. (1994) 'Introduction' in K. Tester (ed.) *The Flâneur*, London: Routledge, pp. 1–21.

Thomas, H. (1995) *Dance, Modernity and Culture: Explorations in the Sociology of Dance*, London: Routledge.

Thomas, M. J. (1995) 'Preface', in M. J. Thomas (ed.) *Gower Handbook of Marketing*, Aldershot: Gower, pp. xxv–xxvi.

—— (1996a) 'Consumer market research. Does it have validity? Some postmodern thoughts', paper presented to the Swedish Marketing Federation, Stockholm, October.

—— (1996b) 'Postmodern marketing for dummies', paper presented at Georgetown University Business School, Washington, February.

Thompson, C. J. (1993) 'Modern truth and postmodern incredulity: a hermeneutic deconstruction of the metanarrative of "scientific truth" in marketing research', *International Journal of Research in Marketing* 10(3): 325–38.

—— (1996) 'Caring consumers: gendered consumption meanings and the juggling lifestyle', *Journal of Consumer Research* 22 (March): 388–407.

—— (1997) 'Buy Brown's book!', *European Journal of Marketing* 31(3/4): 253–62.

——, Arnould, E. and Stern, B. B. (1997) 'Exploring the *différence*: a postmodern approach to paradigmatic pluralism in consumer research', in S. Brown and D. Turley (eds) *Consumer Research: Postcards From the Edge*, London: Routledge, pp. 150–89.

—— and Hirschman, E. C. (1995), 'Understanding the socialised body: a post-structuralist analysis of consumers' self-conceptions, body images and self-care practices', *Journal of Consumer Research* 22 (September): 139–53.

—— and Holt, D. (1996) 'Utopian consumer desires and the new traditionalist lifestyle', paper presented at ACR conference, Tucson, October.

——, Pollio, H. R. and Locander, W. B. (1994) 'The spoken and the unspoken: a hermeneutic approach to understanding the cultural viewpoints that underlie consumers' expressed meanings', *Journal of Consumer Research* 21 (December): 432–52.

Thompson, D. (1996) *The End of Time: Faith and Fear in the Shadow of the Millennium*, London: Sinclair-Stevenson.

Thornton, W. H. (1994) 'Cultural prosaics as counterdiscourse: a direction for cultural studies after Bakhtin', *Prose Studies* 17(2): 74–97.

Thorpe, V. (1996) 'Shop assistants get anti-violence video as "store rage" soars', *Independent on Sunday*, 22 September: 10.

Tjosvold, D. and Wong, C. (1994) 'Working with customers: cooperation and competition in relational marketing', *Journal of Marketing Management* 10(3): 297–310.

Todorov, T. (1970) *Introduction à la littérature fantastique*, Paris: Éditions due Seuil.

—— (1990 [1978]) *Genres in Discourse*, trans. C. Porter, Cambridge: Cambridge University Press.

Tolstoy, I. (1990) *The Knowledge and the Power: Reflections on the History of Science*, Edinburgh: Canongate.

Tong, R. (1989) *Feminist Thought: A Comprehensive Introduction*, London: Routledge.

Tornroos, J.-A. and Ranta, T. (1993) 'Marketing as image management – a postmodern reformulation of the marketing concept', in D. Brownlie *et al.* (eds) *Rethinking Marketing*, Coventry: Warwick Business School Research Bureau, pp. 166–75.

Tucker, W. T. (1974) 'Future directions in marketing theory', *Journal of Marketing* 30 (April): 30–5.

Turner, G. (1996) *British Cultural Studies: An Introduction*, London: Routledge.

Tyler, S. (1986) 'Post-modern ethnography: from document of the occult to occult document', in J. Clifford and G. E. Marcus (eds) *Writing Culture: The Poetics and Politics of Ethnography*, Berkeley: University of California Press, pp. 122–40.

—— (1987) *The Unspeakable: Discourse, Dialogue and Rhetoric in the Postmodern World*, Madison: University of Wisconsin Press.

Ulmer, R. (1994) *Alfons Mucha*, Bonn: Benedikt Taschen.

Vaile, R. S. (1949) 'Towards a theory of marketing – a comment', *Journal of Marketing* 12 (April): 520–2.

Valence, G., d'Astous, A. and Fortier, L. (1988) 'Compulsive buying: concept and measurement', *Journal of Consumer Policy* 11(4): 419–33.

van den Bulte, C. (1994) 'Metaphor at work', in G. Laurent, G. L. Lilien and B. Pras (eds) *Research Traditions in Marketing*, Dordrecht: Kluwer, pp. 405–25.

van Maanen, J. (1988) *Tales of the Field: On Writing Ethnography*, Chicago: University of Chicago Press.

—— (1995) 'An end to innocence: the ethnography of ethnography', in J. van Maanen (ed.) *Representation in Ethnography*, Thousand Oaks: Sage, pp. 1–35.

van Raaij, W. F. (1993) 'Postmodern consumption: architecture, art and consumer behavior', in W. F. van Raaij and G. J. Bamossy (eds) *European Advances in Consumer Research*, *vol. 1*, Provo: Association for Consumer Research, pp. 550–8.

Vargish, T. (1991) 'The value of humanities in executive development', *Sloan Management Review* 32(3): 83–91.

Vattimo, G. (1991 [1985]) *The End of Modernity: Nihilism and Hermeneutics in Postmodern Culture*, trans. J. R. Snyder, Baltimore: Johns Hopkins University Press.

Veeser, H. A. (ed.) (1989) *The New Historicism*, New York: Routledge.

—— (ed.) (1992) *The New Historicism: A Reader*, New York: Routledge.

—— (1996) 'Introduction: the case for confessional criticism', in H. A. Veeser (ed.) *Confessions of the Critics*, New York: Routledge, pp. ix–xxvii.

Venkatesh, A. (1992) 'Postmodernism, consumer culture and the society of the spectacle', in J. F. Sherry and B. Sternthal (eds) *Advances in Consumer Research*, *vol. XIX*, Provo: Association for Consumer Research, pp. 199–202.

—— (1994) 'Business beyond modernity: some emerging themes', *Organisation* 1(1): 19–23.

—— (1995) 'Ethnoconsumerism: a new paradigm to study cultural and cross-cultural consumer behavior', in J.A. Costa and G.J. Bamossy (eds) *Marketing in a Multicultural World: Ethnicity, Nationalism and Cultural Identity*, Thousand Oaks: Sage, pp. 26–67.

——, Sherry, J. F. and Firat, A. F. (1993) 'Postmodernism and the marketing imaginary', *International Journal of Research in Marketing* 10(3): 215–23.

Vice, S. (1995) 'Addicted to love', in L. Pearce and J. Stacey (eds.) *Romance Revisited*, London: Lawrence & Wishart, pp. 117–27.

Walcott, R. (1995), '"Out of the Kumbla": Toni Morrison's *Jazz* and pedagogical answerability', *Cultural Studies* 9(2): 318–37.

Wallace, D. F. (1996) *Infinite Jest: A Novel*, Boston: Little Brown.

Walle, A. (1996) 'Macromarketing and postmodernism: a strategic alliance', unpublished manuscript.

Wallendorf, M. and Arnould, E.J. (1991), '"We gather together": consumption rituals of Thanksgiving Day', *Journal of Consumer Research* 18 (June): 13–31.

—— and Brucks, M. (1993), 'Introspection in consumer research: implementation and implications', *Journal of Consumer Research* 20 (December): 339–59.

Watkins, S. A., Rueda, M. and Rodriguez, M. (1992) *Feminism for Beginners*, Cambridge: Icon Books.

Waugh, P. (ed.) (1992a) *Postmodernism: A Reader*, London: Edward Arnold.

—— (1992b) *Practising Postmodernism, Reading Modernism*, London: Edward Arnold.

Webster, F. E. (1992) 'The changing role of marketing in the corporation', *Journal of Marketing* 56(4): 1–17.

Webster, R. (1996) *Studying Literary Theory: An Introduction*, 2nd edn, London: Arnold.

Weir, D. (1996) 'Trawlers, snoopers and branding popes', *The Times Higher* 13 September: 28.

Weitz, B. A. and Jap, S. D. (1995) 'Relationship marketing and distribution channels', *Journal of the Academy of Marketing Science* 23(4): 305–20.

Wensley, R. (1995) 'A critical review of research in marketing', *British Journal of Management* 6 (December): S63–S82.

Wernick, A. (1991) *Promotional Culture: Advertising, Ideology and Symbolic Expression*, London: Sage.

Westbrook, R. A. and Black, W. C. (1985) 'A motivation-based shopper typology', *Journal of Retailing* 61(1): 78–103.

Wheale, N. (ed.) (1995) *The Postmodern Arts: An Introductory Reader*, London: Routledge.

Widdicombe, R. (1994) 'Discovering legends in his own lifetime', *The Sunday Times*, 4 September, Section 10: 10–11.

Wilde, O. (1995) *The Works of Oscar Wilde*, Bristol: Parragon.

Williams, L. A. and Burns, A. C. (1994) 'The halcyon days of youth: a phenomenological account of experiences and feelings accompanying spring break on the beach', in C.T. Allen and D.R. John (eds) *Advances in Consumer Research, vol. XXI*, Provo: Association for Consumer Research, pp. 98–103.

Williams, R. H., Painter, J. J. and Nicholas, H. R. (1978), 'A policy-oriented typology of grocery shoppers', *Journal of Retailing* 54(1): 27–42.

Williamson, J. (1978) *Decoding Advertisements: Ideology and Meaning in Advertising*, London: Marion Boyars.

—— (1986) *Consuming Passions: The Dynamics of Popular Culture*, London: Marion Boyars.

Willmott, H. (1993) 'Paradoxes of marketing: some critical reflections', in D. Brownlie *et al.* (eds) *Rethinking Marketing*, Coventry: Warwick Business School Research Bureau, pp. 207–21.

Wilson, D. T. (1995), 'An integrated model of buyer–seller relationships', *Journal of the Academy of Marketing Science* 23(4): 335–45.

Winterson, J. (1996) *Art Objects: Essays on Ecstasy and Effrontery*, London: Vintage.

Wolf, M. (1992) *A Thrice Told Tale: Feminism, Post-modernism and Ethnographic Responsibility*, Stanford: Stanford University Press.

Wolfinbarger, M. F. and Gilly, M. C. (1996), 'An experimental investigation of self-symbolism in gifts', in K. P. Corfman and J. G. Lynch (eds) *Advances in Consumer Research*, vol. *XXIII*, Provo: Association for Consumer Research, pp. 458–62.

Wolpert, L. (1992) *The Unnatural Nature of Science*, London: Faber & Faber.

Wood, G. (1996) 'Private dancer', *The Observer Life*, 6 October: 37–8.

Worthington, S. and Horne, S. (1996) 'Relationship marketing: the case of the university alumni affinity credit card', *Journal of Marketing Management* 12(1–3): 189–99.

Wright, P. (1986) 'Schemer schema: consumers' intuitive theories about marketers' influence tactics', in R.J. Lutz (ed.) *Advances in Consumer Research*, vol. *XIII*, Provo: Association for Consumer Research, pp. 1–3.

Wright, T. (1989) 'Marketing culture: spectacles and simulation', in T.L. Childers *et al.* (eds) *Marketing Theory and Practice*, Chicago: American Marketing Association, pp. 326–8.

York, P. and Jennings, C. (1995) *Peter York's Eighties*, London: BBC Books.

Young, E. and Caveney, G. (1992) 'Introduction', in E. Young and G. Caveney (eds) *Shopping in Space: Essays on American "Blank Generation" Fiction*, London: Serpent's Tail, pp. v–viii.

Young, J. (1993) *Nietzsche's Philosophy of Art*, Cambridge: Cambridge University Press.

Young, R. J. C. (1996) *Torn Halves: Political Conflict in Literary and Cultural Theory*, Manchester: Manchester University Press.

Zaltman, G. (1996) 'Metaphorically speaking: new technique uses multidisciplinary ideas to improve qualitative research', *Marketing Research* 8(2): 13–20.

—— and Coulter, R. H. (1995), 'Seeing the voice of the customer: metaphor-based advertising research', *Journal of Advertising Research* 35 (July–August): 35–51.

——, LeMasters, K. and Heffring, M. (1982) *Theory Construction in Marketing: Some Thoughts on Thinking*, New York: John Wiley & Sons.

I don't want to go home